Ukraine between war and peace

Jacques Baud

UKRAINE BETWEEN WAR AND PEACE

Max Milo

Max Milo, Paris, 2023
www.maxmilo.com
ISBN: 9782315010820

1. Understanding the conflict

The way in which a crisis is understood determines the way in which it is resolved. This statement, which I often repeat, seems simple. Yet we are unable to do so. This was already the case with George W. Bush's "war on terror", which all Western countries rushed to follow in Afghanistan, Iraq and elsewhere, where we supported the aggressor (even though we knew he was lying).

All these wars have been lost, our soldiers, the civilian victims of war (including those of terrorist attacks) have died for only one reason: we did not want to understand these conflicts, their nature, and their actors before we got involved.

You can't win a war by convincing yourself that you've won.

Learning the lessons of a conflict should not only allow us to revisit our doctrines of engagement and the orientation of our armament policies, but also - and this is essential - to avoid the emergence of new conflicts. To think that a conflict is the product of a single cause ("Putin is crazy!") is childish. Conflicts are always the result of a cluster of causes, whose relative importance varies over time.

The identification of these causes and their interactions is the task of the intelligence services and of those who are supposed to enlighten our decision-makers. However, in France more than elsewhere, the thinking on the conflict, whether it comes from "pro-Russians" or "pro-Ukrainians", is not based on facts, but on convictions. The problem is not limited to military conflicts, but to all crises. We remember the statement of Olivier Véran, Minister of Health, on February 18, 2020, whose intonations strangely recalled General Gamelin in 1939...

> *I don't need to check that France is ready. France is ready! And it is ready because we have an extremely solid healthcare system[1].*

In France, military "experts" such as Generals Dominique Trinquand, Michel Yakovleff, and colonels such as Pierre Servent or Michel Goya are in this tradition. They base their judgment on their perception (even their prejudices) and not on facts. This pleases our media, but it leads to defeat.

This phenomenon is exemplified by the French Senate's information report, published in February 2023[2]. It is built on prejudices, unfounded accusations, and rumors, while elements essential to the understanding of the conflict have been dismissed. Each event is described as if it had fallen from the sky, without reason. The result is a fatalistic reading of the problems, which is necessarily emotional, which is understood only through "punch lines" and which makes in-depth solutions impossible.

We can already predict that it will satisfy those who speak on television, but will perpetuate the mistakes that have been made over the last thirty years and that have systematically led to disasters. The problem is that this report has the ambition to guide the reflection for the future of the French armed forces.

That being said, the Swiss Annual Security Report[3], published in September 2022, suffers from exactly the same shortcomings.

In the western French-speaking world, our reading of the Ukrainian conflict suffers from a cruel lack of honest, scientific and academic reflection. In Europe, more than in the United States, problems are judged without being analyzed in order to condemn and not to find solutions. This is true both for those who adhere to the official narrative and for those who reject it. Everyone seems to see it as a reflection of their own concerns, without really asking whether it corresponds to the reality on the ground.

We adapt the facts to our conclusions instead of adapting the conclusions to the facts. This is the way political problems in all fields seem to be treated.

---

1. Alexandra Bensaid & Nicolas Demorand, "Olivier Véran on the coronavirus: "France is ready because we have an extremely solid health system"", *France Inter*, February 18, 2020
2. Cédric PERRIN & Jean-Marc TODESCHINI, "Ukraine: one year of war. What lessons for France?", Senate Committee on Foreign Affairs, Defense and Armed Forces, Information Report No. 334, February 8, 2023
3. https://www.newsd.admin.ch/newsd/message/attachments/72369.pdf

2. The actors

2.1. The United States

The conflict in Ukraine is often presented as a conflict between Russia and NATO. This is partly true, but it would be more accurate to say that it is a conflict between the United States and Russia. NATO being, conceptually, only the armed arm of the American strategy in Europe (and perhaps in Asia too, as we shall see).

The understanding of the Ukrainian conflict inevitably starts from the study of the global American strategy, which the Americans call *"Grand Strategy"*. It is imbued with a complex combination of philosophical, societal, political and military elements that have been the subject of numerous books. We will not go into detail here and focus on some of the salient aspects.

There is a messianic dimension to American culture that stems from its religious past, which assumes that the United States is the bearer of a moral and economic truth that justifies its presence in the world. Both paternalistic and missionary, the United States believed it had a role to play in the development of the world. This sentiment emerged at the end of World War II with the accession of the United States to nuclear power, and it became even more pronounced after the fall of communism in 1989 and the Gulf War in 1991.

In his book *"The Grand Chessboard,"* Zbigniew Brzeziński gives us a glimpse of the American perception of the world. But, as relevant and interesting as it is, this reading must be qualified. In 1997, when he wrote his book, Brzeziński was no longer "in business." His vision is essentially that of the 1980s. For example, he does not perceive the emerging structural weakening of the United States, nor the growing role of China in a globalized system. It also fails to take into account the emerging economic powers (Brazil, Russia, India, China, South Africa or BRICS) and their potential to challenge Western leadership.

That being said, he correctly observes that the relationship between Ukraine and Russia is of a special nature. He shows how US policy can use Ukraine as a lever to affect Russia and that the goal is less to develop Ukraine than to prevent Russia's re-emergence as a superpower.

The real element that allows us to understand the "Grand Strategy" of the United States in the post-Cold War era is the "Wolfowitz doctrine".

2.1.1. The Wolfowitz doctrine

Europeans have a poor understanding of American domestic and foreign policy. Many have stuck to a 1940s reading that linked Americans and Europeans in a community of civilization and destiny.

Since 1945, spared by the war, the American continent has been able to benefit from an industrial and technological advantage that it had never had before. But with the onset of the Cold War and the possession of nuclear weapons, the idea of a community of destiny evolved into a form of protective paternalism of which the Marshall Plan and NATO are the expression. The United States gradually felt that it had a mission to lead the free world in its crusade against tyranny.

This perception culminated with the fall of communism in the USSR. A fall in which the West had nothing to do with. It was the communist system that imploded and not the somewhat far-fetched idea that the West had pushed the USSR into exorbitant military spending.

On March 7, 1992, the *New York Times* published a draft of the Pentagon's *Defense Planning Guidance 1994-1998*, which outlines a post-Cold War strategy for the United States[4]:

---

4. "Excerpts From Pentagon's Plan: 'Prevent the Re-Emergence of a New Rival,'" *The New York Times*, March 8, 1992 (https://www.nytimes.com/1992/03/08/world/excerpts-from-pentagon-s-plan-prevent-the-re-emergence-of-a-new-rival.html)

Our first objective is to prevent the re-emergence of a new rival, on the territory of the former Soviet Union or elsewhere, which represents a threat of the order of that which the Soviet Union once represented.

After the dissolution of the Soviet Union and the success of the first Gulf War, the United States appeared all-powerful. This strategy advocates maintaining its dominant position in the world, even at the expense of its closest allies:

While the United States supports the goal of European integration, we must seek to prevent the emergence of uniquely European security arrangements that could weaken NATO, particularly the Alliance's integrated command structure.

This document triggered an outcry, forcing the Department of Defense to water down its final version of April 16, 1992. It remains known as the "*Wolfowitz Doctrine*" and continues to permeate American strategy today. It has the particularity of announcing that in order to achieve these objectives, the United States cannot rely on UN mechanisms:

While the United States cannot become the world's policeman and assume responsibility for solving all international security problems, neither can we allow our critical interests to depend solely on international mechanisms that may be blocked by countries whose interests may be very different from our own.

Wolfowitz is obviously referring to the United Nations Security Council, which allows the other permanent members (P5) to oppose the United States, thanks to the veto power. He concludes that the United States must be able to act outside this mechanism. This is what happened in 2001 for the war in Afghanistan and in 2003 for Iraq. Thus, with the Wolfowitz Doctrine, the United States distanced itself from the "law-based international order" (LBIO) that emerged from the Second World War, to define a more flexible "rules-based international order" (RBIO)[5].

---

5. https://diplomaticopinion.com/2021/05/10/the-rules-based-international-order/

It is on the basis of this doctrine that the United States will base its war on terrorism, foreign kidnappings, the practice of torture, its interventions in the internal affairs of its adversaries (for example by supporting materially and financially the opposition movements), and to encourage secessionist movements in certain countries.

2.1.2. The trap of Thucydides

As long as the United States had the material, economic and military capacities to ensure its role as leader of the Western world, the Wolfowitz doctrine was consistent with a kind of natural order of things. But this did not last.

The fall of the Berlin Wall heralded a new era. Whereas the Cold War had been driven by the notion of "division", the idea of globalization was to emerge from that of "integration", as Thomas Friedman explained[6]:

> *The symbol of the Cold War system was a wall, which divided us all. The symbol of the globalization system is the World Wide Web, which unites us all.*

In synergy with technological evolution, globalization is the system of movement and ubiquity, whereas the Cold War was essentially a static system, symbolized by the notion of "blocs".

The end of the cold war is the most important event of the end of the 20th century, but it is only one element of a convergence of factors at that time. Technological evolution, the fall in the cost of communications, economic integration mechanisms, free trade agreements, industrial relocation and the resulting (imperfect) social harmonization, give rise to the notion of a "global village" with growing interdependencies.

Particularly in the United States, globalization is not simply seen as an economic phenomenon, but above all as a mental attitude, a philosophy. Its ambition is to reshape the world into a network of actors who are both partners and competitors, whose relationships are determined by their comparative advantage.

---

6. Thomas L. Friedman, "From supercharged financial markets to Osama bin Laden, the emerging global order demands an enforcer. That's Americas new burden," *The New York Times Magazine*, March 28, 1999.

Initially, globalization proposed better international cooperation and interdependence as a guarantee of stability. Everyone contributed to the global edifice according to their means. This was a noble idea, but it has drifted. Western countries quickly began to exploit the differences in resource costs to their advantage without fulfilling the promise of development for the countries of the South. Only countries like China and India, with their high level of education and almost unlimited manufacturing capacity, were gradually able to acquire the necessary know-how.

The world began to divide itself into a financialized West and a manufacturing "rest of the world." In the 2000s, as in the Vietnam War era, entangled in costly wars, the U.S. focused on maintaining its military-industrial complex, and gradually abandoned civilian industry to the "rest of the world."

The United States has failed to evolve with its own globalization project and has thus been overtaken by it. Its society is increasingly polarized[7]. Poverty and deprivation are on the rise. There are more prisons than universities in the country[8] and the quality of education is in free fall[9]. The prison system has become an economic activity[10] and generates a turnover of nearly 74 billion dollars per year, more than the GDP of 133 countries in the world[11]! Let's remember that, according to the 13th amendment of the United States Constitution, slavery has not been abolished for prisoners, and that many American companies take advantage of this to produce at low cost. The financialization of the economy has led to the gradual disappearance of know-how and skills, resulting in a backwardness in terms of innovation[12]. The offshoring of cheap services,

---

7. https://www.edelman.com/trust/2023/trust-barometer
8. Christopher Ingraham, "The U.S. has more jails than colleges," *The Washington Post*, January 6, 2015 (https://www.washingtonpost.com/news/wonk/wp/2015/01/06/the-u-s-has-more-jails-than-colleges-heres-a-map-of-where-those-prisoners-live/)
9. Christopher Ingraham, "The U.S. has more jails than colleges. Here's a map of where those prisoners live," *The Washington Post*, January 6, 2015.
10. L. B. Wright, "The American Prison System: It's Just Business," *Fordham Journal of Corporate & Financial Law*, December 9, 2018 (https://news.law.fordham.edu/jcfl/2018/12/09/the-american-prison-system-its-just-business/#_ednref8)
11. Brian Kincade, "The Economics of the American Prison System," *smartasset.com*, November 1, 2022 (https://smartasset.com/mortgage/the-economics-of-the-american-prison-system)
12. Steve Denning, "Why U.S. Firms Are Dying: Failure To Innovate," *Forbes*, February 27, 2015; Danny Vinik, "America's innovation crisis," *Politico*, October 14, 2016; Walter Isaacson, "How America Risks Losing Its Innovation Edge," *TIME Magazine*, January 3, 2019; Jordan Bar Am, Laura Furstenthal, Felicitas Jorge & Erik Roth, "Innovation in a crisis: Why it is more critical than ever," *McKinsey & Company*, June 17, 2020

such as call centers or credit card management, has been replaced by the offshoring of high value-added managerial or engineering services[13].

America's wealth no longer comes from its ability to manufacture goods, but from its ability to generate financial profits. For example, McDonald's® ice cream machines make more money when they break down than when they work[14]. Today, the United States has the most power outages of any industrialized country[15].

A model of economic and industrial development in the 1960s, the United States is now in decline. The growing gap between its geostrategic dominance and its economic performance is gradually pushing it into the "Thucydides trap." In other words, unable to rise, they seek to lower others. Europe is following the same path.

This explains Joe Biden's statement during his March 31, 2021 speech[16]:

> *The rest of the world is closing in [on us] and closing in fast. We can't allow this to continue.*

The winner of this economic competition is undoubtedly China. That is why it has become the main adversary of the United States.

But the Americans have another fear. They see themselves in competition with three "challengers": China, a powerful adversary that is on the verge of overtaking them; Europe, an important power, but not an adversary of their size; and Russia, which they see as an important power because it is nuclear, but far from being a threat to their leadership. In the short and medium term, with the exception of China, none of these "challengers" is really in a position to compete individually with the United States in terms of influence and power.

So why this obsession of the United States to literally "destroy" Russia? Simply because they know that inevitably, Russia must get closer to one or the other of its main adversaries (Europe or China) giving them a

---

13. Anna Huffington, *Third World America*, Crown Publishers, New York, 2010, pp. 27-29
14. Andy Greenberg, "They Hacked McDonald's Ice Cream Machines-and Started a Cold War," *Wired*, April 20, 2021
15. Ula Chrobak, "The US has more power outages than any other developed country. Here's why.", Popular Science, August 17, 2020 (https://www.popsci.com/story/environment/why-us-lose-power-storms/)
16. "Remarks by President Biden on the American Jobs Plan," Carpenters Pittsburgh Training Center (Pittsburgh, Pennsylvania), *whitehouse.gov*, March 31, 2021

decisive advantage, thanks to its position, its size and its inexhaustible energy resources.

It is the alliance with Russia that will determine the balance of great powers in the future. By forming a "Eurasian bloc" with Europe, Russia would confront the United States with two adversaries (Eurasia and China) strong enough to challenge its global leadership in the long run. By partnering with China, Russia would certainly strengthen it into a strong "Asian bloc," but the United States would retain its European ally and thus have only one real adversary, caught between the two.

This is why the American strategy towards Russia during the Ukrainian crisis, seeing that it had literally pushed it into the arms of China, is not really incongruous.

The ideal, for the United States, remains a fragmented world over which it can exercise its hegemony. This is why keeping Europe away from Russia has long been a US priority. As early as September 1982, in a *Special National Intelligence Estimate* (SNIE) classified as SECRET, the CIA had already mentioned the risk of a too close relationship between Europe and the USSR based on energy resources[17]. That same year, President Ronald Reagan had (already!) authorized a clandestine operation to destroy the Bratsvo gas pipeline[18], forty years almost to the day before the destruction of the Nord Stream 1 and 2 gas pipelines!

A Europe with abundant and cheap energy would eventually mean a loss of influence for the United States. With the fall of communism, the risk of a rapprochement between Europe and Russia beyond a simple supply of energy has only reinforced this prospect.

Significantly, Europe's "dependence" on Russia did not really appear in the European discourse until the arrival of Donald Trump. His objective is then to make the United States great again (*"Make America Great Again!"*). Unable to rise, it is necessary to keep the heads of potential competitors under water. This is why the Trump administration quickly

---

17. "The Soviet Gas Pipeline in Perspective," Special National Intelligence Estimate, SNIE 3-11/2-82, *Central Intelligence Agency*, September 3, 1982 (http://insidethecoldwar.org/sites/default/files/documents/NIE 3-112-82 The Soviet Gas Pipeline in Perspective September 21, 1982.pdf)
18. David E. Hoffman, "Reagan Approved Plan to Sabotage Soviets," *The Washington Post*, February 27, 2004 (https://www.washingtonpost.com/archive/politics/2004/02/27/reagan-approved-plan-to-sabotage-soviets/a9184eff-47fd-402e-beb2-63970851e130/)

applied sanctions to China, to Germany for Nord Stream 2 and literally to the whole planet for Huawei.

Russia's role in the American strategic perception

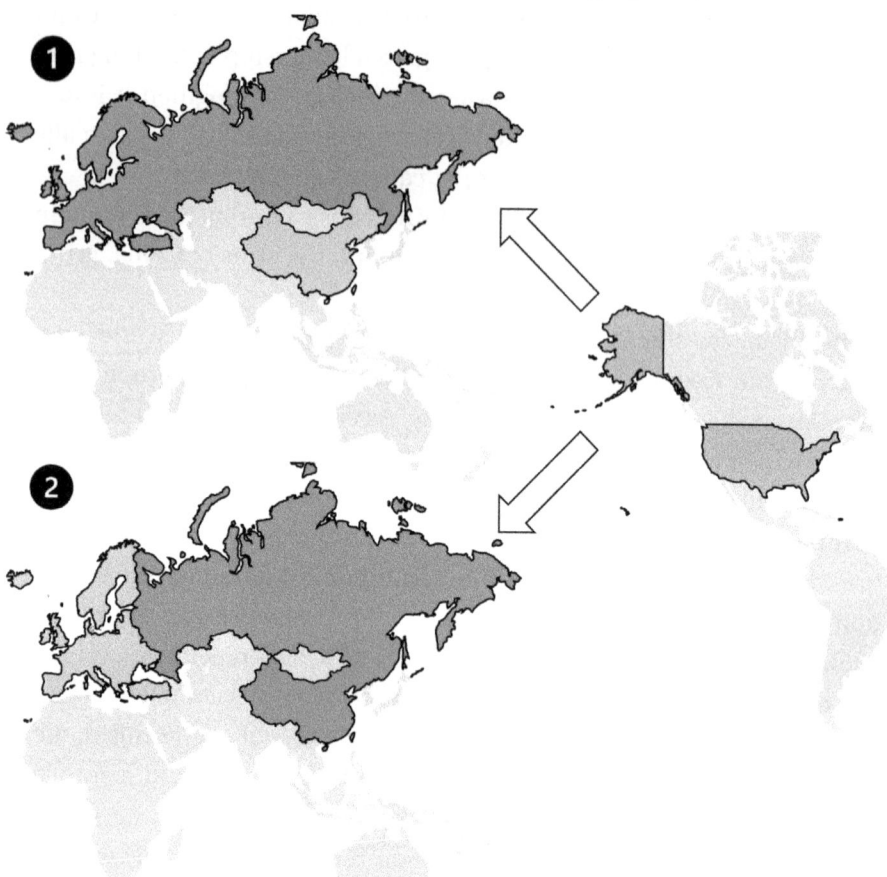

Figure 1 - U.S. perception of Russia's role as a pivot, which could give its rivals (Europe and China) a decisive advantage. Russia, as a source of strategic materials, could give Europe the advantage in a Eurasian bloc (1) or China in an Asian bloc (2).

In order to reduce their adversaries, the United States systematically undertakes to fragment them. It is the old Roman principle of *divide and impera* (divide and rule) that they applied in the former Yugoslavia, Iraq, the Middle East and Syria, and that they are already trying to apply in China.

This is also the strategy advocated by Israel in the Middle East (Yinon plan[19]). It is a perfect illustration of the idea of a "rules-based international order", which is being put in place in defiance of the United Nations Charter.

Russia has perceived this risk; and its determination to resist it is systematically mocked by those who reject international law. Yet the threat is real. Under the title "Decolonization of Russia"[20] a project has been developing in Europe since the early 1990s[21] under the patronage of the United States. It aims to dismember Russia into 19 or 34 independent states (depending on the model) according to their ethnic components. It is strange to note that it is supported by the same politicians who want more integration in Europe! Our politicians, encouraged by our media, are trying to do in Russia what they tried to do in Africa and elsewhere...

A first *Forum of Free Nations of Russia* was held in Warsaw in May 2022, followed by a second one in Prague on July 23-24, 2022, a third one in Gdansk on September 23-25, 2022 and a fourth one on January 30, 2023 in the European Parliament, in Brussels

Paradoxically and ironically, our propaganda systematically contradicts what the Ukrainian leaders say. Thus, on the Swiss state media RTS, Vladimir Putin's "paranoia" is regularly mentioned, as by Michel Eltchaninoff, philosopher[22], or Patrick Lemoine, psychiatrist[23]. But on March 3, 2023, Oleksiy Danilov, secretary of the Council of Defense and National Security of Ukraine, declared on this same media[24]:

> *The West must prepare for the decolonization of Russia. Russia will soon cease to exist within its present borders. This does not depend on us. The beginning of Russia's collapse was caused by Putin on February 24, 2022. [...] The processes that led to the collapse of the USSR are now underway in today's Russia.*

---

19. "To Clean Break: A New Strategy for Securing the Realm," *The Institute for Advanced Strategic and Political Studies*, July 1996, (http://www.informationclearinghouse.info/article1438.htm)
20. Casey Michel, "Decolonize Russia," The Atlantic, May 27, 2022 (https://www.theatlantic.com/ideas/archive/2022/05/russia-putin-colonization-ukraine-chechnya/639428/)
21. https://www.csce.gov/international-impact/events/decolonizing-russia
22. https://www.rts.ch/info/culture/livres/13114631-michel-eltchaninoff-poutine-peut-passer-de-la-theorie-aux-actes-tres-facilement.html
23. https://www.rts.ch/info/monde/12951473-megalomane-sous-cortisone-parano-la-sante-mentale-de-vladimir-poutine-analysee-par-un-psychiatre.html
24. https://www.rts.ch/info/monde/13818312-lukraine-demande-des-armes-des-armes-et-encore-des-armes.html

2. The actors

It confirms what he had already stated a month earlier in *The Kyiv Independent*, that the disintegration of Russia is the goal of Ukraine[25]. This is perfectly consistent with what Oleksei Arestovich said in March 2019: the destruction of Russia is the condition for Ukraine to join NATO and enter the Western community on a full footing. Whether this is an objective reality or a vision of the mind is certainly debatable, but it is the vision and reading of the American and Ukrainian leaders.

Map of the post-Russian free states - Decolonization and reconstruction of Russia[26]

Figure 2 - Map shown on freenationsrf.org with a 34-state partition.

---

25. Alexander Query, "Danilov: 'Ukraine's national interest is Russia's disintegration," *The Kyiv Independent*, February 6, 2023 (https://kyivindependent.com/national/danilov-ukraines-national-interest-is-russias-disintegration)
26. https://freenationsrf.org/

Singularly, while the Anglo-Saxon media quite regularly evoke the project of dismantling Russia[27], the French-speaking media systematically conceal the events and facts that could contradict their narrative.

The management of this crisis shows that neither the Americans nor the Europeans have any compassion for Ukraine. Moreover, Kevin McCarthy, the successor of the highly publicized Nancy Pelosi as Speaker of the House of Representatives, has agreed to reduce aid to Ukraine in exchange for the votes necessary for his election[28]! In fact, he will refuse Zelensky's invitation in March 2023. This shows what our "values" are all about!...

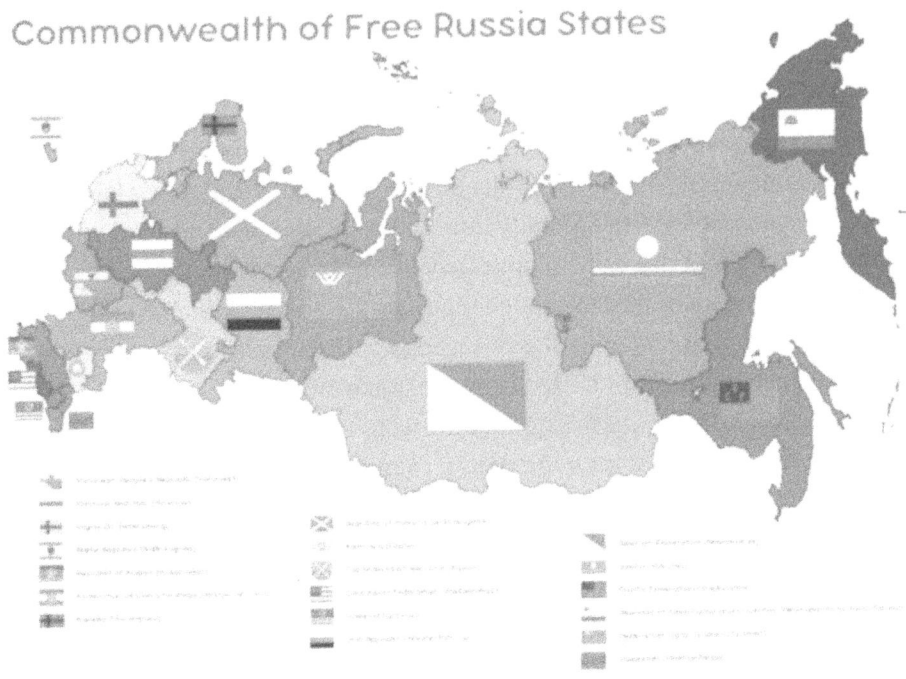

Figure 3 - Map presented at the Forum of Free Nations of Russia on July 23-24, 2022 in Prague. It shows another version of the partition of Russia broken down into 19 independent states.

---

27. Anchal Vohra, "The West Is Preparing for Russia's Disintegration," *Foreign Policy*, April 17, 2023 (https://foreignpolicy.com/2023/04/17/the-west-is-preparing-for-russias-disintegration/)
28. Josie Ensor, "Kevin McCarthy 'agreed to cut aid to Ukraine' to secure US speaker role", *The Telegraph*, January 7, 2023 (https://www.telegraph.co.uk/world-news/2023/01/07/kevin-mccarthy-fails-14th-ballot-speaker-us-house/)

2.1.3. The RAND Corporation Strategy (2019)

The observation of events in Ukraine and around Russia since 2020 highlights a very coherent pattern. Contrary to what journalist Jean-Philippe Schaller asserts, one does not have to be an agent of Putin to read the strategy outlined in 2019 by the *RAND Corporation*[29] *"for the United States and its allies"*, with the objective of *"putting Russia under tension and unbalancing it"*[30].

This is a set of two documents prepared by the Pentagon's main think tank: *"Extending Russia: Competing from Advantageous* Ground[31]*"* and *"Overextending and Unbalancing* Russia[32]*"*. They total about 350 pages and outline a complex strategy to create situations of social and economic tension that place Russia permanently on the defensive, on several fronts at once, to destabilize and weaken it politically internally and externally.

Its principle is based on the myth - very widespread in France[33] - that the USSR collapsed as a result of a "surge" in its capabilities, caused by Ronald Reagan's "Star Wars" project... The problem is that this is false. As a CIA report of the time already noted, the USSR never engaged in this race[34]. The USSR did not collapse because of Western action, it was the communist system that imploded, because it was not viable.

The myths that make up our knowledge of Russia are at the root of the unfortunate - and stupid - decisions we make today.

What is striking about this document, which has about 30 major recommendations, is that at *no point* does it mention the promotion of human rights or the rule of law. It is clear here that it is not about promoting democracy, improving the situation in Russia, or helping Ukraine, but about advancing American interests.

---

29. The RAND Corporation is a think-tank created by the Pentagon at the beginning of the Cold War to develop strategies against the USSR.
30. James Dobbins *et al*, "Overextending and Unbalancing Russia," *RAND Corporation* (Doc. No. RB-10014-A), 2019.
31. James Dobbins, Raphael S. Cohen, Nathan Chandler, Bryan Frederick, Edward Geist, Paul DeLuca, Forrest E. Morgan, Howard J. Shatz, Brent Williams, "Extending Russia: Competing from Advantageous Ground," *RAND Corporation*, 2019
32. James Dobbins & others, "Overextending and Unbalancing Russia," *RAND Corporation*, 2019 (Doc Nr RB-10014-A), 2019
33. Thierry Wolton, *Le KGB en France*, Grasset, 1986.
34. "Moscow's Response to US Plans for Missile Defense," Internet archive (web.archive.org/web/20170119110741/https://www.cia.gov/library/readingroom/docs/DOC_0006122438.pdf).

However, it is often forgotten that the RAND Corporation warned policymakers against implementing this strategy, as it could provoke Russian intervention in Ukraine:

> *[...] Such an action could also have a significant cost for Ukraine and for the prestige and credibility of the United States. It could result in disproportionate human and territorial losses for Ukraine, as well as refugee flows. It could even lead Ukraine to a disadvantageous peace.*

So we knew very well, as early as 2019, that our policy of destabilizing Russia by relying on Ukraine could generate a catastrophe...

Options to destabilize Russia

Geopolitical options	Probability of success	Benefits (United States)	Costs and risks (Russia)
Provide lethal aid to Ukraine	average	high	high
Increase support to Syrian rebels	low	average	high
Promoting liberalization in Belarus	low	high	high
Intensify links with the South Caucasus	low	low	average
Reduce Russian influence in Central Asia	low	low	average
Destabilizing Transnistria	low	low	average

Figure 4 - RAND Corporation analysis of options for destabilizing Russia in geopolitical matters. It recognizes many elements that were attempted by the United States in 2020-2023. But we also see that the RAND Corporation had identified that these actions would have a low probability of success. The problem is that our politicians do not read and are generally uneducated. This explains the failure of the Western strategy. [Source: "Overextending and Unbalancing Russia," RAND Corporation, 2019 (p. 4).

2. The actors

2.2. The Ukraine

2.2.1. *The objectives of Ukraine*

We know the goals of Ukraine from the interview given by Oleksei Arestovich, a close adviser to Zelensky, on March 18, 2019: it is to enter NATO, and then enter the European Union. The problem is that the tensions with Russia, NATO can not accept Ukraine into its fold without running the risk of activating Article 5 of the Atlantic Charter. It is a bit like taking out an insurance policy for a risk that has a 100% probability of occurrence!

The Minsk agreements could have made a decisive contribution to calming these tensions and making it easier for Ukraine to join NATO. But the confessions of Angela Merkel and François Hollande show that the West sought to maintain these tensions, the interest of Ukraine being only a secondary objective.

Ukraine's entry into NATO is therefore only possible if Russia is unable to threaten it. It is therefore necessary to make it suffer a crushing defeat that will destroy its economy, provoke a revolution and a change of regime, or even the dismantling of Russia into smaller entities. This is exactly what Arestovich says: *"Our price for joining NATO is a war against Russia and its defeat"*. He even gives the probable date of this war: *"2021 or 2022"*[35]!

But the price will be higher than expected, as we will see.

In March 2022, during an interview on CNN, Zelensky himself acknowledged that he had been manipulated and instrumentalized by the Americans to join NATO[36]:

> *I asked them personally to say frankly if they were going to accept us into NATO in a year or two or five, to say it directly and clearly, or just say no [...] And the answer was very clear, you will not be a member of NATO, but publicly, the doors will remain open.*

---

35. "Predicted Russian - Ukrainian war in 2019 - Alexey Arestovich", YouTube, March 18, 2022 (https://youtu.be/1xNHmHpERH8)
36. Chandelis Duster, "Zelensky: 'If we were a NATO member, a war wouldn't have started,'" cnn.com, March 20, 2022 (https://edition.cnn.com/europe/live-news/ukraine-russia-putin-news-03-20-22/h_7c08d64201fdd9d3a141e63e606a62e4)

This mechanism that should lead to the collapse of Russia and later to the expansion of NATO is not a Ukrainian creation, but an American one.

It is a question of pushing Russia into a conflict, which should allow the massive and brutal application of a deluge of sanctions. It is about isolating Russia in a form of "strategic mobbing" aimed at banning it from the international community and thus bringing about regime change. Published in April 2019, the two documents describe exactly what we will see in 2022-2023.

As Oleksei Arestovich explains, Ukraine's membership in NATO must necessarily involve the destruction of the Russian state or the overthrow of its government (with Western help). In other words, for Ukraine the total defeat of Russia is an *"enabling objective"*, while for the United States it is an *"end goal"*.

It is to push them to revolt that Western sanctions also hit Russian citizens. In September 2022, Volodymyr Zelensky declared that he would only agree to negotiate with Russia if Vladimir Putin was no longer in power[37]. He issued a decree a few days later, forbidding any negotiations with Russia until Vladimir Putin left[38]. In other words, peace negotiations do not depend on the situation in Ukraine, but on that of Russia. This confirms that the West is not looking for Ukraine's victory, but for Russia's defeat.

As stated by Oleksei Arestovich in March 2019, this is the price Ukraine has to pay. Therefore, for our politicians, it does not matter what the price is. As Republican Senator Lindsey Graham says, it's about letting the Ukrainians fight to the last[39]. This is the same formulation used by François Hollande during an interview where he was tricked by comedians Lexus and Vovan who pretended to be Petro Poroshenko[40]. It is a quasi-millennialist vision, which the West has been quick to embrace, that pushes a country to self-destruction in order to create a renewal of the European geostrategic space.

---

37. "Ukraine Will Not Negotiate with Russia as Long As Putin Is In Power: Zelensky," *Barron's/AFP*, September 30, 2022 (https://www.barrons.com/news/ukraine-will-not-negotiate-with-russia-as-long-as-putin-is-in-power-zelensky-01664548507)
38. Vladimir Socor, "Zelenskyy Bans Negotiations with Putin," *Eurasia Daily Monitor* (Volume 19, No. 147), October 5, 2022 (https://jamestown.org/program/zelenskyy-bans-negotiations-with-putin/)
39. https://youtu.be/HkbwZCqn7BY
40. https://youtu.be/D8FDgJsrRt0?t=549

2.2.2. The Ukrainian strategy

Ukraine knew that an offensive against the Donbass would trigger a reaction from Moscow. As Oleksei Arestovich makes abundantly clear in March 2019, it entered this conflict knowing that it would have to fight. But it seems that Volodymyr Zelensky was lured by American promises that massive sanctions would bring Russia to its knees very quickly and that after brief battles, Ukraine would be victorious, The sanctions against Russia were part of the Ukrainian and Western strategy.

Process leading to Ukraine's accession to NATO

Intensification of strikes against the population of Donbass

Russia's intervention

Triggering of massive sanctions against Russia

Economic collapse of Russia

Popular discontent
Revolts and overthrow of Vladimir Putin

Decolonization process of Russia

Membership of Ukraine in NATO possible

Figure 5 - Ukraine's accession to NATO requires the disappearance of Russia as a geostrategic power. The process of destroying Russia as a strategic power and allowing Ukraine's integration into NATO. This process is described by the RAND Corporation and Oleksei Arestovitch, advisor to Volodymyr Zelensky in 2019. It explains why the West attaches more importance to the defeat of Russia than to the victory of Ukraine. Victory whose criteria could never be articulated.

This is why, although the West knew there would be a Russian intervention, no precautionary measures were taken to evacuate the Ukrainian population from the predicted combat zone. In fact, the Ukrainian government believed that the Russians would be stopped by the economic, societal and political consequences of their intervention before they could even carry it out.

But the resilience of the Russian economy and society decided otherwise. The fighting has literally swallowed up the Ukrainian army. Today, Zelensky is caught between the demand for victory imposed on him by his political class, which will not accept a negotiation after so many sacrifices, and a desperate fight.

This is the reason why Volodymyr Zelensky can afford to be demanding with the Westerners. With the risk that this will generate growing irritation. For example, American parliamentarians have asked Joe Biden to stop arms deliveries[41]. But by promising a quick victory, the Americans have clearly acquired a debt towards Ukraine. That is why Joe Biden and Jens Stoltenberg were forced to promise aid *"for as long as it takes"* to Zelensky[42].

2.3. Russia

2.3.1. *Russia's objectives*

Whatever our preferences, judging a conflict - and even more so, a war - with bias leads to bad decisions. This is what happened with our reading of Russia's objectives, which created an artificial image of Russian foreign policy and strategy and thus pushed Ukraine toward an irreparable deterioration of the situation.

For Russia, the war started already in 2014, and the Minsk agreements were supposed to end it. It was the determination of the Ukrainians,

---

41. Kelley Beaucar Vlahos, "Republican lawmakers to Biden: no more 'unrestrained aid' to Ukraine," *Responsible Statecraft*, April 20, 2023 (https://responsiblestatecraft.org/2023/04/20/republican-lawmakers-to-biden-no-more-unrestrained-aid-to-ukraine/)
42. Patsy Widakuswara, "Biden to Vow 'As Long as It Takes' Support for Ukraine on War Anniversary," *Voice of America*, February 17, 2023 (https://www.voanews.com/a/biden-to-vow-as-long-as-it-takes-support-for-ukraine-on-war-anniversary-/6968536.html)

Germany, France, the United States and Britain not to implement them that led to a new phase of the conflict, which pushed the Russians to intervene. This new phase had no other purpose than to impose by force what the Minsk Agreements should have brought: security for the people of Donbass. This is why the Russians see their intervention as a *"Special Military Operation"* (*Spetsialnaya Voïennaya Operatsya* or SVO).

On February 24, 2022, Vladimir Putin stated the two objectives of this operation: "demilitarization" and "denazification". He derived these terms from the four objectives formulated by the *Allied Control Authority* in July 1945 at the Potsdam Conference for Germany.

Having failed to listen to and understand Vladimir Putin, the West has systematically advised and helped Ukraine in the wrong direction. In a somewhat cynical way, one could say that the Russians should thank our media who have done everything to make Ukraine take the wrong decisions. In fact, the West has favored the narrative over the reality on the ground.

Firstly, the objectives expressed by Vladimir Putin are not linked to a physical element (territory, city, etc.), but to a dynamic element (destruction of forces). This means that the way to achieve the objective is linked to the evolution of forces on the ground and not to a pre-established political project.

Second, one must understand the philosophical framework within which the Russians operate. They have a Clausewitzian perspective, in which war and (foreign) policy have the same purpose. Thus, the achievement of operational and military objectives can be exploited to achieve strategic and political objectives. This means that the objectives achieved on the ground will be used as a lever to achieve other objectives, for example, the neutrality of Ukraine.

2.3.1.1. Western alternative narratives on causes - the false friends

In order to understand the dynamics of the conflict (and if possible to resolve it) it is therefore necessary to carefully distinguish between the causes of the military intervention and the objectives that this intervention would allow to achieve.

Our irrepressible tendency to replace the discourse of the protagonists by our own "impressions" detached from the facts invariably leads us to a deterioration of the situation. This applies to the media that relay the ideas of Ukrainian neo-Nazis, but also to analysts who are sometimes considered "pro-Russian". These so-called experts have developed a whole series of discourses that seek to explain the Russian intervention, not on the basis of what the Russians have said, but on that of their own perceptions or expectations. Peace is not built on chimeras, but on facts.

2.3.1.1.1. The Russian intervention would be the expression of a conflict of civilization

Propagated by both the far right and the far left, this narrative explains the war in Ukraine as a confrontation between a traditionalist civilization inspired by religion and a "wokist" West[43]. This is not true. If there are indeed two "great" ways of understanding society on the European continent, its fault line is not on the Russian border, but between Western Europe (the "old Europe" according to Donald Rumsfeld) and Eastern Europe (the "new Europe"). Like Russia, the Baltic countries, Poland, Belarus, Hungary or Ukraine belong to a more traditional culture that has a healthier and more balanced vision of society. Russia is not fighting a war of civilization. One could even say that it is the opposite. Westerners feel that only their way of seeing things is right and that the rest of the world must adopt the same worldview. Russians, on the other hand, believe that every society has a positive aspect, and that there is no need to impose one way of seeing.

2.3.1.1.2. The Russian intervention would be caused by the extension of NATO to the East

This is the justification given by the anti-NATO community. This is not true. It is important here to distinguish between the reasons for tension between the West and Russia and the reason why the latter decided to intervene in Ukraine.

Russia sees the possibility that Ukrainian territory could be used by NATO to deploy troops and weapons systems as an existential threat. On November 30, 2021, Vladimir Putin warned NATO against such a

---

43. https://www.rts.ch/info/monde/13163399-alexandre-soljenitsyne-a-la-source-des-discours-de-vladimir-poutine-sur-lukraine.html

deployment, and stated that this would represent a red line for Russia that would provoke a strong response[44].

Since the end of the Cold War, NATO has slowly moved closer to the Russian border. Western promises not to expand the Alliance to the East were never kept because they were not backed by a treaty. At first, the Russians did not perceive NATO expansion as a threat. In the early 1990s, they even held out the hope of being part of a NATO that had been redesigned as a system of collective security based on cooperation rather than confrontation, along the lines of the OSCE. This position was maintained by Vladimir Putin in the early 2000s. This changed in 2002, when the Americans, under President George W. Bush, began to withdraw from all disarmament treaties.

Unlike Westerners, whose strategic thinking is rooted in a balance of forces, Russians think in terms of *"correlation of forces"* (Соотношение Сил), a phrase too often translated in the West as *"balance of forces."* While Westerners see war as a clash of forces, Russians understand war as a combination of factors that range from the tactical to the strategic, with objectives that fit together in political and strategic coherence. The notion of "correlation of forces" thus reflects a holistic vision of war that Westerners do not have. This is why the West has failed in Vietnam, the Middle East, the Sahel and in the fight against terrorism.

Thus, NATO expansion was not a problem for the Russians as long as the United States respected arms control agreements. It was their gradual withdrawal from these agreements, followed by the decision to deploy missiles in Eastern Europe, which created Russian concern, expressed in the speech of February 10, 2007 in Munich. Vladimir Putin then noted that the West was playing with international law, not only in the Middle East, but also in Europe. It is not, therefore, as Benoît Vitkine, Le Monde's Moscow correspondent, claims, a *"hostile speech against the unipolar world and therefore against the* United States"[45], but the translation of a concern, faced with a West that seems to set no limits.

---

[44]. "Putin says NATO troops in Ukraine would be a 'red line' for Moscow," *PBS*, November 30, 2021 (https://www.pbs.org/newshour/world/putin-says-nato-troops-in-ukraine-would-be-a-red-line-for-moscow)

[45]. Caroline Roux in the program "C dans l'air" of October 17, 2021 ("Poutine, maître du jeu #cdanslair 17.10.2021", *France 5/YouTube,* October 18, 2021) (1h33'30")

Until the beginning of 2022, Russia considered the evolution of NATO as a political problem, which should have a diplomatic solution. Therefore, in mid-December 2021, it submitted proposals to the United States and NATO. But with the deterioration of the situation in Donbass in February, Russia decided to intervene for the benefit of the people of Donbass and to seize the opportunity to exploit a victory in Ukraine as leverage to find a solution for both the security of the Russian-speaking people of Ukraine and for its own security.

2.3.1.1.3. The Russian intervention would aim at reconstituting the tsarist empire or the Soviet Union (we don't really know)

This is the narrative carried by neo-Nazis (or similar) in the Baltic states, Poland and Ukraine. It is a form of conspiracism, based on the writings of Alexander Dugin, whom the tabloid press[46] and our state media[47] describe as *"a close friend of Vladimir Putin"*[48]. This is simply a lie, because not only does it appear that the two men have never met[49], but Dugin sees Putin as a "liberal" and openly criticizes him[50]. He was even reportedly expelled from Moscow University for his extremist comments in 2014, according to the Ukrainian media outlet *Euromaidan Press*[51]. Our media is lying once again, but it was probably their rhetoric that encouraged Ukrainians to carry out a terrorist attack against him in August 2022. This could explain why our media did not condemn this act!

Vladimir Putin (ex-member of the KGB, of course!!) is also said to be nostalgic for the former USSR, declaring that *"the destruction of the USSR was the greatest geopolitical catastrophe in the history of the 20th*

---

46. https://www.thesun.co.uk/news/19571946/putins-guide-alexander-hospital-bomb-killed-daughter/
47. https://www.rts.ch/info/monde/13319945-la-fille-dun-ideologue-russe-proche-du-kremlin-tuee-dans-lexplosion-dune-voiture-a-moscou.html
48. Katherine Bayford, "Alexander Dugin was never Putin's brain," *Unherd*, August 22, 2022 (https://unherd.com/thepost/alexander-dugin-was-never-putins-brain/)
49. Pjotr Sauer, "Alexander Dugin: who is Putin ally and apparent car bombing target?", *The Guardian*, August 21, 2022 (https://www.theguardian.com/world/2022/aug/21/alexander-dugin-who-putin-ally-apparent-car-bombing-target)
50. https://irrussianality.wordpress.com/2017/09/13/interview-with-alexander-dugin/
51. "Putin's ideologist, chauvinist philosopher Dugin fired from work," *Euromaidan Press*, June 28, 2014 (https://euromaidanpress.com/2014/06/28/putins-ideologist-chauvinist-philosopher-dugin-fired-from-work/)

century[52]". This phrase is periodically used in the media, such as *RTS*[53], *Le Monde*[54], *Le Figaro*[55] or *France 24*[56], to illustrate his ambition to restore the "greatness" of the USSR. This is propaganda. In reality, the sentence is taken from a speech of April 25, 2005, where Putin does not regret the Soviet regime, but the *chaotic way in* which the transition to democracy took place for Russian society[57]. Unlike Alexander Lukashenko, President of Belarus, Vladimir Putin is not nostalgic for the communist world. On the contrary, he has promoted very "Western" economic policies. Moreover, Alexander Solzhenitsyn and Alexander Dugin, who are described as his sources of inspiration, were virulent opponents of the Soviet system.

2.3.1.1.4. Russian intervention would deny the existence of the Ukrainian people

The Ukrainian far-right propaganda is relayed by our journalists who attribute to Vladimir Putin the idea that Ukraine *"is a country that does not exist and that he does not recognize the existence of Ukraine as a country."*[58]

In support of this argument, an article by Vladimir Putin published on July 12, 2021, entitled *"On the historical unity of Russians and Ukrainians"* is invariably cited[59]. The journalist Paul Gogo (nomen est omen), correspondent of *La Libre* in Moscow, sees in it a conspiracy by Vladimir Putin to unite the two countries by force[60].

In fact, those who have taken the trouble to read this article can see that at no time does Vladimir Putin speak of annexation or even of reuniting Ukraine with Russia. He reminds us that Russians and Ukrainians share a common heritage, but he unambiguously recognizes the existence

---

52. "Comment un homme a changé la Russie", *la-croix.fr*, April 26, 2005
53. https://pages.rts.ch/la-1ere/programmes/signature/5679174-jacques-allaman-poutine-ou-le-passe-d-une-illusion.html
54. "The fall of the Soviet empire, twenty-five years later," *lemonde.fr*, September 8, 2016
55. "Vladimir Fedorovsky: 'The fall of the USSR is still a trauma...'", *lefigaro.fr*, December 16, 2016
56. "Putin, the unavoidable boss of Russia," *France 24*, March 18, 2018.
57. http://en.kremlin.ru/events/president/transcripts/22931
58. Isabelle Mandraud in the program "C dans l'air" of January 11, 2022 ("Poutine rêve d'URSS, l'Ukraine sous tension #cdanslair 11.01.2022", *France 5/YouTube*, January 12, 2022) (08'55")
59. "Article by Vladimir Putin 'On the historical unity of Russians and Ukrainians'", *france.mid.ru*, July 12, 2021 (https://france.mid.ru/fr/presse/russes_ukrainiens/)
60. Paul Gogo, "Vladimir Putin's disturbing article on Ukraine", *La Libre*, July 16, 2021 (updated July 18, 2021) (https://www.lalibre.be/international/europe/2021/07/18/linquietant-article-de-vladimir-poutine-sur-lukraine-HOFONP6JYZCNHBHCZZPRMDE4TQ/)

and sovereignty of Ukraine and defines it as a *"free state"*. His intention is clearly to make Ukraine understand that it has no reason to discriminate between its citizens based on their origin.

What the ultra-nationalist or neo-Nazi media and journalists are hiding is that with this article, Vladimir Putin is responding to the *"Law on Indigenous Peoples of Ukraine"* which was just adopted on July 1st, 2021[61]. This law is reminiscent of the Nuremberg racial laws of the 1930s, and grants different constitutional rights to Ukrainian citizens, depending on their ethnic origin.

Since 2014, political life has been influenced by extreme right-wing elements, which have considerable leverage through corruption and violence. Those who try to deny their existence under the pretext that they would not have a parliamentary majority or that Volodymyr Zelensky is Jewish, have understood nothing about the situation in Ukraine. These elements advocate the "racial purity" of Ukrainians ("Idea of Nation"), a discourse which does not appear verbatim in our media, but which our journalists seem to have largely espoused, as we shall see below.

The article in *La Libre*[62] reflects a phenomenon that has been observed since 2014: the belief that the authorities in Kiev and "the idea of nation" are supported by the population as a whole.

2.3.1.1.5. The Russian intervention would be motivated by hatred of the West, of Europe and/or of their democracy

Vladimir Putin is said to have started a war against the West out of hatred for democracy. This argument is based on the allegation that Vladimir Putin started this war in 2014 because he opposed the treaty between Ukraine and the European Union[63]. This is disinformation pure and simple. In 2013, when it wanted to join the EU, Ukraine wanted a solution that would have better taken into account its traditional economic ties with Russia. It was José-Manuel Barroso, then president of the European

---

61. "Принят Закон 'О коренных народах Украины'", *rada.gov.ua*, July 1, 2021 (https://www.rada.gov.ua/ru/news/Novosty/Soobshchenyya/211516.html)
62. Paul Gogo, "Vladimir Putin's disturbing article on Ukraine", *La Libre*, July 16, 2021 (updated July 18, 2021) (https://www.lalibre.be/international/europe/2021/07/18/linquietant-article-de-vladimir-poutine-sur-lukraine-HOFONP6JYZCNHBHCZZPRMDE4TQ/)
63. Bemjamin Haddad, in the program "C dans l'air" of February 21, 2022 ("Ukraine: what does Putin really want? #cdanslair 21.02.2022", *France 5/YouTube*, February 22, 2022) (04'02")

Commission, who himself imposed a choice on Ukraine, while Russia had offered a compromise solution[64].

In reality, neither Russia nor Vladimir Putin was opposed to the EU. On the contrary, Russia saw the opportunity to have a counterweight to American hegemony. This is why Russia has always been in favour of creating an autonomous European defence capability, which the United States has systematically opposed (Wolfowitz doctrine).

2.3.1.2. The real reasons for the military intervention

The different narratives seen above are neither the motives nor the cause of the Russian military intervention in Ukraine. They are only *"enabling factors"* that exist in the background and that contribute to widening the gap between the West and Russia, but that Russia has never considered as justifying a military confrontation.

These narratives make the war in Ukraine a fatality that cannot be influenced by negotiations. That is why they are (re-)appearing on our media in order to show that there is no point in opening a dialogue[65]. These are revisionist constructions of events, which are based on no concrete evidence and are similar to conspiracy theories.

The tensions between Ukraine and Russia result from two main problems. A geostrategic problem, the interest of the Americans to extend NATO to Ukraine, and a social problem, the treatment of the Russian minority in Ukraine, to which Russian society as a whole is sensitive.

The geostrategic problem was deliberately created by the Americans, by piloting the Maidan coup and placing in power an ultra-nationalist and neo-Nazi minority whose actions were known to lead to tensions in the country, including rapprochement with NATO. Six years earlier, on February 1st, 2008, William Burns, then U.S. ambassador to Moscow (now director of the CIA) sent a confidential memo to Washington warning:

> [NATO's expansion into Ukraine] could potentially split the country in two, leading to violence or even, according to some, civil war, which would prompt Russia to decide whether to intervene.

---

64. "Barroso reminds Ukraine that Customs Union and free trade with EU are incompatible", *ukrinform*, February 25, 2013
65. https://www.france24.com/fr/émissions/vu-de-russie/20221216-vu-de-russie-une-guerre-civilisationnelle-contre-un-occident-satanique

In February 2014, the new authorities in Kiev resulting from Euromaidan converged these two problems. But for the Russians, both problems had to be solved by diplomatic solutions.

The languages that divide Ukraine

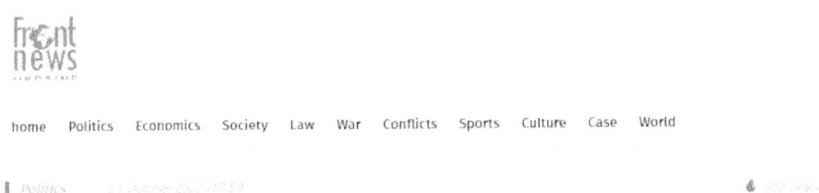

Figure 6 - The exclusion of the Russian language from the official languages in 2014 and then the continuation of a policy of ethnic cleansing to eradicate Russian culture in Ukraine is the source of the internal tensions that the Minsk agreements should have resolved. No Western politician has expressed opposition to this policy since 2014, allowing hatred to fester.

Vladimir Putin counted on a) the implementation of the Minsk agreements (with the commitment of Germany and France) to resolve the issue of minorities in the Donbass, and b) a discussion on the basis of proposals to NATO and the United States in December 2021.

But neither the Ukrainians nor the West, led by Germany and France, had any intention of implementing the Minsk agreements. In June 2022, Petro Poroshenko confessed that he had signed the Agreements only to allow Ukraine to rearm[66] and was even tricked by journalists on the phone about this[67]. Coming from Poroshenko, whose xenophobic remarks against his own Russian-speaking citizens were known (but did not elicit any reaction in our media…), such duplicity was predictable.

The real surprise came on November 24, 2022, from Angela Merkel in the magazine *Der Spiegel*. She confirms that Ukraine did not sign the Minsk agreements in order to apply them, but to gain time and get its army back on its feet and she reveals that she herself signed them

---

66. "Minsk deal was used to buy time - Ukraine's Poroshenko," *The Press United*, June 17, 2022 (https://thepressunited.com/updates/minsk-deal-was-used-to-buy-time-ukraines-poroshenko/)
67. https://twitter.com/i/status/1593290123718053888

without really intending to apply them[68]. A confession that she will confirm on December 8 in *Die Zeit*[69], and which will be followed by a similar confession from François Hollande, former president of France[70]. The picture will be completed on February 9, 2023, when Volodymyr Zelensky confesses in turn to *Spiegel* that he had told Emmanuel Macron and Angela Merkel that he would not implement these agreements[71].

This confirms that Germany and France were accomplices of Ukraine, and were not willing to fulfill the task for which they had committed themselves. So much for the honor of countries that claim to have "European values" but have no word. Not only does this confirm - and reinforce - Vladimir Putin's statements, but it shows the "rest of the world" the duplicity of the West, with a significant impact on the nature of our relations with other continents.

To this is added stupidity and incompetence. In June 2022, the verbatim of the telephone conversation of February 20, 2022 between Emmanuel Macron and Vladimir Putin was published. Not only did it show that the French president had simply never read the Minsk agreements, of which he was supposed to be the guarantor, but that he had had this conversation in the presence of a journalist[72]. Vladimir Putin will keep the image of a boaster who does not know his files and who cannot be trusted.

In other words, the main Western players in the Minsk agreements admit to having committed themselves with the idea of not respecting their signature. They have lied to the Russians, to the people of Donbass and to the Ukrainian people. With the help of our media, they have done everything to prevent solutions. For example, until February 2022, researchers and journalists systematically used the term "separatist" to

---

68. https://www.spiegel.de/panorama/ein-jahr-mit-ex-kanzlerin-angela-merkel-das-gefuehl-war-ganz-klar-machtpolitisch-bist-du-durch-a-d9799382-909e-49c7-9255-a8aec106ce9c
69. https://www.zeit.de/2022/51/angela-merkel-russland-fluechtlingskrise-bundeskanzler
70. Theo Prouvost, "Hollande: 'There will only be a way out of the conflict when Russia fails on the ground'", *The Kyiv Independent*, December 28, 2022 (https://kyivindependent.com/national/hollande-there-will-only-be-a-way-out-of-the-conflict-when-russia-fails-on-the-ground)
71. "Putin ist ein Drache, der fressen muss," *Der Spiegel*, February 9, 2023 (https://archive.is/Q5Eol#selection-4281.0-4323.21)
72. "'Who cares about the proposals of the separatists!': when Emmanuel Macron phoned Vladimir Putin to avoid war in Ukraine", *franceinfo / AFP*, June 25, 2022 (https://www.francetvinfo.fr/monde/europe/manifestations-en-ukraine/on-s-en-fout-des-propositions-des-separatistes-quand-emmanuel-macron-telephonait-a-vladimir-poutine-pour-eviter-la-guerre-en-ukraine_5220382.html)

refer to the autonomists of Donbass, who were ready to remain under the authority of Kiev, as it was provided in the Minsk agreements.

As for the Russian proposals of December 2021, concerning the enlargement of NATO to Ukraine, they were immediately rejected by the West, without any discussion.

In order to understand the Russian position, we must recall the situation of the people of Donbass.

2.3.1.2.1. The situation of the Russian-speaking minority in Ukraine

For the Russians, since 2014, the Russian-speaking population of Donbass has been the victim of a war that Vladimir Putin has called "genocide"[73]. The term seems excessive to us, as it is usually associated with major cases, such as the Jewish Holocaust. Our media widely criticized Vladimir Putin's use of this word, but did not hesitate to use it themselves a year later to describe the transfer of children to Russia, intended to save them from the bombing of the city of Donetsk[74].

For the media that propagate nauseating ideologies in the West, the discrimination against Russian-speaking Ukrainians is only Kremlin propaganda. In reality, they are hiding the reality.

In early July 2021, just after the adoption of the *Law on Indigenous Peoples of Ukraine*, Oleg Seminsky, from the presidential party "Servants of the People" and deputy of the Rada, declared[75]:

> *Russians are not an indigenous people in the sense of the law, so they will not be able to fully enjoy all human rights and fundamental freedoms defined by international law and provided for by the Constitution and laws of Ukraine.*

---

73. https://www.ohchr.org/FR/ProfessionalInterest/Pages/CrimeOfGenocide.aspx
74. Salomé Kourdouli, "Who is Maria Lvova-Belova, Russian organizer of the deportation of Ukrainian children?", *rtbf.be*, February 21, 2023 (https://www.liberation.fr/international/europe/qui-est-maria-lvova-belova-organisatrice-russe-de-la-deportation-denfants-ukrainiens-20230221_FXYNDQNEVFE7RNIY2PXMJNLCN4/)
75. "Нардеп від "Слуги народу" Семінський заявив про "позбавлення конституційних прав росіян, які проживають в Україні"," AP News, July 2, 2021 (https://apnews.com.ua/ua/news/nardep-vid-slugi-narodu-seminskii-zayaviv-pro-pozbavlennya-konstitutciinikh-prav-rosiyan-yaki-prozhivaiut-v-ukraini/)

This is the Ukrainian variant of the Nuremberg Laws of 1935, which covers exactly what a Euromaidan activist told the BBC in March 2014[76]: the notion of "*one nation, one people and one country*". This is the "*Idea of Nation*", which the superimposed letters "I" and "N", forming the emblem of the AZOV regiment, symbolize. In other words, Ukraine belongs only to Ukrainian-speaking Ukrainians, while others (such as Ukrainians of Russian origin) cannot be fully part of it.

Strangely enough, no media, nor any European government protested against this law which penalizes Ukrainian citizens for what they are and not for what they do. This is exactly what we have been trying to fight since the 1930's, so that ethnicity is no longer a criterion in the way laws are applied.

The abuses suffered by the Russian-speaking minority in Donbass are a legitimate reason for intervention. This is why our media deny their existence. This is the case of the RTS, which only sees propaganda from the Kremlin[77]. In March 2022, in a surreal exchange with Gennady Gatilov, the Russian ambassador, the Swiss journalist Philippe Revaz denied the existence of the victims of Donbass, in a mixture of bad faith and imbecility and in a rather abject manner, made fun of the crimes of the neo-Nazi militias in Ukraine[78].

For, to claim that Vladimir Putin started a war on February 24, 2022, one must deny everything that preceded. Yet the Russian president was clear[79]:

> *The purpose of this operation is to protect the people who, for the past eight years, have been subjected to humiliation and genocide by the Kiev regime. To this end, we will seek to demilitarize and denazify Ukraine, as well as bring to justice those who have perpetrated numerous bloody crimes against civilians, including citizens of the Russian Federation.*

---

76. "Neo-Nazi threat in new Ukraine: NEWSNIGHT," *BBC Newsnight/YouTube*, March 1st, 2014 (https://youtu.be/5SBo0akeDMY)
77. "TO meet the Azov regiment, accused by Russia of being infested with "neo-Nazis"?", *rts.ch*, April 16, 2022 (https://www.rts.ch/info/monde/13004251-a-la-rencontre-du-regiment-azov-accuse-par-la-russie-detre-infeste-de-neonazis.html)
78. https://www.rts.ch/play/tv/redirect/detail/12961433
79. "Address by the President of the Russian Federation," The Kremlin, February 24, 2022 (http://en.kremlin.ru/events/president/news/67843)

The existence of neo-Nazis in Ukraine according to the American media

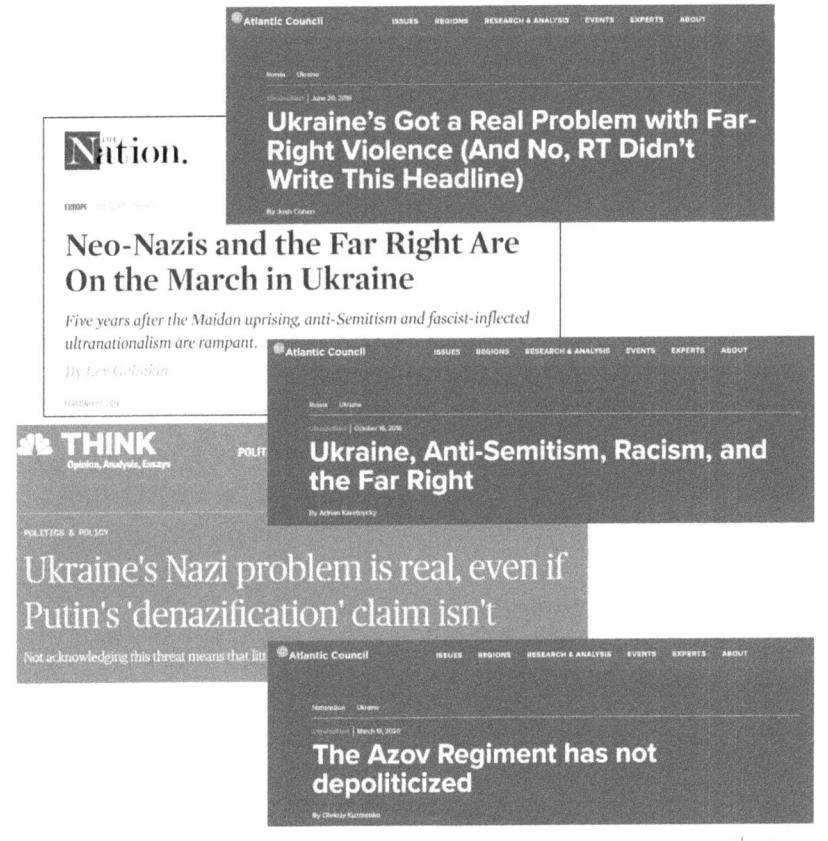

Figure 7 - For journalist Jean-Philippe Schaller of RTS, the presence of neo-Nazis in the Ukrainian ranks is only an invention of Russian propaganda. This is not the opinion of most of the media and it shows that the hatred towards Russians goes far beyond the respect of facts...

Ukrainian neo-Nazi militias that operated in the Donbass region consider Russian speakers as *"Untermenschen"*. By their silence on these crimes, our media - and our politicians - show that they have adopted the same language and are in line with the ideological line adopted by Ukraine after the February 2014 coup. But because they do not want to be equated with neo-Nazis, they seek to minimize their importance in the Ukrainian security and repressive system.

The *Atlantic Council*, a media outlet linked to NATO and the U.S. government, had long warned that *"The Azov Regiment has not depo-*

liticized[80]" and that *"Ukraine has a real problem with far-right violence (and no, RT did not write that headline)*[81]". In March of this year, *NBC News* wrote that *"the Nazi problem in Ukraine is* real"[82], contrary to RT's claim[83], while the American centrist media outlet *The Hill* says it has nothing to do with Kremlin propaganda[84]. Our media obviously have very curious political preferences[85] and I would like to believe that they do not have neo-Nazi sympathies, but their analyses do not show this. We have already seen that some journalists of the Swiss public service entertain theories about an Islamist conspiracy that would threaten the West and would aim to "replace us"[86], and inspired Anders Breivik, responsible for the Utoya massacre[87]!

This disregard for Russian-speaking Ukrainian victims is mirrored today with respect to "Ukrainian-speaking" victims. Western resistance to any form of negotiation between Ukraine and Russia is largely due to the perception that the war causes casualties only among Russians: the Ukrainians are fighting a victorious war without casualties.

2.3.1.2.2. Respect for international law

The Russian intervention in Ukraine is invariably described as a violation of international law, particularly because it is "unprovoked and unjustified". But is this really the case?

The events between March 2021 and February 2022 in Ukraine suggest that a situation was sought in which Russia would be forced to intervene. It is likely that the events in Georgia in 2008 served as a model.

---

80. Oleksiy Kuzmenko, "The Azov Regiment has not depoliticized," Atlantic Council, March 19, 2020 (https://www.atlanticcouncil.org/blogs/ukrainealert/the-azov-regiment-has-not-depoliticized/)
81. Josh Cohen, "Ukraine's Got a Real Problem with Far-Right Violence (And No, RT Didn't Write This Headline)," *The Atlantic Council*, June 20, 2018 (https://www.atlanticcouncil.org/blogs/ukrainealert/ukraine-s-got-a-real-problem-with-far-right-violence-and-no-rt-didn-t-write-this-headline/)
82. Allan Ripp, "Ukraine's Nazi problem is real, even if Putin's 'denazification' claim isn't," NBC News, March 5, 2022 (https://www.nbcnews.com/think/opinion/ukraine-has-nazi-problem-vladimir-putin-s-denazification-claim-war-ncna1290946)
83. https://www.rts.ch/info/monde/13532090-poutine-na-pas-un-discours-de-desinformation-mais-un-discours-carrement-faux.html
84. Lev Golinkin, "The reality of neo-Nazis in Ukraine is far from Kremlin propaganda," *The Hill*, November 9, 2017 (https://thehill.com/opinion/international/359609-the-reality-of-neo-nazis-in-the-ukraine-is-far-from-kremlin-propaganda/)
85. https://youtu.be/bEv4-IJsl9k
86. Sylvain Besson, *La Conquête de L'Occident. Le Projet secret des islamistes*, éditions du Seuil, Paris, October 7, 2005.
87. https://www.qub.ac.uk/Research/GRI/mitchell-institute/FileStore/Filetoupload,818003,en.pdf

In August 2008, Western promises of NATO membership encouraged the Georgian government to bomb the Russian-speaking population of Tskhinvali in South Ossetia. An attack that a report commissioned by the European Union[88] deemed illegal and disproportionate[89]:

The question arises whether the use of force by Georgia in South Ossetia, starting with the bombing of Tskhinvali on the night of August 7-8, 2008, was justifiable under international law. It was not.

It was therefore the Georgian government that provoked the Russian intervention, as noted by Heidi Tagliavini, the Swiss ambassador in charge of the fact-finding mission on the events of 2008[90]:

From the Mission's point of view, it was Georgia that started the war by attacking Tskhinvali (in South Ossetia) with heavy artillery on the night of August 7-8, 2008.

It is thus the responsibility to protect (R2P) that pushed Dimitri Medvedev (and not Vladimir Putin, as claimed by the host Caroline Roux on *France 5*[91]) to decide to intervene.

After the dissolution of the USSR, large Russian-speaking minorities found themselves unwillingly on the territory of new countries with exacerbated nationalism and treated with disdain and distrust by the new countries. In some countries, differentiated statuses have been created for ethnic nationals and Russian speakers, who - sometimes - are not even considered citizens. This situation has led Russia to be concerned about the fate of these minorities and to conclude treaties with these countries to guarantee the rights of Russians.

In Ukraine, the *Treaty of Friendship*, signed on May 31, 1997, was to guarantee Russian speakers *"the protection of the ethnic, cultural,*

---

88. "Quotes from EU-sponsored Georgia war report", *Reuters*, September 30, 2009
89. Andrew Rettman, "EU-sponsored report says Georgia started 2008 war", *euobserver.com*, September 30, 2009
90. Timothy Heritage, "Georgia started war with Russia: EU-backed report", *Reuters*, September 30, 2009 (https://www.reuters.com/article/us-georgia-russia-report-idUSTRE58T4MO20090930)
91. Caroline Roux in the program "C dans l'air" of October 17, 2021 ("Poutine, maître du jeu #cdanslair 17.10.2021", *France 5/YouTube*, October 18, 2021) (53'04")

linguistic and religious originality of national minorities on their territory[92]." The abolition of the Kivalov-Kolesnichenko law on February 23, 2014, was a violation of this treaty and triggered protests throughout southern Ukraine, and led Crimea to claim its January 1991 status under Moscow, which it had just before Ukraine's independence in December.

Because the regular Ukrainian army was reluctant to fight its Russian-speaking compatriots, the new government in Kiev, with the help of Western countries, set up paramilitary militias, composed of ultra-nationalist and neo-Nazi fanatical militants to supplement the military. From then on, Kiev's abuses against Russian-speaking Ukrainians have multiplied and are well known and documented. It is not surprising that one year after its annexation to Russia, the population of Crimea *"preferred Moscow to Kiev"*, according to the American magazine *Forbes* in 2015[93].

There was a negotiated solution to this situation: the Minsk agreements. By becoming *Resolution 2202 (2015)* of the UN Security Council, not only the two guarantor powers for Ukraine (Germany and France), but also the other four permanent members of the Security Council, and a fortiori, the other UN member countries, had to help Ukraine implement it.

Not only did the West declare that it had no intention of enforcing these agreements, but it did absolutely nothing to protect the people of the Donbass and - on the contrary - armed the Ukraine. Clearly, the West has deliberately refused to enforce international law.

By the end of March 2021, after Volodymyr Zelensky issued a decree ordering the recapture of Crimea and the south of the country[94], troops were deployed to the borders of the Donbass. From that moment on, OSCE observers noted an increase in jamming against their drones patrolling along the ceasefire line[95]. For the Russians, the indicators for a Ukrainian operation against Crimea and the Donbass are perceived as a new threat against the Russian-speaking minorities.

---

92. https://apps.dtic.mil/dtic/tr/fulltext/u2/a341002.pdf
93. Kenneth Rapoza, "One Year After Russia Annexed Crimea, Locals Prefer Moscow To Kiev," *Forbes*, March 20, 2015 (https://www.forbes.com/sites/kenrapoza/2015/03/20/one-year-after-russia-annexed-crimea-locals-prefer-moscow-to-kiev/)
94. https://www.president.gov.ua/documents/1172021-37533
95. https://twitter.com/Eire_QC/status/1383830469695860749

*Number of explosions recorded by OSCE in Donbass
(August 2020 - February 2022)*[96]

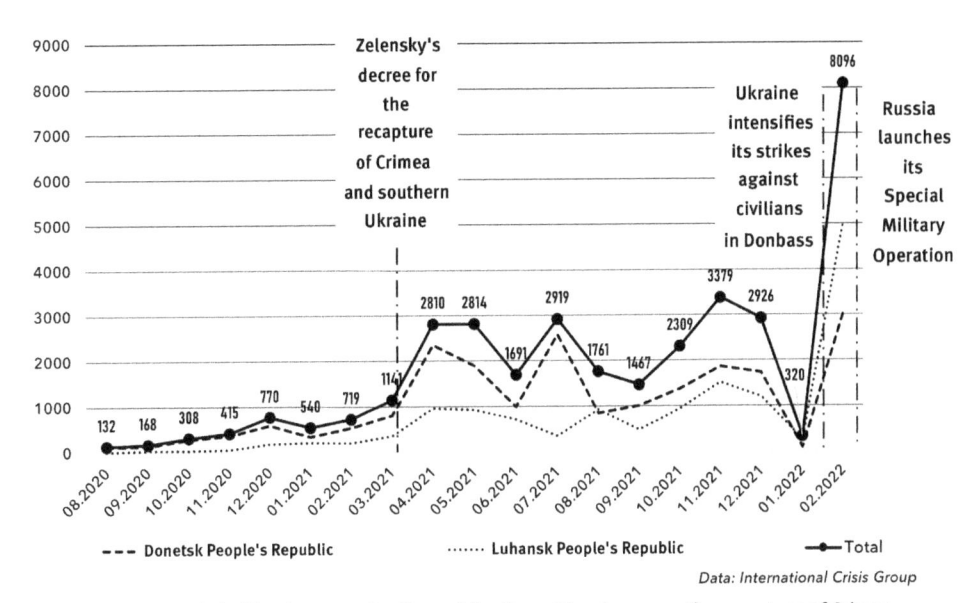

Figure 8 - It is in March 2021, after the publication of the decree on the recapture of Crimea and the south of the country, the beginning of the Ukrainian deployment on the borders of the Donbass and a first intensification of bombing, that the Russians expect a Ukrainian operation. That is why they are deploying troops in their Southern Military District from April 2021.

It was this threat that prompted Russia to activate its forces in the Southern Military District as early as April 2021 with "contingency planning" to prepare for intervention in Ukraine should the threat materialize. This happened in mid-February 2022, with the intensification of artillery preparation against the Donbass[97].

It is likely that the Russians saw an opportunity to turn an operational success in protecting the people of the Donbass into a strategic success by not allowing Ukraine to join NATO. Some will say that R2P was merely a pretext for Russia. It is possible, but we did everything to give it this pretext, which is perfectly legitimate in itself.

---

96. https://www.crisisgroup.org/content/conflict-ukraines-donbas-visual-explainer
97. "Transcript of Vladimir Putin's speech announcing 'special military operation' in Ukraine," *The Sydney Morning Herald*, February 24, 2022 (https://www.smh.com.au/world/europe/full-transcript-of-vladimir-putin-s-speech-announcing-a-special-military-operation-20220224-p59zhq.html)

2. The actors

Because in this perspective, thanks to the conditions created by Ukraine and its Western allies, the Russian intervention has become legitimate. That is why the victims of Donbass are never mentioned, because the objective of the Western narrative is to derationalize the Russian decision.

In fact, Russia has only applied the principle of "responsibility to protect" (R2P), defined as follows by the United Nations[98]:

> *The responsibility to protect (often referred to as "R2P") rests on three equal pillars: the responsibility of each state to protect its population (Pillar I); the responsibility of the international community to assist states in protecting their population (Pillar II); and the responsibility of the international community to protect when a state is clearly failing to protect its population (Pillar III).*

In other words, the responsibility to protect lies primarily with the state vis-à-vis its population (Pillar I) (in this case, Ukraine), but when they do not do so, and the international community (Pillar II) does not help them to do so (such as Germany and France, which were guarantors of the implementation of the Minsk agreements), external actors are empowered to do so under Article 51 of the United Nations Charter (Pillar III). This is what the Russians have done.

Simply put: if our diplomats had fulfilled their mission, enforced IHL and R2P between 2014 and 2022, and sought to enforce the Minsk agreements, we would not be where we are.

Because we ignored the real causes of the conflict in Georgia, we did not pay attention to the events that were likely to create the same effects in Ukraine. But we "had" to ignore these root causes in order to claim that the Russian reaction is irrational, unjustified or "unprovoked". In fact, it was the conspiracy theory developed by our media that contributed to the outbreak of the war in Ukraine.

---

98. https://www.un.org/fr/chronicle/article/la-responsabilite-de-proteger

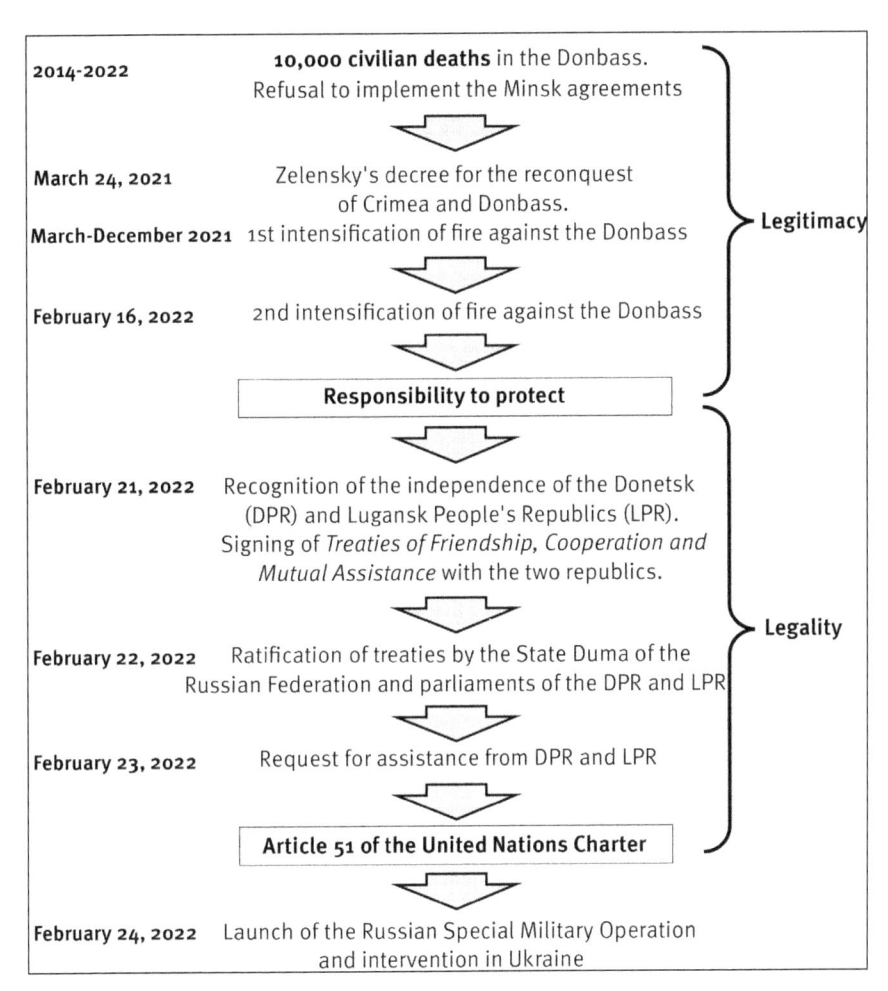

```
2014-2022          10,000 civilian deaths in the Donbass.
                   Refusal to implement the Minsk agreements
                                    ⬇
March 24, 2021     Zelensky's decree for the reconquest
                   of Crimea and Donbass.                        ⎫
March-December 2021  1st intensification of fire against the Donbass  ⎬ Legitimacy
                                                                  ⎪
February 16, 2022  2nd intensification of fire against the Donbass ⎪
                                    ⬇                              ⎭
                   ┌─────────────────────────────────┐
                   │   Responsibility to protect     │
                   └─────────────────────────────────┘
                                    ⬇
February 21, 2022  Recognition of the independence of the Donetsk
                   (DPR) and Lugansk People's Republics (LPR).
                   Signing of Treaties of Friendship, Cooperation and
                   Mutual Assistance with the two republics.
                                    ⬇                              ⎫
February 22, 2022  Ratification of treaties by the State Duma of the ⎬ Legality
                   Russian Federation and parliaments of the DPR and LPR
                                    ⬇
February 23, 2022  Request for assistance from DPR and LPR
                                    ⬇
                   ┌─────────────────────────────────┐
                   │ Article 51 of the United Nations Charter │
                   └─────────────────────────────────┘
                                    ⬇
February 24, 2022  Launch of the Russian Special Military Operation
                   and intervention in Ukraine
```

Figure 9 - The process that led to the decision to intervene in Ukraine. This is the scenario that the Russians openly explained and presented in our media between February 15 and 24. But it was quickly forgotten, because it shows that the Russians had a perfectly rational approach to launch their operation. Moreover, it is the only process that is consistent with the military actions on the ground.

2.3.2. War as a continuation of politics

The objective of "demilitarization" was to destroy the military potential of Ukraine that threatened the population of Donbass. One could say that this goal has already been achieved twice before the spring of 2023:

- In June 2022, the material potential of the Ukrainian army[99] and a large part of the human potential are destroyed. On June 12, 2022, President Zelensky signed a decree authorizing the engagement of units of the Territorial Defense (*Terroborona*) in the fighting[100]. It was at this time that *Radio France International* (RFI) declared that the Ukrainian army had exhausted its equipment and armaments of Soviet or Russian origin and was therefore completely dependent on Western aid[101].
- By the end of 2022, the human potential is practically destroyed. The Ukrainian authorities amended the law on recruitment, which broadened the spectrum of mobilizable personnel[102]. At the same time, the military law was tightened to discourage desertion and punish insubordination more severely[103]. There was an upsurge in forced recruitment, which seemed to concern minorities in particular, the Magyar minority[104]. We will come back to this.
- In the spring of 2023, the "third" Ukrainian army, made up of reservists, foreign volunteers and Western equipment, is ready for a spring counter-offensive that raises many uncertainties…

The objectives stated by Vladimir Putin on February 24, 2022 were clear and relatively limited. The situation allowed Russia to go beyond these objectives in order to have space for negotiation. For example, on March 29, 2022, Moscow withdrew the troops encircling Kiev as a goodwill gesture after Volodymyr Zelensky made his proposal in the Istanbul negotiations. The West saw this as a retreat, but in reality, with

---

99. "Zelenskiy Asks NATO Allies for Modern Heavy Weapons, More Financial Support," *RFE/RL's Ukrainian Service*, June 29, 2022 (https://www.rferl.org/a/ukraine-zelenskiy-nato-modern-weapons-financial-supprot/31921346.html)
100. "Country policy and information note: military service, Ukraine, June 2022 (accessible)," *gov.uk*, July 17, 2022 (https://www.gov.uk/government/publications/ukraine-country-policy-and-information-notes/country-policy-and-information-note-military-service-ukraine-june-2022-accessible)
101. "Ukraine dependent on arms from allies after exhausting Soviet-era weaponry", *RFI*, June 10, 2022 (https://www.rfi.fr/en/ukraine-dependent-on-arms-from-allies-after-exhausting-soviet-era-weaponry)
102. Stefan Korshak, "Ukrainian Cabinet's New Conscription Rules: War-critical Workers May Avoid Draft," *Kiyv Post*, January 31, 2023 (https://www.kyivpost.com/post/11701)
103. "Zelensky Signs Controversial Law Toughening Punishment for Desertion in Army," *AFP/Kiyv Post*, January 25, 2023 (https://www.kyivpost.com/post/11498)
104. Füssy Angéla, "Mint a barmokat, úgy fogdossák össze a férfiakat Kárpátalján - Nézze meg helyszíni videóriportunkat!", *PestiSracok*, January 23, 2023 (https://pestisracok.hu/mint-a-barmokat-ugy-fogdossak-ossze-a-ferfiakat-karpataljan-nezze-meg-helyszini-videoriportunkat/)

only 22,000 troops, Russia never deployed enough to take a city of nearly 3 million people.

Having troops encircling Kiev had an operational function (to fix Ukrainian forces), but also a strategic function as a *bargaining chip*. The withdrawal at the end of March 2022 was therefore most likely planned a long time ago[105], but the Russians turned it into a political asset. They have withdrawn troops from an area of secondary importance to them in order to strengthen their position in the Donbass area, where their priority objective is. This is a way of turning operational success into strategic success.

One can imagine that the Russians see the spring offensive expected by the West in 2023 in the same way. In the event of an offensive, they would seek to obtain higher gains than they would like, so that they could use them in a later negotiation.

As Serguei Lavrov reminded us in his July 20, 2022 interview with several Russian media, Russia's objectives are not geographical or territorial. As Vladimir Putin said on February 24, it is a matter of "demilitarization", in other words, neutralizing the military threat to the Donbass. This obviously translates into an advance on the ground, but the ground is not the objective. As Lavrov says, if the West provides missiles with a range of 300 km to Ukraine in order to achieve their objective, Russian forces will have to advance 300 km to destroy these missiles or have a 300 km buffer zone[106].

2.3.3. Russia ready to negotiate from the start

The inability of our "armchair strategists" to understand a logic different from their own is exactly at the origin of our economic, political and military failures. For example, Patrick Martin-Genier, who is regularly seen on *France 5* or *LCI*, declares that "*Vladimir Putin does not want to*

---

105. Jonathan Spicer & Gleb Garanich, "Russia pledges to reduce attack on Kyiv but U.S. warns threat not over," *Reuters*, March 29, 2022 (https://www.reuters.com/world/europe/ukraine-sets-ceasefire-goal-new-russia-talks-breakthrough-looks-distant-2022-03-29/).
106. "Foreign Minister Sergey Lavrov's interview with RT television, Sputnik agency and Rossiya Segodnya International Information Agency, Moscow, July 20, 2022", *Embassy of the Federation in Russia in Germany*, July 21, 2022 (https://russische-botschaft.ru/de/2022/07/21/foreign-minister-sergey-lavrovs-interview-with-rt-television-sputnik-agency-and-rossiya-segodnya-international-information-agency-moscow-july-20-2022/)

negotiate anything, he wants to exterminate the Ukraine[107]". This is a pure and simple lie, based on nothing.

In reality, Vladimir Putin has always favored a negotiated solution. These were the Minsk agreements, whose implementation he has repeatedly demanded! It is because the Westerners (Germany and France in the lead) refused to implement them, and because Ukraine was preparing to adopt a military solution as early as March 2021, that we have moved to a more confrontational mode.

On February 25, 2022, the Russians advanced dramatically, destroying most of Ukraine's critical military capabilities in one day. Realizing that the planned scenario would turn to Ukraine's disadvantage, Volodymyr Zelensky called for negotiations[108]. He contacted Igniazio Cassis, the Swiss Minister of Foreign Affairs, to arrange mediation and a peace conference[109].

Russia declared itself ready to discuss and a first round of talks was held in Gomel, near the Belarusian border. But the European Union did not agree and arrived on February 27, with a 450 million euro arms package to encourage Ukraine to fight[110].

A "witch hunt" then began in Ukraine, targeting those who supported the negotiation process. Denis Kireyev, a member of Ukrainian military intelligence (GUR), who was part of the negotiating team, was assassinated on March 5 by the Ukrainian secret service (SBU)[111], as Kyrylo Budanov, director of the GUR, would later confirm[112]. Other assassinations followed. On March 2, Vlodymyr Struk, mayor of Kreminna,

---

107. "War in Ukraine: Vladimir Putin "does not want to negotiate anything, he wants to exterminate Ukraine", says an expert on Europe", *franceinfo*, March 12, 2022 (https://www.francetvinfo.fr/monde/europe/manifestations-en-ukraine/guerre-en-ukraine-vladimir-poutine-ne-veut-rien-negocier-il-veut-exterminer-l-ukraine-affirme-un-specialiste-de-l-europe_5006026.html)
108. Olga Rudenko, "Ukraine ready to negotiate with Russia," The Kyiv Independent, February 25, 2022 (https://kyivindependent.com/national/ukraine-ready-to-negotiate-with-russia/).
109. Arthur Rutishauser, "Schweiz will Friedenskonferenz in Genf organisieren", *Tages Anzeiger*, February 26, 2022 (https://www.tagesanzeiger.ch/schweiz-will-friedenskonferenz-in-genf-organisieren-129475547083)
110. Maïa de La Baume & Jacopo Barigazzi, "EU agrees to give €500M in arms, aid to Ukrainian military in 'watershed' move," Politico, February 27, 2022 (https://www.politico.eu/article/eu-ukraine-russia-funding-weapons-budget-military-aid/).
111. https://www.timesofisrael.com/ukraine-reports-claim-negotiator-shot-for-treason-officials-say-he-died-in-intel-op/
112. Vlasta Lazur, "'Денис Кірєєв - співробітник ГУР, якого вбили в автівці СБУ, а тіло викинули на вулицю' Інтерв'ю з Кирилом Будановим," Radio Svoboda, January 22, 2023 (https://www.radiosvoboda.org/a/вбивство-кірєєва/32233661.html)

was eliminated by the SBU after having established contacts with the Russians. The Anglo-Saxon press reported on this at[113], but no French-speaking journalist condemned it. On March 7, Yuriy Prilipko, mayor of Gostomel, was assassinated after trying to negotiate an evacuation of civilians with the Russians.

A month later, the same scenario is repeated. Volodymyr Zelensky makes a proposal that includes the neutrality of Ukraine, the ban on nuclear weapons on its territory, the non-violent resolution of the situation in Crimea and Sevastopol, the identification of the Donetsk and Lugansk regions as "separate zones", the renunciation of NATO membership and the deployment of foreign military bases and contingents on its territory[114]. The Russians are ready to discuss it and a resolution of the crisis is expected[115].

But once again the European Union and Great Britain threatened Zelensky with withdrawal of support and arms shipments if he persisted in negotiating. So he withdrew his proposal. The Ukrainian media *Ukraïnskaya Pravda* then noted that the West was the main obstacle to peace[116].

In March 2022, the Russians achieved their objective of "denazification", with the encirclement of Mariupol. In June, they reach their objective of "demilitarization". We can therefore say that from June 2022, the Russians would have had no reason not to want a negotiated solution.

But it is at this point that the situation becomes complicated. Seeing that they have lost the game, the West begins to deliver weapons to Ukraine, in order to keep the conflict "active". Western propaganda talks

---

113. Kaya Terry, "Pro-Russian mayor of city in eastern Ukraine who welcomed Putin's invasion is found shot dead in the street after being kidnapped from his home," *The Daily Mail*, March 3, 2022 (https://www.dailymail.co.uk/news/article-10571663/Pro-Russian-mayor-city-eastern-Ukraine-shot-dead-kidnapped-home.html)
114. "Zelensky says Ukrainian neutrality on the table ahead of fresh talks with Russia in Turkey," France 24, March 27, 2022 (updated March 28, 2022) (https://www.france24.com/en/europe/20220327-live-kyiv-accuses-russia-of-destroying-fuel-and-food-storage-depots-in-ukraine); "Ukraine ready to discuss adopting neutral status in Russia peace deal, Zelenskiy says," Reuters, March 28, 2022 (https://www.reuters.com/world/europe/ukraine-prepared-discuss-neutrality-status-zelenskiy-tells-russian-journalists-2022-03-27/).
115. "Russia, Ukraine 'close to agreement' in negotiations, says Turkey," Aljazeera, March 20, 2022 (https://www.aljazeera.com/news/2022/3/20/turkey-says-russia-ukraine-close-to-agreement); "After rejecting ultimatum, Zelensky insists 'meeting' with Putin needed to end war," The Times of Israel, March 21, 2022 (https://www.timesofisrael.com/liveblog-march-21-2022/).
116. https://www.pravda.com.ua/eng/news/2022/05/5/7344206/

about Ukrainian "counter-offensives" and that Russia "lost the war", but the opposite is true.

Ukraine and the West are captives of the *"sunk cost fallacy"* theory[117]. Known in economics, this theory describes the tendency to persist in an action whose costs exceed its benefits, but in which one has already invested significant resources[118]. The problem is that this type of obstinacy inevitably leads to a higher final price, even if the objective is achieved. This is the price the Ukrainians paid in Mariupol, Severodonetsk and Lysychansk...

The longer the conflict goes on, the more resources and territory Ukraine loses. The Russians believe that the worse the situation gets for Ukraine, the more it will lose in a negotiation process and the more difficult it will be. This is exactly what Sergei Lavrov and Vladimir Putin said in July 2022: *"The longer the conflict goes on, the more* difficult *the negotiations will be"*[119].

On August 18, 2022, President Tayyip Erdogan met with Volodymyr Zelensky in Lvov and offered to arrange a meeting with Vladimir Putin[120] and to mediate with Moscow[121]. But on the 24th, Boris Johnson paid an impromptu visit to Zelensky to declare that *"this is not the time to propose some lame plan for* negotiation*"*[122] and provided additional aid of £54 million for weapons.

On September 14, 2022, in her State of the Union address, Ursula von der Leyen declared that *"this is a time for determination, not appeasement"*[123]. At this point, the Europeans are convinced by propaganda that

---

117. https://youtu.be/GCmfXMMhRzk
118. Caeleigh MacNeil, "Sunk Costs: a trap influencing our decisions?", *asana*.com, January 10, 2022 (https://asana.com/fr/resources/sunk-cost-fallacy)
119. "Putin warns negotiations will get harder longer conflict in Ukraine continues," Radio New Zealand, July 8, 2022 (https://www.rnz.co.nz/news/world/470559/putin-warns-negotiations-will-get-harder-longer-conflict-in-ukraine-continues)
120. "Erdogan offers Zelensky opportunity to organise meeting with Putin", *Ukraïnska Pravda*, August 19, 2022 (https://www.pravda.com.ua/eng/news/2022/08/19/7363969/)
121. Grzegorz Kuczyński, "Lviv Summit Confirms Erdogan's Diplomatic Offensive," *Warsaw Institute*, August 22, 2022 (https://warsawinstitute.org/lviv-summit-confirms-erdogans-diplomatic-offensive/)
122. Tom Balmforth & Andrea Shalal, "UK's Boris Johnson, in Kyiv, warns against 'flimsy' plan for talks with Russia," *Reuters*, August 24, 2022 (https://www.reuters.com/world/europe/uks-johnson-kyiv-warns-against-flimsy-plan-talks-with-russia-2022-08-24/)
123. "State of the Union Address 2022 by President von der Leyen", *European Commission*, September 14, 2022 (https://ec.europa.eu/commission/presscorner/detail/fr/speech_22_5493)

Kiev is on a winning streak and they have invested so much in this conflict that they cannot go back.

Believing that the West cannot lose face in this exercise and that they will continue to support Ukraine all the more as their own economic situation deteriorates, the Russians change their strategy. They decide to systematically destroy the Ukrainian potential. This is what General Sourovikine explains in October[124].

Support for negotiations among the Russian population [%].

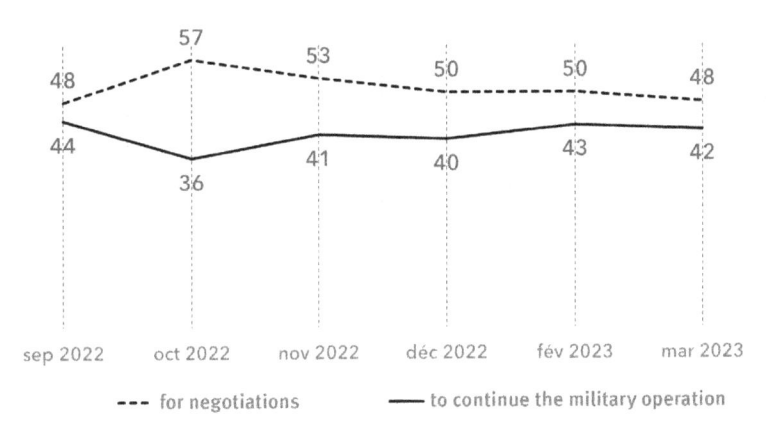

Figure 10 - The Russian population's willingness to negotiate is weakening. Arms shipments to Ukraine, terrorist attacks on Russian soil and the sabotage of Nord Stream 2 have increased support for the military operation in Ukraine. [Source: Levada Center]

In November 2022, driven by the impending failure of the mid-term elections, the American government seems to have understood this dynamic and encourages Volodymyr Zelensky to negotiate[125]. However, on the set of RTS, Claude Wild, the Swiss ambassador in Kiev, asserts that it is Russia that is asking to negotiate, because it is in a weak position[126]. Nothing could be further from the truth. In fact, it is exactly the opposite. For the Russians, neither the Ukrainians nor the Westerners are trus-

---

124. "Суровикин: российская группировка на Украине методично "перемалывает" войска противника", *TASS*, October 18, 2022 (https://tass.ru/armiya-i-opk/16090805)
125. Missy Ryan, John Hudson & Paul Sonne, "U.S. privately asks Ukraine to show it's open to negotiate with Russia," *The Washington Post*, November 5, 2022 (https://www.washingtonpost.com/national-security/2022/11/05/ukraine-russia-peace-negotiations/)
126. https://www.rts.ch/play/tv/redirect/detail/13567586?startTime=383

2. The actors

tworthy interlocutors. On December 9, during his press conference in Bishkek (Kyrgyzstan), Vladimir Putin declared that the level of trust with the West was "*almost at* zero"[127].

The Russians are not opposed to negotiation, but since October 2022, they have come to terms with the fact that the West is dragging them into a war of attrition and they are in no hurry. They will only negotiate if they have solid guarantees that Ukraine and the West will not try to do again what they did with the Minsk agreements.

In Russia, opinion remains more or less on the same line as the government. The figures of the Levada Center[128] (considered a foreign agent in Russia) are very close to those of a "secret" poll, revealed by the Russian opposition media *Meduza*, whose origin and authenticity could not be verified[129].

In other words, the prolongation of the conflict desired by the West seems to strengthen popular support for the Russian government. While in European countries, people are demonstrating for their countries to stop fuelling the conflict, in Russia, it seems that popular support for Vladimir Putin remains strong.

---

127. Kevin Liffey, "Putin says loss of trust in West will make future Ukraine talks harder," *Reuters*, December 9, 2022 (https://www.reuters.com/world/europe/putin-says-loss-trust-west-will-make-future-ukraine-talks-harder-2022-12-09/)
128. https://www.levada.ru/2023/03/02/konflikt-s-ukrainoj-otsenki-fevralya-2023-goda/
129. https://meduza.io/en/feature/2022/11/30/make-peace-not-war

3. Geostrategic considerations

3.1. The Russian threat to Europe

The historical tendency to expansion that is attributed to Russia today is merely an extrapolation of our understanding of the Marxist thinking that guided Soviet policy. In this reading, the USSR saw itself as the spearhead of the class struggle and engaged in a permanent and systemic war with the West, which was part of a historical process. Until the death of Stalin, the strategic military thinking of the USSR was dominated by the idea that its security would be guaranteed only by a victory of socialism over capitalism, and that the confrontation between the two systems was inevitable. Soviet strategists speak of the principle of "inevitability of war".

However, the USSR's intention to invade Europe seems to have been a myth, as a study by the *Staff College* at Ft. Leavenworth in the United States[130] demonstrates. It is based on declassified Soviet documents, articles and minutes of meetings, which indicate that the Soviet leadership had no intention of invading Europe[131]. Instead, they feared that if it appeared weak, the West might have seized the opportunity to attack the USSR[132].

---

130. Dr. Mahir J. Ibrahimov, Mr. Gustav A. Otto & Col Lee G. Gentile, Jr, "Cultural Perspectives, Geopolitics & Energy Security of Eurasia: Is the Next Global Conflict Imminent?", US Army Command and General Staff College Press, Fort Leavenworth, 2017 (https://www.armyupress.army.mil/Portals/7/combat-studies-institute/csi-books/cultural-perspectives.pdf)
131. Raymond Garthoff, Deterrence and the Revolution in Soviet Military Doctrine, The Brookings Institute, Washington D.C., 1990, p. 11
132. Vladislav Zubok, The Kremlin's Cold War: From Stalin to Khrushchev, Harvard University Press, Boston, 1997, p. 20

Today more than ever, the Russian military threat against Europe is a fiction carefully maintained to encourage hatred in our countries. It is not clear why Russia would seek to attack its main customer for hydrocarbons and its main source of manufactured goods.

It is both brandished and contradicted by our media, our politicians and the same people who, in February 2022 already[133], then in March[134], in June[135], in October[136], in November[137], in December 2022[138] and in February 2023[139], affirmed that Russia had already lost the war against a Ukraine that lacks equipment and weapons!

This threat is all the less understandable as European countries are ready to sacrifice part of their own defence capabilities to replace Ukrainian equipment systematically destroyed by Russia. This so-called threat has not prevented Estonia from giving all its artillery to Ukraine, nor Latvia from doing the same with all its portable anti-aircraft missiles STINGER[140]. This shows, if it were necessary, that these countries bordering Russia are not afraid of being the object of an attack.

The idea that Russia is a threat to our society is quite recent, as is the idea of our "energy dependence", which did not seem to be a problem for Europeans until Donald Trump used it as an argument to prevent the construction of the Nord Stream 2 gas pipeline.

---

133. Jean-Baptiste Jeangène Vilmer, "Why Putin has already lost the war," *Le Grand Continent*, February 27, 2022 (https://legrandcontinent.eu/fr/2022/02/27/pourquoi-poutine-a-deja-perdu-la-guerre/)
134. "Invasion of Ukraine: 'Russia has lost the war'", *Le Journal de Montréal*, March 2, 2022 (https://www.journaldemontreal.com/2022/03/02/invasion-de-lukraine-la-russie-a-perdu-la-guerre)
135. Ian Bremmer, "Russia has already lost the war," *The Echo*, June 18, 2022 (https://www.lecho.be/opinions/general/la-russie-a-deja-perdu-la-guerre/10396613.html)
136. Paul Véronique, "General Michel Yakovleff: 'Putin has lost the war, but he has not yet understood it'", *L'Express*, October 20, 2022 (updated October 22, 2022) (https://www.lexpress.fr/monde/europe/general-michel-yakovleff-poutine-a-perdu-la-guerre-mais-il-ne-l-a-pas-encore-compris_2182214.html)
137. "Ukraine: 'Russia has already lost this war,' says historian Jean-François Colosimo," Public Sénat, November 25, 2022 (https://www.publicsenat.fr/article/politique/ukraine-la-russie-a-deja-perdu-cette-guerre-estime-l-historien-jean-francois)
138. "François Hollande: 'Vladimir Putin has already lost the war in Ukraine'", *Le Soir*, December 26, 2022 (https://www.lesoir.be/485229/article/2022-12-26/francois-hollande-vladimir-poutine-deja-perdu-la-guerre-en-ukraine)
139. Jonathan Littell, "Putin has already lost the war, but we are not doing what is necessary to force him to accept it," *Le Monde*, February 24, 2023 (https://www.lemonde.fr/idees/article/2023/02/24/jonathan-littell-on-laisse-poutine-croire-qu-il-n-a-pas-perdu-la-guerre_6163122_3232.html)
140. "Latvia to deliver all available Stinger MANPADS to Ukraine", *Ukraïnska Pravda*, April 21, 2023 (https://www.pravda.com.ua/eng/news/2023/04/21/7398940/)

3.2. The "values"

3.2.1. From "law-based international order" to "rules-based international order"

Since the early 2000s, in order to wage their war on terrorism, the United States and Great Britain have sought to create an alternative international order that gives them a free hand. The aim is to reduce the authority of international institutions. To this end, the "law-based international order" (LBIO) that emerged from the Second World War is being replaced by a "rules-based international order" (RBIO).

Clearly, international relations are no longer governed by rules of law recognized and accepted by all, but by rules established unilaterally. These rules can be "values" (the famous "Western values"), but also national interests. The OIBR is therefore broader and includes other elements than law, such as social norms or principles (often of Western origin). At first glance, this seems more attractive, but the problem is that the rules - unlike the law - are less clear.

As the *Australian Institute of International Affairs* (AIIA) says[141]:

> *Contrary to popular belief, a rules-based international order is not a continuation of the past, but a replacement for an order based on international law. The decline of the ideal of a politically neutral international law is a dangerous development.*

Inspired by Israeli policy, this approach has led the United States to withdraw from all arms control treaties. It is also what allowed the Americans to kidnap citizens on the territory of European countries without their approval, or the use of torture in Europe.

The United States sees the United Nations in opposition to its unipolar vision of the world, where it represents the model to follow. This is why, faced with the rise of China and Russia, and their cohesion in the UN Security Council, the United States is trying to set up an alternative

---

141. Prof. Shirley Scott, "In Defense of the International Law-Based Order," Australian Institute of International Affairs (AIIA), June 7, 2018 (https://www.internationalaffairs.org.au/australianoutlook/in-defense-of-the-international-law-based-order/)

system for managing the international order, based around countries that are favourable to them. This is the basis of the *"Democracy Summit"*, launched by Joe Biden in December 2021, whose main objective is to *"strengthen democracy and defend against authoritarianism".* Yet, of the 111 countries invited, only 19 were *"full democracies"* as defined by the *Economist Intelligence Unit* (EIU). The other 92 were (again according to the EIU) *"failing democracies"* (such as the United States itself, France and Belgium), *"hybrid regimes"* and *"authoritarian regimes"*[142].

In fact, there is a tendency to replace a world order based on international law, with the UN system as the keystone, by a system of "values", the keystone of which would be American thinking.

A May 17, 2017 memo to then-Secretary of State Rex Tillerson sheds light on the exploitation of our "values" for geopolitical purposes[143]:

> *(...) In the case of U.S. allies such as Egypt, Saudi Arabia, and the Philippines, the Administration is absolutely right to emphasize good relations for a variety of important reasons, including counterterrorism, and to face honestly the difficult trade-offs in human rights.*
>
> *(...) Compared to our rivals, the dilemma is far less important. We don't want to support America's adversaries abroad; we seek to pressure, compete with, and thwart them. For this reason, we should consider human rights an important issue in U.S. relations with China, Russia, North Korea, and Iran. This is not just out of moral concern for the domestic management of these countries. It is also because pressuring these regimes on human rights is a way to impose costs on them, to apply counter-pressure, and to regain the initiative strategically.*

In other words, we do not use our values to disseminate them, but as leverage to influence our opponents or to impose policy changes on them. Moreover, we use these "values" in an extremely selective way. For example, we have cordial ties with the United States, yet between 1947

---

142. "Democracy Index 2020 - In sickness and in health?", *The Economist Intelligence Unit*, 2021 (https://www.eiu.com/n/campaigns/democracy-index-2020/)
143. https://www.politico.com/f/?id=00000160-6c37-da3c-a371-ec3f13380001

and 1989, they attempted 72 times to overthrow governments: 6 times openly and 66 times through clandestine operations, of which only 26 were successful[144]. Not to mention the (very likely) involvement of the United States in the destruction of critical European infrastructure (Nord Stream 1 and 2), which Jens Stoltenberg, NATO Secretary General, did not hesitate to call an "act of war"[145].

The discourse on our values is variable. For example, on the occasion of the Ukrainian crisis, Joe Biden repeated over and over that *"nations have the freedom to choose their own path and to choose with whom they want to partner*[146]*."* He is a liar. The U.S. imposes sanctions on countries that buy Russian weapons, under the *Countering America's Adversaries Through Sanctions Act* (CAATSA), and has, for example, sanctioned China for acquiring Russian weapons systems! Thus, 33 countries[147] have been placed under sanctions or have suffered retaliation, in order to dissuade them from buying Russian military equipment[148]. But France is no better: the origin of the rift between Bamako and Paris has little to do with the rule of law (Paris was quite happy with a coup d'état in 2020), but with an arms contract between Mali and Russia[149].

So we are not fighting for the respect of international law, but for the maintenance of Western supremacy. This is very different, and the Ukrainian conflict has made this difference clear to the world.

---

144. Lindsey A. O'Rourke, "The U.S. tried to change other countries' governments 72 times during the Cold War," *The Washington Post*, December 23, 2016.
145. Katya Adler, "A journey to the site of the Nord Stream explosions", BBC News, November 18, 2022 (https://www.bbc.com/news/world-63636181)
146. Shane Harris, Robyn Dixon, Rachel Pannett & Emily Rauhala, "Biden says U.S. has not verified a pullback of Russian troops from Ukraine's border, despite Moscow's claims," *The Washington Post*, February 15, 2022
147. They are: Algeria, Angola, Armenia, Azerbaijan, Belarus, Cameroon, China, Egypt, Ghana, India, Indonesia, Iran, Iraq, Kazakhstan, Kyrgyzstan, Malaysia, Mexico, Morocco, Myanmar, Nepal, Nicaragua, Nigeria, Pakistan, Peru, Philippines, Qatar, Saudi Arabia, Serbia, South Korea, Turkey, United Arab Emirates, Uzbekistan, and Vietnam
148. John V. Parachini, Ryan Bauer, Peter A. Wilson, "Impact of the U.S. and Allied Sanction Regimes on Russian Arms Sales," *RAND Corporation*, 2021
149. Georges François Traoré, "Les vraies raisons de la brouille: Bah N'Daw aurait communiqué aux Français des documents de contrat d'armement", *maliweb.net*, May 26, 2021; Georges Ibrahim Tounkara, "Assimi Goïta, l'homme au center de la transition au Mali", *dw.com*, May 26, 2021

3.2.1.1. The arrest warrant against Vladimir Putin

On March 14, 2023, the *International Criminal Court* (ICC) issued an arrest warrant for Vladimir Putin for the abduction, detention and deportation of approximately 6,000 Ukrainian children to Russia.

3.2.1.1.1. The International Criminal Court (ICC) or justice "à la carte"

The ICC is an international court created by the Rome Statute of 1998, which came into force in 2002. Its power can only be exercised over countries that recognize its jurisdiction. Some countries, such as the United States, Israel, Ukraine, Russia, China or India do not recognize it.

In the 2000s, Western countries pressured African countries to sign the Rome Statute, using the financial support they provided[150]. However, it very quickly became apparent that the ICC was mainly exercising its powers over countries that were not part of the Western world. While the justice system should be independent and impartial, it has been invoked only to judge personalities from countries that are adversaries of the West. This is what has caused many African countries to withdraw. War crimes committed by Western countries in Afghanistan, Iraq or Syria have not been dealt with by the ICC.

On June 11, 2020, President Donald Trump issued an executive order (*Executive Order 13928*), which authorizes the freezing of assets and banning the families of ICC officials[151].

On September 2, 2020, the U.S. administration even adopted sanctions against judges of the *International Criminal Court* (ICC) "*involved in the ICC's efforts to investigate U.S. personnel*" for war crimes[152]!... Thus, anyone making a contribution in the form of "services" to individuals designated for sanctions - the Prosecutor or his top aide - could be subject to civil and criminal penalties[153].

---

[150]. Mwangi S. Kimenyi, "Can the International Criminal Court Play Fair in Africa?", *Brookings Institution*, October 17, 2013 (https://www.brookings.edu/blog/africa-in-focus/2013/10/17/can-the-international-criminal-court-play-fair-in-africa/)
[151]. "Factsheet: U.S. Sanctions on the International Criminal Court," *Center for Constitutional Rights*, April 2, 2021 (https://ccrjustice.org/factsheet-us-sanctions-international-criminal-court)
[152]. "US Sanctions on the International Criminal Court," *Human Rights Watch*, December 14, 2020 (https://www.hrw.org/news/2020/12/14/us-sanctions-international-criminal-court)
[153]. "Factsheet: U.S. Sanctions on the International Criminal Court," *Center for Constitutional Rights*, April 2, 2021 (https://ccrjustice.org/factsheet-us-sanctions-international-criminal-court)

In April 2021, just after the election of the new leadership of the ICC[154], now chaired by Polish (!) judge Piotr Hofmański, the Biden administration revoked *Executive Order 13928*, but obtained from the ICC so that it would not investigate war crimes committed by the US military in Afghanistan[155]... So much for the impartiality of the judiciary...

To this end, in August 2022, the United States enacted the *American Service-Members' Protection Act* (ASPA), which is a law that prevents the ICC from indicting and arresting American citizens. It even authorizes the U.S. government to use any means necessary - including military force - to free Americans who have been arrested[156]. The U.S. has even made it clear that countries that cooperate with the ICC in arresting U.S. citizens will be subject to retaliation. For example, U.S. law allows for the withdrawal of U.S. military assistance to countries that ratify the Rome Statute[157].

The ICC is theoretically independent, but it is not. It has repeatedly demonstrated that it serves the interests of the Western community rather than justice. This is the difference between a "law-based international order" and a "rules-based international order".

During my many years in international bodies, I was surprised to see how war crimes committed in African countries provoked more reactions than those committed by Westerners. It is therefore not really surprising that the ICC has a bad reputation in Africa, where it is seen as a tool for imposing Western law, not for justice. In fact, despite the hundreds of war crimes and crimes against humanity committed by Western armies (United States, Great Britain, France, Poland, Ukraine, Canada, etc.) in countries that were unjustly, illegally and illegitimately attacked, it is almost exclusively Africans who have been brought before this court[158].

---

154. https://www.icc-cpi.int/news/new-icc-presidency-elected-2021-2024
155. Andrea Germanos, "Critics Fume as ICC Excludes US From Probe Into Afghan War Crimes," *commondreams.org*, September 27, 2021; "Statement of the Prosecutor of the International Criminal Court, Karim A. A. Khan QC, following the application for an expedited order under article 18(2) seeking authorisation to resume investigations in the Situation in Afghanistan", www.icc-cpi.int, September 27, 2021 (https://www.commondreams.org/news/2021/09/27/critics-fume-icc-excludes-us-probe-afghan-war-crimes)
156. Todd Buchwald, "Unpacking New Legislation on US Support for the International Criminal Court," *Just Security*, March 9, 2023 (https://www.justsecurity.org/85408/unpacking-new-legislation-on-us-support-for-the-international-criminal-court/)
157. "U.S.: 'Hague Invasion Act' Becomes Law," *Human Rights Watch*, August 3, 2002 (https://www.hrw.org/news/2002/08/03/us-hague-invasion-act-becomes-law)
158. https://en.wikipedia.org/wiki/International_Criminal_Court

The arrest warrant against Vladimir Putin will probably have negative consequences... but probably more for the West than for Russia. Because by issuing an arrest warrant, even before having concrete elements to justify it, the ICC has shown that it only provides "à la carte" justice, with political objectives. Once again, the West has shown the world that the institutions it has created serve its own interests and not those of the world.

The ICC judges have missed an opportunity to demonstrate their integrity: their credibility and legitimacy in the "rest of the world" is not very high and will certainly continue to weaken. Their refusal to condemn crimes committed by Western countries confirms a widely shared feeling that they are not applying justice impartially, but are exploiting justice for political interests.

3.2.1.1.2. The substance of the charge

As for the substance, American investigative journalists[159] were interested in the merits of the accusations against Russia.

The ICC's mandate is based on a report published in the United States on February 14, 2024[160], which the Swiss channel RTS attributes to Yale University[161], suggesting that it is the result of a scientific and impartial approach. However, this is not the case.

In fact, this report was prepared by the *Humanitarian Research Lab* (HRL) of Yale University, under the guidance of the *Conflict Observatory* of the U.S. government. The Conflict Observatory is an arm of the *Office of Conflict and Stabilization Operations*. It was specifically created by the U.S. Department of State on May 17, 2022 to address the intervention in Ukraine[162].

This is a far cry from the impartial approach suggested by the term "humanitarian", since the report was financed by the US government[163].

---

159. Jeremy Loffredo & Max Blumenthal, "ICC's Putin arrest warrant based on State Dept-funded report that debunked itself," *The Grayzone*, March 31, 2023 (https://thegrayzone.com/2023/03/31/iccs-putin-arrest-state-dept-report/)
160. "Russia's Systematic Program for the Re-Education & Adoption of Ukraine's Children," *Humanitarian Research Lab at Yale School of Public Health*, February 14, 2024 (https://hub.conflictobservatory.org/portal/sharing/rest/content/items/97f919ccfe524d31a241b53ca44076b8/data)
161. https://www.rts.ch/play/tv/redirect/detail/13792813
162. https://www.state.gov/promoting-accountability-for-war-crimes-and-other-atrocities-in-ukraine/
163. Carly Olson, "Russia has relocated 6,000 Ukrainian children to camps in Russian territory, a report finds," *The New York Times*, February 15, 2023 (https://www.nytimes.com/2023/02/15/world/europe/russia-ukraine-children-camps.html)

Moreover, its methodology is questionable, as it is based only on indirect (second-hand) information:

> *This methodology has its limitations. Yale HRL explicitly relies on open source information for its work and does not conduct interviews with witnesses or victims.*

In fact, our "experts" have only taken information from the Internet!

As for our media, they mention the secret nature of these actions, but carefully omit to specify that the parents of the children fear being called collaborators:

> *Many Ukrainian families do not wish to share their experiences publicly, as they fear being considered collaborators with Russia.*

That being said, it is good that the international community is concerned about children. But we must care about *all* children. No one held the government of Kiev accountable for bombing its own citizens between 2014 and 2022... Similarly, no one reacted when it was revealed that sanctions against Iraq had caused the death of 500,000 children, as justified by Mrs. Madeleine Albright, US Secretary of State in 1996[164]. Again, our media are loudly offended by the rumors propagated by Ukraine, but keep silent - and thus accept - the crimes against Arab children.

This is the problem of war crimes in Ukraine. They are condemned without even knowing if they were really committed by Russians. Because you only have to look at the map to see that the areas occupied by Russian forces are Russian-speaking areas and that we do not really see why or how Russia would try to alienate a population that is already largely won over. As Ignazio Cassis, Swiss Minister of Foreign Affairs[165] states:

> *These are not war crimes until a court of law says so.*

---

164. 60 Minutes show, "Madeleine Albright," *newmedia7/YouTube*, August 5, 2016. (https://www.youtube.com/watch?v=FbIX1CP9qr4) (In reality, it appears that the figure was more like 130,000 dead children; which is enough to be outraged about...except for our journalists, politicians, and judiciary!)
165. "Ignazio Cassis: 'These are not war crimes until a court decrees it'", *rts.ch*, April 7, 2022 (https://www.rts.ch/info/suisse/13002882-ignazio-cassis-ce-ne-sont-pas-des-crimes-de-guerre-tant-quun-tribunal-ne-la-pas-decrete.html)

In other words, whether the rumors are verified or not, those who are outraged against Russia for rumors that have not been confirmed, but who have never been outraged for the dead Iraqi children, fall into the category of "supremacists". For them, the life of an Iraqi boy is worth 1,000 times less than that of a Ukrainian boy. Not very surprising, since the idea of a "superior people" dominates the ideology of the Ukrainian government and those who support it.

Blinken, Nuland, Baerbock, Albright... the crises are managed by individuals who have a profound disregard for others and for human life...

3.2.1.1.3. The arrest warrant against Vladimir Putin

Several anomalies make the arrest warrant against Vladimir Putin an act more political than judicial.

First of all, neither Russia, Ukraine nor the United States have ratified the Rome Statute. In other words, not only do they not recognize the jurisdiction of the ICC, but the ICC has no jurisdiction over them. It is interesting to note that Joe Biden welcomed this decision before clarifying that the United States does not recognize the ICC.

Secondly, we are surprised that this mandate does not cover the case of Boutcha! After a year, it seems that no evidence has been found to incriminate the Russians. Apparently, the commission of inquiry set up by the Europeans, from which the Russians have - naturally - been excluded, is not able to deliver conclusive accusations[166]. Moreover, while any trifling matter can feed propaganda against Russia, Boutcha's crimes seem to have strangely disappeared from our media.

Third, this arrest warrant is not based on any serious investigation, but only on presumptions, unilateral statements by Ukraine and second-hand information. We will come back to this.

Fourth, one can expect international justice to be impartial in the matters it must decide. This is not the case. For example, neither the ICC nor our media have considered as "genocide" the transfer of Russian-speaking Ukrainian children to Ukrainian-speaking areas in order to make them lose their Russian culture, as shown in a report by RTBF's

---

166. "UN Commission: too early to draw conclusions on war crimes in Ukraine," *Euronews / AP/ AFP*, June 15, 2022 (https://fr.euronews.com/2022/06/15/commission-de-lonu-trop-tot-pour-ti-rer-des-conclusions-sur-des-crimes-de-guerre-en-ukraine)

"19:30", where the teacher explains that she has to make them forget Russian in order to make them speak Ukrainian[167].

The accusation of war crimes is demanding. Especially if it is expressed so loudly. It imposes its conditions on both the accused and the accuser. Either one condemns all the crimes or none of them, because condemning only one side, loudly and without nuance, without reacting to the others, means *that one accepts the other crimes*. This goes far beyond a simple "double standard" and does not only concern judicial institutions. This is what we saw with the terrorist attacks in Russia that none of our media (among others: *RTS, RTBF, LCI, France 5*) condemned. But there are no good and bad war crimes.

The problem is that the Russians know the reality of things. They know that Russian speakers in Donbass are not full citizens in Ukraine, that since 2014 the Ukrainian army has been shelling the civilian population of Donbass, and that Russia's initiative was simply to get children away from the war zones since 2014. The report of the American journalists shows that the "camps" where the children were sent are actually hotels, set up for music lessons.

There is no doubt that this maneuver will have no effect on governance in Russia. On the contrary, it may confirm to the Russian population that the West is trying to overthrow power in Russia. Vladimir Putin will emerge with the image of a courageous man who is not afraid to confront Western countries.

The objective is to make peace negotiations more difficult. Not only do these judges not seek justice, they try to prevent peace. By doing this, the ICC has condemned Ukraine to death, because it is not Russia that is in a weak position.

Crimes of any kind are condemned by all value systems. The particularity of Western values is the impartial and just treatment of these crimes. We do not recognize the law of retaliation, but give the accused the right to defend himself. This is the essence of our values. However, none of our media, journalists or even our governments take offense at the fact that the Russians are totally excluded from commissions of inquiry into the crimes of which they are accused (e.g. in the MH-17,

---

167. https://www.rtbf.be/article/en-ukraine-le-desamour-pour-la-langue-russe-vue-comme-celle-de-lagresseur-10971374

Skripal, Navalny, Boutcha, Nord Stream, etc. cases). This incoherence on the essence of what made the values of the West is discrediting us, and rightly so.

In reality, if we had confidence in our values and in our accusations, we would respect the rules that we have set for ourselves and that we want to be universal. The reality, unfortunately, is that our western society is in the hands of supremacists who think that we are superior to others... This is what is destroying us.

3.2.2. A new look at neo-Nazism and extremism

After the Cold War, instead of building relations on the basis of deeper cooperation with Russia, the idea that it continued to pose a threat was artificially maintained. In countries that had national interests overseas, the new geostrategic landscape allowed them to develop projection forces. But in countries that did not have a tradition of intervening outside Europe, the disappearance of the Warsaw Pact threat meant that the very need to maintain an army was called into question. This was particularly true of Germany and Switzerland[168]. More generally, the United States understood that the "*Swords to Ploughshares*" initiatives could call into question its military presence in Europe.

In this context, the countries of Eastern Europe play an essential role. Their treatment of their Russian minorities, fueled by a hatred and fear of Russia, justifies seeing it as a threat. Instead of building relations on constructive cooperation with a demanding Russia, the West has done everything possible to continue to see it as a potential threat.

Thus, we have tolerated - and even integrated - the values of those countries that continue to venerate their past of fighting the Soviets with the help of the Third Reich. We have tolerated that in 21st century Europe, countries continue to have citizens who have more rights than others, because of what they are, not what they do. The hatred against Vladimir Putin remains impregnated with the "naziabonde" ideology that our media has had to try to hide in order to preserve its narrative.

It was therefore necessary to hide the fact that the Ukrainian power was deeply supremacist. To this end, it is enough to declare that the problem

---

168. https://www.bk.admin.ch/ch/f/pore/vi/vis179.html

does not exist, as the Swiss journalist Jean-Philippe Schaller does in his program *Geopolitis*[169].

It is important here to be precise about the terms used. Our fact-checkers show us that there are no "Nazis" in Ukraine. This is true. Nazism is a political ideology from the 1930s that does not need to be described here. "Neo-Nazism", on the other hand, is more of a societal phenomenon than an ideology in its own right. It is a heterogeneous assembly of ideologies that combine hatred of everything and everyone in a kind of theatrical representation of violence, by associating Nazi symbolism with it. It is to distinguish them from "Nazis" that they are called "neo-Nazis". This is the term Vladimir Putin regularly uses and not the word "Nazi", as the Swiss RTS claims[170]. Some use the term "ukronazi" to emphasize the Ukrainian nationalist dimension and the references to the Nazi forces of World War II, which are very present.

The term "neo-Nazi" expresses the racialist character of its followers in Ukraine, who see a hierarchy among the country's citizens based on their ethnic origin.

That is why no one mentions the *"Law on Indigenous Peoples"* in Ukraine and why we arm movements there that advocate the racial purity of the country. None of our media and their journalists have reacted to this law which penalizes citizens not on the basis of who they are. Since 1948 we have tolerated the treatment of Arabs as "inferior" citizens in Palestine, why should we be indignant that Russian speakers are treated in the same way in Ukraine?

We have even allowed social networks like Facebook and Instagram to override basic rules of tolerance to accept "posts" advocating violence against *"Russians and Russian occupiers"*[171]. This includes calls for the murder of Vladimir Putin and Alexander Lukashenko and violence perpetrated by neo-Nazis[172].

---

169. https://youtu.be/bEv4-IJsl9k?t=414
170. "Putin does not have a speech of disinformation, but an outright false speech," *RTS.ch*, November 19, 2022 (https://www.rts.ch/info/monde/13532090-poutine-na-pas-un-discours-de-desinformation-mais-un-discours-carrement-faux.html)
171. Munsif Vengattil & and Elizabeth Culliford, "Facebook allows war posts urging violence against Russian invaders", *Reuters*, March 11, 2022 (https://www.reuters.com/world/europe/exclusive-facebook-instagram-temporarily-allow-calls-violence-against-russians-2022-03-10/)
172. "Facebook and Instagram Say It Is Okay to Support Nazism in Ukraine, and They Modify Terms Allowing Advocacy for Death to Russians," *The Conservative Treehouse*, March 10, 2022 (https://theconservativetreehouse.com/blog/2022/03/10/facebook-and-instagram-say-it-is-okay-to-support-nazism-in-ukraine-and-they-modify-terms-allowing-advocacy-for-death-to-russians/)

The logical consequence of this situation is that in the United States[173], in Belgium[174], in Switzerland[175], in all circles anti-Semitism is increasing[176]. As in this whole Ukrainian crisis, it seems that Westerners have difficulty seeing beyond the end of their noses. For the violence that we have tolerated, and even that our media have stimulated, has triggered three distinct phenomena that tend to converge towards anti-Semitism:

- In order to remove all the flaws from Ukraine and to erase the racist character of its policy towards linguistic minorities, our media had to literally "whitewash" the extremists who make up its volunteer units and turn a blind eye to the extremism that fuels Ukrainian nationalism. This is what we saw with the program *Geopolitis*. A right-wing Swiss politician even attacked me on his *Facebook* page by saying that the volunteers who left to join the Ukrainian paramilitary were democrats! In reality, many share what this Euromaidan activist said: *"Putin is not even a Russian. He is a Jew!*[177]*"*

- As Western countries line up plans to support Ukraine and find that their economies can no longer keep pace, some annoyance is beginning to be felt with Volodymyr Zelensky's demands. Especially in the United States, there are a growing number of commentators on the conflict who note that the main instigators and most staunchly opposed to any political solution since 2014 are of the same religion as Zelensky. This is the case of Victoria Nuland, Antony Blinken, but also of many figures who are in the inner workings of the US administration. Without going into more detail here, it seems that the

---

173. Herb Scribner, "Antisemitism is on the rise in the U.S., surveys say," *Axios*, February 13, 2023 (https://www.axios.com/2023/02/13/antisemitism-ajc-poll-survey-rise-online)
174. "Is antisemitism on the rise in Brussels?", VRT.be, February 27, 2023 (https://www.vrt.be/vrtnws/en/2023/02/27/is-antisemitism-on-the-rise-in-brussels/)
175. "The number of anti-Semitic incidents rose by 6% in 2022, the vast majority of them happening online, Jewish groups said on Tuesday", *Swissinfo*, February 28, 2023 (https://www.swissinfo.ch/eng/society/anti-semitism-cases-on-the-rise-in-switzerland--especially-online/48321170)
176. Douglas Belkin, "Antisemitism Is Rising at Colleges, and Jewish Students Are Facing Growing Hostility," *The Wall Street Journal*, December 14, 2022 (https://www.wsj.com/articles/antisemitism-is-rising-at-colleges-and-jewish-students-are-facing-growing-hostility-11671027820)
177. Shaun Walker, "Azov fighters are Ukraine's greatest weapon and may be its greatest threat," *The Guardian*, September 10, 2014 (https://www.theguardian.com/world/2014/sep/10/azov-far-right-fighters-ukraine-neo-nazis)

Jewish community is increasingly caught in the crossfire between Republicans and Democrats.

- The reshaping of the geostrategic and geopolitical landscape of the Middle East, which could become more hostile to the Jewish state, especially with the advent of a far-right government. A major U.S. ally in the Middle East, Israel is seen as a permanent foreign policy problem by much of the so-called U.S. Deep State.

In order to support Ukraine, we had to twist the arm of our values; because its internal politics is very far from being democratic, contrary to what our media claims. The ban on media[178] and opposition political parties[179] is totally ignored here. On February 4, 2023, a Ukrainian mechanic from the Nikolayev region was arrested by the SBU for "liking" two posts in 2022 on the social network *VKontakte*, which was favorable to Vladimir Putin. This "like" was interpreted as *"dissemination of material justifying the armed aggression of the Russian Federation against Ukraine"* (Article 436-2 of the Criminal Code, Part 2) and he faces up to 8 years in prison. The indictment does not mention any espionage activities. But on February 15, he was suspected of providing information to the *"Witches' Empire of Russia"*, a secret society, which the SBU considers to be an espionage network[180].

---

178. "Ukraine: President bans opposition media Strana.ua and sanctions editor-in-chief", European Federation of Journalists, August 26, 2021
179. "NSDC bans pro-Russian parties in Ukraine", Ukrinform, March 20, 2022 (https://www.ukrinform.net/rubric-polytics/3434673-nsdc-bans-prorussian-parties-in-ukraine.html)
180. Oleg Chernish, "Чи міг український "сільський чаклун" стати шпигуном для російських відьом. Історія одного злочину," BBC News Ukrainian Service, April 16, 2023 (https://www.bbc.com/ukrainian/articles/clmdjyrl08do)

Combating the glorification of Nazism, neo-Nazism and other practices that contribute to contemporary forms of racism, racial discrimination, xenophobia and related intolerance

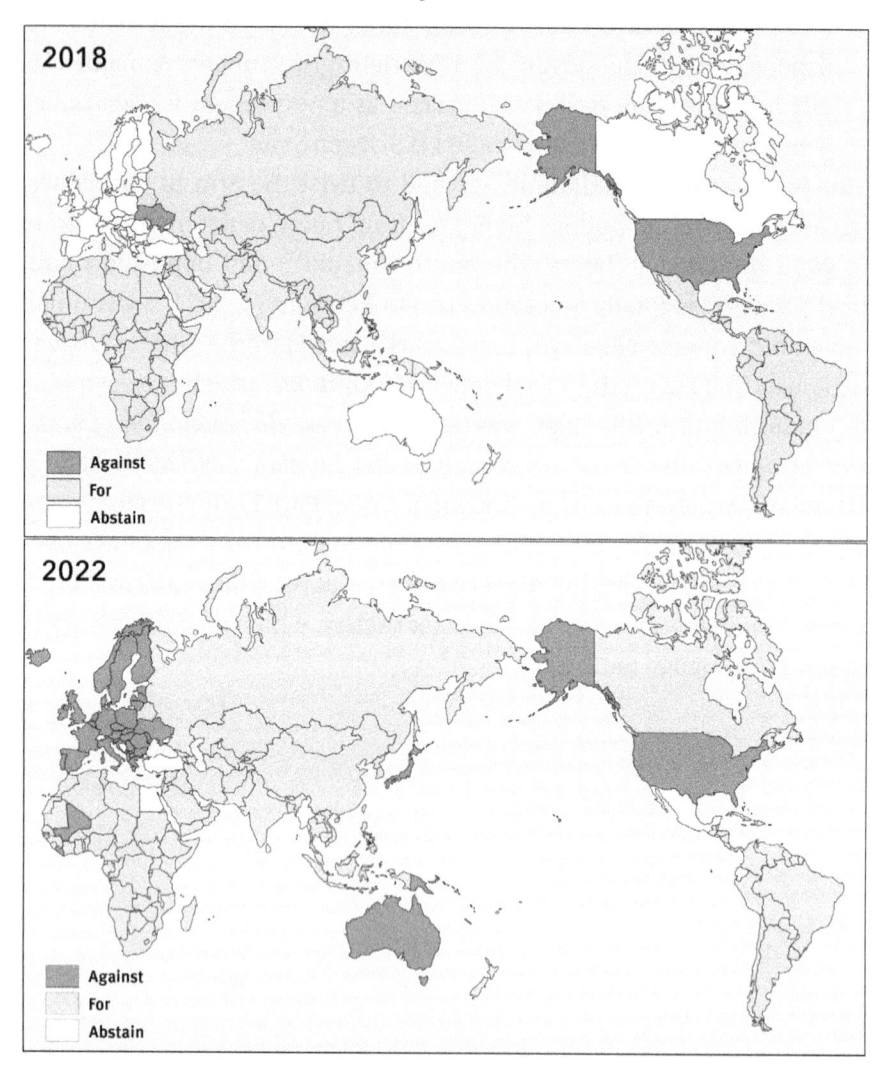

Figure 11 - Every year, Russia presents a resolution against the glorification of Nazism to the United Nations General Assembly for a vote. Until 2022, only two countries rejected this resolution, the United States and Ukraine. In 2022, under the pretext that Russia had declared to fight against Nazism in Ukraine, the Western countries joined the opposing countries. So much for our values...

3.2.3. A new perception of terrorism

In July-August 2022, a campaign of purge (read: eliminations) conducted by the security service (SBU) in the territories occupied by the Russian-speaking coalition was observed in Ukraine. This is a terrorist campaign targeting pro-Russian Ukrainian personalities and officials. It comes after major changes in the leadership of the SBU[181], in Kiev[182], and in the regions, including Lvov, Ternopol[183] since July. The aim was to eliminate Russian-speaking Ukrainians accused of supporting Russia. It was in the context of this same campaign that Darya Dugina was eliminated on August 21, probably by the Ukrainian security services[184]. We find the same phenomenon eight months later, with the assassination of the journalist-blogger Vladlen Tatarsky, on April 1st, 2023 in Saint Petersburg.

The purpose of these campaigns is not clear. Is it to divert attention from the military failures in Ukraine itself? Is it to give the illusion that Russia is destabilized and thus revive Western aid that is beginning to tire?

Still, none of our journalists, media or governments has condemned these bomb attacks against Russian journalists. These journalists are no more and no less than the journalists of Charlie Hebdo. There is no such thing as good and bad terrorism: terrorism is a method. Either one approves the method or one condemns it. One can approve of the cause that leads to terrorism (like the Palestinians), without approving the method. One cannot condemn it when it comes from the Arabs and accept it when it comes from Israel, Ukraine or the United States! So we have media that support terrorism!

In the same vein, the calls for murder by American politicians such as Senator Lindsay Graham or Luxembourg's Foreign Minister Jean Asselborn, who have not been condemned by anyone, show that we are not worth much. This means that our media and our politicians accept that we kill on the basis of our personal judgment. Why should the Islamic

---

181. https://www.republicworld.com/world-news/russia-ukraine-crisis/zelensky-dismisses-dy-head-of-security-service-of-ukraine-and-replaces-several-officials-articleshow.html
182. https://www.kyivpost.com/ukraine-politics/zelensky-replaces-leadership-of-sbus-dept-of-information-and-analytical-support-decrees.html
183. https://en.interfax.com.ua/news/general/852306.html
184. Julian E. Barnes, Adam Goldman, Adam Entous & Michael Schwirtz, "U.S. Believes Ukrainians Were Behind an Assassination in Russia," *The New York Times*, October 5, 2022 (https://www.nytimes.com/2022/10/05/us/politics/ukraine-russia-dugina-assassination.html)

State not have the same right? As we can see, such a way of thinking is totally unacceptable! Could we apply the same logic to those politicians and journalists who approved them?

On April 13, 2023, the program "C à vous" of *France 5* evokes the internal situation in Russia through the case of children who would have been arrested by the security services for having circulated propaganda images. Our journalists draw the conclusion that the country is sliding towards fascism (which means that this was not the case before!). It's possible, but in 2015 in France, simply not "being Charlie" was considered "apology for terrorism."[185] An 8 year old child was even arrested because he had declared at school that he "wasn't Charlie"[186]!

These cases illustrate exactly what non-Europeans rightly criticize us for: we have institutionalized the *"law of the strongest"* which advocates *"do as I say, but not as I do"*. France is far from being exemplary in terms of human rights. In a crisis situation, France declared that it would no longer respect human rights[187]. Why should it not be the same in other countries, which also have a terrorist threat?

3.3. The sanctions

Sanctions have become a privileged tool in the foreign policy of Western countries and have gradually replaced diplomacy in order to bring their partners to align themselves with their decisions. Their logic is to create an intolerable pressure for the targeted populations and to push them to provoke a change of policy in their country[188].

They extend the foreign policy of our countries to influence the domestic policy of other countries. In other words, they are a way of

---

185. Grégoire Bézie, "'No, I'm not Charlie': where freedom of expression ends," *France 3 Corse*, January 16, 2015 (updated June 10, 2020) (https://france3-regions.francetvinfo.fr/corse/2015/01/16/non-je-ne-suis-pas-charlie-la-ou-s-arrete-la-liberte-d-expression-634010.html)
186. Caroline Politi, "Enfant de 8 ans entendu pour apologie du terrorisme: 'Il n'y a pas de poursuites'", *L'Express*, January 29, 2015 (https://www.lexpress.fr/societe/justice/enfant-de-8-ans-entendu-pour-apologie-du-terrorisme-il-n-y-a-pas-de-poursuites_1646040.html)
187. "State of emergency: France warns it will not respect human rights," *AFP/Le Point.fr*, November 27, 2015 (https://www.lepoint.fr/societe/etat-d-urgence-la-france-previent-qu-elle-ne-respectera-pas-les-droits-de-l-homme-27-11-2015-1985317_23.php)
188. Richard Nephew, *The Art of Sanctions - A View from the Field*, Columbia University Press, New York, 2018

circumventing Article 2 of the UN Charter, which establishes the principle of non-interference in the internal affairs of States. This is why the only legal sanctions are those decided by the UN Security Council. This is also the reason why Russia and China do not use them as retaliation to the sanctions applied to them.

The sanctions applied to Russia after February 24, 2022, were intended to create "shock and awe" in order to cause its collapse[189]. This is the same expression used by the Americans in 2003 to describe their strikes before the invasion of Iraq. According to the business media *Bloomberg*, they were intended to be *"the economic equivalent of a nuclear bomb"*[190].

They were therefore not intended to "punish" Russia or to influence its policy, but to cause its collapse, even before its intervention was successful. This was stated by Bruno Le Maire, the French Minister of the Economy, and Annalena Baerbock, the German Minister of Foreign Affairs. The idea was that after the start of the Ukrainian offensive against the Donbass, which has been in preparation since March 2021, Russia would intervene to protect the Russian-speaking population. It would then become possible to strike a decisive fatal blow through sanctions. That is why these sanctions were massive and applied simultaneously before Russia could react.

In this scenario, the United States and the European Union used Ukraine as bait. As Oleksei Arestovich explained already in March 2019, Ukrainians were lured into a war that was supposed to be extremely short and decisive. The West simply played with the lives of Ukrainians by exploiting their nationalism.

---

189. Daniel Flatley, "How Biden's Shock-and-Awe Tactic Is Failing to Stop Russia," *Bloomberg*, February 24, 2023 (https://www.bloomberg.com/news/features/2023-02-24/russia-sanctions-to-stop-putin-s-war-in-ukraine-became-300b-distraction#xj4y7vzkg)
190. Daniel Flatley, "How Biden's Shock-and-Awe Tactic Is Failing to Stop Russia," *Bloomberg*, February 24, 2023 (https://archive.is/pRivV#selection-3483.0-3515.30)

Number of sanctions applied to Russia (as of February 22, 2023)

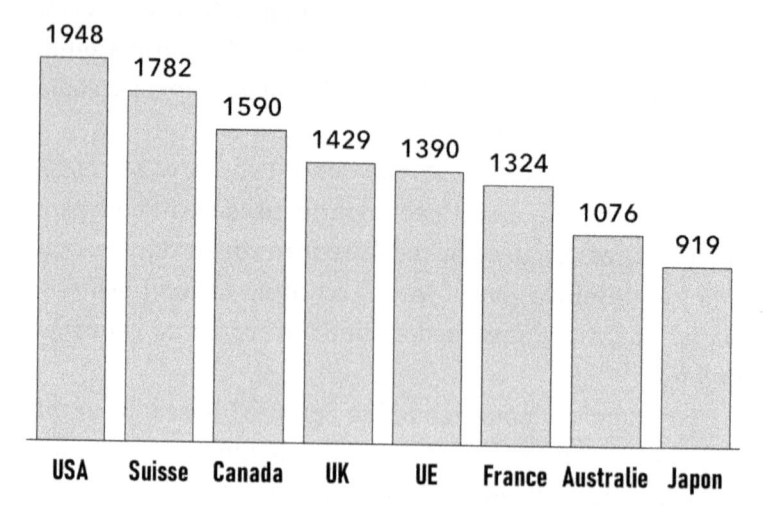

USA	Suisse	Canada	UK	UE	France	Australie	Japon
1948	1782	1590	1429	1390	1324	1076	919

Figure 12 - Sanctions applied to Russia since February 24, 2022. Until October 2022, Switzerland was the country that had adopted the most sanctions. [Source: Castellum AI]

Sanctions have thus become a weapon of war, designed to achieve war aims[191]. In the Ukrainian conflict, they were intended to achieve the total defeat of Russia, even before the guns spoke, through its collapse. This means that those who associated themselves with these sanctions became *de facto* and *de iure* cobelligerents in the Ukrainian conflict.

On the other hand, it can be seen that the sanctions have instead helped to strengthen the unity of the country and close the ranks behind Vladimir Putin. This is, in fact, a risk that was foreseen by the RAND Corporation already in 2019, based on observations in 2014:

> *International sanctions have not improved Russia's behavior and have even allowed the regime to plausibly blame the West for the economic difficulties of ordinary citizens.*

---

191. Nicholas Mulder, *The Economic Weapon: The Rise of Sanctions as a Tool of Modern War*, Yale University Press, Cornell University, January 25, 2022 (https://yalebooks.yale.edu/book/9780300259360/economic-weapon/)

3.3.1. The effectiveness of sanctions on the Russian economy

The form and nature of the sanctions against Russia had everything to achieve their objective. On March 1st, 2022, Bruno Le Maire, French Minister of Finance, declared[192]:

> *The sanctions are effective, the economic and financial sanctions are even very effective.*

Obviously, and as usual, he does not know his files. His ministry has not done any analysis of the Russian economy. For as early as the summer of 2022, serious experts see that the sanctions have not worked. If our leaders had read better the strategy of the RAND Corporation that they followed, they would have noted that the American think tank had already noted the ineffectiveness of sanctions against Russia[193]:

> *Russia's economic weaknesses are considerable, but the counterintuitive effect of sanctions shows that weaknesses should not be confused with vulnerabilities that the United States could exploit to its advantage.*

This is why the EU is beginning to string together packages of sanctions, each as ineffective as the next, even banning the sale of toilets to Russia[194]... On December 29, 2022, the British magazine *The Economist* (probably an "agent of Putin" for the Swiss journalist Jean-Philippe Schaller!) declared that *"the world's ninth-largest economy had done much better than* expected"[195]:

> *Currently, the Russian economic system is in better shape than expected. At the same time, Europe, burdened by high energy prices, is entering a recession.*

---

192. "'We will cause the collapse of the Russian economy,' says Bruno Le Maire," *France 24/YouTube*, March 1st, 2022 (https://youtu.be/Ntzacqlm-Ac)
193. "Extending Russia: Competing from Advantageous Ground," *RAND Corporation*, 2019 (p.28).
194. James Crisp, "EU stops selling toilets to Russia as punishment for invading Ukraine," *The Telegraph*, February 16, 2023 (https://www.telegraph.co.uk/world-news/2023/02/16/eu-toilet-ban-russia-ukraine-invasion-export-sanctions/)
195. "In 2022 Russia kept the economic show on the road," *The Economist*, December 29, 2022 (https://www.economist.com/finance-and-economics/2022/12/29/in-2022-russia-kept-the-economic-show-on-the-road)

Nicholas Mulder, author of a book on U.S. sanctions, notes that they have a history of ineffectiveness and seem to act more as a "boomerang effect." Regarding Ukraine, he observes[196]:

> [Western countries] have abandoned the idea that this influences Russian decision-making. Instead, they see it as a war of economic attrition.

This explains the statement of Josep Borrel, in March 2023[197]:

> There's not much more we can do from a sanctions perspective, but we can continue to increase our financial and military support [to Ukraine].

The problem is that the number of countries under sanctions is only increasing, because sanctions operate on a "ratchet" mechanism that does not reverse. The countries under sanctions understood that no matter what they did, the sanctions would remain. So they eventually adapted and learned to live cut off from Western countries. Today, countries like Iran and Russia are already under so many sanctions that they no longer fear anything. So they actively collaborate.

The collapse predicted by European economists has not happened. In its January 2023 assessment, the IMF estimates that Russia has an economy that is responding better than expected to sanctions and will perform better than the countries that sanctioned it in 2024[198].

The problem is that until 2022, our brilliant economists limited themselves to comparing Russia's economy to that of Italy or Spain. But that's a bit simplistic. The 2014 sanctions sounded an alarm bell for the Russian government, which focused on "hardening" its economy.

---

196. Ben Holland, "Sanctions Are the Economic Weapon with a History of Backfiring," *Bloomberg*, January 29, 2022 (https://archive.is/FR6Kz#selection-3341.0-3407.16)
197. Alexandra Brzozowski, "'Not much left' on Russia sanctions, other support needed now, says EU's Borrell", *EURACTIV.com*, March 10, 2023 (updated March 11, 2023) (https://www.euractiv.com/section/defence-and-security/interview/not-much-left-on-russia-sanctions-other-support-needed-now-says-eus-borrell/)
198. www.imf.org/fr/Publications/WEO/Issues/2023/01/31/world-economic-outlook-update-january-2023

Thus, for the balance of payments, the latest edition of the *CIA Factbook* ranks Russia fourth in the world, France 26th and the United States 209th[199]! With a public debt that represents 25% of its GDP, it ranks Russia 183rd in the world, while France is 14th (123.01%) and the United States 11th (126.39%)[200].

Less financialized than Western countries, Russia has a more robust, more balanced economy with a larger share of the real economy in its GDP. This is the main reason why it has withstood sanctions well, which no Western country could have absorbed in this way.

Structure of GDP by economic sector (2017)

Countries	Agriculture	Industry	Services
Russia	4.7 %	33.0 %	62.3 %
European Union	1.6 %	25.1 %	70.9 %
United States	0.9 %	19.1 %	80.0 %
Germany	0.7 %	30.7 %	68.6 %

Figure 13 - The structure of Russian gdP shows a much larger share of agriculture and manufacturing than its major European partners. It can be seen that the West has gradually abandoned its production capacities and has largely created its dependence on the outside world by developing the service sector.

On April 1st, 2023, on the LCI channel - which is undoubtedly the most active channel in disinformation about Russia - the journalist Quentin Bérichel explains that the Russian economy is collapsing[201]. He is a liar. Because one month earlier, in its report on the *Global Russia Manufacturing Purchasing Managers' Index* (PMI), the American agency *Standard & Poor* noted *"the strongest improvement in industrial production conditions for six years in February"*[202]:

---

199. https://www.cia.gov/the-world-factbook/field/current-account-balance/country-comparison
200. https://www.cia.gov/the-world-factbook/field/public-debt/country-comparison
201. "Russia's economy is (finally) taking the brunt of the sanctions," *LCI*, April 1st, 2023 (https://youtu.be/7bh1ZX0H0E4)
202. www.pmi.spglobal.com/Public/Home/PressRelease/947832c3086449a48a90e75cc273bf64

The latest data indicate a solid improvement in the health of the Russian industrial sector, the most marked in just over six years. This improvement extends the current ten-month growth streak.

Improved operating conditions were aided by a sharp increase in production in February. The increase in output accelerated from January and was slightly faster than the average for the period. The Russian manufacturing firms monitored showed that the recovery was related to import substitution and a further increase in new orders.

While in March 2022 the European Union decided to exclude a number of Russian banks from the SWIFT interbank payment system[203], a year later it was the Russian government that banned its banks from using it[204]. By 2022, Wall Street had advised Western governments against disconnecting Russian banks from SWIFT[205]. To satisfy Kiev, European leaders did not listen. As a result, the Americans no longer have any visibility into payments to and from Russia.

As for the latter, in 2014, after a first wave of sanctions, it created its own alternative system, the *System for Transfer of Financial Messages* (SPFS), which has been operational since 2022[206]. This system is connected with China's *Cross-Border Interbank Payment System* (CIPS), which should help reduce the hegemony of the dollar in international transactions[207].

So we are very far from a collapse of the Russian economy. Quite the contrary. *Newsweek* magazine even predicted at the end of January 2023

---

203. "Russian banks banned from SWIFT", *UK P&I*, March 2, 2022 (https://www.ukpandi.com/news-and-resources/articles/2022/russian-banks-banned-from-swift/)

204. "Russia bans SWIFT," *RT*, March 20, 2023 (https://www.rt.com/business/573298-russia-bans-swift-use/)

205. Daniel Flatley, Katherine Doherty & Hannah Levitt, "Wall Street Counsels Washington Against Kicking Russia Off SWIFT," *Bloomberg*, February 25, 2022 (https://www.bloomberg.com/news/articles/2022-02-25/wall-street-counsels-washington-against-kicking-russia-off-swift?leadSource=uverify%20wall)

206. Huileng Tan, "China and Russia are working on homegrown alternatives to the SWIFT payment system. Here's what they would mean for the US dollar," *Business Insider*, April 19, 2022 (https://www.businessinsider.com/china-russia-alternative-swift-payment-cips-spfs-yuan-ruble-dollar-2022-4)

207. "Moscow, Beijing working on SWIFT workaround," *Reuters*, March 16, 2022 (https://www.reuters.com/article/ukraine-crisis-russia-china-idUKL5N2VJ39Z)

that the Russian economy could be more successful than that of the United States by 2025[208]!

Growth prospects for 2023-2024

Dernières projections de croissance des Perspectives de l'économie mondiale

(PIB réel, variation annuelle en pourcentage)	2022 ESTIMATION	2023 PROJECTIONS	2024
Production mondiale	3,4	2,9	3,1
Pays avancés	2,7	1,2	1,4
États-Unis	2,0	1,4	1,0
Zone euro	3,5	0,7	1,6
Allemagne	1,9	0,1	1,4
France	2,6	0,7	1,6
Italie	3,9	0,6	0,9
Espagne	5,2	1,1	2,4
Japon	1,4	1,8	0,9
Royaume-Uni	4,1	-0,6	0,9
Canada	3,5	1,5	1,5
Autres pays avancés	2,8	2,0	2,4
Pays émergents et pays en développement	3,9	4,0	4,2
Pays émergents et pays en développement d'Asie	4,3	5,3	5,2
Chine	3,0	5,2	4,5
Inde	6,8	6,1	6,8
Pays émergents et pays en développement d'Europe	0,7	1,5	2,6
Russie	-2,2	0,3	2,1

Figure 14 - International Monetary Fund projections for 2023-2024 show that Russia will grow faster than the Eurozone countries. [Source: IMF]

The sanctions announced as a result of the SVO included the freezing of Russian public and private ("oligarch") assets deposited in European and American banks. Initially estimated to be around $600 billion[209],

---

208. Brendan Cole, "Russia's Economy Forecast to Outperform U.S. Within Two Years," *Newsweek*, January 31, 2023 (https://www.newsweek.com/russias-economy-forecast-outperform-us-within-two-years-1777788)
209. Richard Partington, "Russia 'preparing legal action' to unfreeze $600bn foreign currency reserves", *The Guardian*, April 19, 2022 (https://www.theguardian.com/business/2022/apr/19/russia-preparing-legal-action-to-unfreeze-600bn-foreign-currency-reserves)

this wealth was re-evaluated at 300 billion euros (April 14, 2023)[210]. However, it has emerged that the EU judicial authorities have only been able to identify 33.8 billion euros of the 250 billion euros held in Europe. The remaining funds have not been traced and likely remain under Russian control[211].

In January 2023, Ursula von der Leyen stated that she wanted to "seize, not freeze" these assets and give them to Ukraine[212]. But in reality, apart from the fact that the EU has not been able to locate these funds, the legality of seizing funds from the Russian reserve is questionable. There is no legal framework in Europe to support such a decision[213]. The European Commission has even ruled that Russian assets should be returned to their owners once the conflict is over[214].

Furthermore, it is possible that rumors of a confiscation of Russian assets have scared off investors in other countries, although no official information confirms this at this stage. This could explain the massive withdrawals (mainly in the last quarter of 2022) of some 133 billion USD from Credit Suisse, causing the bank to collapse in March 2023[215].

Blinded by our own propaganda and what happened in 2014, when sanctions had a marked effect on the Russian economy, our experts overestimated the outcome of the 2022 sanctions. Clearly, trying to prevent trade with a country like Russia, which is a major supplier of raw materials, agricultural products and fertilizers, primarily to countries in the Southern Hemisphere and Asia, is very different from the same policy against a "consumer" country.

---

210. https://www.consilium.europa.eu/en/policies/sanctions/restrictive-measures-against-russia-over-ukraine/sanctions-against-russia-explained/
211. Oleksiy Yarmolenko, "Delfi: The EU cannot find the frozen €300 billion of the Russian Central Bank, which they want to give to Ukraine", *Babel.ua*, February 21, 2023 (https://babel.ua/en/news/90794-delfi-the-eu-cannot-find-the-frozen-300-billion-of-the-russian-central-bank-which-they-want-to-give-to-ukraine)
212. Elisabeth Braw, "Freeze-Don't Seize-Russian Assets," *Foreign Policy*, January 13, 2023 (https://foreignpolicy.com/2023/01/13/putin-sanctions-oligarchs-freeze-seize-assets/)
213. "Should Russia's frozen assets be seized to rebuild Ukraine?", *Swissinfo.ch*, February 23, 2023 (https://www.swissinfo.ch/fre/politique/faut-il-saisir-les-actifs-gel%C3%A9s-de-la-russie-pour-reconstruire-l-ukraine-/48307052)
214. Wester van Gaal, "EU: Russian assets to be returned in case of peace treaty", *EU Observer*, November 30, 2022 (https://euobserver.com/ukraine/156496)
215. Anna Cooban, "Credit Suisse got its lifeline. Investors are unconvinced," *CNN*, March 17, 2023 (https://edition.cnn.com/2023/03/17/investing/credit-suisse-shares-drop-despite-lifeline/index.html)

Strangely enough, no one anticipated the resistance of the Russian economy, the impact of sanctions that could have had at the global level (at the expense of the countries of the southern hemisphere) and the lack of international support for the policy of the Western countries.

3.3.2. Sanctions on petroleum products

The logical effect of the sanctions on oil products was to prevent Russia from selling its products in order to finance its operation in Ukraine. These restrictions have certainly led to a decrease in the volumes sold by Russia. But, by virtue of the law of supply and demand, this reduction in supply on the market has very logically caused an increase in prices, and therefore in Russia's revenues. According to *Bloomberg*, in April 2022, the increase in prices gave Russia an additional income of more than 9 billion dollars[216].

On LCI, General Dominique Trinquand, who is as brilliant in oil technology as he is in operational art, explains that with the departure of Western oil companies, Russia is no longer able to ensure normal production[217]. This is simply not true.

Three days earlier, *Bloomberg* reported that Russian diesel exports were at an all-time high[218].

First of all, it should be remembered that after the sanctions on oil equipment in 2014, Russia started manufacturing this equipment itself... and is now an exporter[219]! In fact, despite the sanctions, Russia increased its oil production capacity in 2022 by increasing the number of wells by 7%, bringing the total to 7,800 wells[220]. Moreover, contrary to our general's assertion and according to a British newspaper, the Russian oil sector *"is operating largely as it did before [the sanctions].*

---

216. "Russia expects to earn $9.6 billion more in April due to high oil prices," *Reuters*, April 5, 2021 (https://www.reuters.com/business/energy/russia-expects-earn-96-bln-more-april-due-high-oil-prices-2022-04-05/)
217. https://youtu.be/7bh1ZX0H0E4
218. Jack Wittels & Prejula Prem, "Russia's Diesel Exports Heading for Record Despite EU Sanctions," *Bloomberg*, March 27, 2022 (https://www.bloomberg.com/news/articles/2023-03-27/russia-s-diesel-exports-heading-for-record-despite-eu-sanctions#xj4y7vzkg)
219. "A Russian oil and gas equipment manufacturing company is interested in the Norwegian market," *ernergi24.no*, June 3, 2021 (https://energi24.no/betalt-innhold-arkiv/a-russian-oil-and-gas-equipment-manufacturing-company-is-interested-in-the-norwegian-market)
220. Tim McNulty, "Putin enjoys oil boom as Russia sanctions fail to dent Kremlin coffers", *Express (UK)*, February 14, 2023 (https://www.express.co.uk/news/world/1734625/Vladimir-Putin-Russian-oil-Ukraine-war-sanctions)

Russia has been able to preserve most of its know-how, assets and technologies in the field of oil services[221]*.*

The cap on Russian oil prices decided by the G7 and then the European Union at the beginning of 2023 has had several disastrous, though perfectly predictable, effects. First, Russia has declared that it will only sell its oil to countries that respect the market price. In other words, this means that potentially the already tight energy market is likely to contract further, with a general increase in the price of hydrocarbons.

Second, the decision of the West to intervene in a market that is regulated by OPEC+ was seen by Middle Eastern countries as an insult to their economic sovereignty. This explains - at least in part - the refusal of Arab countries to comply with Western injunctions to increase production levels.

Paradoxically, one year after the adoption of sanctions against Russia, European countries remain the main importers of Russian oil products. The exceptions to the regime adopted by the EU are so numerous that they have not really affected imports. The problem is that nowadays, European countries use intermediaries to mask the Russian origin of the products, for an additional cost paid by the West. So we had the disadvantages of sanctions, without the expected effect[222].

According to an April 2023 report by the *Centre for Research on Energy and Clean Air* (CREA), Western countries imported 42 billion euros worth of petroleum products from countries that increased their imports of Russian crude oil in the 12 months following the invasion of Russia[223]. This means that not only did Western countries not prevent Russia from exporting its oil products, but they paid more for their imports than if they had paid Russia directly. This is an asymmetrical pattern, in which not only do Western countries fail to achieve their objective, but their economies suffer as a result.

---

221. Tim McNulty, "Putin enjoys oil boom as Russia sanctions fail to dent Kremlin coffers", *Express (UK)*, February 14, 2023 (https://www.express.co.uk/news/world/1734625/Vladimir-Putin-Russian-oil-Ukraine-war-sanctions)
222. Shweta Sharma, "EU is still largest importer of Russian oil due to loophole in sanctions, report claims", *The Independent*, April 19, 2023 (https://www.independent.co.uk/news/world/europe/eu-largest-importer-russia-oil-ukraine-war-b2321756.html)
223. https://energyandcleanair.org/wp/wp-content/uploads/2023/04/CREA_Press-release_The-laundromat_EU-G7-and-Australias-indirect-imports-of-Russian-oil-revealed.pdf

3.3.3. The lack of microprocessors

On April 1st, 2023, on the French television channel LCI, the journalist Jean Quatremer explains that the sanctions are hitting the Russian economy so hard that the Russians have to *"butcher washing machines to obtain* electronic *chips*[224]*".* He is a liar.

Imports of microprocessors / semiconductors into Russia (2021-2022)

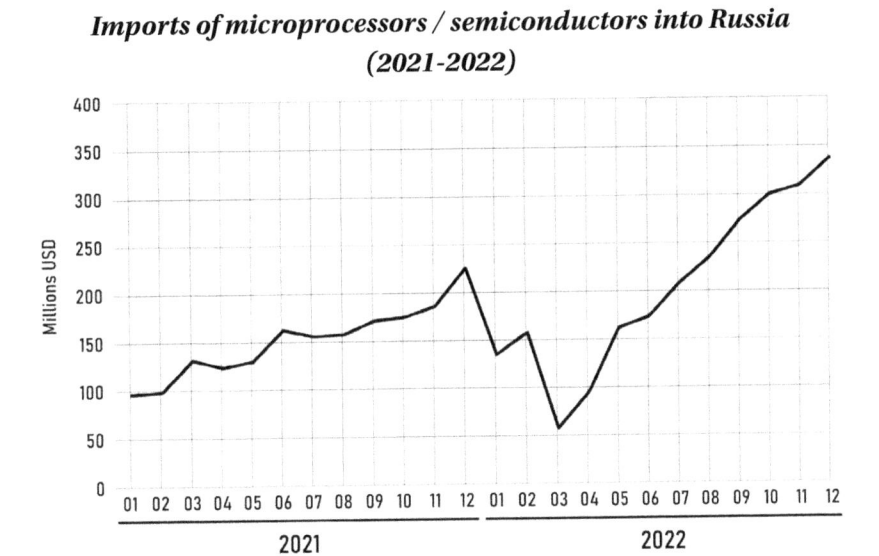

Figure 15 - Contrary to what Western disinformation claims, Russia increased its semiconductor imports in 2022. It has simply switched suppliers. From sourcing primarily from the West, Russia has turned to Asia. In a globalized economy, sanctions are no substitute for effective diplomacy. [Source: Free Russia Foundation]

In January 2023, the Washington-based *Free Russia Foundation* released a report on the effectiveness of sanctions against Russia. It found that Russian microprocessor imports increased from $1.82 billion in 2021 to $2.45 billion in 2022 (for the entire year). China has become Russia's main source of microprocessor supply. In 2022, China, Hong Kong, Germany, the Netherlands, and Finland were the top suppliers by value; China, Hong Kong, Estonia, Turkey, and Germany led in the number of transactions[225].

---
224. https://youtu.be/7bh1ZX0H0E4?t=491
225. "Effectiveness Of U.S. Sanctions Targeting Russian Companies and Individuals," *Free Russia Foundation,* Washington DC, January 2023 (https://www.4freerussia.org/effectiveness-of-u-s-sanctions-targeting-russian-companies-and-individuals/?ref=en.thebell.io)

3.3.4. The sanctions on Nord Stream

It should be remembered that Germany halted the *Nord Stream 2 (NS2)* project *before* Russia launched its offensive in Ukraine. This interruption, wanted by Donald Trump, was applauded by Western conspiracy theorists, who saw in this pipeline the *"Putin's gas pipeline"*. Thus, the French daily *Libération*[226] invented a conspiracy theory according to which Vladimir Putin would have sought to put Europe *"at the mercy of Moscow"* thanks to its natural gas. This is totally false.

In 2014, after sanctions were applied to Russia, Vladimir Putin understood that the objective of the West was to weaken his country. He also realized that the endless disputes related to "leaks" from the gas pipelines crossing Ukraine would increase and that his dependence on Europe was putting his economy at risk. He therefore decided to abandon the construction of new gas pipelines to Europe[227].

In 2016, in order to begin its energy transition and get out of coal, Angela Merkel managed to convince Vladimir Putin to build NS2, following the route of Nord Stream 1 (NS1), to avoid the hazards of a supply transiting through Ukraine.

But in the summer of 2017, the Trump administration implemented a strategy to isolate Russia by driving it out of its traditional markets[228]. As early as 2018, Trump pressured Germany to give up the NS2[229], and then applied sanctions against companies involved in its construction in January 2020[230]. Donald Trump's policy is supported in Europe by environmentalists and Eastern European Russophobes. On January 20, 2021, 58 European parliamentarians (mainly from the former Eastern

---

226. Christophe Bourdoiseau, "L'Allemagne gèle le 'gazoduc de Poutine'", *Libération*, February 22, 2022 (https://www.liberation.fr/international/europe/lallemagne-gele-le-gazoduc-de-poutine-20220222_2P4HYGUGOBHE5OO4SG7U6POQFA/)
227. Michael Birnbaum, "Putin cancels new natural gas pipeline to Europe in a surprise move," *The Washington Post*, December 1st, 2014 (https://www.washingtonpost.com/world/europe/putin-cancels-new-natural-gas-pipeline-to-europe-in-a-surprise-move/2014/12/01/c1955c90-73ee-11e4-95a8-fe0b46e8751a_story.html)
228. Sarah McFarlane, Georgi Kantchev, "Gas: Trump ready to step on Russian toes in Europe," *L'Opinion*, July 29, 2018. (https://www.lopinion.fr/international/gaz-trump-pret-a-marcher-sur-les-plate-bandes-russes-en-europe)
229. Dpa, "Trump kritisiert Deutschland wegen Ostsee-Pipeline" ("Trump criticizes Germany over Baltic Sea pipeline"), *merkur.de*, April 3, 2018.
230. "Donald Trump approves U.S. sanctions on companies collaborating on Nord Stream 2 pipeline," *Agence Europe*, January 3, 2020.

European countries, with a few "Westerners" such as Bernard Guetta) proposed stopping the German-Russian project[231].

On June 14, 2022, Gazprom reduces the flow of gas to Germany by 40 percent. RTS states that *"Russia is increasingly using the gas weapon to put pressure on the Europeans"*. For what purpose? The Swiss media obviously does not specify this, nor does it explain the reason for this reduction. This is a gratuitous accusation, which insinuates that Russia is waging an economic war against the West, in order to *"tighten the market for raw materials and drive up prices"*[232].

In fact, what the Swiss media is hiding is that Siemens, the company responsible for the maintenance of the NS1 turbines, had to repair one of these turbines in one of its workshops in Canada. The problem is that - at first - Canada refuses to return the turbine to Germany because of the sanctions against Russia. Without the turbine, Gazprom cannot operate the pipeline normally and is reducing its capacity by 40% for technical reasons[233]. In other words, not only is Canada imposing sanctions on Germany, but the reduction in Russian deliveries is the result - once again - of internal problems in the Western camp. So the Swiss media lied... once again!

In mid-July and after lengthy negotiations, Canada agreed to Germany's request to return the turbine, which provoked the anger of Zelensky, who summoned the Canadian ambassador to admonish him[234]. But the problem did not end there. Despite the Canadian agreement, the turbine was late in arriving, and the Russians had no guarantee that they would see it again. In addition, there are other turbines due for maintenance in Canada as early as the end of July 2022, and the Westerners have not defined any clear policy. Therefore, on July 14, 2022, Gazprom sent a

---

231. *Joint Motion for a Resolution Pursuant to Rule 132(2) and (4) of the Rules of Procedure on the Arrest of Aleksei Navalny*, European Parliament, January 20, 2021 (2021/2513(RSP)).
232. https://www.rts.ch/info/monde/13181278-le-robinet-de-gaz-russe-pour-leurope-est-progressivement-coupe.html#timeline-anchor-1655470920416
233 "Russia lowers gas flows to Europe with part stuck in Canada," The Associated Press, June 14, 2022 (https://apnews.com/article/russia-ukraine-canada-business-baltic-sea-8558b02f065d79bd5d9f725188239c98); Huileng Tan, "Russia is cutting 40% of one key pipeline's natural-gas supply to Germany because a piece of equipment is stuck in Canada due to sanctions," Business Insider, June 15, 2022 (https://www.businessinsider.com/russia-cuts-gas-supply-germany-siemens-equipment-stuck-canada-sanctions-2022-6?r=US&IR=T)
234. "Canadian ambassador in Kiev summoned following 'unacceptable' transfer of turbines," *Le Figaro* / AFP, July 11, 2022 (https://www.lefigaro.fr/flash-actu/l-ambassadeur-du-canada-a-kiev-convoque-a-la-suite-du-transfert-inacceptable-de-turbines-20220711)

letter to the German authorities announcing that it will be able to invoke "force majeure" after the planned maintenance work on NS1 between July 11 and 21.

In addition, despite Gazprom's request to Siemens, the Canadians refuse to give the Russians the description of the work done on this first turbine. In the absence of these documents, Russia did not authorize the return of the turbine and its reinstallation in the compressor station. Based on the 1982 experience, the Russians feared that the Canadians had sabotaged the turbine before returning it. Result: NS 1 is working at a fraction of its capacity.

Finally, in December 2022, *Reuters* announces that Russia has started to produce itself the turbines necessary to circulate gas in the pipelines[235]. Reuters thus demonstrates that the Swiss media has lied to us about everything (it is obviously not the only one!) and that the sanctions have only stimulated Russian industrial production.

3.3.5. Fertilizers and cereals

In May-June 2022, the West suddenly became concerned about Ukrainian grain exports. They accused Russia of organizing a blockade of Ukrainian ports on the Black Sea. This is obviously not true, because it is the Ukrainians themselves who have mined their ports, in order to prevent an amphibious attack from Russia.

Indeed, in mid-June 2022, David Arakhamia, a close adviser to Zelensky, stated that the Ukrainian military *"strongly opposes the idea of demining Ukrainian Black Sea ports in exchange for allowing grain exports through Russia"*[236]. But that did not stop *RTS from* writing on June 27 that *"transport ships have been blocked in port since February because of sea mines and Russian warships* off the coast."[237]

---

235. "UPDATE 1-Russia's Power Machines completes first high-power gas turbine to replace imported equipment," *Reuters*, December 26, 2022 (https://www.reuters.com/article/russia-gasturbine/update-1-russias-power-machines-completes-first-high-power-gas-turbine-to-replace-imported-equipment-idUKL8N33G0Q5)
236. Dave Lawler, "Ukraine suffering up to 1,000 casualties per day in Donbas, official says," *Axios*, June 15, 2022 (https://www.axios.com/2022/06/15/ukraine-1000-casualties-day-donbas-arakhamia)
237. https://www.rts.ch/info/monde/13202280-un-missile-russe-touche-un-centre-commercial-du-centre-de-lukraine-faisant-craindre-un-lourd-bilan.html

In fact, it appears to be yet another attempt by the Ukrainian government to find a reason for Western intervention in the conflict, as the *Washington Post* suggests[238]. This has led to accusations that Russia is using *the "weapon of hunger"* and thus holding the countries of the southern hemisphere hostage[239]. In reality, Russia has not prevented Ukraine from exporting its grain (most of which can go to Europe by land). It is indeed the Western sanctions that have hindered Russian grain exports.

The West claims *urbi et orbi* that fertilizers and food products are not sanctioned. Thus, Josep Borrell, head of EU foreign policy, says[240]:

> *The Russian agricultural sector is not targeted. Our sanctions do not prohibit the import of Russian agricultural products or fertilizers, nor do they prohibit payment for these Russian exports.*

However, these products hardly manage to leave Russia. In fact, if these products are not sanctioned, the transport, the companies that export them, as well as the means of payment are! This is why these products are rotting in European ports instead of supplying the countries that need them, because no European economic actor dares to transport them.

As for the Ukraine, the export of its cereals by boat, it is not directed towards the countries of the South which are in shortage, but towards the countries of the Northern hemisphere.

It is the same problem with air flights. With the skies closed to Russian planes, Russia has also closed its skies to Western planes. The result is an asymmetrical situation: these sanctions hit Westerners harder than Russians. In fact, they benefit Asian airlines - especially Chinese ones - which do not have to bypass Russian skies, while their Western counterparts have to make costly and time-consuming detours. But the

---

238. Karoun Demirjian, Alex Horton & Stefano Pitrelli, "Russia's grain blockade may require U.S. intervention, general suggests," *The Washington Post*, May 26, 2022 (https://www.washingtonpost.com/national-security/2022/05/26/russia-ukraine-grain-blockade/)
239. "Moscow accused of using "hunger as a weapon of war" Access to the comments Discussion", *Euronews / AFP*, June 25, 2022 (https://fr.euronews.com/2022/06/25/moscou-accusee-dutiliser-la-faim-comme-arme-de-guerre)
240. Vince Chadwick, "Exclusive: Internal report shows EU fears losing Africa over Ukraine," devex.com, July 22, 2022 (https://www.devex.com/news/exclusive-internal-report-shows-eu-fears-losing-africa-over-ukraine-103694)

Americans are bad players: in order to compensate for this comparative advantage, they plan to impose a tax on them[241]!

Ukrainian grain recipients as of April 21, 2023 [tons].

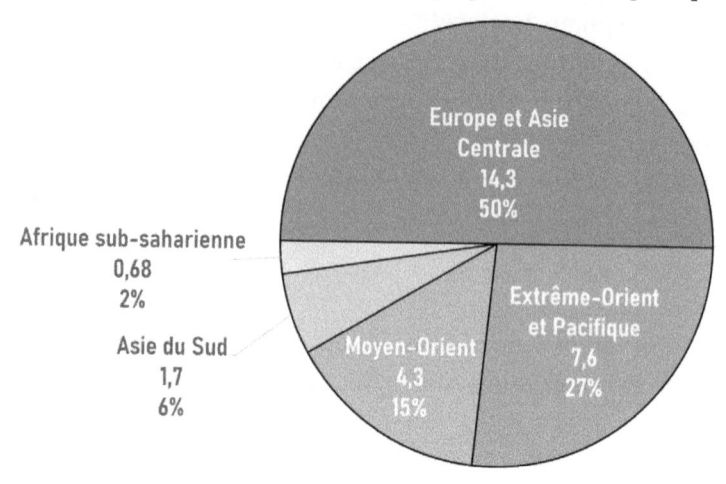

- Europe et Asie Centrale 14,3 — 50%
- Afrique sub-saharienne 0,68 — 2%
- Asie du Sud 1,7 — 6%
- Moyen-Orient 4,3 — 15%
- Extrême-Orient et Pacifique 7,6 — 27%

Figure 16 - While Western countries have accused Russia of preventing grain deliveries to Southern Hemisphere countries, only 2% of Ukrainian deliveries are to Sub-Saharan Africa. [Source: https://www.un.org/en/black-sea-grain-initiative/vessel-movements]

The proposal to reopen the European sky to Russian traffic is on the table, but the Russians are not in a hurry: in any case, with the sanctions on some Russian citizens, the means of payment (credit cards and banking system) and exports, the Russians have no interest in going to Europe!

3.3.6. The isolation of Russia

The strategy of the United States and the European Union was to isolate Russia on all political, economic and diplomatic levels. It was a form of "strategic mobbing" aimed at causing the collapse of the Russian economy and discouraging other countries from coming to its aid. This has not worked[242].

---

241. Kate Kelly & Mark Walker, "Banned from Russian Airspace, U.S. Airlines Look to Restrict Competitors," The New York Times, March 17, 2023 (updated March 18, 2023) (https://www.nytimes.com/2023/03/17/us/politics/russia-us-airlines-ukraine.html)
242. Josh Holder, Lauren Leatherby, Anton Troianovski & Weiyi Cai, "The West Tried to Isolate Russia. It Didn't Work," The New York Times, February 23, 2023 (https://www.nytimes.com/interactive/2023/02/23/world/russia-ukraine-geopolitics.html)

Western sanctions play a decisive role in this strategy. A central element of this scheme was to cut Russia off from the SWIFT interbank payment system in order to prevent it from trading with the outside world and to drive it into bankruptcy. This was to lead to social unrest, which was to fuel a revolutionary movement with the aim of "regime change".

But of course, to imagine that a country that supplies raw materials and energy would be isolated from the world was all the more absurd given that the Russian economy is healthy. In 2021, Russia's public debt was 17% of its GDP, placing it 182nd (out of 198 countries) in the world. By comparison, France's foreign debt was 112% of its GDP at the time, and the United States 128%[243].

The system of sanctions is not limited to those affecting Russia, but also to those that could be applied to third countries that do not associate themselves with American and European decisions. Indeed, quite quickly, the West had to realize that the countries of the southern hemisphere would not follow them in applying sanctions[244].

The Ukrainian crisis has shown that the West has only sanctions as a foreign policy tool. The pressure - not to say blackmail - that African countries were subjected to during the UN votes on Russia showed that partnerships with the West are a dangerous game[245]. Unexpectedly, the pressure on African countries to fall in line tends to backfire on the West[246].

Unlike the 1960s-2020s when the West led the way because of its economic supremacy, China is now a much more interesting partner for the "rest of the world."

While in some countries of the "new Europe," such as Poland or the Baltic states, hatred of the Russians dominates political thinking, in other countries, such as Slovakia, ties to Russia remain strong. Thus, in

---

243. https://en.wikipedia.org/wiki/List_of_countries_by_public_debt
244. Sharon Wajsbrot, "Opec refuses to replace Russian oil," *Les Echos*, May 5, 2022 (updated May 6, 2022) (https://www.lesechos.fr/finance-marches/marches-financiers/lopep-se-refuse-a-remplacer-le-petrole-russe-1405149)
245. Krista Larson, "Africa leader warns of pressure to choose sides in Ukraine," *AP News*, September 20, 2022 (https://apnews.com/article/russia-ukraine-united-nations-general-assembly-macky-sall-f7b8ec5e6092dc439adc1230e4f64d1d)
246. Robbie Gramer & Jack Detsch, "Western Allies Pressure African Countries to Condemn Russia," *Foreign Policy*, May 5, 2022 (https://foreignpolicy.com/2022/05/05/western-allies-pressure-african-countries-to-condemn-russia/)

September 2022, a poll showed that the majority of Slovaks would rather see a Russian victory[247].

In February 2023, the United Nations General Assembly (UNGA) passed a 141-7 resolution calling for an immediate cessation of hostilities and Russia's withdrawal from Ukraine. The numbers suggest overwhelming support for the Western position. But the reality is more subtle.

The objective of the West is to obtain the collapse of Russia through its isolation. To achieve this, they seek to impose their decisions and to sanction those who do not agree with them. The votes at the UNGA are subject to enormous pressure on the countries of the South, which is combined with blackmail[248]. Thus, what appears to be a success against Russia in the short term, is a failure on the strategic level and in the medium and long term. African countries have understood that their dependence on the West is a major vulnerability. This is what the Sahelian countries have understood, and they have undertaken to expel foreign armed forces from their territory.

The "abstentions" (formal or through the "empty chair" policy) are a way of expressing the refusal to align with Western positions, without openly confronting each other. This is why abstentions carry more weight than our media would have us believe.

Contrary to Josep Borrell's assertion, Africans are very knowledgeable about European affairs, often better than European citizens themselves. But they do not want to be involved in this conflict which does not concern them in any way. It always comes back to the same question: why is this conflict more reprehensible than those we have created in Africa or in the Middle East?

---

247. Michal Hudec, "Most Slovaks want Russia to win Ukraine war", *EURACTIV.sk*, September 15, 2022 (https://www.euractiv.com/section/politics/short_news/most-slovaks-want-russia-to-win-ukraine-war/)
248. "Western Allies Pressure African Countries to Condemn Russia," *Foreign Policy*, May 5, 2022 (https://foreignpolicy.com/2022/05/05/western-allies-pressure-african-countries-to-condemn-russia/)

Countries under US sanctions (2022)

Figure 17: Countries under U.S. sanctions now tend to work together. Sanctions are most often aimed at imposing policies, so they are unlikely to be eased.

Request for immediate cessation of hostilities (February 2023)

Figure 18 - United Nations member countries calling for an immediate end to Russian intervention Several countries complained that they were pressured by Western countries to vote.

3. Geostrategic considerations

**Countries that have adopted sanctions against Russia
(February 2023)**

Figure 19 - Countries that have adopted sanctions against Russia.

3.3.6.1. The triangular relationship between Russia, India and China

At the G20 meeting in March 2023 in New Delhi, the Americans tried to pressure India to have a condemnation of Russia in the final declaration. The U.S. put India in an impossible situation: since Russia was part of the G20, such a final declaration was unlikely to be issued, leaving the only prospect of concluding the G20 without a final declaration.

In fact, the Americans were counting on the spectacular rapprochement between Russia and China - India's old enemy - to push for this declaration. But India did not "bite". In the West, when it comes to China or Russia, the emphasis is on differences. In Asia, and more broadly in a world aware of its responsibilities (which excludes the West as a whole), the emphasis is on what brings people together.

China and India have differences and both are close to Russia. India has understood perfectly well (unlike Western mono-neuron leaders) that the Sino-Russian rapprochement is not directed against it, but against American aggressiveness. But not only does India see in this rapprochement an opportunity to improve its own situation, but the United States is beginning to behave as an adversary of India as well.

On March 31, 2023, Russia published its foreign policy concept, which had not been changed since 2016[249]. Interestingly, Russia no longer sees itself as a European country, but as a "vast Eurasian and Euro-Pacific power." In other words, it has begun its pivot to the East. Russia, which we have prevented from becoming a bridge between the West and the East, is going to consolidate an already very strong bloc that will become the epicenter of our planet's development in a very short time.

We did with Russia exactly what the EU did with Ukraine in 2013: instead of seeing it as a bridge, it was seen as a gap.

3.3.6.2. China

Economically, Western sanctions have had three major effects: to encourage Russia to develop an industrial base for consumer products that it did not have, to push it to develop links with China that it did not have before, and to reduce its dependence on foreign capital. The incentive to develop indigenous capacity in many areas has helped manage employment better.

China has been a partner of Russia for several years now. The industrial ties between the two countries are historical and important. The ideological quarrels of the 1960s and 1980s have been forgotten, as have the territorial disputes.

Russia has understood that its transactions with the EU are systematically placed in a political and ideological context and are thus subject to sanctions in a totally unpredictable way. It has also understood that the development of China and the explosion of the Asian market is an opportunity: more stable, more predictable, more resistant to sanctions, paying more and seeking to reduce its dependence on the United States, it is clearly more attractive. This is why Russia has built a vast network of pipelines and is beginning to supply so many resources that will no longer be available to Europe.

Since the presidency of Donald Trump, the Americans have become more forceful towards China and are playing with the Taiwan issue - as they played with Ukraine - to bring it into a conflict that would weaken it. The Chinese are aware of this and the situation in Russia has inevitably led to a rapprochement between the two countries.

---

249. https://mid.ru/en/foreign_policy/fundamental_documents/1860586/?lang=fr

It is interesting that for China, the West justifies its support for Taiwan's independence, while in Ukraine, it refutes the historical and political elements that make Crimea a territory that has never felt Ukrainian and that the Ukrainians have never really considered "Ukrainian" (especially through their infrastructure investments).

In April 2023, the statements of the Chinese ambassador to France on the set of the French channel LCI triggered a polemic[250]. In reality, the interview shows the level of ignorance of the journalist, as the ambassador's statements are far from being false.

China is accused of supporting Russia with a double standard because of the Crimea situation. But these are very different situations.

The fundamental difference between Crimea and Taiwan is that Taiwan, like China, considers that there is only one China and that Taiwan is a province. This is what the "1992 Consensus" says[251], which the United States recognizes and which is the subject of a joint declaration of December 16, 1978[252]. In other words, Taiwan's independence is a Western construct.

Crimea, on the other hand, although it was "given" in 1954 by Khrushchev to Ukraine, then a member of the USSR, has always been Russian, after having been in the hands of the Tatars, about whom we will speak again below. This donation has never been ratified by the parliaments of Russia, Ukraine and the USSR. But, more importantly, Crimea obtained to be removed from the Ukrainian bosom in order to be directly subordinated to Moscow by a popular referendum on January 20, 1991[253]. The new configuration of the USSR was validated by the referendum of March 17, 1991, led by Moscow, which confirmed the maintenance of the Union. Ukraine will become independent only 9 months later, while the separation from Crimea has been consummated. After a legal battle, it is in 1995, that Ukraine abolishes the constitution of Crimea and overthrows by force its president.

So, contrary to what Darius Rochebin claims in his questioning of the Chinese ambassador, the latter is right. The situation of the two countries is fundamentally different. It is the Western discourse, which evacuates

---

250. https://youtu.be/8XYDYf1gmtA
251. https://fr.wikipedia.org/wiki/Consensus_de_1992
252. http://us.china-embassy.gov.cn/eng/zmgx/zywj/lhgb/200310/t20031023_4917623.htm
253. NdA: with a participation of 81.3% of the population.

parts of history and "simplifies" its explanation in order to support a clearly destabilizing policy of the US and the EU, which seeks military involvement in the region[254].

The West has done everything to make Russia and China feel similarly situated and feel the need to strengthen each other through an even more robust partnership.

3.3.7. The stability of Russia

Popularity of Vladimir Putin since October 2021

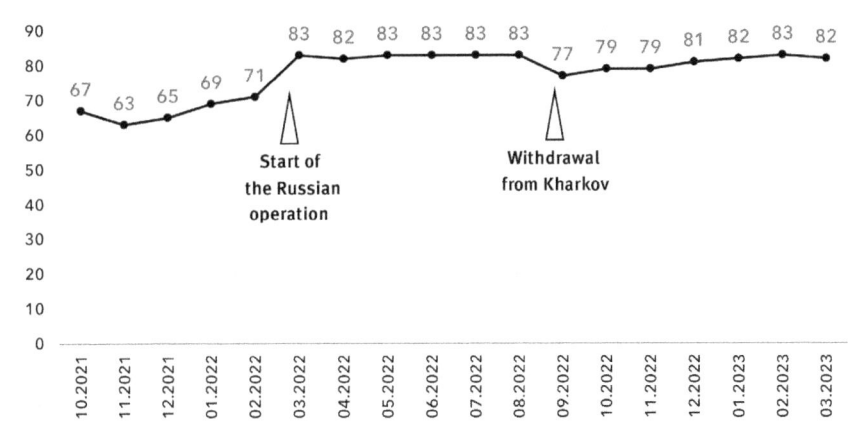

Figure 20 - Vladimir Putin's popularity rating has remained relatively stable since February 2022. An inflection was observed after the withdrawal from the Kharkov region by Russian-speaking forces in September. The Russian population is generally supportive of his government's actions. [Source: Levada Center (considered a foreign agent in Russia)

The same is true for support for the Russian special operation (SVO) in Ukraine, which remains very strong and has been reinforced by Western arms deliveries.

Our media is playing with numbers and dates to create misinformation. This is the case of the controversial Swiss media *Heidi News*, which tries to show that the government falsifies polls on support for the SVO. It refers to the approval rate of 58.8%, measured on February 26-28, 2022 by

---

254. "EU's Borrell asks European navies to patrol Taiwan Strait", EURACTIV.com / AFP, April 23, 2023 (https://www.euractiv.com/section/eu-china/news/borrell-asks-european-navies-to-patrol-taiwan-strait/)

the *Russian Field*, an institute rather close to the opposition to Vladimir Putin[255]. The Swiss media compares this figure to 71 per cent, measured by the *VTsIOM* polling institute, which is close to the Russian government, on March 5, 2022[256]. The difference seems too large to be honest, but the Swiss media obviously does not mention the rates measured by *VTsIOM* on March 5-7, 2022 which show an increase to 64% approval[257]. The Swiss media obviously does not mention that the opposition to the SVO measured by *Russian Field*, which was 34% at the end of February, increased to 22% at the beginning of March, a value higher than that given by *VTsIOM* (21%). So there is no evidence that the government is falsifying the figures as Heidi News claims.

Support for the action of the armed forces in Ukraine [%]

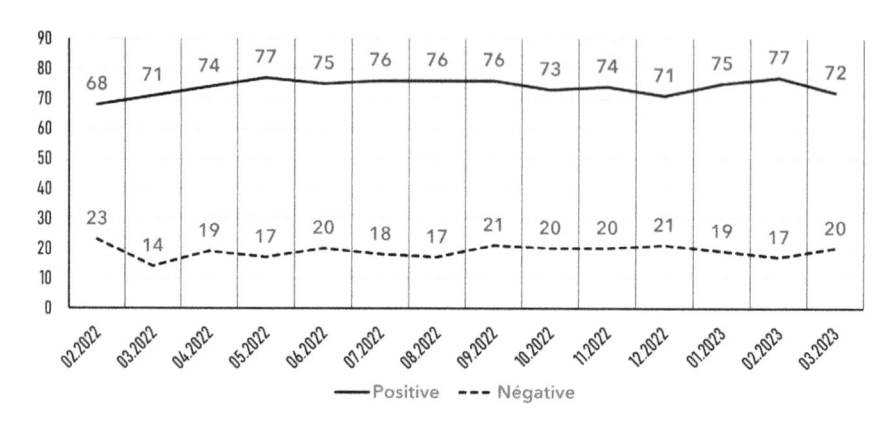

Date	Positive	Negative
02.2022	68	23
03.2022	71	14
04.2022	74	19
05.2022	77	17
06.2022	75	20
07.2022	76	18
08.2022	76	17
09.2022	76	21
10.2022	73	20
11.2022	74	20
12.2022	71	21
01.2023	75	19
02.2023	77	17
03.2023	72	20

Figure 21 - It can be seen that support for the SVO is steadily increasing. A slight inflection was noted at the end of 2022, especially after the withdrawal from Kharkov, which was very poorly explained to the population. In other words, the Russian authorities are not under pressure from their public, as Western governments are beginning to be. [Figures: Levada Center]

These figures can be compared with those of the *Levada Center* - considered a "foreign agent" - which kept regular statistics throughout the SVO, systematically asking the same questions, which is not the case with

---

255. https://web.archive.org/web/20220310065852/https:/russianfield.com/netvoine
256. https://wciom.ru/analytical-reviews/analiticheskii-obzor/armija-i-obshchestvo-na-fone-specialnoi-voennoi-operacii
257. https://web.archive.org/web/20220308171955/https://russianfield.com/zamir

Russian Field[258] mentioned by the Swiss media. The jump in popularity of the SVO between late February and early March 2022 appears to be a fact and not a manipulation of the numbers, as *Heidi News* suggests. In March 2023, according to the Levada Center, support for the special military operation in Ukraine is 72%[259].

Despite the misinformation and manipulations of our media, the Russian public is overwhelmingly behind its authorities. What emerges from the polls is that Russians support the SVO while wanting peace and a negotiated exit from the conflict, which has been the position of the Russian government since the war began in 2014.

It is also interesting to note that according to Russian Field, the majority of Russians blame the conflict on the West.

Responsibility for the deterioration of the situation according to the Russian population (as of February 26-28, 2022)

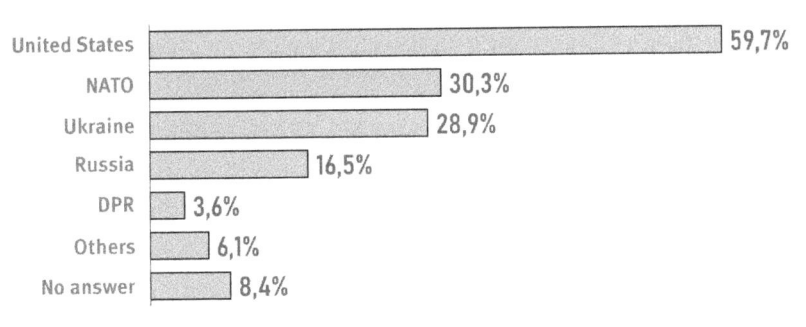

United States	59,7%
NATO	30,3%
Ukraine	28,9%
Russia	16,5%
DPR	3,6%
Others	6,1%
No answer	8,4%

Figure 22 - Responses to the question "Who do you think is behind the escalation of relations with Ukraine?" according to the Russian Field polling institute close to the opposition in Russia. The question was asked at the very beginning of the SVO. As can be seen, the population has a position very close to that of the Russian government.

Nevertheless, there will be in Russia - as in the West - a certain fatigue with regard to the hostilities. But it seems that this fatigue remains more favorable to Russia both internally and externally. The West's insistence on bringing down Russia and its government, including calls for murder by some Western leaders, only strengthens support for Vladimir Putin.

---

258. https://russianfield.com/projects
259. https://www.levada.ru/2022/12/23/konflikt-s-ukrainoj-otsenki-dekabrya-2022-goda/

Worthless politicians without any values, such as Lindsay Graham, Republican senator[260], or Jean Asselborn, Luxembourg Minister of Foreign Affairs, who declared on *Radio 100.7* in Luxembourg, that *"It would be all we could wish for, that he be effectively eliminated physically, so that it stops"*[261]. So individuals who did not lift a finger to enforce the Minsk agreements, because the conflict was killing Russian speakers, are now calling for murder! We are governed by individuals who are worthless.

These stupid statements have only strengthened the ranks of the Russians around their president. On the contrary, they show that our leaders are unable to anticipate problems intelligently and can only envisage muscular solutions.

3.4. Strengthening NATO and the EU

Some will say that the conflict in Ukraine has strengthened the Atlantic Alliance (NATO) and the European Union (EU). This is not so sure.

First of all, NATO has had only an extra role in this crisis. NATO member countries have contributed to supporting Ukraine individually, but NATO as an organization has had only a marginal role. NATO helped restore the Ukrainian army in 2014, within the framework of the *Euro-Atlantic Partnership* (EAPC). Let us recall here that the EAPC included Ukraine, of course, but also Russia, Belarus and Switzerland. The purpose of this parallel structure to the Alliance was to help the so-called "partner" countries to improve their defence institutions. NATO's intervention to reorganize and train the Ukrainian army was therefore part of a "normal" context.

The point here is that in this crisis, the Allies have shown only a façade of unity. They have acted in a totally erratic manner, ranging from destroying the Nord Stream 1 and 2 gas pipelines against Germany to sabotaging the dialogue initiatives proposed by Turkey.

---

260. Lexi Lonas, "Graham calls for 'somebody in Russia' to take Putin out," *The Hill*, March 4, 2022 (https://thehill.com/homenews/senate/596843-graham-calls-for-somebody-in-russia-to-take-putin-out/)
261. Guillaume Oblet, "Jean Asselborn: 'Éliminer physiquement Vladimir Poutine'", *Le Quotidien*, March 2, 2022 (updated March 3, 2022) (https://lequotidien.lu/politique-societe/jean-asselborn-eliminer-physiquement-vladimir-poutine/)

This can be explained by the fact that NATO is not a collegial structure, but an assembly of countries that have placed themselves under the protection of a superpower, which therefore has real decision-making power. In other words, in this crisis, NATO has shown that it is only an instrument of American policy.

It should be noted that since 2014, NATO has been unable to address the dispute between Ukraine and Russia - both members of the Euro-Atlantic Partnership Council (EAPC) - within its own institutions. Yet, the EAPC *"which includes 50 countries, is a multilateral forum for dialogue and consultation on political and security issues between NATO member and partner countries"*[262].

As for the EU, it has shown that it is only capable of fuelling the conflict by supplying arms and nipping in the bud attempts at negotiations desired by Ukraine. It has shown a remarkable inability to try to calm the situation.

This is because the EU does not have a common foreign policy. The *Common Foreign and Security Policy* (CFSP) has remained a pious hope since the late 1980s. The existence of a foreign minister, in the person of Josep Borrell, is reduced to the function of a sterile spokesman. Without a common foreign policy, there can be no *Common Security and Defence Policy* (CSDP). The Nord Stream affair and the way the Ukrainian crisis has been handled show that the EU is navigating at a loss, without any real objectives. Its sanctions have had effects that its experts had not been able to identify beforehand.

A fundamental criterion, repeatedly invoked by Russia since 2007, is the indivisibility of security. This is a principle that has been accepted by OSCE members and was sealed in the Istanbul Document (1999)[263] and the Astana Declaration (2010)[264]:

The security of each participating state is inextricably linked to that of all the others.

When the German government announced a record defense budget of 100 billion for 2023, the media exulted: "Putin wanted to weaken

---
262. https://www.nato.int/cps/fr/natohq/topics_49276.htm
263. https://www.osce.org/files/f/documents/0/2/39570.pdf
264. https://www.osce.org/files/f/documents/b/3/74987.pdf

Europe," but it is getting stronger! To what extent did Vladimir Putin have this objective? What is certain is that Germany had to revise its copy. The devaluation of the Euro against the dollar and the inflation resulting from the sanctions against Russia have sounded the death knell for this extraordinary budget. In October 2022, the German business newspaper *Handelsblatt* announced that the Ministry of Defence would make deep cuts in planned spending[265].

3.4.1. Relations between NATO and Russia

We have only remembered the 1962 Cuban Missile Crisis as a case of American sensitivity to having potentially hostile missiles in their immediate vicinity. But we often forget that the origin of this crisis was the 1961 deployment of American PGM-19 JUPITER nuclear missiles in Turkey. At the time, the Americans did not yet have the technology to build intercontinental missiles, and the JUPITERs were only an improved version of the German V2s, with a range of 2,400-2,700 km.

The Americans do not like it when people do to them what they do to others. The Soviets understood this and started to deploy missiles in Cuba. Finally, the Americans, caught in their game, had to withdraw their missiles from Turkey… The USSR won.

However, NATO was in direct contact with Soviet territory as early as 1952 with the accession of Turkey and was already touching Russian territory in 1949 with Norway. The problem is therefore not that NATO touches the Russian border, but what the West does there.

The Baltic countries joined NATO in 2004, without this really creating a problem for Russia. In fact, the problem came from the United States. As early as 2002, by gradually withdrawing from all arms control treaties, Bush and Trump also got out of their obligations. As early as 2004, they began negotiating with the new NATO members (Poland, Czech Republic and Romania) to station missile launchers there. This is what triggered Moscow's concern.

This concern is reinforced by two observations. Firstly, the attitude of the Americans, who, since 1991, have launched a large number of

---

265. Martin Greive, Martin Murphy & Frank Specht, "Regierung kürzt mehrere Rüstungsprojekte", *Handelsblatt*, October 24, 2022 (https://www.handelsblatt.com/politik/deutschland/bundeswehr-sondervermoegen-regierung-kuerzt-mehrere-ruestungsprojekte/28761788.html)

military operations against sovereign countries in defiance of international law, without encountering the slightest condemnation from their Western allies. Secondly, the Mk41 launchers in question are capable of firing anti-ballistic (defensive) or nuclear (offensive) missiles. The site of Radzikowo (Poland), chosen for their installation, is 800 km from the Russian border and 1,300 km from Moscow. This proximity goes exactly against the principles of the ABM Treaty, which aimed to allow for negotiation until the last few seconds before a fatal decision.

However, the Russians know that the West does not respect their word or the agreements they have signed. This is why Washington's assurances on a purely defensive use of these launchers are received with legitimate scepticism in Moscow. This is what motivated Vladimir Putin's tough speech in Munich in 2007.

The Russian concern is not only legitimate, but it is symmetrical in the West, as the *RAND Corporation* points out[266]:

> *If placing strike assets in close proximity to Russia would reduce the amount of time Russian military leaders have to detect and respond to air and cruise missile attacks, it would leave U.S. and allied leaders with even less time to detect and respond to Russian missile attacks against assets currently located at those bases. This combination of mutual vulnerability and risk of surprise attack could be seriously destabilizing in a crisis, especially if tactical nuclear weapons are also stored at nearby sites.*

Thus, contrary to what we are told by the generals on our television sets, the problem of the Russians is not so much to have tanks on their border, but nuclear weapons.

This is what will motivate Vladimir Putin's declaration in March 2023 to accede to Alexander Lukashenko's request to deploy nuclear weapons on Belarusian territory. Technically, this decision has no impact, as these weapons have ranges that allow them to be fired from Russian territory. On the other hand, it is a political message.

---

266. James Dobbins, Raphael S. Cohen, Nathan Chandler, Bryan Frederick, Edward Geist, Paul DeLuca, Forrest E. Morgan, Howard J. Shatz, Brent Williams, "Extending Russia: Competing from Advantageous Ground," RAND Corporation, 2019

3.4.2. Ukraine's membership in NATO and the EU

3.4.2.1. Ukraine's membership in NATO

At the 2008 NATO Summit, it was decided to consider Georgia and Ukraine for NATO membership. However, the decision of NATO is not enthusiastic, because it is known that it is provocative in nature and will strengthen the feeling of encirclement of the Russians.

In August 2008, the scenario that led to Russia's intervention to protect the Russian-speaking population of South Ossetia from the disproportionate attack[267] of the Georgian government[268] probably served as a model for the Ukrainian crisis of 2022.

After 2014, relations between Ukraine and its neighbors are far from harmonious. The new far-right government views ethnic groups as inferior to "ethnic" Ukrainians. The result is very high ethnic tensions.

In addition to the Russian-speaking community, which is the largest, the Magyar minority has been subjected for many years to[269] abuses by Ukrainians[270], with the blessing of Western countries[271]. Thanks to the complacency of the Western media, the persecution of this minority by Ukrainian extreme right-wing organizations has increased[272]. This is the main reason why Hungary opposes Ukraine's membership in the Atlantic Alliance, as explained by the *Washington Times*[273], whose article is reproduced on the website of the Hungarian Embassy in the United States[274]. In March 2023, Peter Szijjarto, Hungary's foreign minister, stated that his government *"would not support any concrete steps towards integration (on the part of Ukraine) into NATO or the EU"*

---

267. Andrew Rettman, "EU-sponsored report says Georgia started 2008 war", *euobserver.com*, September 30, 2009
268. "Quotes from EU-sponsored Georgia war report", *Reuters*, September 30, 2009
269. https://youtu.be/9b07devNZU0
270. "Budapest summons Ukrainian ambassador over 'raids' on ethnic Hungarian organisation", *Euractiv.com / Reuters*, December 1st, 2020 (https://www.euractiv.com/section/europe-s-east/news/budapest-summons-ukrainian-ambassador-over-raids-on-ethnic-hungarian-organization/)
271. Mariann Őry, "Foreign Minister Warns EU about Acts against Hungarians in Ukraine," *Hungary Today*, January 24, 2023 (https://hungarytoday.hu/foreign-minister-warns-eu-about-atrocities-against-hungarians-in-ukraine/)
272. https://hhrf.org/on-our-radar/hungarians-in-ukraine/
273. Balazs Tarnok, "Why is Hungary 'blocking' Ukraine's NATO accession?", The Washington Times, June 25, 2021 (https://m.washingtontimes.com/news/2021/jun/25/why-is-hungary-blocking-ukraines-nato-accession/)
274. https://washington.mfa.gov.hu/eng/news/why-is-hungary-blocking-ukraines-nato-accession

until the situation improves. In order to hide the Ukrainian crimes, our media associate this refusal with the so-called proximity between Viktor Orban and Vladimir Putin[275]!

In April 2023, NATO is cracking down on Ukraine's entry into the Alliance. While extremist Eastern European countries such as the Baltic states and Poland are pushing for membership, the United States, Germany and Hungary are opposed. The *Financial Times* talks about deep differences within NATO[276]. In fact, this situation was provoked by Volodymyr Zelensky himself, who put the Alliance on the spot by making his presence at the Vilnius summit (July 11-12, 2023) conditional on a concrete declaration in favour of Ukraine.

3.4.2.2. Ukraine's accession to the EU

Contrary to the ramblings of our "experts" Russia has never opposed the accession of Ukraine to the EU[277] and it does not intend to change its policy in the future[278]. In 2013, it was the European Union that opposed Ukraine's continued relations with Russia. It refused the Russian proposal to accommodate the economic interests of Ukraine and Russia and that Ukraine be simultaneously part of two agreements. It was José-Manuel Barroso who demanded that Ukraine make a choice[279].

At the end of March 2022, when Volodymyr Zelensky made his proposals for negotiations with Russia, the latter made it clear that it would oppose Ukraine's membership in NATO, but not in the EU[280].

---

275. "Ukraine's Hungarians stuck between Kyiv and 'pro-Putin' Orban," *France 24*, March 21, 2023 (https://www.france24.com/en/live-news/20230321-ukraine-s-hungarians-stuck-between-kyiv-and-pro-putin-orban)
276. "US opposes offering Ukraine a 'road map' to Nato membership," *Financial Times*, April 8, 2023 (https://www.ft.com/content/c37ed22d-e0e4-4b03-972e-c56af8a36d2e)
277. Elena Teslova, "Russia not worried about Ukraine's EU candidate status: Putin," *Anadolu Agency*, June 17, 2022 (updated June 18, 2022) (https://www.aa.com.tr/en/world/russia-not-worried-about-ukraines-eu-candidate-status-putin/2616606)
278. Joe Walsh, "Russia-Ukraine Peace Talks: Russia Willing To Let Ukraine Join EU If It Stays Out Of NATO, Report Says," Forbes, March 28, 2022 (https://www.forbes.com/sites/joewalsh/2022/03/28/russia-ukraine-peace-talks-russia-willing-to-let-ukraine-join-eu-if-it-stays-out-of-nato-report-says/).
279. "Barroso reminds Ukraine that Customs Union and free trade with EU are incompatible," *ukrinform*, February 25, 2013 (https://www.ukrinform.net/rubric-economy/1461921-barroso_reminds_ukraine_that_customs_union_and_free_trade_with_eu_are_incompatible_299321.html)
280. Joe Walsh, "Russia-Ukraine Peace Talks: Russia Willing To Let Ukraine Join EU If It Stays Out Of NATO, Report Says," *Forbes*, March 28, 2023 (https://www.forbes.com/sites/joewalsh/2022/03/28/russia-ukraine-peace-talks-russia-willing-to-let-ukraine-join-eu-if-it-stays-out-of-nato-report-says/)

The accession of Eastern European countries has systematically been preceded by their accession to NATO. This is neither a written rule nor an immutable process, but it was probably perceived as a problem by Ukraine. For its open conflict with Russia as early as 2014 made it virtually impossible for it to join NATO, due to the risk of invoking Article 5 of the Atlantic Charter. This, by the way, is what the Americans told Zelensky[281]. But this should not prevent membership in the EU. At least in theory. Because the problem today is that if Ukraine is admitted into the EU, a whole cascade of problems could affect Europe.

First, it would require the EU to substantially fund the reconstruction of the country. Already today, Ukraine is supported at arm's length by the EU.

Secondly, as long as the endemic problems of corruption are not solved, investors will not rush to come to Ukraine.

Hungary has long been divided on the Ukrainian question. Contrary to what the so-called experts of French media like *France 5* or *LCI* claim, it is not because Viktor Orban is a dictator, but simply because minorities are persecuted in Ukraine. This has been the case for many years for the Hungarian minority. At the beginning of 2023, it was observed that these minorities were the first to be targeted by forced recruitment[282]. This explains Hungary's anger[283] and why 97% of Hungarians are opposed to European sanctions against Russia[284].

That said, the integration of Ukraine into the EU, proclaimed urbi et orbi, still seems far away. In April 2023, Poland, Hungary, Slovakia have banned the import of Ukrainian grain.

---

281. Chandelis Duster, "Zelensky: 'If we were a NATO member, a war wouldn't have started,'" cnn.com, March 20, 2022 (https://edition.cnn.com/europe/live-news/ukraine-russia-putin-news-03-20-22/h_7c08d64201fdd9d3a141e63e606a62e4)

282. Füssy Angéla, "Mint a barmokat, úgy fogdossák össze a férfiakat Kárpátalján - Nézze meg helyszíni videóriportunkat!", *PestiSracok*, January 23, 2023 (https://pestisracok.hu/mint-a-barmokat-ugy-fogdossak-ossze-a-ferfiakat-karpataljan-nezze-meg-helyszini-videoriportunkat/)

283. Chris King, "Shocking claims of ethnic Hungarians being forcibly drafted into Ukrainian military in Transcarpathia," *Euro Weekly News*, January 24, 2023 (https://euroweeklynews.com/2023/01/24/shocking-claims-of-ethnic-hungarians-being-forcibly-drafted-into-ukrainian-military-in-transcarpathia/)

284. Robert Semonsen, "97% of Hungarians Reject Brussels' Sanctions Against Russia," *The European Conservative*, January 17, 2023 (https://europeanconservative.com/articles/news/97-of-hungarians-reject-brussels-sanctions-against-russia/)

3.4.3. Sweden's and Finland's membership in NATO

In May 2022, in the emotion and hysteria triggered by the Russian offensive in Ukraine, Sweden and Finland expressed their intention to be candidates for entry into NATO. Many see this as a nod to Vladimir Putin. Jens Stoltenberg, Secretary General of the Alliance, says that *"Putin wanted less NATO, but he got the opposite*[285]*".*

If we stick to the map of Europe, this is correct, but a closer look shows that it is simplistic. Our politicians see the Ukrainian crisis as a soccer match where everyone is trying to score points at the expense of Russia. But the reality is more nuanced.

First, the leaders of the two Scandinavian countries were incredibly dilettantic in failing to consult with the various members of the Alliance beforehand - and Turkey in the first instance - to gauge their support.

Clearly, Turkey does not want to bring into the Alliance countries that might challenge its policy towards the Kurds, which it considers existential. Nothing has been said yet, but Turkey knows how to be firm with its NATO allies, and it is likely that it will not give up its demands on Sweden, whose policy towards the Kurds is diametrically opposed.

One of the most delicate points for Sweden is certainly the extradition of Kurds considered terrorists by Ankara. We would thus be in a paradoxical situation, to say the least, where a "democratic" country would hand over to a country it considers "autocratic" individuals to whom it has granted protection in the name of the fight against autocracy!

Strategically, the Swedish and Finnish decision highlights the analytical weakness of their and the Europeans' leadership. They think that in case of conflict, American nuclear power would protect them better than their neutrality. They make two errors in reasoning.

First, they are based on the idea that Russia attacks its neighbors without reason. This is obviously false, as we have seen. Russia's decision to intervene in Ukraine is far from irrational, even if one does not approve of it. Our annoying habit of not listening to what the Russians tell us and substituting our own reasoning has systematically led us to bad decisions.

---

285. "EU gives 500 million euros more to arm Ukraine," AFP/La Libre, January 23, 2023 (https://www.lalibre.be/international/europe/guerre-ukraine-russie/2023/01/23/lue-accorde-500-millions-deuros-supplementaires-pour-armer-lukraine-3NDE3VBSGFCJNHNNRW2CP623JQ/)

Second, Sweden and Finland seem to have a very childish reading of American nuclear strategy. The United States would never sacrifice its own national soil by striking Russian soil for the sake of Sweden or Finland. In other words, these two countries, which met the criteria of neutrality that Russia would want for its direct neighbors, have deliberately and unnecessarily put themselves in Russia's nuclear crosshairs.

For Russia, the main threat could come from the Central European theater of war. In the case of a hypothetical conflict in Europe, with a neutral Scandinavia, Russia did not need to worry about its northern flank. With Finland entering the threat picture, it might be tempted to use theater nuclear weapons to "flank" its operations by striking the Nordic countries preemptively or pre-emptively, with virtually no risk of an American nuclear response.

In June 2022, the Ukrainian media ZN, UA rightly states[286]:

> *Some NATO allies may misinterpret the lessons of this war, given the long-term prospects for European security. Russia will not disappear as a strategic rival, and its military is not as "Potemkin" as it seems.*

On April 4, 2023, Finland becomes the 31st member of the Atlantic Alliance. While its previous president, Sauli Niinisto, had promised a popular referendum[287], this did not happen.

In fact, in both Sweden and Finland, there is little strategic thinking. These are countries that have been viscerally opposed to Russia for a long time and whose governance is particularly childish, as in the Baltic countries. Because it is hard to see why Russia would be interested in going to war with the Scandinavian countries (and even those in Europe, for that matter)... Even during the Cold War, NATO's northern flank never posed a real threat to the USSR and Russia.

---

286. "The Economist: Україні вдається борися з армією Росії, але це не означає, що НАТО теж зможе", ZN,UA, June 10, 2022 (https://zn.ua/ukr/WORLD/the-economist-ukrajini-vdajetsja-borisja-z-armijeju-rosiji-ale-tse-ne-oznachaje-shcho-nato-tezh-zmozhe.html)
287. Tuomas Forsell & Jussi Rosendahl, "Finnish president says joining NATO would require referendum," *Reuters*, October 30, 2017 (https://www.reuters.com/article/us-finland-nato-idUSKBN1CZ2K6)

Possible scheme of a nuclear exchange in the context of a conflict in Europe

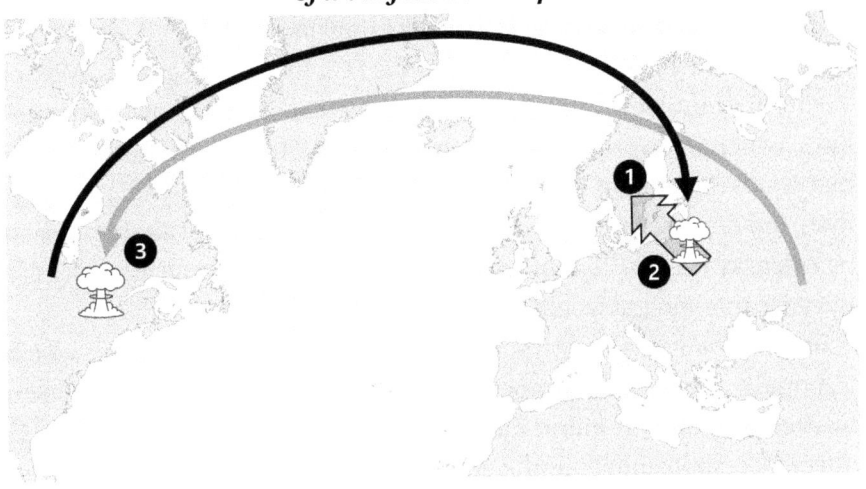

Figure 23 - Assuming Russia attacks NATO member Sweden (1), and the United States retaliates with a nuclear strike on Russian forces (2), Russia could strike U.S. territory (3). Thus, nuclear deterrence will most likely not apply in a case like this, as the United States seeks to safeguard its national soil. In the event of a conflict in Central Europe, with Sweden and Finland members of NATO, Russia might be tempted to "flank" itself with nuclear strikes on these countries. Here again, the United States would be reluctant to strike Russian territory, lest it extend the destruction to its own territory.

The total derationalization of the Ukrainian conflict has led to the conclusion that any country can be attacked at any time at the whim of Vladimir Putin. This is simply silly. The best source of security is always to have good relations with one's neighbors. Russia did not have any disputes with the Nordic countries and they are the ones who thought that they were the center of Russia's attention... The kingdom of heaven belongs to them!

3.4.4. The sabotage of the Nord Stream 1 and 2 gas pipelines

3.4.4.1. Conspiracy theories

On 26 and 27 September 2022, after a series of explosions, leaks were detected on the Nord Stream 1 and 2 gas pipelines near the Danish island of Bornholm. A consensus was quickly established in the West to condemn an act of sabotage[288]. Very quickly, the media spoke of a *"terrorist act*[289]*"* or an *"act of war*[290]*"*.

The question is who did it. Despite the total lack of facts, all eyes are on Russia. On the French television channel LCI, the French general Michel Yakovleff even asserts that Russia could have sabotaged its own gas pipelines, which in any case were no longer useful, in order to demonstrate that it was capable of doing so[291]! The reasoning is simply idiotic: why, then, did the Russians not destroy the Soyuz pipeline in Ukraine, closed by Zelensky in May? To think that the Russians are as stupid as we are is a mistake: this general would do well to read Sun Tzu again.

The alternative is the hypothesis of American responsibility, which is popular in certain European intelligence circles and Anglo-Saxon intellectuals. But in either case, there are no facts that allow one to attribute responsibility for the attack in an indisputable way. In Europe, the anti-Russian conspiracy prevails. On RMC, the "journalist" Nicolas Poincaré, a regular of affabulations about Russia and China, says that a scenario involving the Americans *"is quite unimaginable"* and that it can only be the Russians[292]. On the Swiss channel RTS, Giacomo Luciani, a professor at the *Institut de haute étude internationale et du développement* (IHIED) in Geneva, draws the same conclusion without having the slightest factual element to support it[293].

On the *France 5* channel, when asked who sabotaged the gas pipelines, the journalist Anthony Bellanger, from *France Inter*, answers without hesitation: *"Russia!*[294]*"* In reality, he knows nothing at all and invents a Russian conspiracy. We are in the middle of a conspiracy!

---

288. "Nord Stream leaks: Sabotage to blame, says EU", BBC News, September 28, 2022 (https://www.bbc.com/news/world-europe-63057966)
289. "Nord Stream: explosions, "deliberate acts"... What is known about the leaks of gas pipelines in the Baltic Sea," TF1, September 28, 2022 (https://www.tf1info.fr/international/guerre-ukraine-russie-gazoducs-nord-stream-explosions-sabotages-ce-que-l-on-sait-sur-les-fuites-spectaculaires-en-mer-baltique-2233630.html)
290. Charlotte Lalanne, "Sabotage de Nord Stream: la 'guerre hybride' a bel et bien commencé", L'Express, October 1st, 2022 (updated October 3, 2022), (https://www.lexpress.fr/monde/europe/sabotages-de-nord-stream-la-guerre-hybride-a-bel-et-bien-commence_2181076.html)
291. https://youtu.be/EMD47FFBvTs
292. https://youtu.be/hu1J6aA7c-w
293. https://www.rts.ch/play/tv/redirect/detail/13423556?startTime=176
294. https://youtu.be/K-WzRgrzlLU?t=88

The sabotage of the Nord Stream gas pipelines

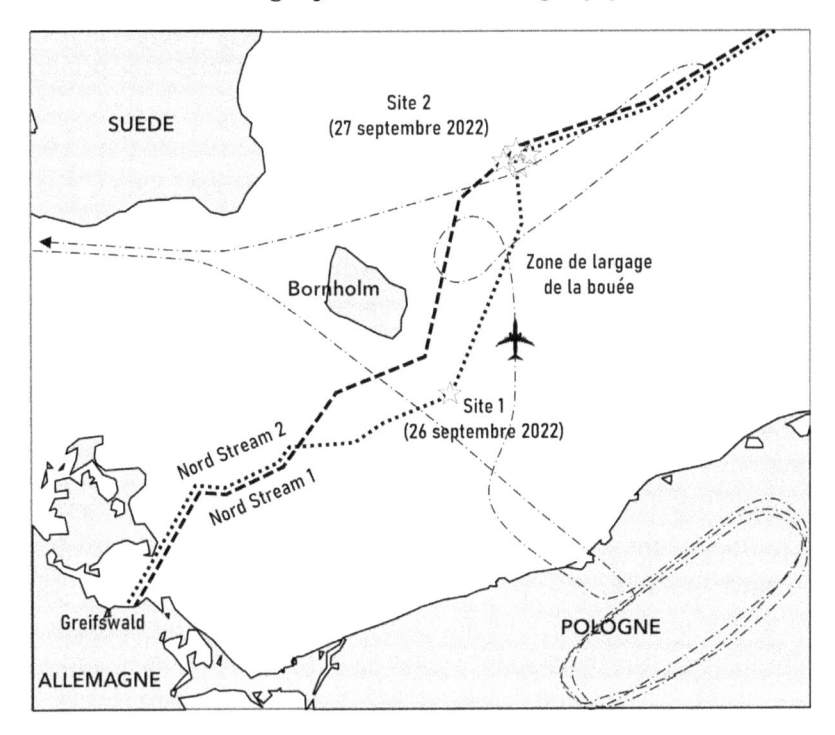

Figure 24 - Sites of the September 26 and 27, 2022 explosions in the vicinity of the Danish island of Bornholm. The explosives were placed on the pipelines between September 17 and September 22, 2022, when the USS Kearsarge left the area. In order to keep the explosions from being too close to the naval exercise, their detonation was delayed. It was controlled by a transmitter placed in a buoy, dropped by a P8 Poseidon aircraft of the US Navy on the morning of the 26th, after having been refueled in flight over Poland by a KC-35R aircraft.

In October 2022, the analysis of Columbia University economist Jeffrey Sachs[295] was called a *"conspiracy theory"* by the *Neue Zürcher Zeitung* (NZZ), a once-respectable Swiss daily newspaper[296]. But the NZZ accuses without any factual basis and draws on an article published the day before by the *Center for European Policy Analysis*[297] (funded by the

---
295. https://youtu.be/nbt-CsSRJl8?t=6695
296. Lia Pescatore, "Nord-Stream-Lecks: kaum Fakten, dafür umso wildere Spekulationen", NZZ, October 18, 2022 (https://www.nzz.ch/amp/wirtschaft/nord-stream-lecks-kaum-fakten-dafuer-umso-wildere-spekulationen-ld.1706600)
297. Mary Blankenship & Bill Echikson, "Conspiracy Theorists, Right-wing Politicians Fuel Nord Stream Disinformation," Center for European Policy Analysis (CEPA), October 17, 2022 (https://cepa.org/article/conspiracy-theorists-right-wing-politicians-fuel-nord-stream-disinformation/)

American arms industry, the *National Endowment for Democracy* (NED) and the American and Estonian governments). A source that is judge and jury, which shows that the NZZ does not work according to the principles of the Munich Charter...

Moreover, it is interesting to note that the NZZ attributes the attack to Russia without any nuance, whereas neither the United States, nor the European Union, nor Germany attributed the sabotage to Russia or to any other country! A conspiracy media that denounces a conspiracy theory... and thus covers up what has all the characteristics of a terrorist attack.

This reasoning illustrates the conspiracy mentality that prevails in the Western media and political class. Because from the beginning, there are many arguments against Russia's action.

First, since it began delivering natural gas to the West in the late 1960s, the Soviet Union and then Russia have never used natural gas as leverage, even at the height of the Cold War. In 1982, the Americans had already sabotaged the Russian gas pipeline Bratsvo[298]. Forty years later, it was the West that announced that it wanted to stop importing Russian gas and oil products so that it would no longer be dependent on its neighbor. In March, Canada's unwillingness to return a turbine for Nord Stream 1, followed by its refusal to give guarantees for the return of other turbines, forced Russia to stop deliveries because it could no longer guarantee the proper functioning of the pipeline.

Secondly, if it wanted to put pressure on the West, it could play with the tap to control the market and thus impose its will. This is the principle of blackmail: to be able to turn back. By destroying the gas pipelines, it automatically excludes itself from any capacity to act and to blackmail the European countries. This is therefore of no interest whatsoever. The accusation against Russia is all the more absurd, since Russia and Turkey have announced that they want to create an "energy hub" to supply gas to Europe[299].

On a more technical level, the island of Bornholm is located in the middle of the strait between Sweden and Poland. Since the Cold War, it has allowed Denmark to monitor the passage of Russian nuclear subma-

---

298. Roman Kupchinsky, "Analysis: The Recurring Fear of Russian Gas Dependency," Radio Free Europe/Radio Liberty, May 11, 2006
299. https://www.reuters.com/business/energy/erdogan-says-he-agreed-with-putin-form-natural-gas-hub-turkey-2022-10-19/

rines between the Baltic Sea and the North Atlantic for NATO. Known in the intelligence services as BALTAP, this strait is covered by the highest density of underwater electronic sensors and electronic listening devices in the entire Baltic. It is hard to imagine that Russian submarine actions could have taken place so close to Bornholm without triggering an alert from the Danish intelligence services.

Russia would have had neither the interest nor the possibility to commit such a sabotage. Of course, the declarations of Russia, a few days after the attack, on the possible repair of the gas pipelines[300] have not been noted by the French-speaking press. Because it would highlight their lies...

3.4.4.2. Examination of the facts

On the other hand, in the Western "camp", there are many potential culprits.

Of these, Germany can probably be excluded. The Nord Stream 1 pipeline was built at the request of Gerhard Schröder, and Nord Stream 2 at the request of Angela Merkel, in order to get away from nuclear power and coal. Moreover, Germany is the country that suffers most from Western sanctions on fossil fuels, and there is talk that it could reach an agreement with Russia to restore gas deliveries.

For their part, the United States and Poland have been opposed to the Nord Stream project from the start. In February 2022, President Biden stated that in the event of a Russian offensive, *"there will be no more Nord Stream 2"*. When asked how this would be done, he replied, *"I promise you that we will be able to do it*[301]*"*. During the construction of the pipeline, the Polish navy repeatedly interfered in a dangerous and irresponsible manner with the Russian ships responsible for the construction site[302]. From the very beginning of the Russian operation in Ukraine, Polish political conduct has been particularly immature,

---

300. "Russia's Novak Says Possible to Repair Nord Stream Pipelines," *Bloomberg News*, October 2, 2022 (https://www.bloomberg.com/news/articles/2022-10-02/russia-s-novak-says-possible-to-repair-nord-stream-pipelines)
301. "If Russia invades Ukraine, there will be no Nord Stream 2, Biden says", *Reuters*, February 8, 2022 (https://www.reuters.com/business/energy/if-russia-invades-ukraine-there-will-be-no-nord-stream-2-biden-says-2022-02-07/)
302. "Poland Denies 'Provocative' Naval Maneuvers Near Nord Stream 2," *The Maritime Executive*, April 2, 2021 (https://maritime-executive.com/article/poland-denies-provocative-naval-maneuvers-near-nord-stream-2)

which is why many Anglo-Saxon military analysts believe that Poland was involved in this attack.

In 2015, the Swedish navy had already intercepted an underwater drone loaded with explosives in the vicinity of the Nord Stream 2[303]. Swedish authorities did not specify the nationality of the underwater vehicle, but it appears to be of Western construction. Moreover, as this event took place just after the events in Maidan, given the atmosphere of the moment, it is very likely that if the underwater vehicle had been Russian, Sweden would have said it was[304]!

Between April and October 2022, the US Navy deployed the USS Kearsarge and its amphibious group[305], for BALTOPS 22 exercises (with sabotage units and underwater demolition specialists) in the Baltic Sea[306]. The websites ads-b.nl and Flightradar24 have in their database the movements of US helicopters in the Baltic Sea and show numerous movements of US helicopters of the MH-60S type in the area of sabotage a few days before the leaks observed[307].

In short, the accusations against Russia are based solely on opinion or prejudice, while those against the United States are based on circumstantial evidence. In both cases, there is no factual evidence to support a hypothesis at this stage.

3.4.4.3. American guilt?

The fact is that the neutralization of Nord Stream 2 has been one of the main thrusts of American foreign policy for almost a decade and especially under Donald Trump. In addition to Joe Biden's statements, which can be interpreted in different ways, it is certain that such sabotage could not have taken place without the knowledge and approval of Denmark

---

303. Mark Iden, "Explosive-Laden Drone Found Near Nord Stream Pipeline," *Pipeline Technology Journal*, November 13, 2015 (https://www.pipeline-journal.net/news/explosive-laden-drone-found-near-nord-stream-pipeline)

304. Bernhard Trautvetter, "Nord-Stream-Anschläge: Warum spricht kaum jemand über die Drohnenfunde?", *telepolis*, October 30, 2022 (https://www.telepolis.de/features/Nord-Stream-Anschlaege-Warum-spricht-kaum-jemand-ueber-die-Drohnenfunde-7324248.html?seite=all)

305. Staff Sgt. Brittney Vella, "22nd MEU Returns from Seven-Month Deployment," marines.mil, October 11, 2022 (https://www.marines.mil/News/News-Display/Article/3184121/22nd-meu-returns-from-seven-month-deployment/)

306. https://www.fehmarn24.de/fehmarn/us-navy-passiert-fehmarnbelt-grosser-flottenverband-der-91809308.html

307. https://www.moonofalabama.org/2022/09/whodunnit-facts-related-to-the-sabotage-attack-on-the-nord-stream-pipelines.html

and Sweden, which have technical control of the underwater space at this location. It is also certain that this sabotage could not have taken place without the political agreement of the United States.

Moreover, the political context in Germany itself would tend to confirm the hypothesis of American responsibility. These sabotages come at a time when the German parliamentary left is calling on the government to enter into negotiations with Russia and is encouraging the population to take to the streets to demand the reopening of Nord Stream[308], which Germany (not Russia) has closed.

Since the beginning of September, demonstrations demanding an end to the sanctions against Russia[309] and the restoration of natural gas supplies[310] have been increasing in Germany. They are not reported by the European media, which seeks to maintain a state of tension. At the same time, Germany is conducting secret negotiations with Russia in order to find solutions[311].

A German shift towards "normalization" with Russia was therefore possible. This is why the United States would have sought to make the current situation irreversible. Apparently, the CIA warned the German authorities of a possible sabotage of the gas pipelines[312]. It is difficult to interpret this warning, but it seems that the American agency was opposed to such sabotage, which could have endangered NATO's cohesion. In any case, it seems that the BND, the German strategic intelligence service, was not informed... Thus, everything looks like an operation carried out by some NATO countries against Germany.

Russia has asked to be part of the joint investigation committee (JIT) set up by Denmark, Sweden and Germany. Predictably, its request was denied. Then, on the basis of a preliminary investigation, Sweden refused to join

---

308. Sevim Dagdelen, "Sturm statt Burgfrieden", Junge Welt, September 5, 2022 (https://www.jungewelt.de/artikel/433948.sturm-statt-burgfrieden.html)
309. "Thousands march in eastern Germany to protest soaring energy prices," aa.tr, September 27, 2022 (https://www.aa.com.tr/en/environment/thousands-march-in-eastern-germany-to-protest-soaring-energy-prices/2696034)
310. Philip Oltermann, "Germany's Die Linke on verge of split over sanctions on Russia," The Guardian, September 19, 2022 (https://www.theguardian.com/world/2022/sep/19/germanys-die-linke-on-verge-of-split-over-sanctions-on-russia)
311. Pepe Escobar, "Who profits from Pipeline Terror?", The Cradle, September 29, 2022 (https://thecradle.co/Article/Columns/16307)
312. https://www.spiegel.de/politik/nord-stream-gasleitungen-cia-warnte-bundesregierung-vor-anschlag-auf-ostsee-pipelines-a-3ab0a183-8af6-4fb2-bae4-d134de0b3d57

the JIT on the grounds that it could not share its information with Germany because of the classification level. On October 6, the Swedish police announced that they had completed their investigation and concluded that there was "serious sabotage"[313], but refused to share their findings for reasons of "national security". This was the content of the German government's response to the parliamentarians' question. In October, Denmark conducted an investigation with the internal intelligence service (PET) and the Danish police[314], but refused to share the results[315].

At the end of October, the Swedish government announces a further investigation by the Swedish armed forces.

At the same time, Russia accused Britain of involvement in the sabotage[316]. It apparently relied on a tweet from Liz Truss, then Foreign Secretary, to Anthony Blinken saying "It's done!" within a minute of the explosions. True or false, the information led to an investigation into the interception of her communications by Russian intelligence services. This one showed that Liz Truss preferred to use her iPhone than the encrypted devices of the GCHQ (the British electronic intelligence service)[317]!

In December 2022, the Washington Post[318] threw a spanner in the works by quoting European officials that Russia was probably not the author of the sabotage...

Obviously, if the investigation had confirmed Russia's responsibility, there would have been a succession of emergency meetings in Europe

---

313. https://sakerhetspolisen.se/ovriga-sidor/nyheter/nyheter/2022-10-06-starkt-misstanke-om-grovt-sabotage-i-ostersjon.html
314. "PET og Københavns Politi nedsætter fælles efterforskningsgruppe i sagen om gaslækager i Østersøen", *Københavns Politi*, October 18, 2022 (https://politi.dk/koebenhavns-politi/nyhedsliste/pet-og-københavns-politi-nedsætter-fælles-efterforskningsgruppe-i-sagen-om-gaslækager-i-østersøen/2022/10/18)
315. Charlie Duxbury, "Nord Stream investigation tests EU intelligence sharing around the Baltic," *Politico*, October 28, 2022 (https://www.politico.eu/article/sweden-denmark-germany-nord-stream-investigation-tests-eu-intelligence-sharing-around-the-baltic/)
316. "Russia Accuses U.K. of Being Involved in Nord Stream Explosions," *The Moscow Times / AFP*, October 29, 2022 (https://www.themoscowtimes.com/2022/10/29/russia-accuses-uk-of-being-involved-in-nord-stream-explosions-a79232)
317. Glen Owen & Dan Hodges, "Liz Truss's personal phone that was hacked by Kremlin agents was so compromised it was locked away in a 'secure location' as experts fear top secret negotiations and private messages may have been leaked," *The Mail on Sunday*, October 29, 2022 (https://www.dailymail.co.uk/news/article-11368619/Liz-Trusss-personal-phone-hacked-Putins-spies-secret-details-negotiations.html)
318. Shane Harris, John Hudson, Missy Ryan & Michael Birnbaum, "No conclusive evidence Russia is behind Nord Stream attack", *The Washington Post*, December 21, 2022 (https://www.washingtonpost.com/national-security/2022/12/21/russia-nord-stream-explosions/)

and within NATO. But this was not the case. So we don't know for sure who actually carried out this attack, but the Germans know that it was not Russia and that it was one of their NATO allies...

If we add that Anthony Blinken, US Secretary of State, called this attack "an incredible opportunity"[319], which certainly no Westerner would have said after the attacks of September 2001, we have a picture of the special status of this sabotage.

On October 13, 2022, while Russia proposes to Turkey the creation of an "energy hub", an attempt to sabotage the TurkStream gas pipeline is intercepted[320]... The authors of this attempt are not known to us, but we can assume that it belongs to the same project, which is to isolate Russia completely and irreversibly.

On February 8, 2023, the American investigative journalist Seymour Hersh revealed that the sabotage of the gas pipelines was carried out by the United States with the help of Norway[321]. Hersh confirms the suspicions of many experts (outside France). The interesting element he brings is the process used by the Biden administration to bypass the American parliamentary control mechanisms.

The sabotage of underwater gas pipelines requires very precise work, both discreet and effective, which must be carried out under very difficult circumstances. The problem is that, since the 1980s, the President of the United States has been required to notify Congress of special operations conducted abroad by the armed forces (Art 50 of the US Code).

The first trick was to recruit divers from a diving school in Panama City, which is a pool of specialists who usually "end up" in the CIA's special services or the American combat swimmers, the SEALs. By employing newly trained divers from outside the *Special* Operations Command (*SOCOM*), President Biden avoided the requirement to report their hiring to Congress. Therefore, on March 23, 2023, when Congressman Sherman asked Anthony Blinken to *"certify that no U.S. government agency was involved,"* he was trying to lie to the American people, because it was

---

319. https://www.state.gov/secretary-antony-j-blinken-and-canadian-foreign-minister-melanie-joly-at-a-joint-press-availability/
320. https://www.aa.com.tr/en/politics/several-arrested-after-attempt-to-blow-up-turkstream-pipeline-russia/2710880
321. Seymour Hersh, "How America Took Out the Nord Stream Pipeline," *Substack*, February 8, 2023 (https://seymourhersh.substack.com/p/how-america-took-out-the-nord-stream)

known from the beginning that this was not the case. So Sherman is a dishonest cheat[322].

The second trick was to exploit Joe Biden's statements during his February 7, 2022 press conference in Washington with Olaf Scholz, where he said that if Ukraine is invaded "there *will be no more Nord Stream 2. We will stop it*[323]"; and that of Victoria Nuland during a State Department press conference that "*if Russia invades Ukraine, somehow Nord Stream 2 will be stopped.*[324]" Both of these statements were taken by the Biden administration as official notification of what was to be done.

The third trick was to place this operation under the umbrella of the 2022 iteration of a naval maritime exercise that takes place annually in the Baltic Sea: exercise BALTOPS 22. This year's exercise included, very appropriately, underwater explosive ordnance disposal training, as announced by the U.S. Navy[325] and NATO...[326]

Seymour Hersh is without a doubt one of the most respected American journalists. A true investigative journalist, he has uncovered numerous cases, thanks to an incomparable network of sources within the Pentagon and the American *Intelligence Community* (IC). Lithuanian-Jewish by origin, it is difficult to see him as a "Putinolater", but let's bet that some French commentators will manage it!

In any case, even if his account is credible, it does not provide answers to certain questions, such as Britain's involvement and Liz Truss' tweet. Nevertheless, Seymour Hersh's investigation is credible and brings to light a number of elements:

- The American decision was made by a core group of five people (Joe Biden; Jake Sullivan, his National Security Advisor; Anthony Blinken, Secretary of State; Victoria Nuland, Deputy Secretary of State; and William Burns, Director of the CIA), outside the institutional mechanisms.

---

322. https://www.c-span.org/video/?c5063543/user-clip-rep-sherman-asks-blinken-nord-stream-sabotage
323. https://youtu.be/OS4O8rGRLf8
324. https://youtu.be/ild-PsPD_Uw
325. "BALTOPS 22, the first Baltic Sea maritime exercise, concludes in Kiel," *US Navy*, June 17, 2022 (https://www.navy.mil/Press-Office/News-Stories/Article/3066830/baltops-22-the-premier-baltic-sea-maritime-exercise-concludes-in-kiel/)
326. "BALTOPS 22 kicks off in the Baltic Sea," *nato.int*, June 8, 2022 (https://shape.nato.int/news-archive/2022/baltops-22-kicks-off-in-the-baltic-sea)

- Democratic safeguards to prevent actions that could potentially lead to a profound deterioration of international relations, or even war, are not working.
- The planning of this incident was initiated several months before the beginning of the Russian intervention in Ukraine, which would tend to confirm that the latter was indeed provoked. The initial idea of the West was to provoke the collapse of Russia through sanctions. This did not work, so in the summer of 2022 they tried to asphyxiate the country by destroying its export infrastructure. This has still not worked...
- At the beginning of 2023, we still have no factual evidence, but circumstantial evidence and a growing body of evidence that the United States was involved in the sabotage, with the complicity of European countries. In any case, Germany was targeted by its own NATO partners in what some have called "an act of war." This raises the question of the substance of relations between Western countries within Europe and NATO: are these relations based on the permanent blackmail of the use of force, even terrorism?
- This case tends to illustrate the fact that Western intelligence is struggling to integrate and continues to serve national interests or interests that are not necessarily in their favour[327]. Already in 2021, Denmark had been pinned down for having authorized the American services to spy on its NATO and EU partners[328]! If we are to believe the statements of journalist Nicolas Poincaré[329], the French intelligence services had no idea of what was going on. Obviously, they work with a white cane!...
- This questions the substance of German democracy, whose leaders accept to be confronted with faits accomplis by their own allies and against their own population. What are the values that Germany stands for? If the Germans accept such authorities, they should not complain about the economic disaster that threatens them...

---

327. Charlie Duxbury, "Nord Stream investigation tests EU intelligence sharing around the Baltic," *Politico*, October 28, 2022 (https://www.politico.eu/article/sweden-denmark-germany-nord-stream-investigation-tests-eu-intelligence-sharing-around-the-baltic/)

328. Charlie Duxbury & Laurens Cerulus, "Vestager dodges tough questions on US spy scandal," *Politico*, June 3, 2021 (https://www.politico.eu/article/margrethe-vestager-unsolved-spy-mystery-nsa-surveillance-edward-snowden/)

329. https://youtu.be/hu1J6aA7c-w?t=171

3.4.4.4. The "pro-Ukrainian" group

On March 7, 2023, the *New York Times* (NYT) published an article, which mentions the responsibility of a "pro-Ukrainian *group*"[330]. On the *same day*, the German media *Die Zeit* gives some additional details about the six members of the commando, who are said to be amateurs[331]. The interesting point here is that the *Times* states that it got its information exclusively from the well-known American "anonymous intelligence official", while *Die Zeit* lists a German prosecutor as its source. Neither newspaper mentions the other's sources...

The revelations of the NYT and *Die Zeit* come four days after Olaf Scholz's visit to Washington. The interview, which lasted only one hour, without witnesses, did not result in a press conference. Apparently, Scholz did not want to use telephone or video communications, but preferred to make the trip, which suggests that the subject of the discussion was important. Was it about these new revelations? Perhaps. In any case, they appear to be a "whitewash" for the United States.

The NYT states that no Americans or Britons were involved in the attack, and that the group acted without the Ukrainian government being informed. Our "experts" in the French media, *France 5*, *LCI* and *BFM TV*, had unquestionably seen the hand of a state in accusing Russia! However, they would be amateurs... and Ukrainians!

However, the theory of a "*pro-Ukrainian group*" propagated by the United States quickly fell apart. On March 27, 2023, the United Nations Security Council rejected the Russian proposal to set up an international investigation to determine the facts[332]. Clearly, the West is trying to avoid revealing a truth that would disturb them.

It should be remembered that the destruction of a hundred meters of a steel pipeline protected by a layer of concrete requires several hundred kilos of explosives on the five sites of the explosions. This requires hours of work at a depth of 60 m, special equipment and decompression bells.

---

330. Adam Entous, Julian E. Barnes & Adam Goldman, "Intelligence Suggests Pro-Ukrainian Group Sabotaged Pipelines, U.S. Officials Say," *The New York Times*, March 7, 2023 (https://archive.ph/4Qmxx)
331. Holger Stark, "Nord-Stream-Ermittlungen: Spuren führen in die Ukraine", *Die Zeit*, March 7, 2023 (https://archive.ph/QWVjd)
332. "UN Security Council rejects Russian demand for Nord Stream probe, *France 24*, March 27, 2023 (https://www.france24.com/en/live-news/20230327-un-security-council-rejects-russian-demand-for-nord-stream-probe)

The 15 m pleasure boat that would have been used for the operation does not seem to be equipped to carry out such operations, nor does it have the capacity to transport the work equipment and probably more than one ton of explosives...

All indications are that this is a story designed to distract from Seymour Hersh's report, which so far provides the most coherent answer to the mystery surrounding the destruction of the gas pipelines.

In early April 2023, the *Washington Post* reported that European diplomats have doubts about alternative narratives[333]:

> At meetings of European and NATO policymakers, officials have adopted a rhythm, said a senior European diplomat: "Don't talk about Nord Stream." Leaders don't see the point of digging too deep and coming up with an embarrassing answer, the diplomat said, echoing the sentiments of several of his peers in other countries who said they would rather not have to deal with the possibility of Ukraine or allies being involved.

3.4.4.5. Epilogue

Whatever the exact course of the operation, it is clear that it was not carried out by Russia. Given the potential implications of such an action, it is absolutely clear that - in any case - it could not have taken place without the approval of the United States, as it constitutes an attack by a NATO country on an infrastructure considered critical by Europe.

The sabotage was most likely carried out by a NATO country, against the interests of Germany, another NATO country. It is therefore comical to observe that on January 11, NATO and the EU decided to set up a structure to improve protection measures against critical infrastructure[334]. In other words, NATO is protecting itself!

---

333. Shane Harris, Souad Mekhennet, Loveday Morris, Michael Birnbaum & Kate Brady, "Investigators skeptical of yacht's role in Nord Stream bombing," *The Washington Post*, April 3, 2023 (https://archive.ph/Xz8wT#selection-693.0-783.14).
334. "NATO and EU set up task force for critical infrastructure resilience and protection," *nato.int*, January 11, 2023 (updated January 12, 2023); (https://www.nato.int/cps/en/natohq/news_210611.htm?selectedLocale=fr)

The hypothesis of a Ukrainian attack would need to be supported by facts to be credible, which is not the case at present. However, it is not totally unrealistic in theory. It would be consistent with the efforts of the Ukrainian leadership to do everything possible to get NATO physically involved in Ukraine. This would have been a false-banner operation, as the Ukrainians have been conducting in the theater of operations. That is why our "experts" immediately pointed the finger at Russia.

As for the United Nations, the Security Council, called upon by China and Russia to investigate the incident, has postponed the session to discuss the matter. The American ambassador argues that *"resources for UN investigations should be saved for cases where states are unwilling or unable to investigate*[335]*"*. This tends to reinforce the suspicion that a NATO country carried out this sabotage against one of its allies.

This would not be the first time, since already in 2021, Denmark's spying activities against its European allies on behalf of the United States were revealed[336], showing that the latter is suspicious of its own allies. All this seems to indicate that NATO functions in a mafia-like manner, with a "godfather" who imposes his law through intimidation.

The counter-narrative proposed by the NYT and the German newspaper Die Zeit, blaming it on a "pro-Ukrainian group" seems to have been sewn up. But it is nevertheless interesting, because it shows a number of facts that demonstrate the lack of integrity of our media.

First of all, he definitively dismisses the responsibility of Russia in this act of war (and terrorism). So, the journalists who accused without hesitation Russia, like Anthony Bellanger, on *France 5*[337], do not have the slightest bit of integrity.

Secondly, it has the clear objective of restoring the virginity of the Atlantic Alliance, which is said to be strengthened, but whose members attack each other with bombings.

Third, that there are forces in Ukraine that the government does not control and that could create a war situation with or within NATO.

---

335. https://news.un.org/en/story/2023/02/1133752
336. "How Denmark became the NSA's listening post in Europe", *France24*, June 1st, 2021 (https://www.france24.com/en/technology/20210601-how-denmark-became-the-nsa-s-listening-post-in-europe)
337. https://youtu.be/K-WzRgrzlLU?t=88

Fourth, this could be one of the signs that the West is slowly beginning to "let go" of Zelensky and Ukraine...

In any case, this affair has become an embarrassment for the West. It has shown that the operation was conceived in tactical terms, by individuals who did not see the strategic implications. In this sense, it is very representative of the way in which the West made its decisions throughout the crisis.

4. Military considerations

The hearing of Colonel Michel Goya, on November 2, 2022, by a commission of the French Senate, is a caricature of our inability to analyze the military situation in Ukraine[338]. He dismisses half of the facts, judges Russian operations according to his own experience within the French Army, ignoring essential aspects of Russian doctrine. For their part, the senators seem more interested in having their thoughts confirmed than in truly understanding the implications of the Ukrainian crisis for national defense.

4.1. The return of conventional warfare

From 1991 onwards, the prospect of a conventional war in Europe gradually faded. The "peace dividend" led to a significant reduction in the military budgets and capabilities of Western countries. The emergence of new technologies and trade liberalization meant a reordering of priorities.

Since the Second World War, armies have been preparing for a so-called third generation war. This was a war that integrated the different weapons into a system, like the Blitzkrieg developed by the Germans. This was the inter-army combat, the mainstay of the schools of war.

After briefly having the appearance of 3rd generation wars, our Middle East wars have rapidly shifted to 4th generation wars, fought by technologically developed armies against more rustic armies, even rudimentary guerrillas.

---

338. https://youtu.be/aZe5diu87sk

Typology of wars according to technologies

Type of war	Brief description
1st generation	Close combat between individuals with simple weapons (sword, shield, etc.)
2nd generation	Use of modern weapons (rifle, machine gun, artillery, aviation), but not yet in an integrated manner (World War I)
3rd generation	Integration of weapons into a combat system (combined arms) (World War II, Blitzkrieg)
4th generation	Non-linear combat by non-state actors (guerrilla, terrorism, etc.) (Iraq, Afghanistan)
5th generation	Non-kinetic combat in the field of information technology and perception management (Ukrainian Army 2022-)

Figure 25 - Typology of wars. The war in Ukraine is a mix between a 3rd generation war (on the Russian side) and a 5th generation war (on the Ukrainian and Western side).

Our military could carry out actions while staying away from the battlefield. Already during the Gulf War (1991), the term "Nintendo war" was used. This way of waging war "at a distance" against weaker opponents, combined with the disappearance of the military threat in Europe, led to a reduction of military potential in Europe.

The problem is that in the meantime, our armies have been engaged in wars against adversaries without heavy equipment, without air power, without great logistical constraints, fighting among populations in a dispersed manner, etc. So today we have a generation of soldiers who are intellectually unsuited to a conflict on European soil. The Russians can bless heaven that the Ukrainian army was trained by NATO officers!

Thus, in Ukraine, the Russians have brought us back to the third generation war, the one for which we were preparing during the Cold War: the confrontation between two armies with comparable equipment and technologies and with similar doctrines of engagement. It is the return of joint operations, where the different components of the ground and air forces work in synergy. Their similarity with the Second World War explains why there are many tactical/operational references.

Army personnel of some countries in 1992 and 2022

	1992	2022	Change in %
Germany	476 300	62 800	−86.815
France	453 100	130 000	−71.309
Great Britain	300 100	79 380	−73.549
United States	731 700	485 000	−33.716
USSR / Russia	1 400 000	300 000	−78.571

Figure 26 - Downsizing of the "big" Western countries and Russia. Contrary to popular opinion, this reduction was not a mistake, but simply an adaptation to the post-Cold War landscape. [Source: The Military Balance 1992 and 2022]

The problem is that from the beginning of the Russian operation, the approach of the two belligerents is not symmetrical. While the Russians are fighting a 3rd generation war, the Ukrainians thought they were fighting a 5th generation war. That is, a "non-kinetic" war, where victory was to be achieved through sanctions, actions in cyberspace and influence operations.

After a provocative action by the Ukrainian army, which was supposed to prompt the Russians to launch their operation, the West could unleash an avalanche of sanctions. The Ukrainians and the Americans thought that these sanctions would be enough to cause the economic collapse of the country. The result would have been a crisis that would have forced Vladimir Putin to stop his operation and would have pushed the Russian population to overthrow him. Ukraine was to win the war very quickly and practically without fighting. This is exactly how the Western media presented the conflict in February 2022.

But this idea was based on the parameters of 2014, not 2022. The Russian economy has weathered the attacks very well, the ruble has not collapsed, and support for the government has grown. As a result, the Ukrainians had to fight much longer than they had expected and in a way for which they were not prepared.

The official reports published in 2022 in France and Switzerland show that the reading of the conflict by our governments does not go beyond that of our television sets. They are often produced on the basis of interpretations by pseudo-military experts, who have only a tactical understanding of military action, but are incapable of thinking in operational, or even strategic, terms. This is the main reason for the repeated failures of our armies in the fight against terrorism. We have killed many people, but we have not solved the problem: we are eliminating terrorists, but not terrorism.

The West pushed Ukraine into a 3rd generation war when it expected a 5th generation war. Its forces were prepared to conduct tactical actions toward Crimea and Donbass as early as March 2021, but were unable to conduct operative-level actions and were forced to fight a trench war, as in 1914.

Conversely, thanks to a great mastery of the "Operative Art" (*Operativnoe Iskoustvo*), the Russians exploited the movement to achieve local superiorities and take the initiative. This is why they were able to launch their operation with a lower ratio of forces. They use artillery operationally, while the Ukrainians use it tactically. This is why the ammunition consumption is so different on each side.

Contrary to popular imagery, the art of war requires great creativity. The Ukrainian conflict has highlighted the creativity of the Ukrainians at the tactical level and that of the Russians at the operational/strategic level. The lack of equipment and the suddenness of the conflict forced the Ukrainians to develop new techniques, notably with drones. This allows us to make propaganda on our television screens, but it does not allow us to win a war.

Our image of how the Russians (and formerly the Soviets) fight has always been distorted by the difference in scale of thinking. For example, Westerners see the company as the basic tactical unit of combat, whereas the Soviets (and later Russians) saw the battalion as the basic tactical unit. This had implications for the degree of initiative allowed to junior officers. But the Russians learned from Afghanistan and developed initiative at the lower levels. This is what we see today in Bakhmut, for example.

In the first phase of the offensive, with the relatively small size of the joint forces, commanders had to play more with operational mobility to gain advantage. This is shown by the action towards Kiev, which was not formatted to capture Kiev, and was intended only to prevent the Ukrainian army from strengthening its position in the Donbass.

The way our general officers see and comment on the conflict should worry us more. Of course, the media are only looking for "insights" to support the propaganda they broadcast. But for the military, it is important that the leader be able to apprehend a situation with rigor and flexibility of mind. In the French Senate report, Bruno Clermont, an air corps general, states[339]:

> *The main failure of the Russian military was the misuse of its powerful air force. The Russians proved incapable of conducting an air campaign as NATO would have done under American leadership.*

If the situation in Ukraine were not so serious, this remark would be laughable in its candor. Not only does our general seem to think that there is only one way to wage war, but that it must necessarily be measured against what the Americans are doing. Fortunately, the Russians do not think like him, because in *Newsweek*, an analyst from the *Defense Intelligence Agency* (DIA) - the American equivalent of the *Direction du Renseignement Militaire* (DRM) in France - notes[340]:

> *The manner in which Russia is waging this brutal war does not reflect the widely held view that Vladimir Putin's goal is to destroy Ukraine and inflict maximum damage on the civilian population, and reveals the Russian leader's game of strategic balance.*
> *[...] In 24 days of conflict, Russia carried out some 1,400 strikes and launched nearly 1,000 missiles (by comparison, the United States carried out more strikes and launched more missiles on the first day of the Iraq war in 2003).*

---

339. Cédric PERRIN & Jean-Marc TODESCHINI, "Ukraine: one year of war. What lessons for France?", Senate Committee on Foreign Affairs, Defense and Armed Forces, Information Report No. 334, February 8, 2023 p.33

340. William M. Arkin, "Putin's Bombers Could Devastate Ukraine but He's Holding Back. Here's Why," *Newsweek*, March 22, 2022 (https://www.newsweek.com/putins-bombers-could-devastate-ukraine-hes-holding-back-heres-why-1690494)

The rapid adaptation of both sides to the appearance of new technologies on the battlefield shows that technology is an advantage only in short campaigns. This explains why Ukraine was ready to open negotiations in February-March 2022.

With a prolongation of the conflict, and the adaptation of both adversaries to the innovations of the other, the victory belongs to the one who has more resources. When these resources are technologically similar, it is the human resources that count.

If the Russians occupied the western part of Ukraine, they would face significant popular resistance, where the quality of the fighters would not matter significantly. On the other hand, by staying in the Russian-speaking part of the country, they do not face popular resistance, and the entire burden of defense falls on the armed forces. However, as the conflict progresses, the enormous Ukrainian losses incurred by the West and the waves of mobilization that seek out ever less motivated fighters only reinforce the certainty of a Russian victory.

To sum up, the qualitative aspects of technology are critical for a short campaign, and the quality of the fighters is critical for a long campaign. The strategy imposed by the West on Ukraine has led to its downfall.

4.1.1. Cyberwarfare

Cyber warfare, perceived in the West as one of the pillars of "hybrid warfare" and a major fear of our staffs, does not appear to have played a decisive role in the operations in Ukraine. The fact remains that Ukraine and Russia have enormous potential, given their high levels of education. Ukraine boasts an "IT Army" of up to 400,000 hackers inside and outside the country[341]. The figure is unverifiable and certainly exaggerated, but it doesn't mean much: quality, rather than quantity, defines a "cyber force." But it does feed the myth of popular resistance[342] whose effects on the ground do not live up to its claims.

---

341. Sam Schechner, "Ukraine's 'IT Army' Has Hundreds of Thousands of Hackers, Kyiv Says," *The Wall Street Journal*, March 4, 2022 (https://www.wsj.com/livecoverage/russia-ukraine-latest-news-2022-03-04/card/ukraine-s-it-army-has-hundreds-of-thousands-of-hackers-kyiv-says-RfpGa5zmLtavrot27OWX)

342. Max Smeets & Brita Achberger, "Cyber hacktivists are busy undermining Putin's invasion," *The Washington Post*, May 13, 2022 (https://www.washingtonpost.com/politics/2022/05/13/cyber-attack-hack-russia-putin-ukraine-belarus/)

Here again, Western perceptions have most likely worked against Ukraine by overemphasizing minor aspects, thereby obscuring major ones.

Cyber activities at the beginning of the Russian special military operation

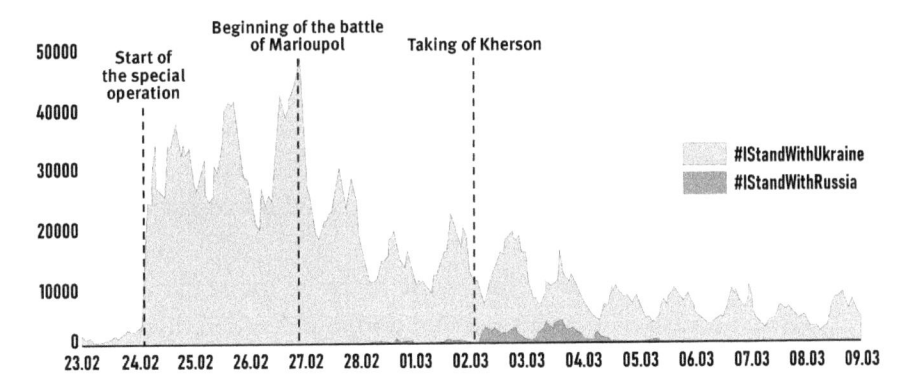

Figure 27 - Examination of cyber activities at the beginning of the Russian operation in February 2022 by the University of Adelaide (Australia)[343] tends to show that the Ukrainians had prepared their cyberoffensive. This tends to confirm that Ukraine was preparing to conduct an offensive against the Donbass before Russia launched its operation.

A study by the University of Adelaide (Australia) on cyber activities in early 2022 in Ukraine shows that the Ukrainians were clearly prepared for an increase in military operations. As early as February 24, Ukrainian bot cyber activities were immediately at a very high level, and it was only a few days later that Russian cyber activities began[344]. This indicates that Ukrainian networks had already prepared their cyber attacks before February 24 in support of their planned operation in the Donbass.

---

343. Bridget Smart, Joshua Watt, Sara Benedetti, Lewis Mitchell & Matthew Roughan, "#IStandWithPutin versus #IStandWithUkraine: The interaction of bots and humans in discussion of the Russia/Ukraine war," *The University of Adelaide*, August 15, 2022 (https://arxiv.org/abs/2208.07038)
344. Bridget Smart, Joshua Watt, Sara Benedetti, Lewis Mitchell & Matthew Roughan, "#IStandWithPutin versus #IStandWithUkraine: The interaction of bots and humans in discussion of the Russia/Ukraine war," *The University of Adelaide*, August 15, 2022 (updated August 20, 2022) (https://arxiv.org/abs/2208.07038)

4.1.2. The disappearance of hybrid warfare

The "hybrid war," which has been the fantasy of Western military pseudo-experts since 2014, seems to be what it has always been: a catch-all "concept," used to give artificial coherence to events that nothing links a priori, of which neither examples nor the objective are known, and whose only purpose was to accredit the thesis of a Russian war in Ukraine. It was a way to make official the Western conspiracy.

The idea of "hybrid warfare" stems from the interpretation of a 2013 article written by Valery Guerassimov, Chief of the Russian General Staff, entitled *"The Value of Science in Foresight*[345]*"*. It is an analysis of the evolution of conflicts in the Middle and Near East and the lessons on how to integrate them into military thinking. It is a methodological approach and not a description of Russian doctrine.

With the Ukrainian crisis of 2014, Westerners are trying to make sense of a "Russian invasion" without Russian troops, a democratic revolution by nationalist far-right militants, the legitimacy of a government that governs without having been elected, etc. A logic is then constructed that brings together cyberwarfare, terrorism, clandestine warfare, conventional warfare and, naturally, information warfare. Guerassimov's article then becomes the key to reading events that are incoherent in reality. Mark Galeotti, a British specialist on Russia, comments on this article and deduces the *"Guerassimov Doctrine"*, which would be the Russian concept of hybrid warfare[346].

In the wake of the Ukrainian propaganda, a Russian "doctrinal base" is literally and artificially created, which the media, such as *Le Temps*[347] or *La Croix*[348], use to condemn Russia. The magazine *Le Point* goes even further, claiming that the doctrine is *"validated by Vladimir Putin"* himself[349]. They are liars: in reality this concept does not exist, and Russia

---

345. Герасимов Валерий, "Ценность науки в предвидении", *vpk-news.ru*, February 26, 2013 (https://vpk-news.ru/articles/14632)
346. Mark Galeotti, "The 'Gerasimov Doctrine' and Russian Non-Linear War," *inmoscowsshadows. wordpress.com*, June 7, 2014
347. Frédéric Koller, "Désinformation, l'offensive russe," *Le Temps*, December 27, 2016
348. Olivier Tallès, "Brussels is alarmed by Russian disinformation," *La Croix*, May 4, 2017.
349. Marc Nexon, "Gerasimov, le général russe qui mène la guerre de l'information," *Le Point*, March 2, 2017

has neither theorized nor invoked it. So much so that in 2015, even NATO is questioning *whether hybrid warfare really exists...*[350]

But pushing our policymakers to misinterpret the adversary's doctrine is extremely dangerous. That's why, in 2018, Galeotti apologized - bravely and intelligently - in an article titled *"I'm Sorry I Created the Guerassimov Doctrine"* published in *Foreign Policy* magazine[351]:

> *I was the first to write about Russia's infamous high-tech military strategy. One small problem: it doesn't exist.*

For Western decision-makers, the concept of "hybrid war" comes in handy to explain everything that our governments fail to control. Thus, Russian hybrid warfare is said to be behind the "yellow vests" crisis, according to an *IFRI* researcher[352], and the natural gas crisis in Europe, according to *Le Figaro*[353]. Conspiracism in the literal sense of the word.

Since February 2022, the "hybrid war" seems to be absent... All the attributes of the "hybrid war", as seen by our experts, were already present in 1942, with different means, and the conflict that is currently taking place in Ukraine is not very different in its substance.

4.1.3. The nuclear question - The core of the problem

In 1945, the USSR had won the race to Berlin and the prestige of victory, but it was bloodless. For some of its Western allies, such as Winston Churchill in Great Britain or certain American generals such as George Patton, this would be an opportunity to continue the war towards Moscow. Stalin was said to have symmetrical intentions towards the Atlantic... The Cold War began.

In 1949, the acquisition of nuclear weapons by the USSR led to the creation of NATO in April, in order to place Western Europe under the

---
350. Dr. Damien Van Puyvelde, "Does hybrid warfare really exist?", *NATO Review*, May 7, 2015.
351. Mark Galeotti, "I'm Sorry for Creating the 'Gerasimov Doctrine,'" *Foreign Policy*, March 5, 2018.
352. Julien Nocetti (with Florian Dèbes & Nicolas Madelaine), "L'informationnel est une arme de guerre clé du Kremlin", *Les Echos/IFRI*, February 25, 2022 (https://www.ifri.org/fr/espace-media/lifri-medias/linformationnel-une-arme-de-guerre-cle-kremlin)
353. Isabelle Lasserre, "Le gaz russe, une arme stratégique dans la guerre hybride de Vladimir Poutine", *Le Figaro*, July 26, 2022 (updated July 27, 2022) (https://www.lefigaro.fr/international/le-gaz-russe-une-arme-strategique-dans-la-guerre-hybride-de-vladimir-poutine-20220726)

American nuclear umbrella. This is still NATO's primary role today. But the relationship between the two superpowers has changed: the United States has lost its nuclear privilege and Russia has acquired a deterrent capability.

At this stage, nuclear war is mainly envisaged at the strategic level. The concern of the two superpowers is to avoid a direct confrontation that could reach the nuclear stage and lead to *Mutual Assured Destruction* (MAD).

NATO was then composed only of the countries of "old Europe", separated from the USSR by more than 1,000 km. This distance gave a possible conflict space to develop conventionally, before resorting to nuclear weapons, the weapon of last resort.

But in 1952, the admission of Turkey into NATO brought the Atlantic Alliance to the border of the USSR and alarmed the Soviets. On May 8, 1955, the entry of the Federal Republic of Germany (FRG) into NATO was decisive. A week later, the Warsaw Treaty Organization (WTO) or "Warsaw Pact" was created.

Contrary to what the pseudo-experts on our television sets say, the function of the VTO is not to create a "sphere of influence". The countries of the East were already ruled by communist parties that were often worse than their Soviet counterparts. The raison d'être of the Warsaw Treaty was to create a "buffer zone" ("glacis" or *Vorfeld* in German), the purpose of which was to recreate a space for a conventional confrontation and to prevent it from becoming nuclear too quickly.

Since the end of the 1960s, the evolution of technology has allowed the miniaturization of nuclear weapons. From then on, the range of available weapon systems allows the intensity of a nuclear exchange to be varied.

The problem is then to keep control of a conflict in order to avoid a nuclear holocaust (MAD). On both sides of the Iron Curtain, doctrines were elaborated in order to graduate the use of nuclear weapons between the tactical and strategic levels.

This is what NATO calls the "flexible response." It is intended to send a clear signal to the Soviets that the United States will not move directly and automatically to a strategic nuclear exchange. The U.S. nuclear strategy retains one constant element: keeping the use of nuclear weapons off U.S. soil.

The geostrategic situation of the United States and Russia is deeply asymmetric. The United States can reach Russian territory with tactical/

operational nuclear weapons, while Russia can only reach American soil with strategic weapons.

In other words, in the event of a major conflict, in order to avoid a strategic nuclear exchange that would affect its territory, the United States would seek to maintain a nuclear conflict in the European theater. To do this, it would carefully avoid directly hitting Russian national soil, so as not to trigger a "strategic duel" with Russia. Therefore, starting in the late 1970s, the United States deployed tactical and theater nuclear weapons in Europe, turning it into a potential nuclear battlefield.

But this asymmetrical situation has become asymmetrical: Russia could use low-level nuclear weapons in Europe, and the United States could only respond by striking its allies. This is what triggers the peace and anti-nuclear movement in Germany and Northern Europe.

The Baltic States, Poland or even countries like Sweden, Finland or even Switzerland, who think that NATO could provide them with additional security, are very much mistaken, because the Americans will never sacrifice Washington, New York or Los Angeles to protect Helsinki or Stockholm. In any case, they would not engage in a strategic nuclear duel with Russia without going through a tactical and operational nuclear phase that would first destroy the European countries.

During the Cold War, the Warsaw Treaty Organization provided a space for a conventional phase in the event of a conflict in Europe. With its disappearance and NATO's advance eastward, this space has disappeared. For this reason, Russia has changed its doctrine of engagement, which allows it to use nuclear weapons more quickly. This situation is the result of two phenomena that took place in parallel in the early 2000s: the expansion of NATO and the denunciation of disarmament treaties by the United States in 2002.

What is astonishing is that Westerners seem not to have perceived this risk. NATO's advance has been seen as a geographical success, but no strategic conclusions have been drawn. However, by moving closer to the Russian border, NATO is also removing an early warning capability.

This is why Russia sees NATO on its doorstep - and in particular in Ukraine - as an existential threat. This has nothing to do with NATO's defensive vocation - or not - because the Alliance runs exactly the same risk, as illustrated by the Ukrainian crisis of December 2021-February

2022. This is what Vladimir Putin tries to explain during his press conference on February 7, 2022, at the end of Emmanuel Macron's visit to Moscow. Ironically, this is what Sweden and Finland have not understood: in the event of war, these countries could be nuclearized first as a preemptive strike...

4.1.4. The Russian nuclear threat

From the very beginning of the Russian intervention, our media claims that Russia is threatening the West with nuclear weapons. This is factually false. To understand this, we must distinguish the context of these allegations.

There are two cases, each of which responds to distinct problems and objectives: the allegations of malicious Western journalists (and other "pseudo-experts") and the accusations coming from Ukraine.

4.1.4.1. Allegations from the West

In this context, the West seeks to present the Russians as brutes, who act irrationally and who are ready to do anything to satisfy the ambition of Vladimir Putin. This is disinformation that comes mainly from conspiratorial circles and media that see the conflict only through the prism of their Russophobia.

It is a matter of distorting Vladimir Putin's words, removing (or denying) the context in which the words were said and explaining them by his failing mental health[354]. This is childish.

In reality, it is the West that has systematically raised the nuclear threat. As early as February 24, 2022, Jean-Yves Le Drian, the French Minister of Foreign Affairs, suggested that NATO could use nuclear weapons[355]. He was followed on February 27, 2022 by Liz Truss, British Foreign Secretary, who spoke of the destruction of the Russian mili-

---

354. Infrarouge program "Menace nucléaire: jusqu'où ira-t-il?", RTS.ch, March 2, 2022 (https://www.rts.ch/play/tv/infrarouge/video/menace-nucleaire-jusquou-ira-t-il?urn=urn:rts:video:12908299)
355. Anthony Audureau/AFP, "Ukraine: Le Drian reminds Putin that 'the Atlantic Alliance is also a nuclear alliance,'" BFM TV, February 24, 2022 (https://www.bfmtv.com/international/ukraine-le-drian-rappelle-a-poutine-que-l-alliance-atlantique-est-aussi-une-alliance-nucleaire_AD-202202240685.html).

tary-industrial complex and the possibility of a direct confrontation between NATO and Russia[356].

This is why, on February 27, 2022, Vladimir Putin announced that his nuclear forces would be placed on a *"special combat alert regime"*[357]. The conspiratorial media then spoke of a threat and sought to create panic. For example, RTS states that Putin *"is clearly brandishing the nuclear threat"*[358].

In fact, Rose Gottemoeller, former Under Secretary for Arms Control in the Obama administration and Deputy Secretary General of NATO, puts Putin's statement in perspective[359]:

> *Putin's order will bring only "three to six additional people" to the nuclear command posts normally staffed with about six people.*

On August 24, 2022, Liz Truss, then British Foreign Secretary and candidate for the post of Prime Minister (which she would occupy only briefly), declared her readiness to use nuclear weapons, even if this led to *"global annihilation"*[360].

Vladimir Putin responded to this irresponsible statement - which the French media failed to note - in his speech of September, 21 2022[361]. He warned the West against the use of weapons of mass destruction and specified that Russia had other very powerful weapons *"more modern than those of NATO."* He does not mention nuclear weapons, but clearly refers to hypersonic weapons, which would allow pre-emptive or even preventive strikes without committing nuclear forces.

---

356. Stephen Mcilkenny, "Liz Truss: Kremlin says decision to put nuclear bases on high alert due to comments made by Foreign Secretary | What did she say about Ukraine crisis?", *The Scotsman*, February 28, 2022 (https://www.scotsman.com/news/politics/kremlin-says-nuclear-bases-on-high-alert-due-to-comments-made-by-liz-truss-3589463)

357. Andrew Roth, Shaun Walker, Jennifer Rankin & Julian Borger, "Putin signals escalation as he puts Russia's nuclear force on high alert," *The Guardian*, February 28, 2022; Runai Tairov, "Путин приказал перевести силы сдерживания в особый режим боевого дежурства," Forbes.ru, February 27, 2022 (https://www.forbes.ru/society/457237-putin-prikazal-perevesti-sily-sderzivania-v-osobyj-rezim-boevogo-dezurstva)..

358. https://www.rts.ch/play/tv/redirect/detail/12908299?startTime=683

359. Stephanie Cooke, "Will Putin Use Nuclear Weapons in Ukraine?", *Energy Intelligence*, March 17, 2022 (https://www.energyintel.com/0000017f-94cd-d81c-a9ff-9ecf7ccf0000)

360. https://www.independent.co.uk/news/uk/politics/liz-truss-nuclear-button-ready-b2151614.html; https://youtu.be/IvH7cgbdazU

361. http://en.kremlin.ru/events/president/news/69390

Threats of the use of nuclear weapons

February 24, 2022
Jean-Yves Le Drian: « I think that Vladimir Putin must also understand that the Atlantic Alliance is a nuclear alliance. »

February 27, 2022
Liz Truss: « I urge the Russians not to escalate this conflict, but we must be prepared for Russia to seek to use even worse weapons. »

February 27, 2022
Vladimir Putin announces that he has put his nuclear forces in a « special combat alert regime ».

August 24, 2022
Liz Truss « ready » to push the nuclear button if necessary, even if it means « total annihilation. »

September 21, 2022
Vladimir Putin: « And those who try to blackmail nuclear weapons should know that the wind can also turn towards them. »

Figure 28 - Despite what the media such as France 5 and RTS say, it is always the West that first brandished the nuclear threat, pushing Vladimir Putin to react.

These are the facts. However, on November 20, 2022, in the program *Géopolitis* "Disinformation, weapon of war", Jean-Philippe Schaller, journalist of the RTS declares that Vladimir Putin uses disinformation *"accusing the West of wanting a nuclear war"*. *"Yet it was Putin who first brandished the nuclear threat. The bigger the better"*. Obviously, the journalist is lying to us (several times in the same program!)[362].

In support of his allegations, our journalist refers to the case of the Ukrainian "dirty bomb". In October 2022, fearing that the Ukrainians were attempting a provocation with a "dirty bomb", Russia made public the rumours of which it was aware. Naturally, Western countries saw this

---

362. https://youtu.be/bEv4-IJsl9k?t=85

as disinformation, which they had not done when Ukraine had made similar accusations in March[363]! But the Russian approach is more subtle.

A "dirty bomb" is nothing more than a conventional explosive (TNT, etc.) around which radioactive material from industry or research has been fixed. When exploding, the bomb disperses radioactive dust, creating a health hazard for people, but with very little material damage. It is a homemade weapon that targets people in a very limited area. It is certainly not likely to trigger a nuclear response.

The idea of the Russians is simply to "cut the grass under the feet" of those who would have the idea to make one. Contrary to what Jean-Philippe Schaller says, we are not in a disinformation operation, but in a preventive action, which seems to have worked...

On the other hand, none of our media reported the deployment of four American strategic nuclear bombers of the type B-52H STRATOFORTRESS on the air base of Moron (Spain) at the end of February 2023 *"to send a message to Russia"*[364]. They also did not report the simulation of a nuclear attack (*"missile strike drill"*), on March 11, 2023, against the city of Saint Petersburg, by one of these aircraft (call name: NOBLE61), from the Gulf of Finland[365]. Reported by the Russian opposition website *Meduza*[366] the same day, the information was - obviously - not taken up by any traditional media. However, it is probably this event that pushed Vladimir Putin, two weeks later, to accede to President Lukashenko's request to deploy nuclear weapons on Belarusian territory[367].

---

363. Richard Stone, "Dirty bomb ingredients go missing from Chornobyl monitoring lab," *Science*, March 25, 2022 (https://www.science.org/content/article/dirty-bomb-ingredients-go-missing-chornobyl-monitoring-lab)
364. Tom Dunlop, "American B-52 bombers overfly Estonia in message to Russia," *UK Defence Journal*, March 3, 2023 (https://ukdefencejournal.org.uk/american-b-52-bombers-overfly-estonia-in-message-to-russia/)
365. David Cenciotti, "Let's Have A Look At B-52's Mission Over The Baltics And Close To Russia Yesterday," *The Aviationist*, March 12, 2023 (https://theaviationist.com/2023/03/12/lets-have-a-look-at-b-52s-mission-over-the-baltics-and-close-to-russia-yesterday/)
366. "An American B-52 bomber capable of carrying nuclear weapons conducted planned maneuvers over the Baltic Sea", *Meduza.io*, March 12, 2023 (https://meduza.io/en/news/2023/03/12/an-american-b-52-bomber-capable-of-carrying-nuclear-weapons-conducted-planned-maneuvers-over-the-baltic-sea)
367. Jones Hayden, "Putin says Russia to deploy tactical nuclear weapons in Belarus," *Politico*, March 25, 2023 (https://www.politico.eu/article/putin-says-russia-to-deploy-tactical-nuclear-weapons-in-belarus-reports/)

Trajectory of the B-52H (NOBLE61)

Figure 29 - On March 11, 2023, the United States conducted a simulated nuclear attack on St. Petersburg from the Gulf of Finland[368].

---

368. https://twitter.com/sentdefender/status/1634633897030950914/photo/1

In fact, an analysis of Vladimir Putin's statements tends to show that he does not believe that the West "wants" a nuclear war, but rather that Western leaders could start a nuclear war because their decisions are impulsive or ill-considered.

Russia's objective is to destroy the Ukrainian military potential. But the West has invented broader objectives; Vladimir Putin would like to seize the resources of Ukraine, he would like to reconstitute the USSR, or even tsarist Russia, etc. But in these conditions, we do not really understand why Russia would seek to nuclearize a territory that it would seek to occupy! The Westerners are trapped by their own rhetoric.

4.1.4.2. Allegations from Ukraine

The allegations coming from Ukraine have another purpose.

From the first hours of the SVO, Russian forces neutralized the Ukrainian air force and the bulk of the anti-aircraft defense. Without air cover, the Ukrainian army is powerless. This is why Zelensky quickly sought to have NATO establish a no-fly zone over the country.

But Westerners are not ready to physically engage in the conflict. It is therefore a matter for Zelensky to find a reason that is sufficiently dramatic or threatening for Europe to feel physically concerned by the conflict and to act.

This is why the Ukrainians evoke the risk of Chernobyl, where however from the first days of its occupation, the Russian and Ukrainian military joined forces to ensure the security of the power station together[369]!

In early March 2022, taking advantage of a minor incident in the Zaporijia nuclear power plant (ZNPP), Zelensky spoke of a danger to Europe[370] and asked for the establishment of an NFZ[371]. But NATO refuses because of the risk of being drawn into a direct confrontation with Russia[372]. Our state media, such as *France 5*, seek to add fuel

---

369. https://t.me/intelslava/20722
370. "Ukraine nuclear plant: Russia in control after shelling", *BBC News*, March 4, 2022 (https://www.bbc.com/news/world-europe-60613438)
371. "Ukraine's Zelenskyy condemns NATO over no-fly zone decision," *dw.com*, March 4, 2022 (https://www.dw.com/en/ukraine-zelenskyy-condemns-nato-over-no-fly-zone-decision-as-it-happened/a-61007081)
372. "Zelensky slams Nato over rejection of no-fly zone," *BBC News*, March 5, 2022 (https://www.bbc.com/news/world-europe-60629175)

to the fire by stating that Vladimir Putin seeks to use the NFZ as a nuclear weapon[373].

Zelensky thus seeks to replay the case of Libya. It is then that the "bombings" of the maternity hospital (March 9) and the theater (March 16) of Marioupol intervene - very opportunely - which will be denied by the Russians, but accompanied by a new request from Zelensky to NATO, which again refuses[374].

In July-August 2022, knowing that NATO would not reverse its decision not to establish an NFZ, Zelensky sought to have the zone demilitarized or to send an international force to the NFZ sector. The NFZ is then the target of artillery fire - obviously - attributed to Russia, which has troops stationed there! The Western discourse is then that Russia seeks to create a nuclear threat on Europe (with what goal?). France 2 even goes so far as to present a damaged chimney on the roof of the ZNPP as a missile[375]! In reality, the remains of projectiles found on the spot are of Western origin. They include HIMARS missiles and American kamikaze drones[376] and British BRIMSTONE [377, 378]. Their firing is followed by the Westerners, who therefore know exactly who is carrying out these attacks against the Energodar power plant.

The Ukrainian strategy was to place the NPPZ at the center of a battle that would force the international community to intervene in one way or another. This is why, on September 1st, 2022, the day an International Atomic Energy Agency (IAEA) mission came to inspect it, Ukraine launched a commando attack against the plant, delaying the deployment of experts. It attempted several attacks in September-October 2022, all unsuccessful, mobilizing 600 men and dozens of barges to cross the Dnieper. These attacks resulted in dozens, if not hundreds, of deaths

---

373. "Nuclear power plants, gas... Putin's other weapons #cdanslair 08.03.2022", *France 5 /YouTube*, March 9, 2022 (https://youtu.be/8Ub97_37vkg)
374. Siobhan Hughes, "Zelensky Asks U.S. Again for No-Fly Zone," *The Wall Street Journal*, March 16, 2022 (https://www.wsj.com/livecoverage/russia-ukraine-latest-news-2022-03-15/card/zelensky-asks-u-s-again-for-no-fly-zone-SA6RQHFsz3NUsT9uE4ru)
375. Emilie Jehanno, "Guerre en Ukraine: Oui, France 2 a confondé une cheminée endommagée avec un missile dans un sujet", 20minutes.fr, August 23, 2022 (https://www.20minutes.fr/arts-stars/medias/3340383-20220823-guerre-ukraine-oui-france-2-confondu-cheminee-endommagee-missile-sujet)
376. https://www.telegraph.co.uk/world-news/2022/07/20/ukrainian-kamikaze-drones-strike-russian-controlled-zaporizhzhia/
377. https://mezha.media/en/2022/05/12/brimstone-in-ukraine/
378. https://t.me/milinfolive/88735

and our media saw nothing but Russian disinformation. They were only confirmed six months later by the *Times* of London[379]. In reality, the concrete elements showing Ukrainian responsibility were known, but our media lied - once again - in order to preserve their narrative.

4.1.4.3. The Russian doctrine

On October 27, 2022, on *France 5*, in a program devoted to the "dirty bomb" that the Ukraine would develop according to the Russians, the criminologist (?) Alain Bauer explains that the Russians consider tactical nuclear weapons as conventional weapons[380]. This is purely and simply a lie.

In reality, Russian doctrine does not speak of *tactical* nuclear weapons. Of course, they have nuclear weapons of varying strengths, which can be used depending on the circumstances and the objectives. But they consider the use of nuclear weapons - regardless of their power - to be strategic in nature, because they can cause a nuclear escalation.

The concept of tactical nuclear weapons was essentially developed by the Americans in order to distinguish between weapons that could be used on the European continent and those that could affect the United States. The idea was that by using weapons on European territory, the Russians (or Soviets during the Cold War) would not retaliate against American territory. Thus, the United States could have used nuclear weapons on the territory of its allies "with impunity."

The Russian nuclear doctrine short-circuits this reasoning by stating that one cannot distinguish between tactical and strategic. Thus, the use of nuclear weapons on European soil (and a fortiori against Russia) could trigger an intercontinental response.

Therefore, Russia considers the use of nuclear weapons only in case of an existential threat to the Russian state, as stated in the presidential decree of June 2, 2020[381]:

---

379. Maxim Tucker, "Ukraine's secret attempt to retake the Zaporizhzhia nuclear plant," *The Times*, April 7, 2023 (https://www.thetimes.co.uk/article/ukrainian-zaporizhzhia-nuclear-power-plant-russia-putin-war-2023-fx82xz3xz)

380. Program "C dans l'air", "Dirty bomb: what is Putin preparing? #cdanslair 27.10.2022", France 5/YouTube, October 28, 2022 (https://youtu.be/1Ub3buKx-yg?t=153)

381. Presidential Decree No. 355 of June 2, 2020 "On the foundations of the state policy of the Russian Federation in the field of nuclear deterrence" (http://www.consultant.ru/document/cons_doc_LAW_354057/752b5672d30c8f49fddf240797c7daca7e53d781/)

The Russian Federation reserves the right to use nuclear weapons in response to the use of nuclear weapons and other weapons of mass destruction against it and/or its allies, as well as in case of aggression against the Russian Federation with conventional weapons, when the very existence of the state is threatened.

As Vladimir Putin made clear at the summit of the Eurasian Economic Union in Bishkek (Kyrgyzstan) in December 2022[382], the principle of nuclear engagement remains "*Launch on Warning*" (LOW). In other words, the launch on warning of nuclear watch systems. To what extent the LOW would allow pre-emptive strikes is a doubt carefully maintained by Moscow, which is in the logic of a policy of deterrence. That said, this new version of the Russian nuclear doctrine for 2020 lowers somewhat the level at which Russia can consider the use of nuclear weapons.

This is probably what motivated President Joe Biden's decision in late March 2022 to abandon the "no-first-use" principle for nuclear weapons[383]. Of course, no Western media reported this major change in U.S. nuclear policy. It is a fundamental decision, yet no one is reporting on it. For example, the annual Swiss Security Report[384] published in September 2022 by the Swiss *Federal Intelligence Service* (SRC) does not say a word about it!

Until then, the United States had considered the use of nuclear weapons only for deterrence purposes (the *"sole purpose"* policy). But Biden's decision "leaves open the option of using nuclear weapons not only in retaliation for a nuclear attack, but also to respond to non-nuclear threats[385].

In other words, the United States and Russia allow each other to use nuclear weapons first, but the Americans can do so at any time, while the

---

382. "Putin says Russia could adopt US preemptive strike concept," *AP News*, December 9, 2022 (https://apnews.com/article/putin-moscow-strikes-united-states-government-russia-95f1436d23b94fcbc-05f1c2242472d5c)

383. Daryl G. Kimball, "Biden Policy Allows First Use of Nuclear Weapons," *Arms Control Today*, April 2022 (https://www.armscontrol.org/act/2022-04/news/biden-policy-allows-first-use-nuclear-weapons).

384. https://www.newsd.admin.ch/newsd/message/attachments/72369.pdf

385. Daryl G. Kimball, "Biden Policy Allows First Use of Nuclear Weapons," Arms Control Association, April 29, 2022 (https://www.armscontrol.org/act/2022-04/news/biden-policy-allows-first-use-nuclear-weapons)

Russians will only do so in case of an existential threat. To simplify (in theory) Russia will use nuclear weapons if - for example - Moscow and the country's institutions are directly threatened, while the United States can use them if one of its military bases is attacked.

By way of comparison, France does not clearly indicate the criteria for the use of its nuclear weapons, considering this to be part of its deterrence strategy. In theory, France could even use these weapons against a conventional threat.

This is the reason why the Russians are much less inclined to use nuclear weapons than the West.

Diagram of nuclear decision and response mechanisms

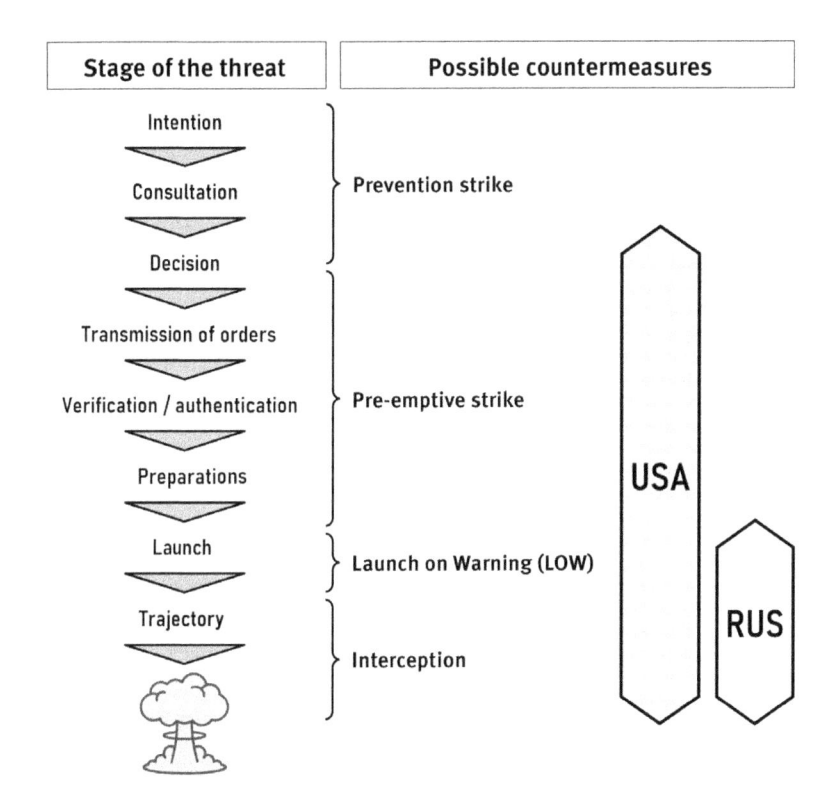

Stage of the threat	Possible countermeasures
Intention → Consultation → Decision	Prevention strike
Transmission of orders → Verification / authentication → Preparations	Pre-emptive strike
Launch	Launch on Warning (LOW)
Trajectory	Interception

USA / RUS

Figure 30 - Joe Biden's decision to abandon the no-first-use policy would allow the United States to conduct preemptive (or even pre-emptive) strikes, while Russia restricts itself to LOW, which some see as part of pre-emptive strikes.

4. Military considerations

4.1.4.4. The deployment of nuclear weapons in Belarus

On March 25, 2023, during a visit by Alexander Lukashenko to Russia, Vladimir Putin declared on the *Rossiya 24* channel that the Belarusian president had asked him to deploy *"tactical nuclear weapons"* on its territory[386]. The reason given was Britain's decision to supply depleted uranium anti-tank shells[387]. But - as always - the reality is more complex.

First of all, Vladimir Putin is only repeating Lukashenko's words, because the Russians do not make a doctrinal distinction between tactical, operational and strategic nuclear weapons. Moreover, the weapons mentioned have ranges of more than 1,000 km, whereas - traditionally - nuclear weapons with a range of 150-500 km are considered tactical.

Three events that our media did not notice explain the Belarusian request.

For several years, Poland has been working to realize its old idea of an Intermarium, put forward by Marshal Józef Piłsudski in the 1920s[388]. It would be an alliance of countries stretching from the Baltic Sea to the Mediterranean Sea to the Black Sea. Based on the idea that neither NATO nor the EU offer an effective solution against Russia, Poland set out to create an alliance that would provide itself with the means to fight their large neighbor. On May 11, 2011, the "Visegrad Battle Group" was created, which brings together forces from Poland, Czech Republic, Slovakia and Hungary, under the command of Poland and independent of the NATO structure[389]. With the conflict in Ukraine, Poland has undertaken to arm itself massively. Its ambition is to have the most powerful army in Europe by 2025[390] with three times the size of the British army[391].

---

386. "Белоруссия давно просит у России ядерное оружие," *Vesti.ru*, March 25, 2023 (https://www.vesti.ru/article/3268612)
387. https://www.rts.ch/play/tv/redirect/detail/13894210
388. Agnes Tycner, "Intermarium in the 21st Century," *The Institute of Wold Politics*, December 23, 2020 (https://www.iwp.edu/articles/2020/12/23/intermarium-in-the-21st-century/)
389. Henrique Horta, "Poland's role in the Intermarium idea", *Blue Europe*, January 11, 2023 (https://www.blue-europe.eu/analysis-en/full-reports/polands-role-in-the-intermarium-idea/)
390. "Polish army to be strongest in Europe in two years - defense minister," *The First News*, April 12, 2023, (https://www.thefirstnews.com/article/polish-army-to-be-strongest-in-europe-in-two-years---defence-minister-37781)
391. "Poland to have army three times size of Britain's in two years, defence minister confirms", *The Telegraph*, April 12, 2023 (https://www.telegraph.co.uk/world-news/2023/04/12/ukraine-russia-war-latest-news-putin-crimea-hungary/)

Belarus plays a pivotal role in the Polish concept[392]. This is why Poland politically, materially and ostensibly maintains the opposition to Belarus with the blessing of the United States. The signing of a joint declaration on January 11, 2023 by Poland, Ukraine and Lithuania, which form the Lublin Triangle and actively support the opposition in Belarus and carry out terrorist actions there, worries Lukashenko[393].

Intermarium and Lublin Triangle

Figure 31 - Poland's foreign policy is oriented towards the realization of an old dream: the construction of the Intermarium. The participation of Ukraine in this project contributes to the distrust of Belarus and Russia.

---

392. Jacek Bartosiak, "Belarus as a Pivot of Poland's Grand Strategy," *The Jamestown Foundation*, December 16, 2020 (https://jamestown.org/program/belarus-as-a-pivot-of-polands-grand-strategy/)
393. "Presidents of Ukraine, Lithuania and Poland signed the Joint Declaration following the Second Summit of the Lublin Triangle in Lviv", *Website of the President of Ukraine*, January 11, 2023 (https://www.president.gov.ua/en/news/u-lvovi-prezidenti-ukrayini-litvi-ta-polshi-pidpisali-spilnu-80313)

Seeing that the situation in Ukraine was deteriorating and that the predicted success against Russia was receding, the United States changed its position and began to work on "regime change" in Belarus. On March 22, 2023, Wendy Sherman, Assistant Secretary of State, received Svyatlana Tsikhanouskaya, leader of the Belarusian militant opposition, to coordinate their actions. The United States then sought to instrumentalize the Belarusian opposition for the benefit of Ukraine, as noted by the American media *The Atlantic Council*[394].

Seeing a military threat emerging, President Lukashenko is seeking Russian support. That is why he is asking Vladimir Putin to deploy nuclear weapons on his territory. This is not only to strengthen the bond and create a community of destiny with Russia, but to raise the price for Western attempts at subversion.

For Russia, this request comes shortly after the American provocation in the Gulf of Finland by a B-52H bomber that we have already mentioned. It is for this reason that the Russian president agreed to the request of his Belarussian counterpart.

We must also be rigorous with the terms. The Swiss expert Alexandre Vautravers says on RTS that this is a transfer of weapons, which would contravene the nuclear non-proliferation treaty (NPT)[395]. This is not true. As the Russian opposition media *Meduza* confirmed on the same day, Vladimir Putin specified that this is not a transfer, but only a deployment[396]. The essential difference is that these weapons remain under the exclusive authority of Russia. In other words, Russia is not doing anything different from the United States, which has nuclear weapons depots in Germany, Belgium, the Netherlands and Turkey.

---

394. Stephen Nix & Mark Dietzen, "The Belarusian opposition can help defeat Putin in Ukraine," *The Atlantic Council*, February 7, 2023 (https://www.atlanticcouncil.org/blogs/ukrainealert/the-belarusian-opposition-can-help-defeat-putin-in-ukraine/)
395. https://www.rts.ch/play/tv/redirect/detail/13894210
396. "Путин пообещал разместить тактическое ядерное оружие в Беларуси. ЕС пригрозил санкциями, Украина потребовала созвать заседание Совбеза ООН", medusa.io, March 26, 2023 (https://meduza.io/feature/2023/03/26/putin-poobeschal-razmestit-takticheskoe-yadernoe-oruzhie-v-belarusi-v-germanii-zayavili-chto-rossiya-prodolzhaet-yadernoe-zapugivanie)

4.2. The Ukrainian conduct of the war

4.2.1. Communication dominates the conduct of operations

Since 1991, Westerners have waged illegitimate wars against opponents who were inferior in technology and numbers. The problem was therefore essentially to convince Western opinions that the opponent was "bad" while masking our own crimes. This is the model that was used to rebuild Ukrainian forces as early as 2014 in preparation for the 2022 conflict by NATO instructors.

Ukraine's goal is the defeat of Russia. Not only to recover its sovereignty over the territories taken by Russia, but also and above all because the key to its entry into NATO is a powerless Russia.

As early as March 2022, Ukrainian intelligence services claim that Russia has no more missiles, because the components of these missiles are manufactured in… Ukraine[397]. This will turn out to be completely false, but they will be caught in their own lie, because Western countries no longer consider it necessary to give Ukraine missiles against this threat. They will realize at the end of the year that this was a mistake. This also shows that the West does not have the intelligence capacity to correct the false information spread by Ukrainian propaganda.

There are two aspects to the answer. The first is that it seems that our media and politicians have systematically attributed Ukrainian weaknesses to Russia. This is a common propaganda "mirror effect" that serves to hide one's own weaknesses behind the supposed weaknesses of the opponent. The conduct of the Ukrainian war is strictly political, while that of Russia is strictly military. This can be seen in the way operations are conducted. That is why we could say from the beginning that Ukraine would lose. I remind you that Russia attacked Ukraine with a numerical inferiority of about 2-3 to 1: Ukraine therefore had all its chances. But paradoxically, nobody in the West really took the war seriously. It was a political and economic war whose objective was not

---

397. Tony Diver, "Vladimir Putin 'running out' of missiles - because parts are made in Ukraine," *The Telegraph*, April 1st, 2022 (https://www.telegraph.co.uk/world-news/2022/04/01/vladimir-putin-running-missiles-parts-made-ukraine/)

to win in Ukraine, but to make Russia collapse. This was said by Oleksei Arestovich in March 2019[398].

For his part, Zelensky thought that sanctions and massive Western support would be enough to bring down Russia, much as the West had defeated Iraq. The problem is that the West has neither the desire nor the capacity to get involved with Ukraine. They have underestimated Russia, its economy and the support of the population for Vladimir Putin. The weapons supplied to Ukraine might have made a difference in a conflict like Iraq, but not against Russia. In 6 months, the West has provided more aid than the Russian defense budget... without success.

The Ukrainians had just under 500 multiple rocket launchers at the beginning of the Russian offensive and lost them. Until March 2023, they received 38 M142 HIMARS and 10 M270 multiple missile systems (MLRS) from the United States and Europe, many of which were destroyed or purchased by the Russians. To claim that this will have an impact on the course of the conflict is wishful thinking.

Especially since the production of HIMARS missiles suffers from the same problems as the production of 155 mm shells. In February 2023, the Americans must recognize that they no longer have missiles to supply to Ukraine without taking them from their own stocks of ammunition[399].

Moreover, the Ukrainians have almost no armour left to carry out offensives. They are therefore using their highly mobile Western artillery assets to conduct a kind of "guerrilla warfare", which consists of intimidating the Ukrainian population in Russian-speaking areas in order to dissuade them from participating in the self-determination referendums. This is the same strategy as the campaign of terrorist attacks against Russian-speaking Ukrainian officials in the Kherson oblast.

This explains the spreading of PFM-1 anti-personnel mines ("butterfly" mines), which look like toys, in the inhabited areas of Donetsk or the firing on the nuclear power plant in Zaporozhie. This is why Zelensky does not want a commission of inquiry on the spot[400]. Our media refuse to reco-

---

398. "Predicted Russian - Ukrainian war in 2019 - Alexey Arestovich", *YouTube*, March 18, 2022 (https://youtu.be/1xNHmHpERH8)
399. Paul McLeary, Lara Seligman & Alexander Ward, "U.S. tells Ukraine it won't send long-range missiles because it has few to spare," *Politico*, February 13, 2023 (https://www.politico.com/news-/2023/02/13/u-s-wont-send-long-range-missiles-ukraine-00082652)
400. https://www.ilfattoquotidiano.it/2022/06/07/energoatom-contro-il-direttore-dellaiea-grossi-mai-invitato-a-zaporizhzhya-vuole-legittimare-la-permanenza-degli-occupanti/6618145/

gnize this strategy and invent fanciful explanations. Thus, according to a French expert, the Russians would shoot at the power plant they control to cut off the electricity flowing to Ukraine[401]! Apparently, the Russians have not found the switch!!!

4.2.2. The absence of popular resistance

The determination of the Ukrainian military to accomplish their mission of defending the country is indisputable. But when it comes to the resistance of the population to the Russian occupation, the emphatic statements hide a more prosaic reality.

The Cornelian choice in front of which Zelensky finds himself today, seems very similar to the one in front of which Marshal Pétain probably found himself in 1940: to choose between the life of the French at the price of the dishonor of a defeat, or to continue the fight at the price of the annihilation of the country. This is perhaps what explains why the French are so "to the point" concerning the Ukraine. But the situation is less similar than it seems. The main difference is that in 1940, the French saw the Germans as invaders with whom they had little in common. Today, Russian-speaking Ukrainian citizens (where Russian forces are located) feel more Russian than Ukrainian, simply because they have never been considered Ukrainians.

As in all Eastern European countries, including Russia, the attachment of the population to their country is very strong. However, in Ukraine, this question takes on a more complex dimension because the attachment to Russia is also very strong. There are two reasons for this.

The first is historical and sociological: economic, familiar and cultural ties with Russia are a daily reality for a large part of the Ukrainian population living in the south and east of the country. This is why, since February 24, 2022, Russia is the country that has received the most Ukrainian refugees.

The second is more political. As we have seen, since 2014, the new authorities in Ukraine have sought to "purify" the country's ethnicity. Laws on languages and the rights of "indigenous people" are only a small part of a policy to push Russian speakers out of the country.

---

401. https://youtu.be/KZDbFcYAbVE?t=1578

Territories taken over by Ukraine in September-October 2022

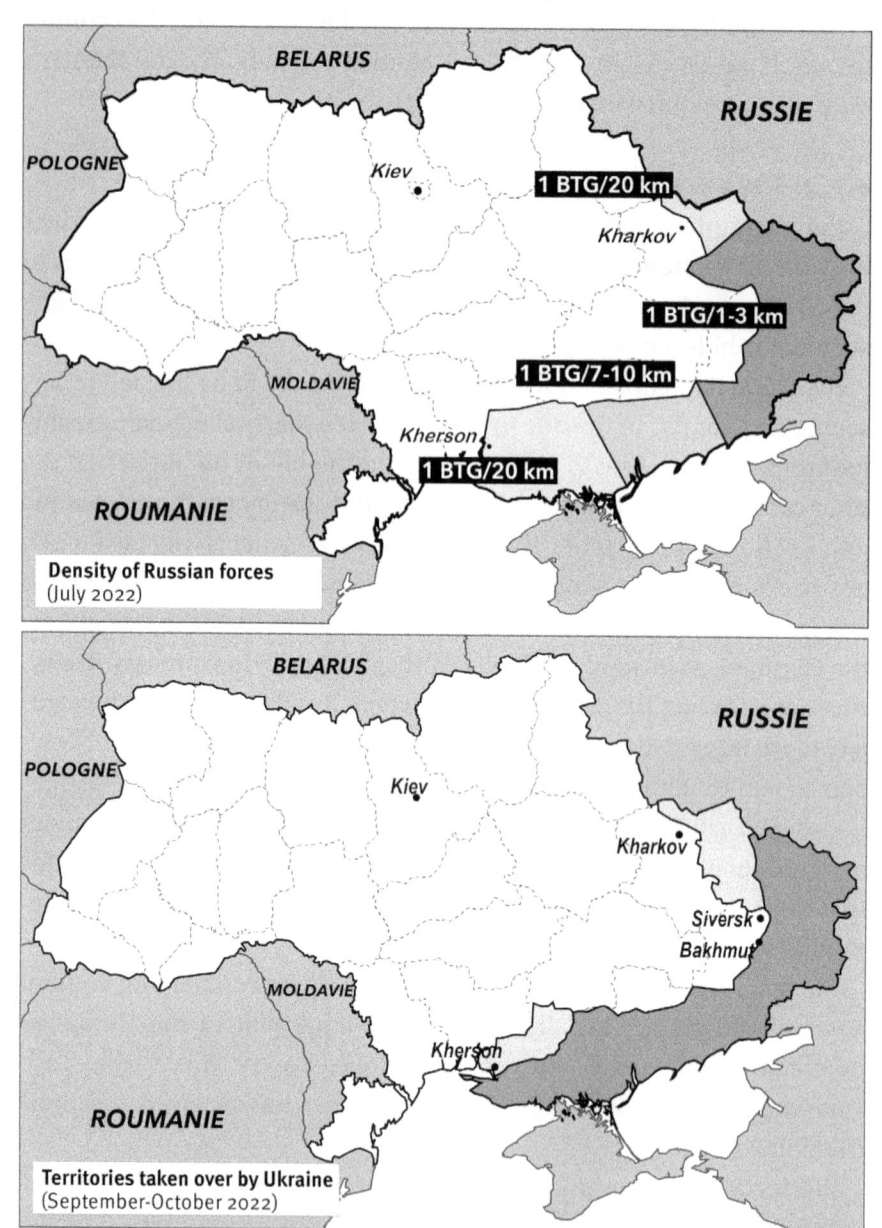

Figure 32 - Since the beginning of the SVO, the Ukrainians have not taken back any territory that had not been left by the Russians beforehand. The priority for Russia from the beginning of the SVO was to remove the military threat to the Donbass, of which neither Kharkov nor Kherson was part. The low density areas (light grey) were the areas where they had no interest in fighting. These are the areas they abandoned in September-October 2022.

This is why, despite Western rhetoric[402], the Ukrainian population is far from unanimous in its support for the government. A survey by the *Kyiv International Institute of Sociology* (KIIS) on Ukrainians' willingness to resist a Russian invasion between December 3 and 11, 2021[403]. It shows that only 50.2 per cent of Ukrainians would resist in some way, of which only 33.3 per cent (or 16.6 per cent of the Ukrainian population) would be willing to take up arms, the majority of whom are in the 50-59 age group. The least interested in taking up arms are the 18-29 year olds, the lifeblood of the military. The breakdown by the four main regions of Ukraine shows that the Russian-speaking areas are much less likely to take up arms.

As we can see, the myth of an armed Ukrainian population is part of the disinformation of our media. There is no doubt that the western part of the country, the cradle of ultra-nationalist supremacism, is extremely anti-Russian. That is why it is very unlikely that Russia would consider occupying the whole country. On the other hand, the Russian-speaking population, which Kiev has never treated as full citizens, is generally supportive of Russia.

As for the action of the armed forces, contrary to what our "experts" say, Ukraine has a huge personnel problem. It has conducted 8 mobilizations since February 2022 and is reaching the end of its potential and is obliged to resort to the forced enlistment of its citizens[404]. This personnel crisis is not new and has prompted the Ukrainian army to call for a tougher law against desertion and refusal to serve[405]. This law was signed by Zelensky in January 2023[406].

---

402. Amy Mackinnon & Jack Detsch, "Ukraine Ready to Fight to 'Last Drop'," *Foreign Policy*, December 8, 2021
403. "Will Ukrainians resist Russian intervention: results of a telephone survey conducted on December 3-11, 2021," *kiis.com.ua*, December 2021
404. Siobhán O'Grady & Kostiantyn Khudov, "As spring offensive nears, Ukraine is drafting reinforcements," *The Washington Post*, April 10, 2023 (updated April 11, 2023) (https://www.washingtonpost.com/world/2023/04/10/ukraine-draft-troops-reinforcements-training/)
405. "Ukraine's Top General Supports Harsher Law for Deserters and Draft-dodgers," *Kyiv Post*, December 20, 2022 (https://www.kyivpost.com/post/5943)
406. "Zelensky Signs Controversial Law Toughening Punishment for Desertion in Army," *AFP/Kiyv Post*, January 25, 2023 (https://www.kyivpost.com/post/11498)

Will to defend in Ukraine

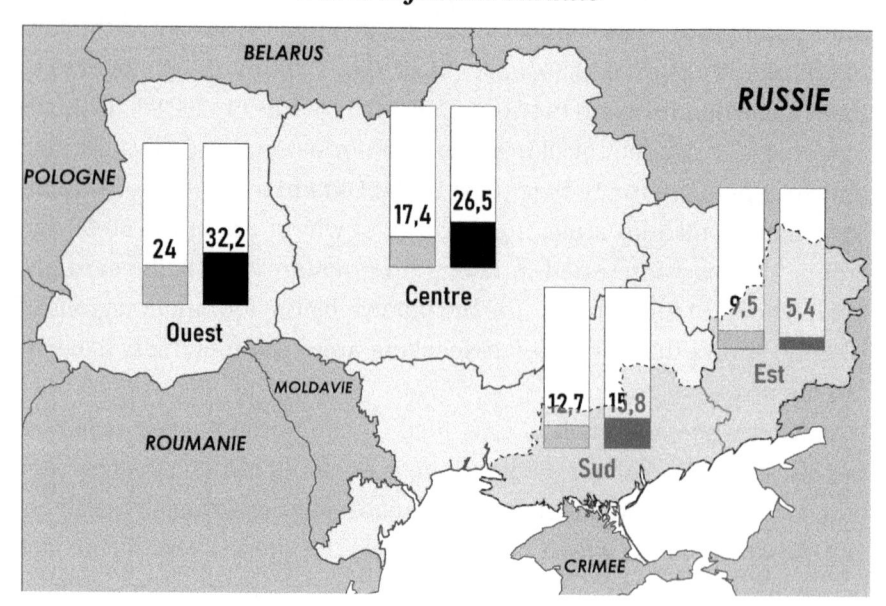

Figure 33 - Proportion of the Ukrainian population [%] ready to take up arms in the event of Russian intervention, based on a KIIS poll in December 2021 (grey) and February 2022 (black). Overlaid and dotted are the territories taken by Russia. As can be seen, the willingness to take up arms decreases steadily from the northwest to the southeast of the country, precisely in the areas where support for Russia is strongest. [Source: https://www.kiis.com.ua/?lang=eng&cat=reports&id=1099&page=1]

A French-speaking Swiss politician who propagates neo-Nazi ideas called me a "Putinolater" for having mentioned the suicides in the Ukrainian army before 2022. Today, he can hurl his insults at British parliamentarians, because they themselves have noted that the suicide rate there is alarming[407]. So we have foolish politicians, who blind themselves with their lies, instead of anticipating the problems!

In 2021 (before the Russian intervention) citizens were again concerned that "non-combat casualties had been higher than combat casualties between 2014 and 2019 and petitioned President Zelensky for an investigation[408]."

---

407. "Ukrainian soldiers are committing suicide due to war stress, says Duncan-Smith," *Politics.co.uk*, January 16, 2023 (https://www.politics.co.uk/parliament/ukrainian-soldiers-are-committing-suicide-due-to-war-stress-says-duncan-smith/)
408. https://petition.president.gov.ua/petition/120726

There is no Ukrainian popular resistance movement in the Russian-controlled territories[409]. While the Russian-speaking population resisted the Ukrainian army and its neo-Nazi supporters, supported, trained and financed by the West, for eight years, nothing similar has emerged against the Russians.

The problem is that during the years 2014-2022, Kiev fought the Donbass autonomists by treating them as invaders. That is why they engaged - with the blessing of the Western media and politicians - artillery against the civilian population. The aim was to make life impossible for them and thus encourage them to return to the fold of Kiev.

The problem is that the strategy for fighting an insurgency must be a careful mix of "carrot and stick. It is necessary to apply force only when it is strictly necessary, and try to seduce the population with incentives. In this phase, Ukraine has been a victim of its own rhetoric. By claiming that Russia was trying to invade it, Ukraine put itself in the position of a country in a defensive situation. However, we can see today that an "invasion" is very different from the situation we had between 2014 and 2022.

In addition to the fact that Kiev has not achieved results on the ground, the government has alienated the Russian-speaking population in the south of the country. In the Donbass, the population has turned to their Russian brothers for generosity and trade that Kiev has denied them. In the rest of the country, the repression against those who rose up to recover their rights was very violent. Moreover, numerous accounts show that after the repatriation of the territories of Kharkov in September 2022 and Kherson in October, "reprisal" operations led to numerous massacres.

In April 2023, the BBC reported that *"the number of Ukrainians suspected or even convicted of working for Russian special services is already in the thousands*[410]*"*. This seems to be a far cry from the rhetoric that Russians are not welcome in Ukraine.

The Russians have understood this mechanism very well and seek to keep the "hearts and minds" of the populations. This is why they are

---

409. Siobhán O'Grady, Serhii Korolchuk & Anastacia Galouchka, "In Slovyansk, conflicted loyalties as Russian forces approach", *The Washington Post*, June 18, 2022 (https://www.washingtonpost.com/world/2022/06/18/ukraine-slovyansk-divided-loyalties-russia/)

410. Oleg Chernish, "Чи міг український "сільський чаклун" стати шпигуном для російських відьом. Історія одного злочину," BBC News Ukrainian Service, April 16, 2023 (https://www.bbc.com/ukrainian/articles/clmdjyrl08do)

welcomed as liberators rather than occupiers. This is also why it is unlikely that they will try to take over the northwest of the country, which is the cradle of Ukrainian nationalism and which would probably pose many more problems.

Kiev-based journalists and diplomats judge the situation in Ukraine from what they see in the west of the country. Because they deny the identity of minorities, they can extrapolate their observations and say that the whole country is behind Zelensky. But this is far from the case.

4.2.3. Conduct of operations

4.2.3.1. The Ukrainian operational strategy

Between 2014 and 2022, Kiev literally laid siege to the Russian-speaking populations of Donbass. Supplies were cut off, including banking services and pension payments, for example. In Crimea, Kiev even cut off the peninsula's drinking water supply. This was to starve the civilian population, as Petro Poroshenko, the then Ukrainian president, explains[411]. It was this situation that made the population of Donbass dependent on humanitarian and financial aid from Russia.

Militarily, Ukrainian forces have built a network of fortifications around the areas held by the autonomists. Dubbed the "Zelensky Line," this network consists of three heavily reinforced defense lines. It was not designed as a defense line (which would pass in front of inhabited areas), but as a siege line, which passes in the middle of urban areas and uses the civilian population as a shield against possible fire from the Donbass. These fortifications will be at the heart of the battles in Severodonetsk, Lysychansk, Soledar or Bakhmut in 2022.

Our media never mentioned this line, which would have shown that Kiev was besieging its own population, and today they minimize its importance in order to claim that the Russians are not capable of seizing simple trenches.

By May 2022, Russian coalition forces were advancing slowly but steadily by about 100 m per day. Ukrainian "counter-offensives" failed and were unable to prevent the Russian advance.

---

411. https://youtu.be/aHWHqj8g7Bk

It is only at the end of 2022, when the situation of the Ukrainian troops is deteriorating, that this battle gets the attention of the media. Volodymyr Zelensky makes it a symbolic issue and ostensibly goes near Bakhmut in December 2022, just before his trip to Washington, during which he will offer Nancy Pelosi a Ukrainian flag signed by fighters of the city.

But in early 2023, the situation of Ukrainian troops in Bakhmut is getting dangerously worse. The upcoming defeat is all the more important as Zelensky and our media have made it a symbol of the Ukrainian defense. A Western discourse then developed which castigated the incapacity of Russian troops to seize such an insignificant objective.

Thus, on January 12, 2023, in the program "C dans l'air" of France 5, Guillaume Ancel, *"former officer of the French army"* (whatever that means), declared that *"Bakhmout is of no military interest"*[412]. In other words, Zelensky and the Ukrainians who built a vast network of fortifications in this area are idiots.

In fact, Ancel has not analyzed anything at all. Like most "experts", he repeats the standard narrative in our media, without understanding, and says what we want to hear[413]. Bakhmut is a small town located in the center of the "Zelensky line". Its importance does not come from its political role, its economic activity or its size (about 70,000 inhabitants), but from its place in the Ukrainian defensive system. It is at the heart of a network of logistical routes essential to Ukrainian defense. If our "expert" had bothered to look at a map, he would have noticed that up to Kramatorsk-Slaviansk the Donbass is a densely built and wooded region. Once this obstacle is crossed, the Russians would have the door open to the Dnieper plains.

Thus, on January 20, according to the German magazine *Der Spiegel*, a report presented to the Bundestag by the German intelligence service (BND) expressed alarm at the level of Ukrainian losses[414] and declared that the fall of Bakhmut would cause the collapse of the entire Ukrainian

---

412. https://youtu.be/1oeN9sF9TEI?t=106
413. Brendan Cole, "Russia's Costly Bakhmut Offensive Has Limited Tactical Value: U.K.," Newsweek, December 3, 2022 (https://www.newsweek.com/russia-ukraine-mod-bakhmut-donetsk-1764368)
414. "Spiegel: German intelligence alarmed by high losses of Ukrainian army in Bakhmut," *The Kyiv Independent*, January 20, 2023 (https://kyivindependent.com/news-feed/spiegel-german-intelligence-alarmed-by-high-losses-of-ukrainian-army-in-bakhmut)

defence[415]. Then, in February, the American magazine *Newsweek* estimated that the fall of Bakhmut could decide the continuation of the war[416], while on March 7, in the *Kyiv Independent*, Volodymyr Zelensky himself declared that "*the capture of Bakhmut [...] 'would pave the way' for other critical urban centers in the* Donetsk *region*"[417].

That being said, Bakhmut has another significance. Despite suggestions from the American military[418], Zelensky refuses to withdraw his troops from the city. He seeks to encourage the West to become more involved in the conflict and considers that a withdrawal from Bakhmut would send the wrong signal[419]. For him, the heroic defence of Bakhmut is also a communication tool to counter weakening Western support.

As TOP SECRET documents "leaked" in April 2023 show, the Americans tried to dissuade the Ukrainians from holding on to Bakhmut and abandoning the city in order to lose fewer men[420]. This has resulted in tensions at the top of the Ukrainian leadership, between the "politicians" and the "military," who would like to follow the Americans' recommendations. This conflicting situation affects the cohesion of the Ukrainian strategic leadership. For example, on March 1st, 2023, while Alexander Rodnyansky, Zelensky's advisor, stated on CNN that Ukraine was not going to sacrifice its soldiers in Bakhmout[421], the *New York Times*

---

415. "German intelligence alarmed by Ukrainian losses in Bakhmut," *Reuters/A News*, January 20, 2023 (https://www.anews.com.tr/world/2023/01/20/german-intelligence-alarmed-by-ukrainian-losses-in-bakhmut)
416. Isabel van Brugen, "Why Bakhmut Could Decide Who Wins Ukraine War," *Newsweek*, February 19, 2023 (https://www.newsweek.com/why-bakhmut-decide-ukraine-war-1782170)
417. Dinara Khalilova, "Zelensky says capture of Bakhmut would give Russia 'open road' to other cities of Donetsk Oblast," *The Kyiv Independent*, March 7, 2023 (https://kyivindependent.com/news-feed/zelensky-says-capture-of-bakhmut-would-give-russia-open-road-to-other-cities-of-donetsk-oblast)
418. Roman Vanian, "United States believes Ukraine should withdraw its forces from Bakhmut in order to advance in another direction," *Ukrainian News*, February 3, 2023 (https://ukranews.com/en/news/912744-united-states-believes-ukraine-should-withdraw-its-forces-from-bakhmut-in-order-to-advance-in)
419. "Ukraine Will Hold Bakhmut, Zelenskiy Vows, Amid Warnings About New Offensive In The East," *RFE/RL's Ukrainian Service*, February 3, 2023 (https://www.rferl.org/a/russia-offensive-ukraine-east/32253748.html)
420. Susannah George & Serhii Korolchuk, "Ukraine defended Bakhmut despite U.S. warnings in leaked documents," *The Washington Post*, April 20, 2023 (https://www.washingtonpost.com/world/2023/04/20/bakhmut-ukraine-war-leaked-documents/)
421. Susie Blann, "Ukraine official: Forces may pull out of key city of Bakhmut," *AP/The Washington Post*, March 1st, 2023 (https://www.washingtonpost.com/world/ukraine-official-says-military-may-pull-back-from-bakhmut/2023/03/01/e2dd402c-b821-11ed-b0df-8ca14de679ad_story.html)

announced on the same day that the Ukrainian president was sending reinforcements to the city[422].

While our media speak of "stalemate", the *Washington Post* speaks of *"sustained progress"* by Russian forces.

By the spring of 2023, the battle for Bakhmut was in its final stages. With a more dynamic operating doctrine and more mobile assets, Ukraine could have cleared its forces from Bakhmut and preserved them, in order to conduct a counteroffensive, as the Russians did in Kharkov in September. The problem is that the Ukrainian army does not really have the means to retake the city after losing it (as the Russians did in Krasnyy Lyman), which is why it is holding on to Bakhmut.

Videos of a Ukrainian mechanized attack on Bakhmut with YPR-765 infantry fighting vehicles supplied by the Netherlands show that the Ukrainians have not mastered joint combat[423]. Our media's emphasis on Ukrainian ingenuity in finding technical solutions has obscured the profound deficiencies in their operational conduct.

The example of Bakhmut illustrates not only the incompetence of the so-called military "experts", who have no experience whatsoever of operational conduct and who come to tell a narrative without understanding themselves what they are saying. But it also shows their deep contempt for Ukrainians, and their determination to distort our perception of the conflict for the sole purpose of satisfying their opinion.

In the West, the conflict is not seen from a human perspective, but exclusively as a political issue. It should be remembered that Zelensky's objective is not the preservation of the lives of his fellow citizens, but the country's entry into NATO, and that this will only be possible if Russia is defeated. Since sanctions have not been enough to bring about Russia's economic and political collapse, the defeat must come from the battlefield, as Josep Borrell says[424].

---

422. "Daily Briefing: War in Ukraine Kyiv Sends Reinforcements to Besieged Bakhmut". *The New York Times*, March 1st, 2023 (updated March 2, 2023) (https://www.nytimes.com/live/2023/03/01/world/russia-ukraine-news)
423. Stetson Payne, "Ukraine Situation Report: Armored Personnel Carriers Make A Charge In Bakhmut," *The War Zone*, March 18, 2023 (https://www.thedrive.com/the-war-zone/ukraine-situation-report-armored-personnel-carriers-make-a-charge-in-bakhmut)
424. https://www.courrierinternational.com/article/vu-de-russie-l-ue-veut-balayer-la-diplomatie-au-profit-de-la-guerre-estime-moscou.

Bakhmut and the "Zelensky line"

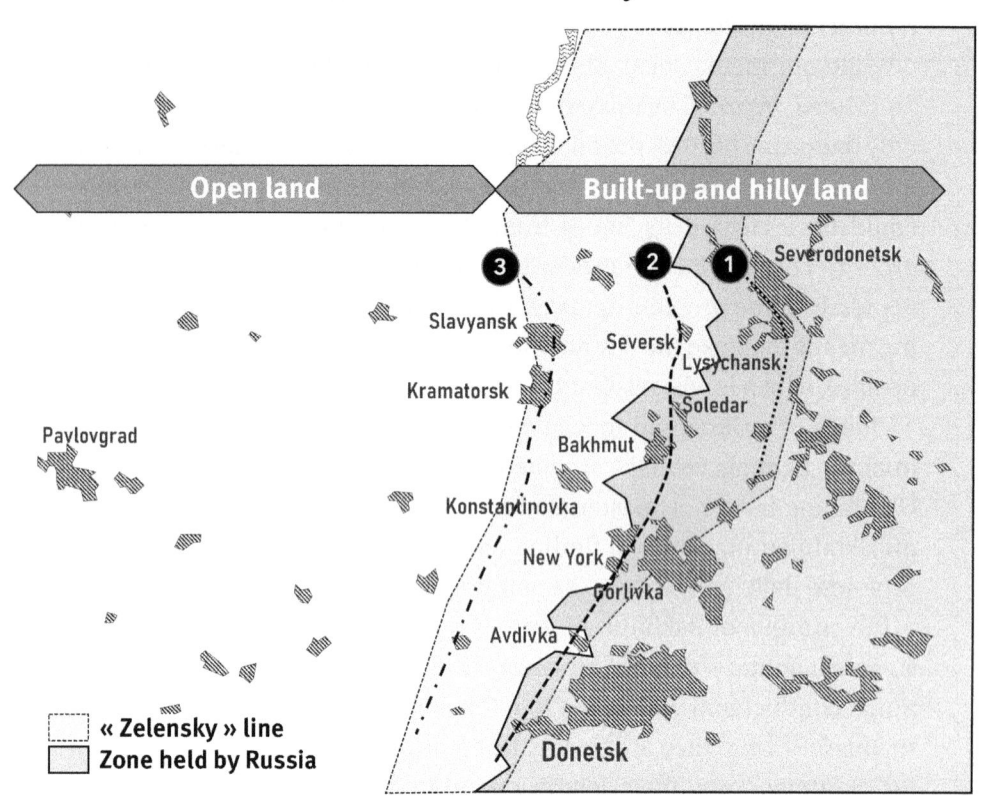

Figure 34 - In the Donbass, in the region of Bakhmut, what is sometimes called the "Zelensky Line" consists of three lines of defense staggered in depth. Considered by our "experts" as insignificant, Bakhmut is at the center of the device set up by the Ukrainians to besiege the Donbass in the Donetsk sector. The Ukrainians relied on the built-up areas for their defense lines. After the third line of defense, the terrain is hardly defensible until the Dnieper.

Focused on defending every square meter, the Ukrainians never had the initiative. By conducting attacks all along the front line, the Russians created pressure that prevented Ukraine from concentrating its forces in one place. The result was the apparent flaw in Ukrainian operational conduct, which is to prefer to hold on to the ground, rather than take the risk of not being able to retake it. Conversely, throughout their operation, the Russians relied on their ability to maneuver and systematically prioritized the lives of their troops over taking territory. Territories that could only be defended with heavy losses were abandoned, even if it meant taking them back later. This is what happened in Kharkov (September 2022) and Kherson (October 2022). The Russian calculation is that lost ground can be recaptured, while human lives cannot be recovered.

Ukrainian defense lines in the Donbass

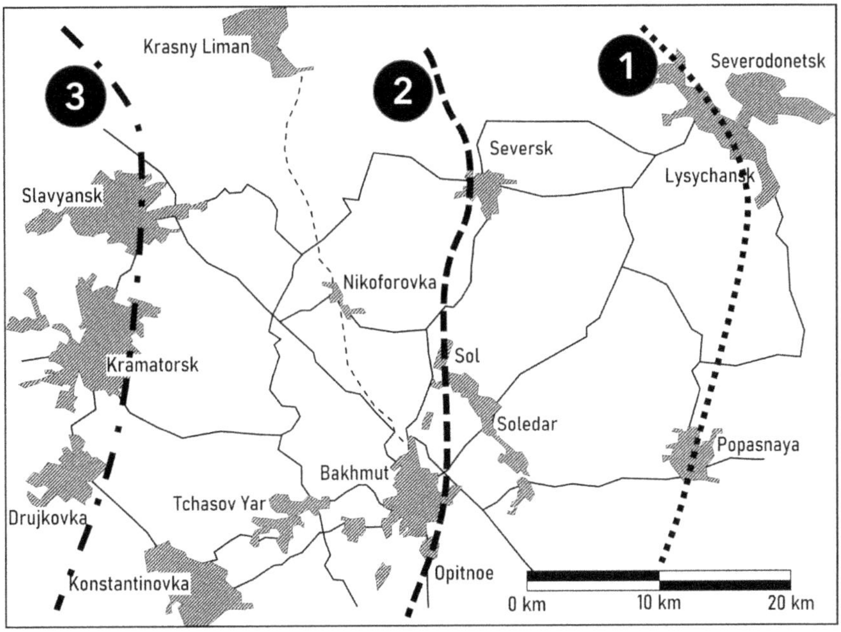

Figure 35 - The first defense line was broken through in early May 2022 at Popasnaya, which opened the door to the fall of Severodonetsk-Lysychantsk. The second is Seversk-Bakhmut and the third is Kramatorsk-Slaviansk. Bakhmut is the last line of defense before Kramatorsk [According to Big Serge Substack].

4.2.3.2. The involvement of Western intelligence

Having very quickly lost control of the sky, the Ukrainian leadership immediately showed its intelligence shortcomings. Apparently, the Ukrainians expected that the populations of the areas occupied by the Russian forces would provide information. But this does not seem to have been the case: between those who have left the area and those who are favorable to the Russians, the Ukrainian army does not have the sources it was hoping for.

So the West had to get involved very quickly. On the strategic level, the United States provides most of the electronic and satellite intelligence that Ukraine receives.

Clearly, the Ukrainians are receiving Western satellite intelligence. Russia is said to have the technical means to blind satellites up to a distance of 1,500 km[425], and which are in the production phase[426]. This includes its KALINA system, based near the city of Zelenchukskaya[427]. However, it does not want to take on the American satellites directly. Not yet. On the other hand, it has stated that commercial satellites could be legitimate targets (e.g., the satellites of the firm Maxar, or Space X)[428]. Ella made the same statement[429] after it was announced that NATO was embarking on a program of military-commercial cooperation in satellite intelligence acquisition through its *Alliance Persistent Surveillance from Space* (APSS) initiative[430].

These are essentially target locations, the coordinates of which are transmitted via Starlink to the command post and then disseminated through the Ukrainian tactical network NETTLE.

With surveillance aircraft, they observe the theater of operations from outside Ukrainian airspace. Participate in airspace surveillance and information gathering along the Russian, Belarusian and Ukrainian borders[431]:

- NATO, with its E-3A NATO AWACS airspace surveillance aircraft and RQ-4D PHOENIX;
- Sweden, with its Gulfstream S102B KORPEN electronic reconnaissance;
- the United States, with RQ4 GLOBALHAWK and MQ9 REAPER surveillance aircraft, RC135V/W RIVET JOINT and RC135U COMBAT

---

425. Chay Quinn, "Russia successfully tests new laser weapon that can 'blind' satellites and destroy drones from three miles away," *Daily Mail*, May 18, 2022 (https://www.dailymail.co.uk/news/article-10829603/Russia-successfully-tests-new-laser-weapon-blind-satellites-destroy-drones.html)
426. Iain Boyd, "Russia is reportedly building a satellite-blinding laser - an expert explains the tech," *Astronomy*, August 1st, 2022 (https://astronomy.com/news/2022/08/russians-is-reportedly-building-a-satellite-blinding-laser--an-expert-explains-the-tech)
427. Bart Hendrickx, "Kalina: a Russian ground-based laser to dazzle imaging satellites," *The Space Review*, July 5, 2022 (https://www.thespacereview.com/article/4416/1)
428. "Russia Says U.S. Satellites Assisting Ukraine Are 'Legitimate' Targets," *The Moscow Times*, October 27, 2022 (https://www.themoscowtimes.com/2022/10/27/russia-says-us-satellites-assisting-ukraine-are-legitimate-targets-a79208)
429. "Russia issues space warning", *RT*, April 12, 2023 (https://www.rt.com/russia/571585-quasi-civilian-satellites-nato/)
430. "NATO's approach to space", *nato.int*, April 12, 2023 (https://www.nato.int/cps/en/natohq/topics_175419.htm)
431. Thomas Newdick, "This Is The Armada Of Spy Planes Tracking Russia's Forces Surrounding Ukraine," *The War Zone*, February 18, 2022 (https://www.thedrive.com/the-war-zone/44337/these-are-the-planes-keeping-watch-on-russian-forces-around-ukraine).

SENT electronic intelligence aircraft, the U2S DRAGON LADY reconnaissance aircraft, and the US Army ARTEMIS electronic reconnaissance aircraft,
- France with Mirage 2000 for specific missions[432].

Western airspace surveillance

Figure 36 - Western reconnaissance flights between January 20 and March 20, 2023, showing constant surveillance of Ukrainian and Russian airspace. Despite the delivery of weapons and the abundance of intelligence available to Ukraine, it is not achieving concrete results on the ground. This map was compiled by Orion Intel, which also has an animated version that allows for a better view of the various intelligence platforms involved[433]. [Source: Orion Intel]

Aerial intelligence activities are carried out along the Ukrainian, Belarusian and Russian borders, from Romania, Poland and the Baltic States; and in the Black Sea, from within a zone (*Intelligence Surveillance Reconnaissance - Operational Area* or *ISR OPAREA*) that stops 15 nautical miles from the coast. An additional line has been defined by the American Secretary of Defense at 40 nautical miles from the coast, intended to avoid the risk of confrontation with Russian aviation.

---
432. Secret American documents
433. https://twitter.com/Orion__int/status/1645456866393346048

The West collects information on the situation in the depth of the theater of operations and provides the Ukrainians with data for artillery fire (M-777 and HIMARS, in particular). In December 2022, the *Wall Street Journal* reported[434]:

> *The United States provided Ukrainian President Volodymyr Zelensky's forces with reams of data on the position and movement of Russian troops and equipment, as well as other combat-related information, as part of an extensive intelligence-sharing agreement that is virtually unprecedented for a non-NATO U.S. ally.*

Since Ukraine is - theoretically - only a "partner" of NATO and the United States (like Switzerland or Russia, before its suspension), it would have only very limited access to classified operational information. The Americans therefore had to significantly relax their intelligence sharing rules for it[435].

The RQ-4 is the heir to the "spy planes" of the 1960s. With a 40-metre wingspan, it has a range of 22,000 km and an endurance of 36 hours. It is equipped with an AN/APY-8 LYNX II synthetic aperture radar (SAR), which allows it to "see" laterally up to a maximum distance of 600 km when it is at an altitude of 20,000 m. The SAR is associated with a *Ground Moving Target Indicator* (GMTI), which is used to detect moving targets and transmit their coordinates in real time to a ground station. By circling in the middle of the Black Sea between the Crimean and Turkish coasts, the RQ-4s can literally cover the entire Ukrainian theater.

For example, on October 29, 2022, the Ukrainian attack on the port of Sevastopol, carried out by a swarm of 9 aerial and 7 naval drones, was coordinated by an American RQ-4B GLOBAL HAWK drone (code name FORTE10), cruising at high altitude off the coast of Crimea. The Ukrainian drones apparently caused only minor damage, according to the Russian authorities, and were all destroyed.

---

434. Warren P. Strobel, "U.S. Has Eased Intelligence-Sharing Rules to Help Ukraine Target Russians," *The Wall Street Journal*, December 21, 2022 (https://www.wsj.com/livecoverage/ukraine-zelensky-biden-congress-washington-trip-russia/card/u-s-has-eased-intelligence-sharing-rules-to-help-ukraine-target-russians-6pgEkPNCQRX8z4KBu4V4)

435. Warren P. Strobel & Michael R. Gordon, "Biden Administration Altered Rules for Sharing Intelligence with Ukraine," *The Wall Street Journal*, March 8, 2022 (https://www.wsj.com/articles/biden-administration-altered-rules-for-sharing-intelligence-with-ukraine-11646744400)

Operational area of Western surveillance devices

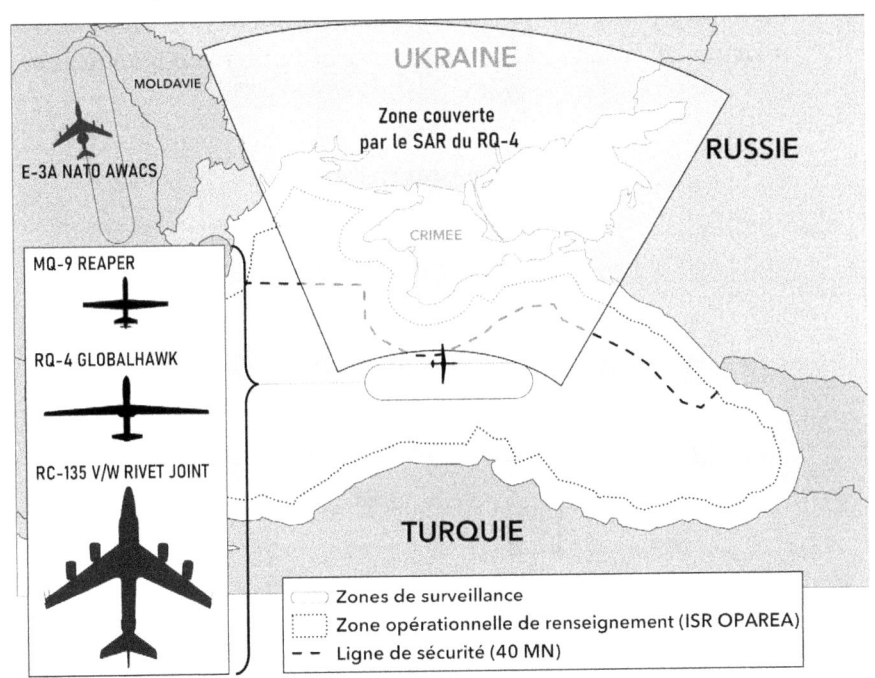

Figure 37 - Main theater surveillance systems from outside Ukrainian airspace according to the secret documents revealed in April 2023.

Other devices, like the MQ-9 REAPER have similar functions, but on a smaller scale. It has a wingspan of 20 m and a ceiling of 15,000 m, its SAR covers a maximum area of about 400 km deep.

It is within the framework of this surveillance that the incident of March 14, 2023, took place off the coast of Sevastopol, between two Russian Sukhoi-27s and an American MQ-9A REAPER drone. The latter was on a reconnaissance mission for Ukrainian forces, as confirmed by the American *National Review*[436]:

> *This downed MQ-9 drone was collecting intelligence on the location and movements of Russian troops, which would have been passed on to the Ukrainians so they could target those forces. We may not*

---

436. Jim Geraghty, "U.S. Drone Becomes a Casualty in the Proxy War with Russia," *National Review*, March 15, 2023 (https://www.nationalreview.com/the-morning-jolt/u-s-drone-becomes-a-casualty-in-the-proxy-war-with-russia/)

like it when Russia shoots down our surveillance drones over international waters, but we should not be surprised that they do. It is a logical, even inevitable, consequence of a proxy war with Russia.

MQ-9A REAPER

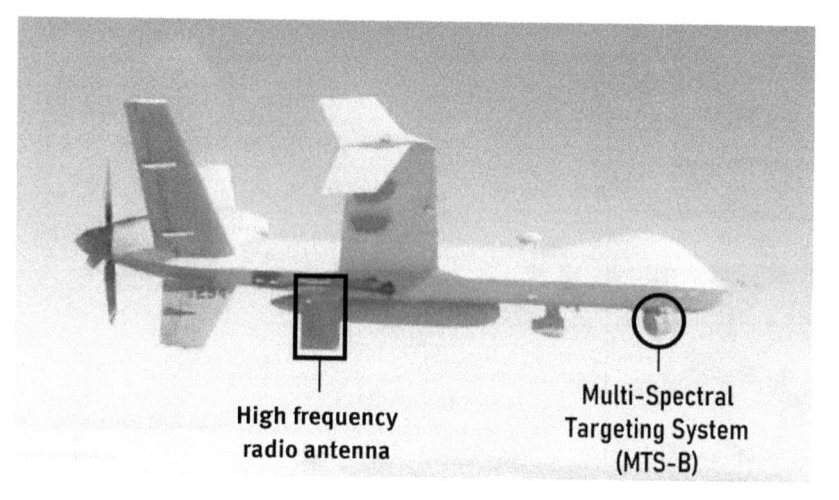

Figure 38 - Image taken by one of the Russian pilots and published by the Russian Ministry of Defence of the MQ-9A REAPER intercepted on March 14, 2023 off Sevastopol. It was equipped with a high frequency antenna and its MTS-B system, which allow the detection and the localization of targets. Flying with its transponder turned off, it is likely that it was on an electronic intelligence mission to support an ongoing Ukrainian operation.

The MQ-9 has a very large blade-shaped antenna mounted on the belly of the aircraft. This type of antenna is typically associated with high frequency radio communications, and can be part of a direction finding system for target location. At the lower front is an AN/AAS-52 multispectral targeting system (MTS-B), comprising a series of optical sensors for targeting. The MTS-B incorporates an infrared sensor, a color TV camera, a monochrome daylight camera, a shortwave infrared camera, a laser designator and a laser illuminator. It was the MTS-B that took the images of the interception by the two Russian fighters.

In early April 2023, the recovery of the wreckage by the Russian Navy allowed for the determination of the resolution of the AN/AAS-52's optronic sensors and the analysis of its performance through different types of weather and distances. The Link-16 data transmission system was also recovered and analyzed to measure its resistance to electronic countermeasures.

This aircraft was flying with its transponder turned off, within the airspace extension notified by Russia at the beginning of its SVO. This suggests that it was in a reconnaissance operation or even a target designation operation for the Ukrainian army.

4.3. The spring counter-offensive (2023)

Since the spring of 2022, Volodymyr Zelensky has been promising a major offensive towards the south of the country, to retake the territories occupied by Russia. This is in fact a continuation of the offensive he planned to carry out in early 2022 and for which he had issued his decree in March 2021.

The Russian intervention in February 2022 prevented him from realizing his project, which was the objective of the SVO. Throughout 2022, there was talk of Ukrainian "counter-offensives". But none of them succeeded in pushing back the Russian coalition. In the summer, Volodymyr Zelensky promised a major offensive with 1 million men[437], but it was postponed to the fall, then to the winter. It was to respond to this threat that Russia carried out its partial mobilization of 300,000 men: it attacked with a force ratio of 23 to 1 in favor of Ukraine and if the latter doubled its numbers, Russia would then be at a disadvantage of 56 to 1.

In 2023, under pressure from the West, the long-awaited offensive is announced for the spring of 2023. It should be conducted by 12 brigades, 3 of which are set up by Ukraine and 9 by Western countries. In April, leaked American documents show that in March, of the nine "Western" brigades, 5 have completed 0% of their training, one is at 10%, one at 20%, one at 40% and one at 60%. As for their equipment, it is only 46% available. Clearly, Ukraine is unlikely to be ready by the

---

437. "Ukraine attacks Russian-held Kherson, plans counterattack", *aljazeerah*, July 12, 2022 (https://www.aljazeera.com/news/2022/7/12/ukraine-strikes-russian-held-kherson-as-kyiv-plans-counterattack)

end of April, which explains the postponement of the offensive to the summer of 2023[438].

Initially, the number of 60,000 men was mentioned for the 12 brigades intended for this major offensive. However, the leaked documents indicate that the maximum number of troops is 30,000, i.e. 50% of the initial planned capacity. In addition, these are essentially new soldiers with no previous combat experience.

It seems that Ukraine is doomed to carry out this offensive or counter-offensive, but at the end of April 2023, there is no telling how it will look. The "leaked" classified American documents give a small idea of the forces involved, but do not allow us to deduce the course of an operation.

However, some points are interesting. These documents mention three "axes": a Northern Axis (Belarus, Belgorod), a Zaporozhie Axis and a Kherson Axis, with an estimate of the forces deployed on each side along these possible axes of operations.

The forces at work in Ukraine

	Ukraine	Russie
Axe Nord	4 250-8 500	5 850
Axe Zaporojie	4 000-8 000	23 250
Axe Kherson	1 250-2 500	15 650

Figure 39 - Forces present on March 1st, 2023 on the possible axes of a spring 2023 offensive. It can be seen that the Americans have very precise figures on the Russians, while for the Ukrainians they have a margin of error of 100%. The reason is that the Americans have no autonomous capacity to establish these figures and must therefore rely on what the Ukrainians tell them. [Source: Document "Assessed Operations in the South", TOP SECRET, March 1st, 2023]

- The Kherson Axis appears to be the least likely for an offensive action because of the Dnieper crossing, which is a major problem. The forces deployed by the Ukrainians seem to argue in favor of a "flank-guard".

---

438. "Ukrainian counteroffensive could begin in summer, PM says," *The New Voice of Ukraine*, April 11, 2023 (https://english.nv.ua/nation/ukrainian-counteroffensive-could-begin-in-summer-pm-says-war-news-50317188.html)

- The Zaporozhie Axis is the one most commentators agree on, consistent with the multiple statements about a recapture of Crimea, which seems to be a central element for the Ukrainian government.
- The Northern Axis, which is an axis that leads us to Russian territory. Incidentally, according to the American documents, this is the only one of the three axes where the forces involved are at parity, or even slightly favorable to Ukraine. Could this be an indication that the Ukrainian offensive favors an attack on Russian territory, not to defeat it, but to destabilize it? This is not impossible, but in the absence of more details, we are in the realm of speculation.

However, it is important not to be misled by the figures. They are very vague on the Ukrainian side and can evolve relatively quickly, but above all, with the proper conduct of operations, an apparently unfavorable balance of forces is not incompatible with success.

But the stubbornness of the Ukrainians to hold static positions, especially in Bakhmut and Avdiivka, plays to the advantage of the Russians who can decimate the Ukrainian forces with their artillery.

In April 2023, the Americans and the Ukrainians know that the offensive proclaimed by our media is very likely to fail. Despite American attempts in late 2022 to get Zelensky to start a negotiation process, he persists.

Volodymyr Zelensky is caught between two fires. On the one hand, he fears that a stalemate in the situation will lead to fatigue in Western support, which is beginning to wane. In fact, this support is waning, but less for logistical reasons than for political reasons. For on the other hand, the West is condemned to success after having prevented Ukraine from negotiating with Russia. After repeatedly claiming that Ukraine had already won the war and that Russia could not win, the West has locked itself into a dead end.

The West and Ukraine are caught by the sunk cost syndrome: it becomes politically impossible to back down after the sacrifices already made, and. The more time passes, the more profound the repercussions of a defeat will be in Ukraine and in the West.

Zelensky's spring offensive is therefore doomed to success on the ground. Having abandoned the negotiations he himself had sought in February, March and August 2022, he is doomed to continue the war. A return to negotiations is a political, and perhaps even a physical, condemnation. For today, the conditions of such a negotiation would be dictated by Russia in a much more intransigent manner than they would have been a year earlier.

Zelensky is therefore forced to continue with his offensive, despite very low prospects of success.

Tanks available for the planned spring 2023 offensive

	Nombre au 24.02.2022	Nombre au 28.02.2023
Leopard 2A4 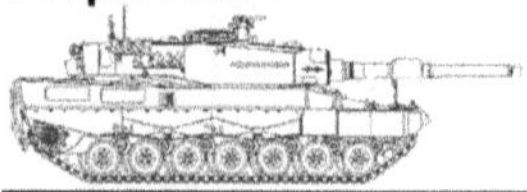	0	32
Challenger 2 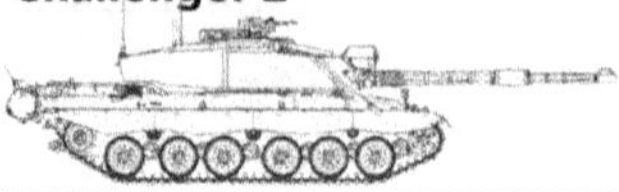	0	14
PT-91 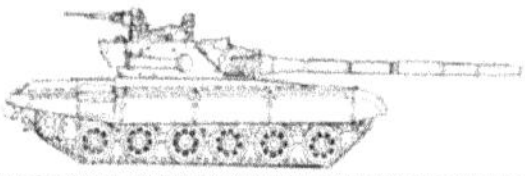	0	31
T-72 	100	38
T-64 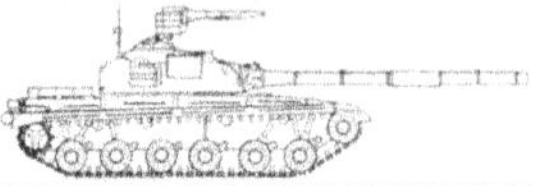	850	43
T-55MS 	0	28
AMX 10 RC 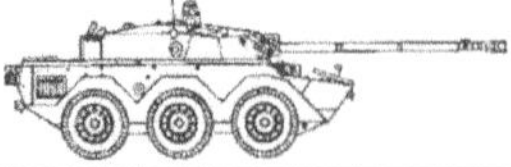	0	14
Total	950	200

Figure 40 - Battle tanks available for the 9 brigades set up by the West, according to secret American documents, "leaked" in April 2023. The AMX-19 RC is not a battle tank, but it is listed as such in the U.S. documents, probably because the Ukrainians want to use it in that role. The figure of 200 does not represent the total number of tanks available to Ukraine, but those that would be committed to this major offensive. They do, however, indicate the level of depletion of Ukrainian forces.

Artillery available for the planned spring 2023 offensive

	Calibre [mm]	Nombre au 28.02.2023
2S1 GVOZDIKA 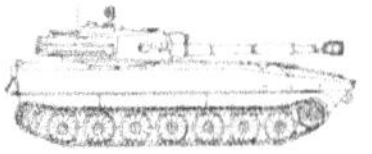	122	10
AS-90 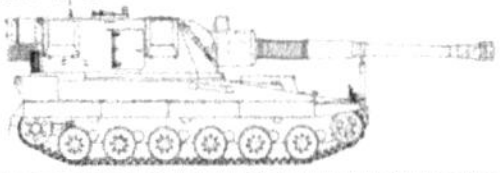	155	20
D-30 	122	46
M-109 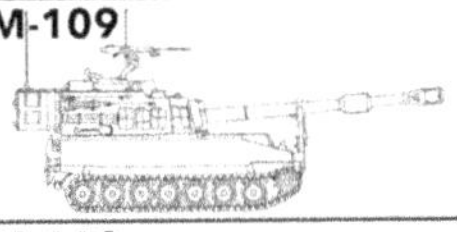	155	18
M-119 	105	36
FH-70 	155	22
Total		152

Figure 41 - Artillery pieces available for the 9 brigades set up by the West for the 2023 offensive. The number of 152 pieces compares to the more than 2,000 artillery pieces that Ukraine had in 2022.

4.4. The "leaked" American secret documents

In early April 2023, the *Washington Post*[439] and the *New York Times*[440], reveal that apparently leaked classified U.S. documents are circulating on

---

439. Dan Lamothe, Ellen Nakashima, Alex Horton, Dalton Bennett, Samuel Oakford & Evan Hill, "Justice Dept. will investigate leak of classified Pentagon documents," *The Washington Post*, April 7, 2023 (https://www.washingtonpost.com/national-security/2023/04/07/pentagon-leak-ukraine-documents/)
440. "Leaked Pentagon Documents Reveal Secrets About Friends and Foes," *The New York Times*, April 8, 2023 (updated April 9, 2023) (https://www.nytimes.com/explain/2023/russia-ukraine-war-documents-leak)

social networks. The alleged leaker is quickly identified as Jack Texeira, a 21-year-old member of the U.S. National Guard.

Apparently, despite his young age and relatively low rank, he has a "TS-SCI" security clearance, one of the highest. This does not mean that he automatically has access to all documents at this classification level, as this access is determined on a need-to-know basis, but it does allow him to move into classified enclosures to do maintenance work on computers[441].

A close examination of the documents shows several things. First, the leak is not the result of hacking. These are photos of summary documents produced by the *Joint Chiefs of Staff* (JCS) for situation briefings and "briefs" produced by the CIA and the *Office of the Director of National Intelligence* (ODNI). The JCS, CIA, and ODNI are three separate institutions and the documents serve different purposes.

This means that whoever took these photos is high enough in the country's hierarchy to have access to all three, and if Jack Texeira released them, he is probably not the leaker. But with more than 850,000 people with TOP SECRET security clearance, including some with TOP SECRET-SCI clearance, there are still many candidates…

These documents are therefore very likely to be authentic. They have been circulating since the beginning of 2023, so it is explicable that some of them have been modified (rather roughly). Overall, they show the weakness of Ukraine and its dependence on Western military aid. In this perspective, one cannot exclude that the revelation of their existence has the objective of calming the ardor of the American "hawks", who seek at all costs to prolong the conflict.

For this reason, commentators suggest that it may have been an organized leak to calm Western expectations of a possible Ukrainian victory. In the United States, the presidential team seems relatively insulated from the military, which has a less partisan view of Ukrainian capabilities and the possible outcome of the conflict. This could explain this very timely leak. Because apparently some of these documents were already circulating in January 2023, but it is only in April that they make the headlines. To what extent this disclosure is an effect of chance is therefore an open question.

---

441. https://www.msn.com/en-us/news/us/why-the-accused-document-leaker-had-high-level-security-clearance/ar-AA19U6R1

In any case, these documents are only a picture of the situation and are not operational. They give no indication of Ukrainian planning for a possible counter-offensive.

Classification abbreviations used in leaked documents

Classification	Signification	Traitement
TS	TOP SECRET	Unauthorized distribution can cause exceptional damage
S	SECRET	Unauthorized distribution can cause serious damage
REL TO FIN, UKR, NATO	Releasable to Finland, Ukraine, NATO	Can be communicated to Finland, Ukraine and NATO
NOFORN ou NF	No Foreign	Cannot be communicated abroad
HCS-P	HUMINT Controlled System-Product	Derived from human sources
SCI-G ou SI-G	Sensitive Compartmented Information – Gamma (SCI-G)	Sensitive information of electromagnetic origin
TK	TALENT KEYHOLE	Satellite information (used only with TS and S)
FGI	Foreign Government Information	Information from a foreign government
RSEN	Risk Sensitive	Risk associated with its distribution (used only with TS and S)
ORCON ou OC	Originator Controlled	Cannot be distributed beyond its initial recipient
FVEY	Five Eyes	Australia, Canada, United States, Great Britain, New Zealand
FISA	Foreign Intelligence Surveillance Act	FISA compatible information
RELIDO	Releasable By Information Disclosure Official	Indication to facilitate sharing with foreign partners

Figure 42 - The classification elements give a small idea of the origin of the information and intelligence that make up these documents.

4.4.1. Military documents

The documents with maps and figures are summaries intended to accompany JCS Intelligence Situation Reports (SITREPs) (J-2). Most of the figures concerning logistics come from information given by the governments that delivered equipment to Ukraine.

Information about Ukrainian troops comes partly from the Ukrainians and partly from Western surveillance systems, as the Ukrainian general staff does not communicate everything to them. The maps showing the deployment of Russian forces come mainly from the *National Geospatial-Intelligence Agency* (NSGA), which provides satellite intelligence, through the *US European Command* (EUCOM) based in Stuttgart. It is only the exploitation of satellite imagery.

Most of these documents have a classification with the annotation FGI, which means that the information comes from a foreign country. Here, presumably, the Ukraine. Moreover, a note aptly warns the reader of the precautions to be taken in interpreting the figures for personnel and equipment losses[442]:

> *Russian (RUS) and Ukrainian (UKR) attrition rates and inventories are unreliable due to information gaps, operations security measures (OPSEC) and information operations (IO), and potential biases in information sharing by the UKR.*

As the *New York Times* noted in June 2022, the Ukrainians are willing to receive Western aid, but they share little information[443]. In fact, they only tell the Americans what they want to tell. In other words, the information coming from Ukraine is far from reliable.

The figures on Russian losses that appear in the classified documents are very close to those given by open sources, such as the Oryx site, which serves as a source for our media. This suggests that the Americans do not have an independent ability to count these losses. The Oryx site (www.oryxspioenkop.com) is generally considered unreliable because of its methodology. Apparently, it simply collects images from social networks without really analyzing their reliability. Although the site states that "its figures significantly underestimate the real nature of Russian casualties," many destroyed materials are counted twice, but appear from different angles. The similarity of the weapons used by the two armies allows for

---

442. Russia/Ukraine - Assessed Combat Sustainability and Attrition, JCS, (SECRET)
443. Julian E. Barnes, "U.S. Lacks a Clear Picture of Ukraine's War Strategy, Officials Say," *The New York Times*, June 8, 2022 (https://www.nytimes.com/2022/06/08/us/politics/ukraine-war-us-intelligence.html)

confusion, even disinformation. The size of the losses mentioned by Oryx does not seem to reflect the situation of the Russian forces on the ground.

4.4.2. The CIA's documents

The CIA documents are in reality only "briefings" usually distributed to certain selected recipients with information from various sources and summarily or not evaluated. It is therefore not "finished intelligence" as such, but "raw intelligence". In other words, it is information that has been reformulated in the form of small notes, but which has not yet been integrated into an analysis. It is the equivalent of a news feed for a normal citizen.

For example, two of these notes mention the February 26, 2023 attack on a Russian A-50U MAINSTAY aircraft at the Matchulishchy air base (Belarus). They appear in two separate "brief" lists. Both have the same reference (Z-G/OO/121322 23) and the same classification (TOP SECRET / SCI-G). However, they present the event in two different ways: one speaks of an action carried out by an SBU agent against the advice of his hierarchy[444]; the other states that it was carried out by the Belarussian opposition, because President Zelensky did not want to provoke President Lukashenko. But in both cases, the drone used for the attack was allegedly supplied by Ukraine. So it seems that the attack was not due to the initiative of the Belarusian opposition.

Examination of the content of these "briefs" shows that a large part of them is derived from information coming from Ukraine (probably the intelligence services) and from diplomats. They do not appear to show a "penetration" of the Russian apparatus by the Americans. These notes are very similar to what can be found on networks like *Telegram*. It is important to remember here that the classification of an information has nothing to do with its relevance or accuracy, but most often serves to mask its origin.

Contrary to what our media claim, these documents reveal a surprising lack of knowledge of the Ukrainian theater by the Americans and their dependence on information coming from Ukraine. Obviously, the

---

444. Phil McCausland & Dan De Luce, "Ukraine agents pursued attacks inside Belarus and Russia, leaked U.S. docs say," *NBC News*, April 11, 2023 (https://www.nbcnews.com/politics/national-security/ukraine-agents-attacks-inside-belarus-russia-leaked-us-documents-say-rcna78973)

Americans have a solid knowledge of what can be observed by satellites, but a very poor knowledge of the operational aspects, both on the Ukrainian and Russian sides.

4.5. The Russian conduct of operations

Russia's goals, announced by Vladimir Putin on February 24, 2022, are demilitarization and denazification of the threat to the people of Donbass.

These goals are thus tied to Ukrainian potential (not territory) and have no time constraints. The objective of denazification would have been reached at the end of March with the encirclement of Mariupol and the objective of demilitarization was reached at the end of spring 2022. That is why, since that time, Volodymyr Zelensky has been asking for weapons and logistical support from the West and has conducted several partial mobilizations to replenish the ranks of the Ukrainian army.

This means that, since the summer of 2022, Russian forces have been eliminating the potential that arrives in the theater of operations. Since the Ukrainians are trying to retake the territory that the Russians have seized, the Russians do not really need to advance, but can just wait for the opponent to destroy him. This is exactly what General Surovikin, newly appointed as the *Commander of the Joint Task Force in the area of the special military operation in Ukraine* in October 2022[445] says:

> *We have a different strategy. [...] We do not seek a high speed of progress, we spare each of our soldiers and methodically "crush" the advancing enemy.*

While our "experts" try to measure military success in kilometers of progress on the ground, the Russians measure it in the number of destroyed opponents.

The problem is that our "experts" and TV generals have a very Western view of warfare. For them, the objective is always material (oil, land, industries, etc.). This is a bit simple. Westerners find it difficult to see

---

[445]. "Суровикин: российская группировка на Украине методично 'перемалывает' войска противника", TASS, October 18, 2022 (https://tass.ru/armiya-i-opk/16090805)

military objectives in anything other than quantitative terms. In the Ukrainian conflict, our "experts" are making exactly the same mistake. However, the Russians have defined an objective of a qualitative nature: the disappearance of a threat. This can only be achieved in two ways: negotiation or the total annihilation of this threat.

4.5.1. Driving structures

Until the end of September 2022, what our media call "the Russians" is only a coalition of the forces of three independent entities: Russia, the DPR and the LPR. There is no unified command, but only coordination by the Russian General Staff. This explains some of the difficulties observed on the ground between fighting units in the Donbass.

From the beginning of October 2022, with the new command structure. All "Russian-speaking" forces are integrated under a single command. The former Donbass militias receive better equipment, are supported by professional military, and supported by the "musicians" of Wagner.

Structure of the Special Military Operation
(February 24, 2022 - October 8, 2022)

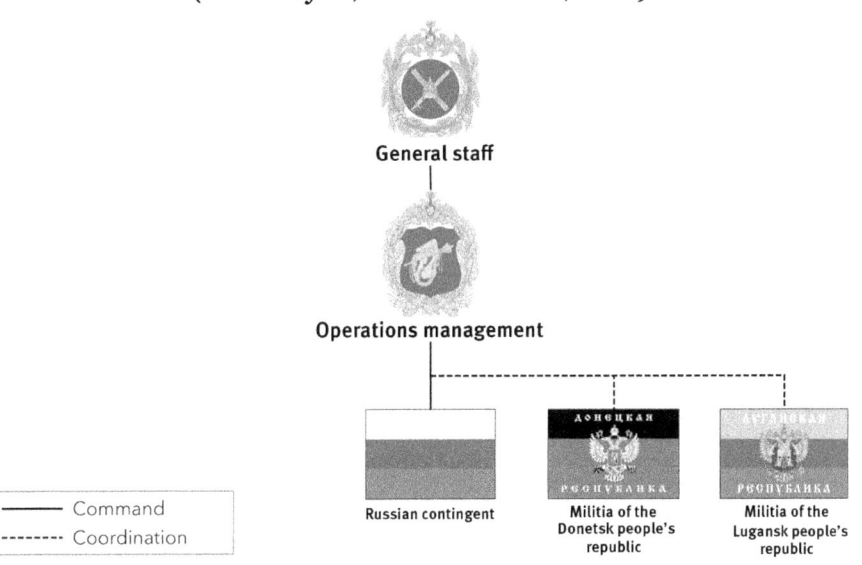

Figure 43 - Until October 2022, the SVO's leadership structure explains what our "experts" have interpreted as weaknesses in the Russian army. In reality, most of the fighting in the Donbass was carried out by the militias of the two Donbass republics, composed of reservists and often with obsolete equipment.

In January 2023, as the West considered expanding its logistical support to Ukraine and providing it with more modern weapons, Russia adjusted its leadership structure, in order to provide the SVO with more resources. This is why the command of the operation is shifting upwards and being assigned to Gherassimov. Contrary to what our military "experts" imagined, it was simply a matter of facilitating access to other resources such as aviation, missiles and even the navy.

While the West "prepares" the battlefield with intensive and prolonged strikes before sending their troops on the ground, the Russians prefer a less destructive, but more troop-intensive approach.

**Structure of the Special Military Operation
(October 8, 2022 - January 11, 2023)**

General staff

Sergueï Sourovikine
Commander of the
Aerospace Forces

**Commander-in-Chief
of the SVO**

Joint forces of the SVO

Figure 44 - After the referendums that allowed four regions of southern Ukraine to join the Russian Federation, all the forces of the Russian-speaking coalition could be placed under a single command. General Sergei Surovikin was then appointed commander-in-chief of Russian forces in Ukraine.

According to a *Defense Intelligence Agency* (DIA) analyst, *"the vast majority of airstrikes take place over the battlefield, with Russian aircraft providing 'close air support' to ground forces. The rest - less than 20 percent, according to U.S. experts - target military airfields, barracks and support depots."* Thus, the phrase *"indiscriminate bombing [that] devastates the city and kills everyone"* echoed by the Western media seems to be contradicted by the US intelligence expert who states [446]

> *If we simply convince ourselves that Russia is bombing indiscriminately, or that it is failing to inflict more damage because its personnel are not up to the task or because they are technically inept, then we are not seeing the conflict for what it is.*

Structure for conducting the Special Military Operation (January 11, 2023 -)

Valerii Gherassimov
Chief of the General Staff

Commander-in-Chief of the SVO

Oleg Salyoukov — Land forces commander

Sergueï Sourovikine — Commander of the aerospace forces

Alekseï Kim — Vice chief of the General Staff

Joint forces of the SVO

Figure 45 - OVS leadership structure as of January 11, 2023. This is to expand access to military resources for the OVS.

---

446. William M. Arkin, "Putin's Bombers Could Devastate Ukraine but He's Holding Back. Here's Why," Newsweek, March 22, 2022 (https://www.newsweek.com/putins-bombers-could-devastate-ukraine-hes-holding-back-heres-why-1690494)

4. Military considerations

In fact, Russian operations differ fundamentally from the Western concept. The West's obsession with having no fatalities in their own forces leads them to conduct very deadly air strikes before engaging their ground troops. This is why, in Afghanistan or in the Sahel[447], the West killed more civilians[448], than the Taliban[449] or the Islamic State[450]. This is why Western countries engaged in Afghanistan, the Middle East and North Africa, no longer publish the civilian casualty figures caused by their strikes.

In Ukraine, the situation is very different. One only has to look at a map of linguistic zones to see that the Russian coalition operates almost exclusively in the Russian-speaking zone, thus in the midst of populations that are generally favorable to it. This also explains the statements of a US Air Force officer: *"I know the media keeps saying that Putin is targeting civilians, but there is no evidence that Russia is doing it* intentionally"[451].

Conversely, it is for the same reason - but in a different way - that Ukraine has deployed its ultra-nationalist paramilitary fighters in major cities such as Mariupol[452]. With no emotional or cultural ties to the local population, these militias can fight even at the cost of heavy civilian casualties. Their atrocities[453], are deliberately concealed by our

---

447. Nathanaël Charbonnier, "Les armées régulières seraient tout aussi meurtrières (voire plus) que les terroristes au Sahel", radiofrance.fr, May 3, 2021 (https://www.franceinter.fr/monde/les-armees-regulieres-seraient-tout-aussi-meurtrieres-voire-plus-que-les-terroristes-au-sahel)
448. "Sahel: les populations craignent plus les bavures des forces de protection que les attaques djihadistes", RTBF.be, April 14, 2021 (https://www.rtbf.be/article/sahel-les-populations-craignent-plus-les-bavures-des-forces-de-protection-que-les-attaques-djihadistes-10740544)
449. Amy Woodyatt & Arnaud Siad, "More civilians are being killed by Afghan and international forces than by the Taliban and other militants," CNN, July 31, 2019 (https://edition.cnn.com/2019/07/30/asia/afghanistan-nato-taliban-intl-scli/index.html)
450. *Midyear Update on the Protection of Civilians in Armed Conflict: January 1st to June 30, 2019*, United Nations Assistance Mission in Afghanistan (UNAMA), July 30, 2019, p. 12; Amy Woodyatt & Arnaud Siad, "More civilians are being killed by Afghan and international forces than by the Taliban and other militants," *CNN*, July 31, 2019
451. William M. Arkin, "Putin's Bombers Could Devastate Ukraine but He's Holding Back. Here's Why," Newsweek, March 22, 2022 (https://www.newsweek.com/putins-bombers-could-devastate-ukraine-hes-holding-back-heres-why-1690494)
452. Roman Goncharenko, "The Azov Battalion: Extremists defending Mariupol," dw.com, March 16, 2022 (https://p.dw.com/p/48aCt)
453. Tim Lister, Celine Alkhaldi, Katerina Krebs & Josh Pennington, "Ukraine promises 'immediate investigation' after video surfaces of soldiers shooting Russian prisoners", CNN, March 27, 2022 (https://edition.cnn.com/europe/live-news/ukraine-russia-putin-news-03-27-22/h_6e158d3f-c5bc5efe7fc3f10b69b7aeee)

media, for fear of losing support for Ukraine, as noted by American media[454].

4.5.2. The Russian mastery of the operative art

Russian military doctrine distinguishes three levels of conduct: "tactics" (*taktika*), "operative art" (*operativnoe iskoustvo*) and "strategy" (*strategiya*). While tactics is considered to be an activity with an essentially technical character and strategy as an essentially intellectual activity with a political character, "operative art" is the art of designing operations.

Operational art is therefore neither a type of operation (as some experts have stated), nor a way of waging war, but the general framework within which military operations are conceived. The Russians see it as the true heart of military action, which is why their military doctrine describes it as an "art", i.e. an activity in which imagination and creativity are encouraged, as the Russian *Military Encyclopedic Dictionary* points out[455].

In the West, "operative art" has not received the same attention in recent years. First of all, the terms "operational" and "operative" are often confused, for the simple reason that the word "operative" does not exist in English. NATO uses the term "operational," which covers two distinct notions in Russian terminology: "operational" expresses a technical state (e.g., operational equipment), and "operative" refers to a level of conduct.

Since 1991, Westerners have fought only counter-insurgency wars, which have been fought almost exclusively at the tactical level. This has had an impact on the design of weapons systems (we will come back to this), but also and above all on military thinking. We have seen the gradual disappearance of operational thinking, which today affects NATO armies and which the Ukrainian army lacks for its conduct of operations.

On the other hand, Russia, which has always had as a priority the defense of its territory, has developed a mastery of operative art that we can see today and which makes the difference with the Ukraine trained by the West.

---

454. "Zelenskyy Worried About Western Financial Support After Video Surfaces Showing Ukraine Military Torturing Russian POW's," The Conservative Treehouse, March 27, 2022 (https://theconservativetreehouse.com/blog/2022/03/27/zelenskyy-worried-about-western-financial-support-after-video-surfaces-showing-ukraine-military-torturing-russian-pows/?utm_source=rss&utm_medium=rss&utm_campaign=zelenskyy-worried-about-western-financial-support-after-video-surfaces-showing-ukraine-military-torturing-russian-pows)

455. https://encyclopedia.mil.ru/encyclopedia/dictionary/details.htm?id=13724@morfDictionary

On February 24, 2022, Russia launches its "special military operation" (Специальная военная операция) (*Spetsial'naya Voyennaya Operatsiya - SVO*) in Ukraine "at a moment's notice." It communicates little about its planning. Nevertheless, observation and study of its military doctrine allow us to sketch the main lines of its operational thinking.

In accordance with Russian military doctrine, the SVO is articulated in two thrusts:

- a main thrust directed to the south of the country in the Donbass region and along the coast of the Sea of Azov. It is led by a coalition (Z) consisting of Russian forces from the Southern Military District through Kharkov and Crimea, with - in the center - forces from the Donetsk and Lugansk Republics, as well as a contribution from the Chechen National Guard for fighting in the urban area of Mariupol; and
- a secondary push on Kiev, led by Russian forces from Belarus (V) and Russia (O).

Russia rigorously applies one of the essential principles of warfare: economy of forces. According to the Pentagon, the Russians have committed about 80 *Battlegroups* (BTGs), totaling about 65,000-100,000 men[456], plus 30,000-40,000 men of the Donbass militias. Ukrainian forces, they then total 200,000 to 250,000[457] men. In May 2022, the Russian coalition (Russia, DPR and LPR) will have 100,000 to 190,000 men and Ukraine will have 700,000[458]. We can therefore see that the Russians have started their operation with a power ratio of 3-4: 1 in favour of Ukraine.

Such a ratio of forces seems to contradict the rules of military art, because it is generally admitted that a superiority of 3 to 1 is necessary for an attack to be successful. In reality, this ratio is very theoretical, because the success of an attack depends on more complex factors. The great battles of history show that it is often an outnumbered attacker who has

---

456. "Senior Defense Official Holds a Background Briefing, April 18, 2022," *defense.gov*, April 18, 2022 (https://www.defense.gov/News/Transcripts/Transcript/Article/3002867/senior-defense-official-holds-a-background-briefing-april-18-2022/)
457. Prasanta Kumar Dutta, Samuel Granados & Michael Ovaska, "On the edge of war", Reuters, January 26, 2022 (https://graphics.reuters.com/RUSSIA-UKRAINE/dwpkrkwkgvm/)
458. "700,000 soldiers defending Ukraine now, Zelenskyy says, as battles rage in the Donbas," Euronews/AP/AFP, May 21, 2022 (https://www.euronews.com/2022/05/21/live-sievierodonetsk-shelling-brutal-and-pointless-zelenskyy-says-as-russia-continues-offe)

won[459]. The Russians did not disprove this paradox, by conducting their operation with highly mobile battle groups, capable of being quickly moved in order to create local superiorities.

Summary concept of the Russian operation (Phase 1)

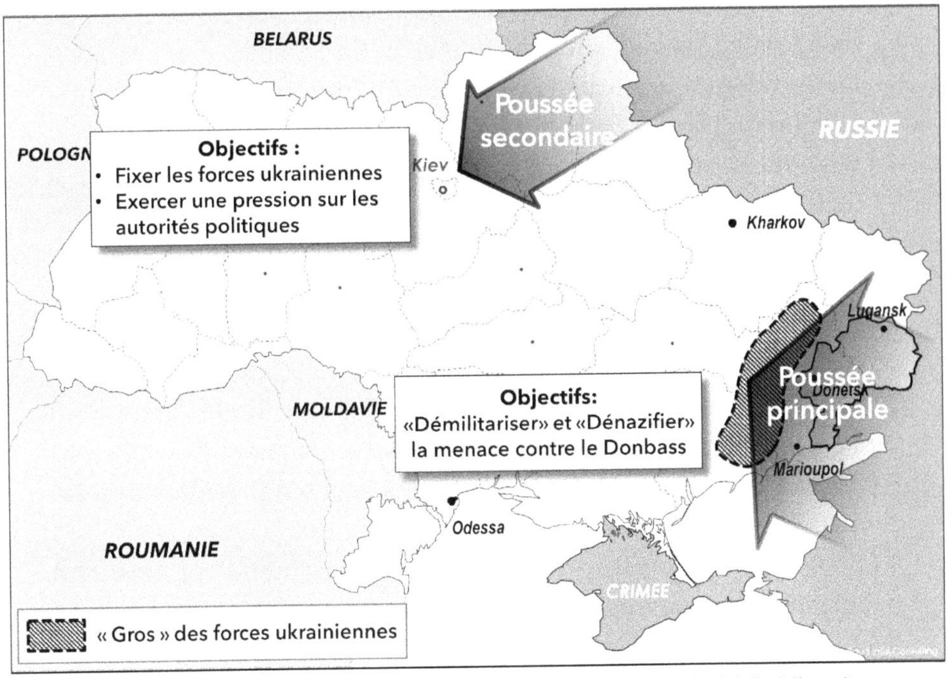

Figure 46 - The general mechanics of the Russian special operation faithfully follows its operational doctrine. It is articulated in a main thrust and a secondary thrust. The role of the secondary thrust is to create conditions favorable to the development of the main thrust.

4.5.2.1. The objectives

The course of operations follows the objectives defined by Vladimir Putin in his televised address on February 24. The intention of Phase 1 is to create favorable conditions for Phase 2, which will be the "pièce de résistance" of what the Russians call "*Special Military Operation*" (SVO).

The mechanics of the operation stem from the fact that the Russian coalition forces are attacking with an unfavorable balance of forces. To

---

459. T.N. Dupuy, *Numbers, prediction, and war: Using history to evaluate combat factors and predict the outcome of battles*, MacDonald & Jane's, January 1st, 1979 (https://www.amazon.com/Numbers-prediction-war-history-evaluate/dp/0672521318) (pp. 12-16)

achieve their objectives, they must be able to create limited superiorities in space and time. This is only possible by preventing Ukrainian forces in the west of the country from reinforcing the bulk of the forces gathered in the Donbass.

The final objective of the SVO is broken down into two objectives located on the axis of the main thrust. These are to neutralize:
- the Ukrainian armed forces regrouped in the Donbass in preparation for the offensive against the DPR and LPR (the objective of "demilitarization"), and
- the ultra-nationalist paramilitary militias of Marioupol (objective of "denazification").

It is therefore necessary to push very quickly in depth towards Kiev during Phase 1, in order to "fix" the Ukrainian forces in the capital sector and hold them back with combat actions. This is the objective of the secondary push towards Kiev.

Did the Russians foresee that this secondary thrust would attract more Western attention than the main thrust? We don't know. Nevertheless, the Western reaction and the media coverage of the Ukrainian defense centered on Zelensky made the Russians' task easier.

Listening only to their prejudices, Western pseudo-experts and politicians have got it into their heads that Russia's objective is to take over Ukraine and overthrow its government. This is what the West has systematically sought to do in the wars it has waged. Trained and advised by NATO experts, the Ukrainian general staff therefore, quite predictably, applied the same logic. They attributed to Russia the objective of regime change in Kiev and thus saw the city as the primary objective of the Russians.

Vladimir Putin's speech is unambiguous: he wants to eradicate the threat to the Russian-speaking population of Donbass, period. Russian military thinking is inspired by Clausewitz, who defined the "center of gravity" (*Schwerpunkt*) as the primary objective of a strategy. The "center of gravity" is the element from which a belligerent derives its strength and ability to act. For the Russians, in the context of the Donbass, the Ukrainian center of gravity is the ensemble of its military and paramilitary forces that threaten the Russian-speaking population. This is therefore the priority objective.

On a more technical level, to create local superiority, one must bring sufficient force into the desired sector, while preventing the adversary from reinforcing his position. This is the objective of "shaping operations". It is a matter of attracting or fixing the adversary's forces in certain sectors, in order to facilitate the execution of decisive operations, i.e. those that allow the objectives to be achieved.

In the first phase of the SVO, the action in the Donbass is a "decisive operation": it must allow the realization of the objectives of "demilitarization" and "denazification". The actions towards Kiev and Kherson-Zaporozhie are at this stage only "shaping operations": they must hold back the Ukrainian forces so that they cannot reinforce the bulk of the troops in the Donbass.

In its communiqué of March 30, 2022, the Russian Ministry of Defense explains this mechanism[460]:

> *The first phase of the special military operation conducted by the Russian armed forces in the Donbass and Ukraine was aimed at forcing the enemy to concentrate its forces, means, resources and combat equipment to defend the major urban areas in these zones, including Kiev. It was to fix them, without storming the cities, in order to avoid civilian casualties, and to inflict such losses on the armed forces of the Kiev regime, that it is not able to use them in the main direction of operation of our forces in the Donbass. All these objectives have been achieved.*

The Russians understand war from a Clausewitzian perspective: war is the pursuit of politics by other means. This is why they move from one to the other in a fluid manner by adapting their political objectives to the evolution of the military situation. In concrete terms, it is a matter of transforming operational successes into strategic successes. This is what happens at the beginning of the SVO, when the Ukrainian side declares itself ready to engage in a negotiation process.

On March 28, with the encirclement of the last square of neo-Nazis in Azovstal, Mariupol, the objective of "denazification" is considered to

---

460. https://z.mil.ru/spec_mil_oper/news/more.htm?id=12415372@egNews

have been achieved and removed from the list of Russian objectives, as reported by the *Financial Times*[461]. This encirclement has two effects:
- It pushed Volodymyr Zelensky to make a written proposal to the Russians in the framework of the Istanbul negotiations. It contains elements considered positive on which they are ready to discuss.
- It allows the Russians to strengthen their position in the Donbass in order to move on to Phase 2 and concentrate their efforts on the objective of "demilitarization". Having now the superiority in its decisive area of operation, Russia can withdraw its troops from the Kiev sector in order to regroup its forces in the Donbass.

Having received Zelensky's proposal, Russia can pass this withdrawal off as a gesture of goodwill. For its part, Kiev passes this withdrawal off as a victory - which is, so to speak, a good thing - but which also has a perverse effect, because the West sees it as a tangible sign of an announced defeat. This encourages them to push Zelensky to withdraw his proposal and to provide him with even more weapons, which will lead to the death of thousands of Ukrainian soldiers, without improving the military situation.

4.5.2.2. The role of aviation

On February 21, 2023, on *France 5*, General Patrick Dutatre declared that the Russians did not know how to use aviation, noting that the air force was not very present in the Ukrainian sky compared to Western actions in the Middle East. He illustrates the fault of the French military - already seen in 1940 - who do not imagine that the adversary can have a different approach to operations. He has understood absolutely nothing.

At the beginning of their offensive, the Russians destroyed the bulk of the Ukrainian air defense in a few minutes, the infrastructure of the military aviation and most of the aircraft.

The problem is that unlike the West, the Russians are not seeking to invade or occupy Ukraine, but to destroy the military potential threatening the populations of the Donbass. In the Middle East, the West wanted to push into the depths of opposing territories, so they needed

---

461. "Russia no longer requesting Ukraine be 'denazified' as part of ceasefire talks," Financial Times, March 28, 2022 (https://www.businessinsider.com/russia-nazi-demand-for-ukraine-dropped-in-ceasefire-talks-2022-3?r=US&IR=T)

an "umbrella". This is not the case with the Russians, who can accomplish their mission without exposing their air assets.

Moreover, as can be seen in Bakhmut, the fighting often takes place at very close range, offering few advantages over artillery. During the strike campaigns conducted by Russia in the depths of Ukraine after the Kerch Bridge attack, missiles were able to reach the targets without endangering Russian pilots.

4.6. Russian failure or success?

Success (or failure) is determined by the achievement (or non-achievement) of the set objectives. The Western discourse on Russia's repeated failures is based almost exclusively on objectives that were never formulated by Russia, but by us! Thus, it is easy to claim that Russia has not achieved them.

So it is with Kiev, which the Americans had designated as a target for Russia, in order to overthrow the Ukrainian government and replace it. Why and by whom? Nobody knows[462]. On March 2, 2022, on *RTS*, Alexandre Vautravers, a Swiss military expert, stated that "*if Kiev has not fallen in the next 48 hours, we will see a 'rotting' of hostilities*"[463]. But our "experts" insist on seeing this as a failure. In May 2022, still on RTS, Claude Wild, the Swiss ambassador in Kiev, declared that the Russians had "*lost the battle of Kiev*"[464].

However, the Russians never declared their intention to take the city and never deployed the necessary forces to do so. They only deployed 20,000-22,000 troops in this sector, while the city was defended by about 60,000 men. Recall that in 1945, in Berlin - then defended by 45,000

---

462. "War in Ukraine: According to the Pentagon, the Russians are ready to take Kiev to 'decapitate' the power there", *20 Minutes.fr/AFP*, February 25, 2022 (https://www.20minutes.fr/monde/3242027-20220225-guerre-ukraine-selon-pentagone-russes-prets-prendre-kiev-decapiter-pouvoir)
463. "Alexandre Vautravers: 'Russia has a weapon just as cruel as the chemical weapon'", *RTS.ch*, March 2, 2022 (https://www.rts.ch/info/monde/12906989-alexandre-vautravers-la-russie-dispose-dune-arme-tout-aussi-cruelle-que-larme-chimique.html)
464. "'No one would have bet a franc on such resistance,' says Swiss ambassador to Ukraine", *RTS Info*, May 24, 2022 (https://www.rts.ch/info/monde/13121067-personne-naurait-parie-un-franc-sur-une-telle-resistance-estime-lambassadeur-suisse-en-ukraine.html)

men - the Soviets attacked the city with 1.5 million men. So there was never a "Battle of Kiev".

The Russian presence around Kiev had two objectives: to fix Ukrainian troops away from the Donbass and to create pressure for negotiations. Both objectives were achieved and by February 25 Zelensky was ready to negotiate with Russia. It was the European Union, by supplying arms, and the neo-Nazi elements in Zelensky's entourage that scuppered the first negotiations in Gomel.

The West did not want to understand what happened, but judged the situation according to what they would have done themselves by choosing the scenario that best supported their discourse. They perceive Russia as the enemy they would like it to be, not as it is. Deliberately or not, our diplomats and journalists have distorted the perception of Western governments and caused unnecessary Ukrainian deaths.

Similarly, our "experts" predicted that Vladimir Putin wanted to make a spectacular and victorious statement for May 9, 2022, the anniversary of the 1945 victory[465], and then for February 24, 2023, the anniversary of the beginning of the SVO... and nothing happened.

In reality, Vladimir Putin never said that he wanted to take Kiev, let alone take it in two days. He never said he wanted to overthrow President Zelensky. He never said that he wanted to take over the whole Ukraine[466]. He never said he was aiming for a victory on May 9. He never said that he wanted to announce this victory at the May 9 parade. He never said that he wanted to "declare war" on May 9 so that he could trigger a general mobilization[467].

Our "journalists" do not analyze anything: they invent! They only project their fantasies, and their prejudices, without any factual analysis.

The "military experts" who parade on our television sets seem to have forgotten what a second lieutenant should know: "Know your enemy!"... And not as we would like him to be, but as he is!

A typical example is the hearing of Colonel Michel Goya by a commission of the French Senate on the lessons of the war in Ukraine. Without any knowledge of Russian military doctrine or the functioning of the Atlantic

---

465. https://www.rts.ch/emissions/infrarouge/13079683-guerre-en-ukraine-la-russie-dans-limpasse.html
466. https://www.rts.ch/play/tv/redirect/detail/13086647?startTime=790
467. https://www.rts.ch/info/monde/13066001-poutine-prendratil-le-risque-de-declarer-la-mobilisation-generale-le-9-mai.html

Alliance, he analyzed the war according to what a French soldier would do! His approach consists in thinking that the war can only be conducted in a French logic. He is making the same mistake as his predecessors in 1914, in 1940 with the terrorist threat in 2015-2016 and in the Sahel. One can even be surprised by the lack of hindsight and the mediocre level of knowledge of the senators who hear our "expert".

Whatever the conflict, each side tends to promote a favorable image of itself and to denigrate its opponent. Ukraine thus has a war communication with which it seeks to minimize its mistakes and maximize those of the Russians. This is a good thing. The problem is that by wanting to support Ukraine we have also adopted its communication and our media have forced us to see the conflict in the same way. There is a perverse effect here, by adopting its way of seeing we helped it to confirm its mistakes and it could not correct them. That is why we observe since 2014, systematically the same defects of the Ukrainian conduct.

Already in 2014-2015, it could be seen that the Ukrainians applied "Western-style" schemes, completely unsuited to the circumstances, against an opponent more imaginative, more flexible and with lighter driving structures. The same phenomenon is repeated today. Finally, the partial vision of the battlefield given by our media has made us incapable of helping the Ukrainian leadership to make the right decisions. It has led us to believe that the obvious strategic objective was Kiev, that "demilitarization" was aimed at Ukraine's membership in NATO, and that "denazification" was aimed at overthrowing Zelensky.

You don't win a war with prejudice: you lose it, and that's what's happening. The Russian coalition has never been "at bay" or "stopped" by a heroic popular resistance: it has simply not done what was expected of it! We did not want to listen to what Vladimir Putin explained to us very clearly. This is why we (i.e. our media and politicians) have thus become - *volens nolens* - the main architects of the Ukrainian defeat that is taking shape. Paradoxically, it is probably because of a few self-proclaimed experts and occasional strategists of our television sets that Ukraine is in this situation today!

In January 2023, the RAND Corporation[468] released a report that found that the conflict in Ukraine was not working to the advantage of either

---

468. Samuel Charap & Miranda Priebe, "Avoiding a Long War," *RAND Corporation*, January 2023 (https://www.rand.org/pubs/perspectives/PEA2510-1.html)

Ukraine or the United States, and that a prolonged war would only exacerbate this trend.

4.7. The role of "volunteers"

The Ukrainian conflict reveals the role of volunteers in combat. It is important here to distinguish between volunteers who enlist as individuals, often with no prior experience, and members of private military companies (PMCs), who are often seasoned combatants.

4.7.1. Individual volunteers

Individual volunteers are not a new phenomenon in Ukraine. As early as 2014, the Ukrainian press had revealed the presence of Russian volunteers to help the autonomists in Donbass. Our media immediately saw the hand of Vladimir Putin in this, but on the eve of the signing of the Minsk agreements, the head of the Ukrainian General Staff declared that there were no Russian regular troops in the Donbass[469]. For his part, the head of the Ukrainian SBU confirmed 9 months later that only 56 individual Russian fighters had been observed in the Donbass[470].

These Russian volunteers were far from the hardened fighters that Russia would have sent if it had sought to influence the fighting in the Donbass in this way. They were clearly young people excited by adventure, but lacking the necessary skills and maturity. Later, Russian veterans joined the Donbass militia, with combat experience in Syria and came up with the idea of creating a private militia, which will become "Wagner."

In 2022, Ukraine will make the same observation with volunteers pouring in from all over Europe. The Ukrainian government announces with great pomp the creation of an *International Legion for the Defense of*

---

469. https://www.dw.com/uk/генштаб-україна-не-воює-з-російськими-регулярними-військами/a-18225044
470. https://www.kyivpost.com/article/content/war-against-ukraine/sbu-registers-involvement-of-56-russian-in-military-actions-against-ukraine-since-military-conflict-in-eastern-ukraien-unfolded-399718.html

Ukraine (LIDU)[471]. It quickly gathers thousands of fighters from all over the world, but their quality is globally bad.

On March 8, 2022, RTBF praises the action of a Belgian volunteer who leaves for Ukraine, and shows us, on the wall of his room, a poster of the *Corps Franc Wallonie* (the Belgian volunteers of the 3rd Reich) and of the *National-Anarchist Movement* (NAM), a radical far-right organization. No doubt one of these "democrats" glorified by the Swiss politician Claude Ruey on his Facebook account! Finally, the democratic ideal of our Belgian volunteer is not impermeable, because he will return eleven days later, without even having been on the ground, shaken by the Russian strike on the base of Yavoriv...[472]

As early as August 2022, the *Kiyv Independent* noted that the International Legion was poorly commanded, with volunteers behaving in a mafia-like manner and launching their volunteers into suicide actions. Military personnel have complained about the crimes committed by foreign volunteers who have come to "break the Russian"[473].

Too young, with no military experience and ill-equipped[474], these volunteers were used as "cannon fodder," as a young British volunteer reported to the *Times of London*[475]. His words were confirmed by many American and Canadian volunteers, who described the disastrous state of the conduct and commitment of these units, often commanded by opportunists with no real experience.

---

471. https://www.president.gov.ua/news/zvernennya-do-gromadyan-inozemnih-derzhav-yaki-pragnut-dopom-73213?ref=kyivindependent.com
472. Arnaud Farr, "La moitié des volontaires partis en Ukraine est rentrée en Belgique : 'On ne voulait pas servir de chair à canon inutilement'", la DH, March 25, 2022 (https://www.dhnet.be/actu/belgique/2022/03/25/la-moitie-des-volontaires-partis-en-ukraine-est-rentree-en-belgique-on-ne-voulait-pas-servir-de-chair-a-canon-inutilement-OG7FSX7WHJAAFHLKLJIBSLDFZE/)
473. Anna Myroniuk & Alexander Khrebet, "Suicide missions, abuse, physical threats: International Legion fighters speak out against leadership's misconduct," *The Kiyv Independent*, August 17, 2022 (https://kyivindependent.com/suicide-missions-abuse-physical-threats-international-legion-fighters-speak-out-against-leaderships-misconduct/)
474. Susie Blann & Elaine Ganley, "Foreign fighters are flocking to Ukraine, where they're searching for weapons and risk being 'cannon fodder,'" *Associated Press/Business Insider*, March 18, 2022 (https://www.businessinsider.com/foreign-fighters-in-ukraine-searching-for-weapons-and-feeling-exposed-2022-3?r=US&IR=T)
475. Debbie White, "Britons fight and die like cannon-fodder in Ukraine, says teenage volunteer," *The Times*, June 1st, 2022 (https://www.thetimes.co.uk/article/dozens-of-british-fighters-thought-to-have-died-amid-ukrainian-foreign-legion-mayhem-8skt76nkw)

4.7.2. Private Military Companies (PMC)

The use of private military companies (PMCs) in war zones is not new. In Iraq, the United States employed up to 100,000 "mercenaries" from 100 PMCs. In Afghanistan, the U.S. Embassy in Kabul was guarded by "mercenaries" and not U.S. military personnel.

Even in Ukraine, CMP's involvement is longstanding. In 2014, to help the Maidan "democratic movement," the German magazine *Der Spiegel* had already mentioned the presence of mercenaries from the firm *Academi* (formerly *Blackwater*, of sinister memory in Iraq and Afghanistan)[476]. The *Bundesnachrichtendienst* (BND) had apparently informed the German government and - at the time at NATO - I had informed a Swiss ambassador to the OSCE, but the information remained a dead letter...

The battle of Bakhmout reveals a formation which was not unknown, but whose fighting value was not really known: the "Wagner".

Our media portrays Wagner's "musicians" as incapable and poorly trained. But this is not the opinion of the *Wall Street Journal*, and of a British volunteer in the Ukrainian forces.

Symbols for Wagner units

Figure 47 - Left: Wagner formation headquarters emblem; Middle: Wagner emblem that appears on their flag; Right: distinctive shoulder badge.

Initially a security company, the Wagner organization in Ukraine has become the equivalent of the Foreign Legion in France. Its soldiers are generally former members of the special forces, often with previous operational experience with the Russian or foreign armed forces. One

---

476. "Ukrainische Armee bekommt offenbar Unterstützung von US-Söldnern," Der Spiegel, May 11, 2014 (https://www.spiegel.de/politik/ausland/ukraine-krise-400-us-soeldner-von-academi-kaempfen-gegen-separatisten-a-968745.html)

can observe the same spirit that one finds among the elite units I have been in contact with: a kind of pride in exposing one's life in combat.

No doubt the "musicians" of Wagner have had significant losses in the fighting in Donbass. But they are effective and have no equivalent on the other side…

4.8. The myth of the role of Western armaments in Ukraine

In February 2022, Ukraine was preparing to launch an operation against the Donbass, with the aim of regaining control of it in order to retake Crimea later, in accordance with the decree of March 24, 2021 of Volodymyr Zelensky. As explained by Oleksei Arestovich in March 2019, Ukraine could not enter NATO as long as the conflict in Donbass was open, and it needed to obtain a defeat of Russia to have that its membership could be considered. But this defeat could only be obtained with a total mobilization of the West with sanctions and massive deliveries of arms.

The problem is that the West, which had armed, educated and trained the Ukrainian army since 2014, thought that with the application of massive sanctions, victory would be achieved quickly and unconditionally.

The objective of defeating Russia will therefore remain the main objective of Zelensky and the Americans throughout the conflict. This explains the statement of Oleksei Reznikov, Ukrainian Minister of Defense, on December 31, 2022, on his Twitter account[477]:

> *At the NATO summit in Madrid in June 2022, it was made clear that over the next decade, the main threat to the alliance would be the Russian Federation. Today, Ukraine is facing this threat. Today we are fulfilling NATO's mission. They are not shedding their blood. We shed ours. That's why they must provide us with weapons…*

Here he is only clarifying what Arestovich said in March 2019. Therefore, Reznikov also states that Ukraine is now part of NATO: this conflict and

---

477. https://twitter.com/i/status/1611458894055833600

Ukraine's sacrifice to destroy the Alliance's hereditary enemy, is the key to its membership in NATO.

4.8.1. Western investment

Between the start of the Russian operation in Ukraine and November 23, 2022, the United States provided approximately $21.8 billion in security assistance to *"help Ukraine preserve its territorial integrity, secure its borders, and improve interoperability with NATO*[478]*."* Of this amount, the Biden administration has committed more than $19 billion in security assistance since the start of the 2022 war.

On February 23, 2023, one year after the start of the SVO, *Statista*'s tally of U.S. military aid to Ukraine shows that in one year it has surpassed in value the military aid to Afghanistan between 2001 and 2021[479]!

At the beginning of November 2022, Germany would like to transfer mobile anti-aircraft systems GEPARD, mounted on LEOPARD 1 chassis, to Ukraine. The problem is that this system is obsolete for service in the Bundeswehr and it has no more ammunition. This ammunition is manufactured in Switzerland. However, Swiss law prohibits the export of war material to a country engaged in an open conflict. Oleksander Scherba, former Ukrainian ambassador to Austria, called Switzerland *"an asshole that watches its neighbor being killed without helping when it could"*[480]. One can understand his reaction perfectly well: he notes that Switzerland accepted without reacting that the Ukrainians of Donbass were killed for eight years, and that all of a sudden it starts to claim international law!...

The problem with arms shipments is the policy adopted by most arms exporting countries to have an end-user clause, which requires the country receiving the arms not to transfer or use them for purposes contrary to their original purpose. These rules are in force within the OSCE, the EU and the member countries of the *Wassenaar Arrangement on Export Controls for Conventional Arms and Dual-Use Goods and Technologies* (WA). Thus, when an "expert" on RTS states that this is a

---

478. "U.S. Security Assistance to Ukraine," *Congressional Research Service*, January 26, 2023 (https://crsreports.congress.gov/product/pdf/IF/IF12040)
479. Martin Armstrong, "Ukraine: U.S. Military Aid Exceeds Costs of Afghanistan," Statista, February 23, 2023 (https://www.statista.com/chart/29375/us-military-aid-to-ukraine-compared-to-past-wars/)
480. https://www.20min.ch/fr/story/pour-lui-la-suisse-est-un-trou-du-cul-qui-regarde-son-voisin-se-faire-tuer-400605828868

problem linked to Switzerland's neutrality, this is incorrect. In reality, it is a rule that has been widely adopted in the West to prevent arms from being re-exported or used for purposes contrary to the security policy objectives of the exporting country. For example, the United States objected to Canada sending 105 Grizzly armoured personnel carriers to the African Union peacekeeping mission in Darfur because their engines were American-made. But peace in Darfur was clearly not a U.S. objective at that point!

4.8.2. An industrial war

The particularity of this conflict is that since the summer of 2022, it has placed Russian and Western industrial capabilities in direct competition. After the destruction of most of the Ukrainian military capabilities in May 2022, the West sought to replace the destroyed equipment.

At first, they collected old Eastern European equipment dating from the Cold War and placed it in a cocoon. But these materials became rare. Often badly maintained, they were hardly usable, but were nevertheless provided to the Ukrainians, for lack of anything better.

In a second phase, the West then supplied obsolete Western equipment from their own reserves. This is the case of the MiG-29 fighters supplied by Poland and Slovakia, which are apparently hardly in working order and which the Ukrainians can only use to "cannibalize" their own damaged aircraft[481].

In a third phase, the Westerners had to take equipment from their own forces. This is the case of the French CAESAR guns, the Estonian artillery, or the British CHALLENGER 2 battle tanks. This shows that the danger of a Russian attack on Europe is only a war rhetoric intended to create panic in our populations.

In a fourth stage, the West tried to produce the necessary materials for Ukraine and to supply it with just-in-time. But here again it is a failure. In March 2023, the European Union decided on a budget of 2 billion euros to finance munitions. One billion was to reimburse the countries that had drawn on their own stocks to support Ukraine, and one billion was

---

481. "Ukraine's top guns need new jets to win the war," *The Economist*, April 23, 2023 (https://www.economist.com/europe/2023/04/23/ukraines-top-guns-need-new-jets-to-win-the-war)

to mobilize European industrial resources to produce 1 million 155 mm shells for Ukraine in 12 months[482].

This sounds like a lot, but it is the equivalent of what Russia fires in 20-40 days! That's why Ukraine has requested 350,000 shells per month from the EU[483].

This phase highlights the inability of the West to sustain a prolonged logistical effort in a high-intensity war.

Western equipment cannot compete with the Russian ability to destroy them. On January 24, 2023, Estonia announced that it would donate all of its 155-mm howitzers, i.e. 24 FH-70s, and 122-mm D-30s of Soviet origin with their ammunition[484]. A week later, on January 31, France offered 12 CAESAR self-propelled howitzers in addition to the 18 it had already supplied to Ukraine[485], while Denmark gave Ukraine all of its 19 CAESAR pieces ordered from France. However, according to the *Moonofalabama* website, which compared these figures with official announcements by the General Staff, the Russian army destroyed 40 howitzers, 32 self-propelled howitzers and 8 multiple rocket launchers during the same week[486]. Although difficult to confirm, these figures tend to show that Western arms deliveries are barely sufficient to compensate for Ukrainian losses.

In fact, Western countries have largely underestimated Russia's capabilities. Their support for Ukraine has become more of a communication exercise than an effective aid. As we can see, they are ready to disarm their own arsenals to meet Ukrainian demand. For example, according to the *Financial Times*, a British member of parliament said that the British army could not last more than five days in the event of a war[487].

---

482. "Ukraine updates: EU agrees €2 billion ammo plan for Kyiv", *Deutsche Welle*, March 20, 2023 (https://www.dw.com/en/ukraine-updates-eu-agrees-2-billion-ammo-plan-for-kyiv/a-65045955)
483. "EU agrees 2-billion-euro ammunition plan for Ukraine," *France 24*, March 20, 2023 (https://www.france24.com/en/live-news/20230320-eu-hammers-out-2-bn-euro-ammunition-plan-for-ukraine)
484. Joe Saballa, "Estonia Sending All Its 155-mm Howitzers to Ukraine," *The Defense Post*, January 24, 2023 (https://www.thedefensepost.com/2023/01/24/estonia-sending-howitzers-ukraine/)
485. "France to supply twelve additional Caesar guns to Ukraine", *France 24*, January 31, 2023 (https://www.france24.com/fr/europe/20230131-en-direct-macron-reçoit-le-ministre-de-la-défense-ukrainien-kiev-réclame-des-avions-de-combat)
486. https://www.moonofalabama.org/2023/01/nato-continues-its-disarmament.html#more
487. George Parker & John-Paul Rathbone, "UK armed forces would last just 'five days' in a war, senior MP warns", *Financial Times*, February 10, 2023 (https://www.ft.com/content/4eb1af29-2491-458c-9f69-e065cba58bbb)

The problem is that the West does not have the capacity to wage war against Russia. Even the support for Ukraine is pushing the NATO countries into a precarious security situation. This shows that Western countries do not seriously consider Russia as a threat to Europe.

4.8.3. The Wunderwaffen

At the end of World War II, with the German army retreating on all fronts, Hitler and his personal staff continued to believe that the situation could be turned around through the use of new weapons. Germany was at the forefront of the development of new technologies and new weapons, which were thought to be "game-changers." Jet planes, missiles, new armored vehicles, these were later called "Wunderwaffen" ("Miracle Weapons"). But the German industry, under bombardment, was no longer able to ensure regular production, while human resources were dwindling. The Wunderwaffen did not prevent the defeat of the Third Reich. 80 years later, the Ukraine is experiencing the same thing as its masters.

By March 2022, as Russian-speaking coalition forces advanced into Ukraine, the Western discourse claimed that Russia was losing the war. The new weapons deployed by the Russian forces, notably the hypersonic missiles, were then christened "Wunderwaffen" by the extremist Western propaganda press, in order to present them as Russia's last resort in the face of an inevitable defeat[488].

Russian successes and the destruction of Ukrainian potential in the first hours of the special operation prompted the West to provide arms to Ukraine from the start. Thus, on February 28, three days after Zelensky called on Russia to negotiate and a process was initiated on the Belarusian border, the European Union urged the Ukrainian president to back down[489] and released 450 million euros in military aid[490].

The multi- and bilateral military aid provided to Ukraine since the beginning of the crisis is considerable: the United States has provided more than 44 billion dollars and the European Union 12 billion euros,

---

488. Volker Pabst, "Moskau zeigt auf seine 'Wunderwaffen'", *Neue Zürcher Zeitung*, March 20, 2022 (https://www.nzz.ch/international/russlands-wunderwaffe-erster-kampfeinsatz-von-hyperschall-rakete-ld.1675519)
489. https://eur-lex.europa.eu/legal-content/FR/TXT/PDF/?uri=CELEX:32022D0338
490. https://www.europarl.europa.eu/RegData/etudes/ATAG/2022/729292/EPRS_ATA(2022)729292_EN.pdf

while bilateral aid totals about 13 billion euros. Thus, in one year of conflict, the West has provided Ukraine with the equivalent of more than 11 times its 2020 military budget.

The record of Western arms supplies is mixed, to say the least. First of all, the weapons delivered have - for the most part - never been used in combat before. This is the case for the German anti-aircraft vehicle GEPARD and even the LEOPARD 2 tanks. Moreover, NATO instructors do not have the experience and knowledge to train Ukrainians to engage these weapons in high-intensity combat.

Major land weapons of Ukraine (2022)

	(1) Situation at 24.02.2022 (BBC)	(2) Russian equipment captured in 07.01.2023 (Oryx)	(3) Provided by the West to 06.01.2023	(1)+(2)+(3) Total as of 06.01.2023	Needs expressed by Zaloujny on 15.12.2022 (Economist)
Battle tanks	 987	533	590	2 110	300
Armored infantry vehicles	 831	928	447	2 206	600-700
Artillery pieces	 1818	194	>467	2 479	500
Multiple rocket launchers	-	52	46	98	

Figure 48 - Major equipment of the Ukrainian army

4.8.4. Training

An essential problem, but totally dodged by our media is the training of Ukrainian personnel. The destruction of the human military potential of the Ukrainian forces has resulted in the gradual disappearance of seasoned military personnel.

By 2023, it can be estimated that Western countries will train about 30-40,000 new Ukrainian military personnel. The problem is that almost no Western instructors have experience in high-intensity conflicts. Apparently, Ukrainian military personnel taken prisoner by the Russians have confided that the training provided by NATO countries is superficial and does not allow them to gain an advantage on the battlefield.

4.8.5. Drones

The use of drones on the battlefield is not new. Since the beginning of the Russian operation, Ukraine has used Turkish-made BAYRAKTAR drones. Although very efficient, these drones did not escape the formidable Russian anti-aircraft defense.

Drones in the Ukrainian theater

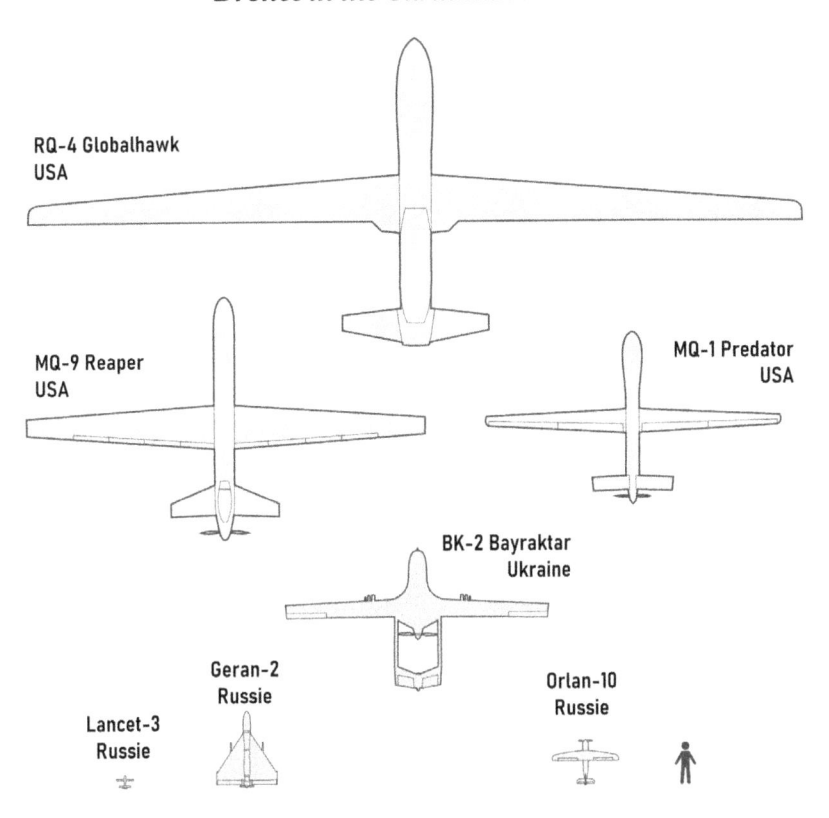

Figure 49 - Main UAV systems engaged in the Ukrainian theater.

4. Military considerations

4.8.5.1. Combat drones

The use of drones in combat is not new. The first prototype "aerial torpedo" dates back to 1918 (Kettering Bug), and observation or grenade-launching drones have been widely seen in the Middle East. But this is probably the first time drones have been used systematically and in established tactics at all levels of leadership.

A particularly important development is the systematic use of "small", inexpensive drones, which can be engaged en masse in order to saturate opposing defences, and which function as mini cruise missiles. These are known as "suicide drones". The Russians use in particular the GERAN-2 of Iranian origin and the LANCET-3 of Russian manufacture.

GERAN-2 has been widely reported in our media for several reasons. Firstly, it is said to originate from Iran, where it is produced under the name SHAHEED-136, which did not fail to strike a chord in 2022, when the country was in the grip of demonstrations. Second, it is an opportunity to say that Russia is running out of drones and has to go begging for them from its "Axis of Evil" allies. Third, it allows the West to accuse Iran of supporting Russia and to impose new sanctions on it[491].

It seems that Russia has purchased several hundred SHAHEED-136s to modify them for use in Ukraine. Information on these modifications remains contradictory, but it seems that the GERAN-2 has been equipped with a hardened satellite guidance system to resist electronic countermeasures. It is a sort of "mini-cruise missile", whose explosive charge has been improved. Its fibreglass hull makes it difficult to detect by radar. Its announced maximum range of 2,500 km is somewhat surprising and its practical range is probably more like 1,000 km.

The GERAN-2, which is made largely from commercially available components, is extremely economical and its destruction requires very expensive means, making it an attrition weapon par excellence. Its production cost is estimated at about 20,000 dollars, while the Ukrainians have to fight them with S-300 missiles of Soviet origin whose unit cost is estimated at 130,000 dollars or American NASAMS missiles

---

[491]. "Switzerland sanctions Iranian drone supply to Russia," *Swiss Government*, November 2, 2022 (https://www.admin.ch/gov/fr/accueil/documentation/communiques.msg-id-91102.html); Daphne Psaledakis & Arshad Mohammed, "New U.S. sanctions target supply of Iranian drones to Russia," *Reuters*, January 6, 2023 (https://www.reuters.com/business/aerospace-defense/us-targets-supply-iranian-drones-russia-new-sanctions-2023-01-06/)

at 500,000 dollars each. A Ukrainian pilot even sacrificed a MiG-29 to shoot down a GERAN-2[492]!

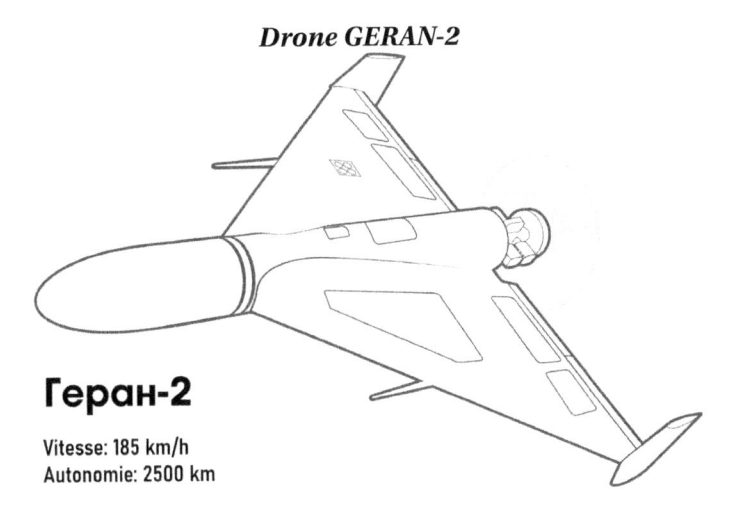

Drone GERAN-2

Геран-2

Vitesse: 185 km/h
Autonomie: 2500 km

Figure 50 - The GERAN-2 (Geranium) UAV is the Russian version of the SHAHEED-136 produced by Iran. Its guidance system has been modified to be invulnerable to electronic countermeasures.

Apparently, according to the Ukrainian General Staff, the Russian LANCET 1 and 3 drones have destroyed or damaged some 200 artillery pieces, mainly M777s. Silent, small and difficult to detect, they are especially effective at night.

In Ukraine, the Russian army works with the "Reconnaissance-Fire Complex" (*Razvedivatel'no-Ognevoï Kompleks - ROK*), which integrates combat systems at the tactical level, and the "Reconnaissance-Fire Complex" (*Razvedivatel'no-Udarnyy Kompleks - RUK*), at the operative level. Their principle is to integrate reconnaissance means with strike elements (artillery, missiles, aviation, airborne troops, special forces, etc.). It requires data transmission systems, which make it possible to compress the OODA (*Observe, Orient, Decide and Act*) loop, well known to the military, so as to react very quickly to the evolution

---

492. Girish Linganna, "Historic! A kamikaze drone downs a fighter aircraft, Ukrainian MiG-29 crashes trying to shoot an Iranian Shahed-136 drone," *Frontier India*, October 13, 2022 (https://frontierindia.com/historic-a-kamikaze-drone-downs-a-fighter-aircraft-ukrainian-mig-29-crashes-trying-to-shoot-an-iranian-shahed-136-drone/)

of the situation in the field. The concept had already started to be developed in Afghanistan. Today, with the help of technology, it has reached maturity.

Russian suicide drone LANCET-3

Ланцет - 3

Vitesse: 110-300 km/h
Autonomie: 40 km
Endurance: ~ 40 min

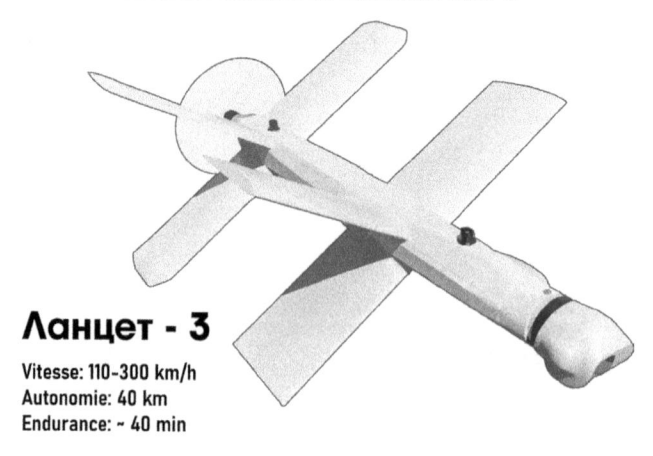

Figure 51 - One of the most effective drones of the Ukraine campaign. Produced by Kalashnikov, the Lancet is a cheap suicide drone that can provide information, before dropping on its target and destroying it with its 5-6 kg of explosives.

Drone KUB

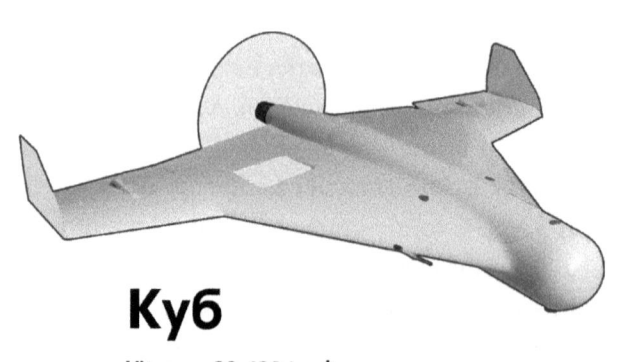

Куб

Vitesse: 80-130 km/h
Autonomie: 40 km
Endurance: ~ 30 min

Figure 52 - The Zala CUB drone is a drone used for the Reconnaissance-Response Complex (RUK).

In the context of the RUK, small, relatively undetectable reconnaissance UAVs such as the KUB provide a view of the battlefield and transmit in real time the coordinates of highly mobile systems such as the Ukrainian CAESAR or HIMARS systems.

4.8.6. "Smart" weapons

Soon, arms supplies to Ukraine exhausted Western potential. Eventually, it was sent weapons under development, such as the GBU-39 GLSDB flying bomb, which can be fired by M270 MLRS or M142 HIMARS multiple rocket launchers[493].

On March 28, 2023, the first GBU-39 bomb launched on Russian territory was intercepted by the anti-aircraft defence. It is a gliding bomb fixed on a propeller allowing its firing from HIMARS or MLRS multiple missile launchers. The radars of the Russian S-300 and S-400 anti-aircraft systems can detect a HIMARS missile at a distance of 80 km and a GLSDB at 30-40 km, given its smaller size. On the other hand, the speed of the GLSDB is three times lower than that of a HIMARS missile, which makes it easier to intercept.

GBU-39 Ground-Launched Small Diameter Bomb (GLSDB)

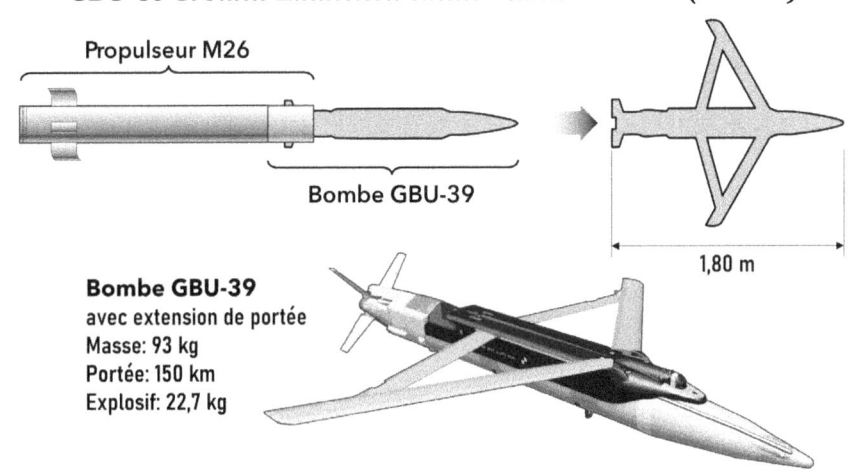

Figure 53 - The GLSDB from Boeing and Saab is still under development. However, it has already been deployed in the Ukrainian theater in March 2023, according to the Russian authorities. The M26 propellant pushes the bomb 32 km; then it detaches and glides to a total distance of 150 km.

---

493. David Axe, "Ukraine's New Rocket-Boosted Glide-Bombs Can Turn Around and Hit Targets on The Backs of Hills, 90 Miles Away," Forbes, February 3, 2023 (https://www.forbes.com/sites/davidaxe/2023/02/03/ukraines-new-rocket-boosted-glide-bombs-can-turn-around-and-hit-targets-on-the-backs-of-hills-90-miles-away/)

Since December 2022, the United States has been supplying Ukraine with JDAM-ER long-range guided bombs. These are essentially kits that can be adapted to aerial bombs, which thus become self-guided. But it is important to remember that they remain gravity bombs without a propulsion system. They are literally gliding bombs, which must be dropped from an altitude of 10-12 km to reach a distance of 80 km.

The JDAM-ER uses the GPS signal to navigate to its target. But secret documents "leaked" in April 2023 indicate that they malfunction and are susceptible to Russian jamming[494]. Furthermore, these bombs hover at a relatively modest speed and are vulnerable to Russian PANTSIR-SM anti-aircraft systems, which can hit very small targets such as drones or HIMARS missiles.

Joint Direct Attack Munition - Extended Range *(JDAM-ER)*

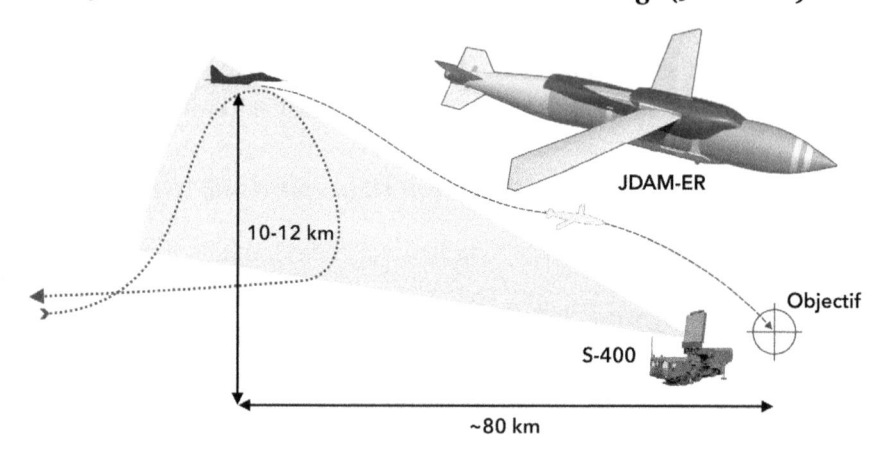

Figure 54 - The JDAM-ER smart glider bomb must be dropped at very high altitude in order to reach a maximum distance of 80 km. But this means that the Ukrainian MiG-29, Su-27 and Su-24 aircraft must expose themselves to the fire of Russian S-300V4 or S-400 missiles. In order to minimize their risk, they have to climb very quickly to the drop altitude, before ducking as quickly as possible. But then they are vulnerable to the TOR-M2 and BUK-M3 systems which lock on to their target more quickly.

---

494. Ellie Cook, "Russian Glider Bombs Spark New Air Defence Woes for Ukraine," *Newsweek*, April 13, 2023 (https://www.newsweek.com/russia-glider-bombs-ukraine-air-defense-jdams-1794155)

The Russians have also developed a number of systems equivalent to those delivered to Ukraine. This is the case of the GROM, which is the equivalent of the JDAM-ER.

Russian gliding bomb GROM

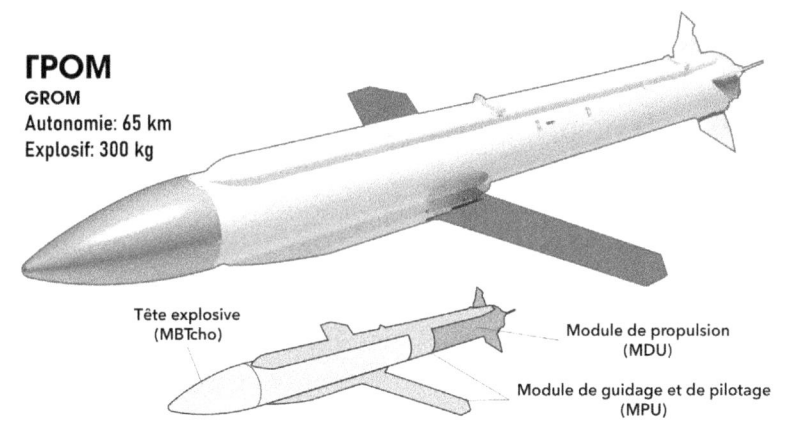

Figure 55 - The GROM bomb is the Russian equivalent of the American JDAM-ER bomb. It is a gravity bomb with retractable wings and a guidance mechanism.

The Russians have found that to combat heavily protected or buried targets, aerial bombs are more effective (and probably less costly) than missiles. They have therefore developed a whole line of "intelligent" gliding bombs, which can be directed autonomously on their target.

But for that, their planes must be able to fly freely in the Ukrainian sky. It was therefore necessary to exhaust Ukraine's anti-aircraft capabilities, in order to allow bombing missions on the front line. This is partly the reason for the campaign of strikes against the country's electrical infrastructure from October 2022. Thanks to our "experts" who found every possible explanation except the right one, the Russian strategy worked. In April 2023, Yuriy Ignat, a spokesman for the Ukrainian air force, noted that the Russians had launched a large-scale bombing campaign *"with a perceptible effect,"* and that Ukrainian anti-aircraft capabilities were insufficient to respond[495].

---

495. Ellie Cook, "Russian Glider Bombs Spark New Air Defence Woes for Ukraine," *Newsweek*, April 13, 2023 (https://www.newsweek.com/russia-glider-bombs-ukraine-air-defense-jdams-1794155)

This explains the apparent decrease in Russian artillery fire in the Donbass since March 2023. The Russian air force is much freer to engage its FAB-500[496] bombs and especially its UPAB-1500B glide bombs. First introduced in 2019, the UPAB-1500B can be engaged from a distance of 40 km, out of range of tactical anti-aircraft systems. Designed after the fighting in Mariupol to fight protected targets, these bombs were used in Avdiivka and Bakhmut.

UPAB-1500B self-guided bomb

Figure 56 - Designed to fight heavily protected infantry, the UPAB-1500B bomb can be dropped out of the range of Ukrainian anti-aircraft defense and can autonomously and accurately direct itself at its target.

4.8.7. Hypersonic weapons

Hypersonic missiles have entered the Ukrainian conflict in force. Their importance in the Ukrainian theater is less important than the change in the balance of power between Russia and the West that they announce. From the very first days of the intervention, KINJAL missiles hit Ukrainian logistic sites. It is likely that at this stage the Russians used them both to test them in combat conditions and to send a signal to the West. Knowing that the West tends to act more on narrative than risk analysis, they certainly meant to.

---

496. Andrew Stanton, "Ukraine Issues Warning About New Modified Russian FAB-500 Aerial Bombs," *Newsweek*, April 8, 2023 (https://www.newsweek.com/ukraine-issues-warning-about-new-modified-russian-fab-500-aerial-bombs-1793298)

The hypersonic missile KINJAL Kh-47M2

Кинжал Х-47М2

Vitesse: Mach 10-12 (~12 500 km/h)
Autonomie: 1'500-2'000 km

1 m

8 m

Figure 57 - The KINJAL hypersonic missile.

While our media tells us all day long that Russia has no capacity for technological development, it has succeeded in developing a whole range of hypersonic missiles (with speeds of 10,000 to 30,000 km/h). Thus, Russia has begun to deploy ZIRCON hypersonic missiles on its ships[497]. Since they are difficult to intercept, these missiles pose a considerable threat to American aircraft carriers, in other words to American force projection capability.

However, the United States has been unable to develop such systems. In March 2023, Lockheed-Martin, which was working on a hypersonic missile as part of the *Air-Launched Rapid Response Weapon* (ARRW) project, abandoned the project after several unsuccessful tests[498]. In other words, Russia has a technological advantage over Western countries and there is no indication that sanctions have affected the production of these weapons.

---

497. Brad Lendon & Anna Chernova, "Putin deploys Russian warship with Zircon hypersonic missile, TASS says," *CNN*, January 5, 2023 (https://edition.cnn.com/2023/01/05/europe/russia-warship-hypersonic-missile-deployed-intl-hnk-ml/index.html)
498. Stephen Losey, "US Air Force drops Lockheed hypersonic missile after failed tests," *Defense News*, March 30, 2023 (https://www.defensenews.com/air/2023/03/30/us-air-force-drops-lockheed-hypersonic-missile-after-failed-tests/)

The hypersonic missile ZIRKON

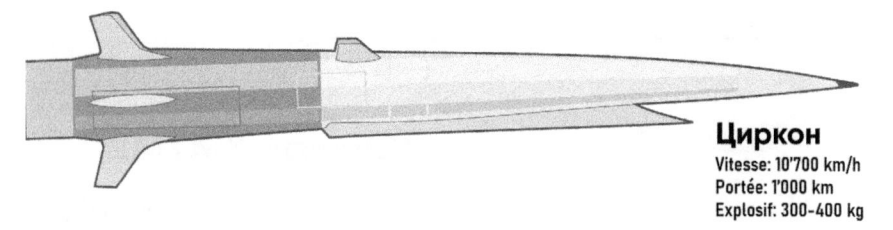

Циркон
Vitesse: 10'700 km/h
Portée: 1'000 km
Explosif: 300-400 kg

Figure 58 - The ZIRKON hypersonic missile does not seem to have been used during the conflict in Ukraine, but it illustrates Russia's technological advance over the West.

4.8.8. Combat tanks

4.8.8.1. An insufficient number

Although our media only talk about Russian defeats and losses, it is clear that by the spring of 2023, Ukraine's tank potential has shrunk to a trickle. Thus, in February 2022, Ukraine had some 800 T-64 tanks and a hundred T-72 tanks. In 2022, Eastern European countries provided Ukraine with about 400 T-72 tanks from their stocks.

Yet classified U.S. documents "leaked" in early 2023 show that Ukraine has only 43 T-64s and 38 T-72s for its major decisive offensive in the spring of 2023. Ukraine probably has more T-64 and T-72 tanks, but apparently not enough to maintain logistical consistency for a major operation.

If we add up the number of tanks that Ukraine had at its disposal on February 24, 2022, those that it captured according to the Oryx site (specially created by the West at the beginning of the Russian operation under the title "Attack on Europe"!)[499], and those officially delivered in 2022, Ukraine would have had more than 2,000 battle tanks. Under these conditions, it is difficult to see how the few LEOPARD 2 tanks delivered in the spring of 2023 could change the situation...

---

499. "Attack On Europe: Documenting Russian Equipment Losses During The 2022 Russian Invasion Of Ukraine," *Oryx*, February 24, 2022 (https://www.oryxspioenkop.com/2022/02/attack-on-europe-documenting-equipment.html)

In February 2022, with about 80 BTGs at the beginning of its operation according to the Pentagon[500], Russia had only about 800-1000 battle tanks. Moreover, if our media and the Ukrainians are to be believed, these tanks would have been obsolete and of lower quality.

However, Russian forces are advancing and from the spring of 2022, the Ukrainians are asking the West for heavy weapons. In 2022, NATO countries provided them with more than 530 tanks of Soviet origin, left in the inventories of Eastern European countries. Although obsolete, this equipment had the advantage of being very similar to the equipment the Ukrainians had lost, thus allowing for rapid deployment.

Number of battle tanks of the Ukrainian army

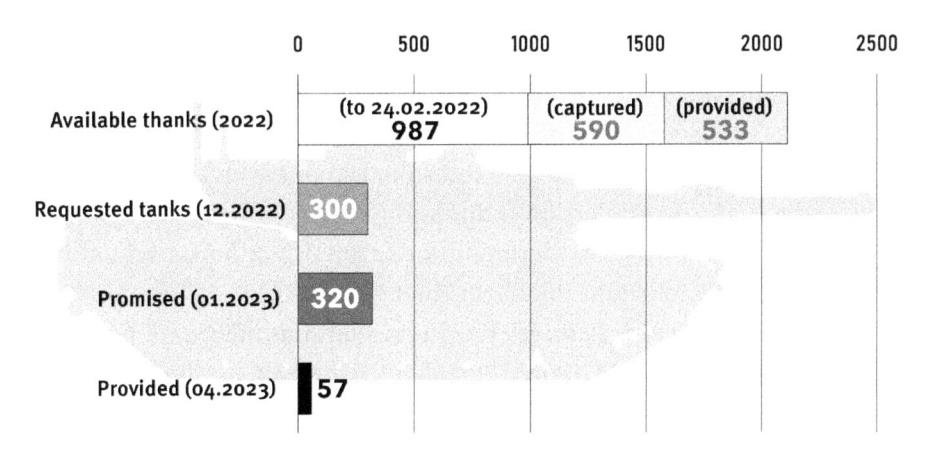

Available thanks (2022)	(to 24.02.2022) 987 — (captured) 590 — (provided) 533
Requested tanks (12.2022)	300
Promised (01.2023)	320
Provided (04.2023)	57

Figure 59 - Comparison of the number of battle tanks in the Ukrainian army and the expressed needs for 2023. The total number of tanks available in 2022 is based on Ukrainian government statements. By downplaying their losses, the Ukrainians have distorted the picture of the conflict, which makes the requirements expressed at the end of 2022 misunderstood in public opinion.

4.8.8.2. Western deliveries

In mid-December 2022, General Valeriy Zaloujny, head of the Ukrainian forces, said in a high-profile interview with *The Economist* that he needed 300 battle tanks, 500-600 armoured infantry and 500 new

---

500. "Senior Defense Official Holds a Background Briefing, April 18, 2022," defense.gov, April 18, 2022 (https://www.defense.gov/News/Transcripts/Transcript/Article/3002867/senior-defense-official-holds-a-background-briefing-april-18-2022/)

artillery pieces[501]. For his part, Mikhailo Podolyak, Ukraine's Minister of Defence, had placed American M1 ABRAMS tanks on his "Christmas list", posted on Twitter[502].

It was with this "shopping list" that Zelensky went to Washington, with the goal of obtaining "*more powerful weapons to enhance Ukraine's ability to launch major offensives against entrenched Russian forces*" in 2023. For its part, the Biden administration wanted to "*discuss how [Zelensky] views diplomacy. Where he stands, and what he needs to do to make sure that Kiev is in the strongest possible position so that we can expedite a negotiation.*"

At this stage, the United States, unlike the Europeans, is seeking to promote a negotiation process. It therefore refused to supply ABRAMS tanks. To justify their decision, the Americans say that these tanks are "*too difficult to maintain and too complex to operate*", as the *Washington Post* explains, and that Ukraine "*already has enough* tanks"[503]. As the major daily noted, Zelensky was unable to convince his ally who had pushed him into the conflict. He will only return to Ukraine with a PATRIOT air defense system and artillery ammunition.

Zelensky then turned to Germany for LEOPARD 2 tanks. While the Americans were reluctant to deliver their M1 ABRAMS to Ukraine, the *Frankfurter Allgemeine Zeitung* (FAZ) revealed that they were pushing Germany to supply LEOPARD 2 tanks[504]. However, Chancellor Olaf Scholz is only willing to deliver them if the United States agrees to supply ABRAMS. At first, an American politician suggested that the United States deliver a single M1 tank in order to provoke the German decision[505]! Illustration of the way Americans perceive their allies.

---

501. https://www.economist.com/zaluzhny-transcript
502. https://twitter.com/Podolyak_M/status/1601146941186117632
503. Karen DeYoung & Missy Ryan, "Amid a show of unity, Zelensky and Biden differ on some war needs," The Washington Post, December 21, 2022 (https://www.washingtonpost.com/national-security/2022/12/21/zelensky-biden-weapons-ukraine-patriots/)
504. https://www.faz.net/aktuell/politik/inland/ukraine-usa-ueberlaesst-deutschland-die-entscheidung-ueber-leopard-2-18516545.html; "US encourages German government to deliver Leopard 2 tanks to Ukraine," *Army Recognition*, December 9, 2022 (https://www.armyrecognition.com/defense_news_december_2022_global_security_army_industry/us_encourages_german_government_to_deliver_leopard_2_tanks_to_ukraine.html)
505. Tal Axelrod, "McCaul calls on US to send 'just one' Abrams tank to Ukraine to spur European support," *abc news*, January 22, 2023 (https://abcnews.go.com/Politics/mccaul-calls-us-send-abrams-tank-ukraine-spur/story?id=96584865)

The sequel was revealed by the *Washington Post* and was hardly reported by the European press[506]. And for good reason!

Anthony Blinken then imagined a scenario worthy of what he was. The United States declared that it would supply 31 M1 battle tanks, in order to obtain Germany's consent. As expected, Scholz allowed Poland to re-export LEOPARD tanks and promised to supply them to Ukraine.

But no sooner has Germany given its approval than the United States comes back and says that its M1s contain technology that must not fall into Russian hands and that the tanks cannot be delivered immediately. In fact, they will be new tanks built especially for Ukraine[507], with inferior protection (because the depleted uranium armor of the American version is classified), which can only be delivered in a year[508] !

In other words, the United States has "rolled Scholz in the flour"! This shows the state of relations between NATO members. We already know that it was a NATO member country that destroyed the Nord Stream gas pipelines; it is Germany that is paying the price of the war waged by the Americans against Russia… The Americans are right: if we have found a "sucker" we might as well exploit it, especially if the German people accept it without question! Each country is responsible for its own destiny. This applies to the Ukrainians, as it does to the Germans.

Charity begins at home! The Westerners do not want to give their most recent and technologically advanced equipment, because they fear that the Russians will get their hands on it.

We can therefore see the reappearance near the front line of vehicles that were largely obsolete for this conflict, such as the American M113 troop carrier, the French VAB or the American M2/3 BRADLEY, whose design was so chaotic that it was turned into a comedy ("*The Pentagon* Wars"[509]).

---

506. Karen DeYoung, Dan Lamothe & Loveday Morris, "Short on time, Biden sought new Ukraine tank plan to break stalemate," *The Washington Post*, January 28, 2023 (https://www.washingtonpost.com/national-security/2023/01/28/inside-story-biden-ukraine-tanks/)
507. "Ukraine will receive Abrams no earlier than the end of 2023," *Militarnyy*, January 29, 2023 (https://mil.in.ua/en/news/ukraine-will-receive-abrams-no-earlier-than-the-end-of-2023/), Lara Seligman, Paul McLeary and Lee Hudson, "U.S. to send Ukraine more advanced Abrams tanks - but no secret armor," *Politico*, January 26, 2023 (https://www.politico.com/news/2023/01/26/us-sends-ukraine-advanced-abrams-tanks-00079648)
508. David Axe, "The Tungsten M-1-How Ukraine's Tanks Will Differ from America's," *Forbes*, January 27, 2023 (https://www.forbes.com/sites/davidaxe/2023/01/27/the-tungsten-m-1-how-ukraines-tanks-will-differ-from-americas/)
509. https://en.wikipedia.org/wiki/The_Pentagon_Wars

Thus, the British fear that the Chobham armour of their CHALLENGER 2 tanks could interest the Russians. After long discussions, the government agreed to deliver 14 of them, provided that the Ukrainians do everything possible to prevent the Russians from capturing them. They thus impose constraints to the Ukrainians. In particular, the CHALLENGERs cannot be used in a sector where the front line threatens to be breached by the Russians[510]. As described by a British official[511]:

> *The first step is to train and work with mission planners to ensure that CHALLENGERS are not used in scenarios where they think collapse is a realistic possibility.*
> *The second step is to ensure, at the tactical level, that the Ukrainians are trained to recover a tank under enemy fire. They certainly do not lack courage.*
> *Other extreme options are being considered, including the use of private military contractors to recover damaged tanks.*

Ukraine will therefore receive M88 armored recovery vehicles specially designed to recover armored tanks in combat condition[512].

As for the LEOPARD 2A4 tanks just received, the Ukrainians undertook to reinforce them with additional reactive armor…

According to Ukrainian sources, it seems that Zelensky is in talks with Western countries to use these tanks in the role for which they were designed.

Thus, not only do these materials require logistics for which Ukraine is not prepared, but each piece of equipment requires its own logistics chain, with the additional requirement of preventing these weapons from falling into the possession of the Russians!

---

510. Inder Singh Bisht, "UK Planning to Avoid Challenger Tank from Falling into Russian Hands," *The Defense Post*, January 30, 2023 (https://www.thedefensepost.com/2023/01/30/uk-challenger-tank-russian/)
511. Jerome Starkey, "SHOCK & ROLL Army hammering out emergency plan to keep Putin's hands off top secret British armour if tanks are damaged in Ukraine", *The Sun*, January 27, 2023 (https://www.thesun.co.uk/news/21191872/army-emergency-secret-british-armour-tanks-war-ukraine/)
512. Christopher Woody & Jake Epstein, "Ukraine is getting a new heavy-duty armored vehicle to haul its damaged tanks off the battlefield, US officials say," Business Insider, January 25, 2023 (https://www.businessinsider.com/ukraine-getting-m88-armored-recovery-vehicles-along-with-abrams-tanks-2023-1?r=US&IR=T)

In December 2022-January 2023, the Western frenzy to obtain battle tanks for Ukraine would have pushed the United States to force Morocco to give Ukraine 20 T-72B tanks, then being upgraded in the Czech Republic[513]. True or false excuse from Rabat? It is difficult to say. In any case, Morocco, a loyal ally of Washington, chose not to speak out to condemn Russia at the United Nations General Assembly on March 3, 2023[514].

4.8.8.3. The expression of Western political weakness

Of the 320 or so tanks promised at the beginning of 2023, only about 50 were assembled in February. In January 2023, Chancellor Olaf Scholz announced the creation of two tank battalions: a LEOPARD 2A4 tank battalion and a LEOPARD 2A6 battalion. Each battalion had 31 tanks, but one month later, only 27 LEOPARD 2A4s (14 from Poland, 8 from Norway and 5 from Spain) and 17 LEOPARD 2A6s (14 from Germany and 3 from Portugal) were finally provided by donors. Finally, at the beginning of April, only 57 tanks were delivered to Ukraine with the promise that other tanks would arrive around the summer of 2023.

However, in Europe, everyone is talking about the Ukrainian spring offensive...

The delivery of Western weapons to Ukraine had a mobilizing effect in Russia. Our media explained that the arrival of German tanks would awaken old memories in Russia. In fact, it is not only the tanks, but also their insignia. On the 80th anniversary of the victory in Stalingrad, Vladimir Putin said:

> *It is unbelievable, but it is a fact: we are again threatened by German LEOPARD tanks bearing crosses.*

Because the Russians know that the Ukrainian tanks have the same symbols as the German tanks during the Polish campaign in 1939. Our

---

513. Ekene Lionel, "Morocco's T-72 tanks were sent to Ukraine without permission," *Military Africa*, January 30, 2023 (https://www.military.africa/2023/01/moroccos-t-72-tanks-were-sent-to-ukraine-without-permission/)

514. Basma El Atti, "Morocco's non-vote on UN condemnation of Putin's war raises controversy", *Arab News*, March 4, 2023 (https://www.newarab.com/news/morocco-chooses-neutrality-uncondemns-putins-war)

media did not mention this, but that is the problem. The Ukrainians must have realized this, because they published a brochure to justify the use of the white cross on their tanks[515].

Distinctive signs on Ukrainian tanks

Figure 60 - Ukrainian tanks have the same distinctive signs as those used by the Wehrmacht during the Second World War. On the left, the white cross used in 1939 for the campaign against Poland. In the middle, the cross used between 1939 and 1945. On the right, the Wolfsangel, symbol of the "Idea of Nation", similar to the emblem of the 2nd SS Panzer Division "Das Reich". (Signs observed on a T-72, apparently in the Kharkov area)[516]

4.8.8.4. Poorly adapted equipment

Russian weapons - and those that were being used in Ukraine until the spring of 2022 - were designed for the defense of the vast territories of the eastern USSR. They can be produced in large quantities, are simple to maintain and to use for conscript armies with limited training time.

Western equipment is of very good quality, but is intended to be used by projection forces, by professional personnel. These are more "refined" systems, whose integration requires the presence of highly specialized personnel. They are more delicate. They are not systems intended for defence, but for attack.

Western equipment therefore arrives with significant logistical constraints. Some systems are obsolete in the West and their ammunition is difficult to obtain (this is the case for the German anti-aircraft tank

---

515. https://www.weareukraine.info/the-backstory-about-the-sense-of-the-white-cross-used-by-the-ukrainian-troops-to-mark-their-vehicles-during-the-latest-counteroffensive-in-the-kharkiv-region/
516. https://i.redd.it/v0s0db1s7tt91.jpg

GEPARD) or some spare parts are simply no longer manufactured, as is the case for the LEOPARD 2A4 tank.

Combat logistics can be carried out relatively easily by exchanging modules, such as the engine block, for example. But more complex repairs can only be carried out by specialized personnel from NATO countries. This implies the establishment of repair centers outside the territory of Ukraine. Apart from the fact that this brings the "repairing" countries into Ukraine's operational logistics chain (and thus as co-belligerents), it poses customs problems. Slovakia, for example, believes that Ukraine should pay import duties, since the country is not a member of the EU.

The tanks supplied by the West are generally from reserves that were mothballed in the early 1990s and have suffered degradation. This equipment must therefore undergo complete overhaul before being sent to Ukraine.

This is why the delivery of LEOPARD 2A4 is delayed and LEOPARD 1 tanks from the 1960s-1990s will be delivered immediately. Other countries, such as Denmark and the Netherlands, do not want to empty their own arsenals and send LEOPARD 1A5 tanks to Ukraine. The problem with the LEOPARD 1 is that it has a 105 mm gun, whose ammunition is practically no longer used in Europe.

Tanks designed for different environments

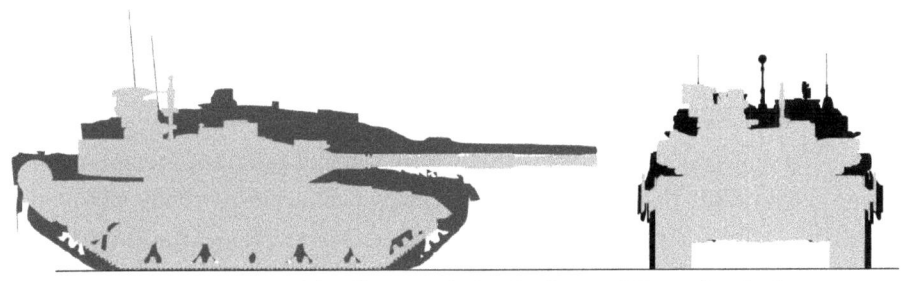

Figure 61 - Comparison of the silhouette of a Russian T-90 tank (in gray) and a German LEOPARD 2 tank (in black). Western tanks are generally designed to fight in Central Europe, with a slightly hilly terrain. They are therefore taller in order to allow for a wider gun travel to be able to fire on the run. Russian tanks are designed to operate in the much flatter Russian territory, and are therefore generally lower. In Ukraine, this means that Western tanks are easier targets to acquire and therefore more vulnerable than their Russian counterparts.

Comparison of Western tanks offered to Ukraine (early 2023)

	Canon	Pression au sol [kg/cm²]	Masse en ordre de combat [t]	Carburant Autonomie [km]
Leopard 2A4 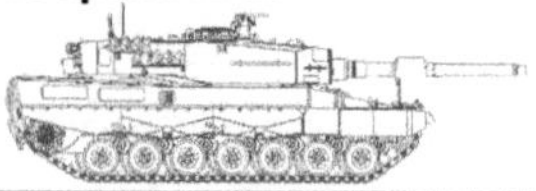	120 mm âme lisse	0,83	55	Polycarburant 550
M1A1 Abrams 	120 mm âme rayée	0,94	57-65	Polycarburant 480
Challenger 2 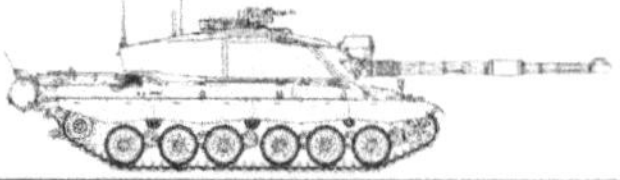	120 mm âme lisse	0,97	65-75	Diesel 450
Leclerc 	120 mm âme lisse	0,90	55	Diesel 550/650
AMX 10 RC 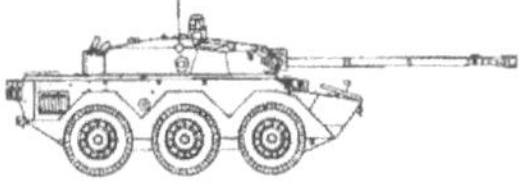	105 mm âme rayée		16,5	Diesel 500-1000

Figure 62 - The battle tanks mentioned at the beginning of 2023 to be given to Ukraine show a great diversity. A major problem is that each tank requires special logistics. Given the small numbers of Western-supplied equipment, one wonders whether the logistical complications become a greater handicap than the advantage these weapons offer. One can imagine that some units will be "single-use" given these difficulties.

An examination of the tanks promised by the West leads to certain conclusions. First of all, it can be observed that the vehicles provided are not of the latest generation. For example, there is a significant difference between the LEOPARD 2A6 (of which 14 were promised by Germany) and the LEOPARD 2A4 (which constitute the majority of the LEOPARDs sent). The A6 version is equipped with a system allowing it to be integrated into a battlefield management system (BMS), whereas the A4 version does not. Moreover, their ammunition is apparently not effective against the Russian T-90s[517].

---

517. Thorsten Jungholt, "Bundeswehr-Kampfpanzern fehlt wirksame Munition," *Die Welt am Sonntag*, April 26, 2015 (https://www.welt.de/politik/deutschland/article140083741/Bundeswehr-Kampfpanzern-fehlt-wirksame-Munition.html)

Russians are not without a sense of humor. The director of the Don Military Museum in Rostov sent an open letter to the German ambassador in Moscow, asking for a LEOPARD 2 for the museum's collection[518], explaining that it would be cheaper than refurbishing a tank recovered from the battlefield in Ukraine[519].

4.8.8.5. Depleted uranium ammunition

On March 20, 2023, Annabelle Goldie, British Minister of Defense, announced that Britain would supply depleted uranium shells to Ukraine. Depleted uranium is a by-product of the process of obtaining nuclear fuel. It is an extremely dense material, which the Americans have been using since the 1990s to make arrow shells. These are very long (60-80 cm) and very thin (3-4 cm in diameter) tubular projectiles designed to pierce tank armor. They are fired by tanks at very high speeds (about 1,700 m/s) and arrive at the target with considerable energy.

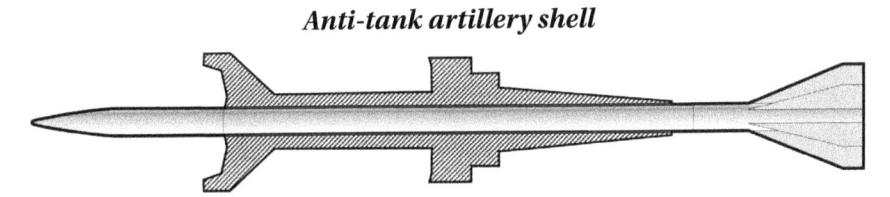

Anti-tank artillery shell

Figure 63 - Armour Piercing Fin Stabilized Discarding Sabot (ADFDS) shells are projectiles that act by kinetic energy. They are most often made of tungsten, but the United States also uses depleted uranium because of its high density and lower cost. The arrow is guided into the barrel by a "sabot" (hatched part) which is detached at its exit. Only the arrow continues towards the target with a very tense trajectory.

On impact, the arrow pierces the armor of the target and explodes into fine particles that are radioactive and extremely toxic. The long-term effect of this type of projectile is to contaminate an area permanently and endanger its occupants. It is an effect comparable to that of a "dirty bomb".

In October 2022, Russia's warning that Ukraine was preparing a "dirty bomb" was greeted as disinformation by our media, which considered it

---

518. https://youtu.be/lMPVV2EnQns
519. https://www.anti-spiegel.ru/2023/offener-brief-an-deutsche-botschaft-russisches-museum-mit-schwarzem-humor/?doing_wp_cron=1678022230.9727001190185546875000

unthinkable that Ukraine would contaminate "its own soil"[520]. However, neither the European ecologists nor the Ukrainians reacted to the idea of permanently contaminating with depleted uranium an area they are trying to reclaim! One might have imagined that national sentiment would have led to a rejection of Britain's offer. But this was not the case...

The reason is quite simple. The important thing for Ukrainians, since 2014, is to have no more linguistic minorities on their territory. This explains the support of the populations of Donbass and southern Ukraine to Russia and the lack of Ukrainian popular resistance in these regions.

4.8.8.6. The Russian potential

At the end of March 2023, videos of T-54/55 tanks transported by rail to Russia were circulating on social networks. That's all it takes to feed Western propaganda, which sees the inadequacies of the Russian army and the success of the Ukrainians. The "experts" of *France 5* were exultant. On the French channel LCI, the "journalist Jean Quatremer concludes that Russia is no longer able to produce tanks[521].

In the *NZZ*, Marcus Keupp, a military expert from the Zurich Polytechnic, predicts that the conflict will end in October 2023 with the defeat of Russia[522]. On the basis of the figures given by our media, he calculates the attrition rate of its tanks and concludes that in October, it will simply not have any more! It is with experts like that that we lose wars!

First of all, our media obviously did not note that Ukraine started to put T-55s back on the battlefield as early as August 2022[523]. This is a modernized version of the Soviet tank produced in Slovenia under the

---

520. "The "dirty bomb", a device that spreads radioactive dust and fear", *RTS.ch*, October 24, 2022 (https://www.rts.ch/info/monde/13489684-la-bombe-sale-un-engin-qui-dissemine-poussieres-radioactives-et-peur.html)

521. https://youtu.be/7bh1ZX0H0E4?t=460

522. Thomas Zaugg & Benedict Neff, "Deswegen sage ich: Russland wird den Krieg im Oktober verloren haben", *NZZ*, March 27, 2023 (https://www.nzz.ch/feuilleton/marcus-keupp-deswegen-sage-ich-russland-wird-den-krieg-im-oktober-verloren-haben-ld.1731488?reduced=-true&mktcval=Twitter&mktcid=smsh); "War in Ukraine: "Putin's army will be defeated by October at the latest", *La Libre*, April 4, 2023 (https://www.lalibre.be/international/europe/guerre-ukraine-russie/2023/04/04/guerre-en-ukraine-larmee-de-poutine-sera-vaincue-au-plus-tard-en-octobre-B252W43RBBGDPB5YSCBUNFDY7Y/)

523. Oleg Danylov, "The M-55S tank: a deep modernization of the Soviet T-55 for the Armed Forces," *Mezha*, September 20, 2022 (https://mezha.media/en/2022/09/20/the-m-55s-tank-a-deep-modernization-of-the-soviet-t-55-for-the-armed-forces/)

designation M-55S. The reason the Ukrainians need them is simply that they have no more battle tanks and the M-55S is a makeshift solution to fill this role.

Disinformation on Russian losses

Figure 64 - Photo from the Oryx site, which records Russian and Ukrainian equipment losses. The image has clearly been (badly) retouched (see the shadow of the man who disappeared). The Oryx site, like many of its counterparts, suffers from a lack of impartiality and intellectual rigor. [Source: Oryx]

There is another reason for the Russians' approach: they are not short of tanks, their production capacity is complete and the use of renovated T-54 or T-55 tanks has nothing to do with the losses suffered. This is a purely technical matter related to the nature of the fighting in Ukraine.

Traditionally, battle tanks are designed to fight other battle tanks. Their fire control and projectiles are designed for this purpose. Arrow-type anti-tank ammunition (APFSDS) is stabilized by fins and can reach maximum velocities when fired from smoothbore guns. These projectiles thus have a very tense trajectory, which gives them a high probability of being hit. In contrast, smoothbore guns are less good at firing explosive projectiles (HE) against "soft" targets at long ranges.

In fact, the Russians found that there were no real tank duels, because the Ukrainians no longer had any tanks. On the other hand, they found that the majority of the fighting is infantry fighting. Therefore, it was necessary to find a kind of mobile artillery fulfilling the same function as the "assault gun" (*samokhodnaya ustanovka*, from World War II). Thanks to their anti-personnel explosive ammunition (HE), the T-54/55 are very well suited to this role and can accurately hit infantry positions at 4,000 m.

Thus, the T-54/55 tank is not used to fight tanks in direct fire, but "soft" targets in indirect fire for infantry units. It thus provides considerable firepower to the infantry on the outskirts of urban areas, to fire on protected positions in buildings, for example.

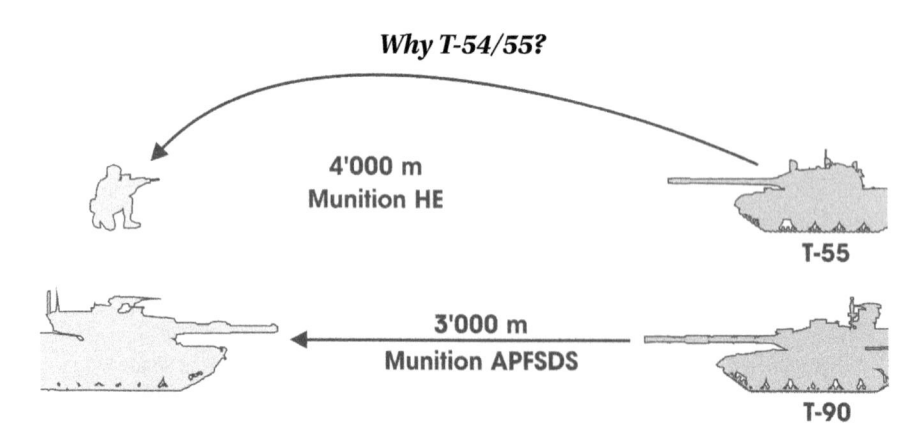

Why T-54/55?

Figure 65 - Although obsolete for tank dueling, the T-54/55 can very well perform the role of "assault guns" to provide fire support to the infantry. The more modern tanks (T-72 and T-90) can thus be reserved for combat against Ukrainian battle tanks.

4.8.9. Artillery

4.8.9.1. A gargantuan consumption

By June 2022, Ukraine had most of its military potential destroyed by Russia, and was therefore dependent on Western supplies. Its 152 mm artillery of Soviet origin is either destroyed or out of ammunition, and it must rely on 155 mm artillery supplied by NATO countries. But by the end of 2022, Ukraine was running out of ammunition and the West was having trouble supplying it.

In Afghanistan, the United States fired about 300 rounds per day[524]. Logically enough, their production capacity is adapted to this consumption. At the end of 2022, Christine Wormuth, Secretary of the US Army, stated that it amounted to 500 shells per day, or about 14,000 155 mm shells per month[525].

According to the *New York Times*, Ukrainian forces fire 2,000-4,000 shells per day[526]. The *Kyiv Post* even mentions the figures of 6,000-7,000 shells per day[527]. According to classified documents "leaked" in April 2023, the Ukrainians are firing an average of 3,500 155mm shells per day[528]. In other words, the Ukrainians fire in 2 to 7 days the equivalent of the American monthly production! The Ukrainians admit that their consumption of artillery shells exceeds the production capacity of the United States[529]!

According to the U.S. State Department, as of March 20, 2023, the United States has supplied Ukraine with 1.5 million 155mm artillery shells, 400,000 105mm shells, 45,000 152mm shells, and 20,000 122mm shells[530].

---

524. Steven Erlanger & Lara Jakes, "U.S. and NATO Scramble to Arm Ukraine and Refill Their Own Arsenals," *The New York Times*, November 26, 2022 (updated November 29, 2022) (https://www.nytimes.com/2022/11/26/world/europe/nato-weapons-shortage-ukraine.html)
525. "Ukraine's artillery shell expenditure outstrips US production," *The New Voice of Ukraine*, December 24, 2022 (https://english.nv.ua/nation/ukraine-s-artillery-shell-expenditure-outstrips-us-production-war-news-50293094.html)
526. John Ismay & Thomas Gibbons-Neff, "Artillery Is Breaking in Ukraine. It's Becoming a Problem for the Pentagon," *The New York Times*, November 25, 2022 (https://www.nytimes.com/2022/11/25/us/ukraine-artillery-breakdown.html)
527. https://www.kyivpost.com/post/51
528. Russia/Ukraine Joint Staff J3/4/5 Daily Update (D+369) (February 28, 2023) (SECRET/NO FORN)
529. Oleksandr Syrskyi, "Ukraine's artillery shell expenditure outstrips US production," *The New Voice of Ukraine*, December 23, 2022 (https://english.nv.ua/nation/ukraine-s-artillery-shell-expenditure-outstrips-us-production-war-news-50293094.html)
530. "U.S. Security Cooperation with Ukraine," Fact Sheet, *U.S. State Department, Bureau of Political-Military Affairs*, March 20, 2023 (https://www.state.gov/u-s-security-cooperation-with-ukraine/); https://crsreports.congress.gov/product/pdf/IF/IF12040

But the West is at the end of its rope and is scrambling to meet the insatiable needs of Ukraine, whose forces are in a very bad position. That is why they have planned to increase their production to 20,000 shells per month in 2023, and have gone to retrieve 300,000 shells from a secret depot in Israel to send them to Ukraine[531]. To replenish their own stockpiles, they plan to buy 155mm shells from South Korea, which refuses to allow the ammunition to be used in Ukraine[532]. The release of "leaked" classified documents in April 2023, show that the U.S. has ordered 330,000 shells and that it takes two and a half months for them to be fully delivered. It is unclear, however, whether these shells went to the United States to "free up" shells for Ukraine or whether they were transferred directly to Ukraine.

Britain, Sweden, Canada and Germany have increased their production of 155-mm shells in order to supply Ukraine. The Americans are seeking to restart production of 152-mm ammunition in the former Warsaw Treaty countries of Bulgaria, Romania, the Czech Republic and Slovakia[533].

In March 2023, France decided to increase to 2,000 rounds the number of 155-mm projectiles it would supply to Ukraine each month[534]; this represents about half a day's firing! The "leaked" classified documents also show that the United States has significantly reduced its ammunition deliveries, probably less for political reasons than because of its production capacity.

In Norway, faced with a 15-fold increase in demand for artillery ammunition, the company Nammo is unable to increase its production of shells because of... TikTok! According to an interview with Nammo's director reported by the *Financial Times* and *Business Insider*, TikTok's data center

---

531. Eric Schmitt, Adam Entous, Ronen Bergman, John Ismay & Thomas Gibbons-Neff, "Pentagon Sends U.S. Arms Stored in Israel to Ukraine," *The New York Times*, January 17, 2023 (https://www.nytimes.com/2023/01/17/us/politics/ukraine-israel-weapons.html)
532. Josh Smith & Mike Stone, "U.S. in talks to buy South Korean ammunition for Ukraine, official says," *Reuters*, November 11, 2022 (https://www.reuters.com/world/asia-pacific/skorea-says-us-will-be-end-user-ammunition-after-report-weapons-ukraine-2022-11-11/)
533. "NATO looking at production of Soviet-era weapons used by Ukraine, says Blinken," The New Voice of Ukraine, November 30, 2022 (https://english.nv.ua/amp/nato-looking-at-production-of-soviet-era-weapons-used-by-ukraine-says-blinken-50287799.html)
534. "War in Ukraine: France will double, to 2000 per month, deliveries of 155 mm shells", BFM Business/AFP, March 28, 2023 (https://www.bfmtv.com/economie/entreprises/defense/guerre-en-ukraine-la-france-va-doubler-a-2000-par-mois-les-livraisons-d-obus-de-155-mm_AD-202303280248.html)

would absorb the electrical energy that would be needed to increase production[535]! Since TikTok is owned by a Chinese company, Nammo's director suggests that there is a conspiracy by China to use electricity to prevent the production of ammunition for Ukraine! Fortunately, ridicule does not kill!

Daily consumption of artillery ammunition

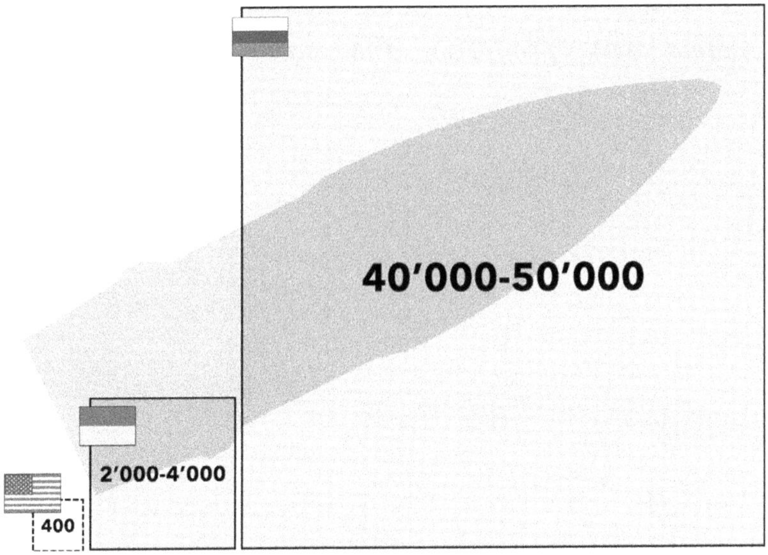

40'000-50'000

2'000-4'000

400

Figure 66 - Representation of the daily consumption of artillery shells in Ukraine and Russia. These are average values. On the left, in dotted line, the daily production of artillery projectiles in the United States. [Source: The New York Times]

As for the Russians, they fire about 40,000-50,000 artillery shells per day according to NATO[536]!

In November 2022, the head of the Estonian intelligence service claims that Russia has already used up two-thirds of its artillery ammunition

---

535. Lindsay Dodgson, "Weapons firm says it can't meet soaring demand for artillery shells because a TikTok data center is eating all the electricity," *Business Insider*, March 27, 2023 (https://africa.businessinsider.com/military-and-defense/weapons-firm-says-it-cant-meet-soaring-demand-for-artillery-shells-because-a-tiktok/y15srh8)

536. Steven Erlanger & Lara Jakes, "U.S. and NATO Scramble to Arm Ukraine and Refill Their Own Arsenals," *The New York Times*, November 26, 2022 (updated November 29, 2022) (https://www.nytimes.com/2022/11/26/world/europe/nato-weapons-shortage-ukraine.html)

reserves. Where do these figures come from? No one knows[537]. But it is probably disinformation: not only does Estonia have a policy of denigrating Russia, but its intelligence services are particularly bad.

The West tends to project Ukrainian weaknesses onto Russia, because there is no evidence that the Russians are short of ammunition. A study by the Jamestown Foundation shows that in 2021, their annual production of artillery shells was four times that of the Americans[538]!

Annual Russian production of 152 mm artillery ammunition

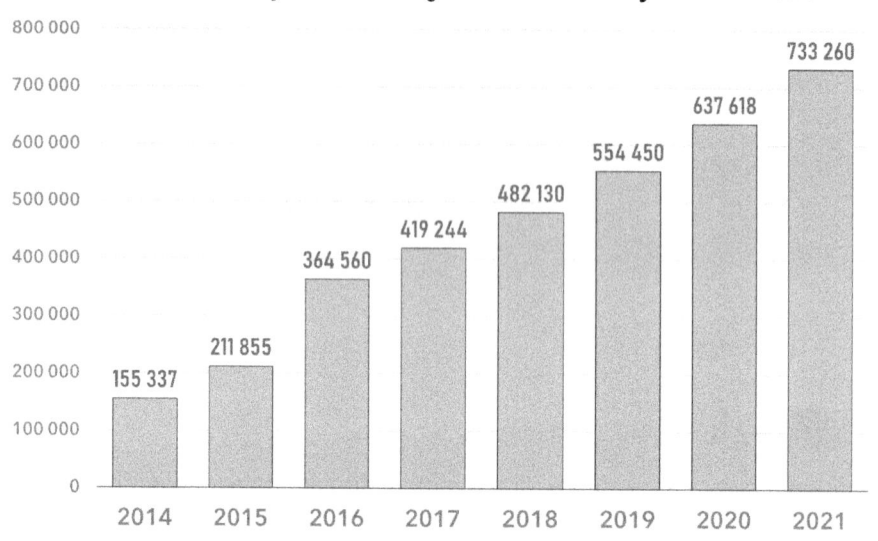

Year	Production
2014	155 337
2015	211 855
2016	364 560
2017	419 244
2018	482 130
2019	554 450
2020	637 618
2021	733 260

Figure 67 - Estimated Russian production of 152 mm ammunition between 2014 and 2021, according to the Jamestown Foundation, a U.S. institution strongly opposed to Russia. These figures, which seek to demonstrate that Russia does not have the means to produce its ammunition, nevertheless manage to show that Russian capacity was more than four times that of the United States.

In reality, it is the Westerners who are struggling to find the ammunition that could allow Ukraine to maintain its pace. On March 20, 2023,

---

537. "Russia has exhausted two-thirds of its ammunition reserves, Estonian intelligence says "*, *The New Voice of Ukraine,* November 25, 2022 (https://english.nv.ua/amp/russia-has-exhausted-two-thirds-of-its-ammunition-reserves-news-50286762.html
538. Hlib Parfonov, "Russia Struggles to Maintain Munition Stocks (Part Two)," *The Jamestown Foundation, Eurasia Daily Monitor,* Volume 19, No. 186 (https://jamestown.org/program/russia-struggles-to-maintain-munition-stocks-part-two/)

the EU decided to finance 1 million shells over 12 months[539], for this purpose, it has managed to mobilize 2 billion euros, one of which will be used to compensate the countries that have drawn on their stocks to help Ukraine. One billion remains, to finance the production of shells. The problem is that this production capacity does not really exist in the EU, and it will be necessary to turn to an external source: Turkey[540]. Predictably, this triggers the anger of France, Greece and Cyprus, who are putting their feet up against the wall. France wants the money to stay in the EU, while Greece and Cyprus refuse to finance the Turkish defence industry[541].

This crisis has shown that not only has Europe lost its global political and industrial leadership, but that it is deeply divided on many issues. In fact, the only thing that unites Europe is Russophobia.

4.8.9.2. Multiple missile launchers

With the destruction of the Ukrainian artillery potential in the spring of 2022, the West was forced to provide multiple missile launchers. Their performance is not radically different from that of their Russian counterparts. However, like the M142 HIMARS, they can fire ammunition with a non-ballistic trajectory, which makes defence against these missiles more difficult. Presented as miracle weapons, they have not radically changed the situation. The Russians quickly learned to decentralize their ammunition depots and adapted the software of their anti-aircraft systems to respond effectively against these missiles.

The American missile launchers can launch several *Guided Multiple Launch Rocket Systems* (GMLRS) missiles of "small" calibre or an *Army Tactical Missile System* (ATACMS) missile of larger calibre. The ATACMS has a range of 300 km and an explosive charge of 200 kg and could allow Ukraine to reach targets on Russian territory, with a high destructive capacity. But the Americans are reluctant to provide Ukraine with

---

539. "Боррель уточнив деталі "історичного рішення" ЄС про закупівлю боєприпасів Україні", Європейська правда, March 20, 2023 (https://www.eurointegration.com.ua/news/2023/03/20/7158323/)
540. "EU cannot agree on how to spend €1 billion on ammunition for Ukraine", *Ukraïnska Pravda*, April 5, 2023 (https://www.pravda.com.ua/eng/news/2023/04/5/7396641/)
541. "Cyprus worried EU's Ukraine ammunition grant could end up in Turkish arms industry", *In-Cyprus*, April 7, 2023 (https://in-cyprus.philenews.com/news/local/cyprus-worried-eus-ukraine-ammunition-grant-could-end-up-in-turkish-arms-industry/)

ATACMS missiles, because they fear that this would lead to a dramatic escalation of the conflict[542]. In fact, according to the *Wall Street Journal*[543] and *The Hill*[544], the launchers delivered to Ukraine have even been secretly modified so that they cannot fire long-range missiles capable of reaching Russian territory.

According to classified American documents 'leaked' in April 2023, the Ukrainians had received 9,584 GMLRS missiles. They are therefore firing an average of 36 missiles, or 6 salvos per day[545]. This is far from being a game-changer. That said, it is likely that the Ukrainians fired a lot of them at the beginning, but that over time they were forced to reduce their consumption so that the Americans could keep up. For the documents indicate that by the end of February they had fired 17, or about 3 rounds per day. Since Ukraine received 38 systems from the United States[546], it can be concluded that a majority of M-142 or a large part of the ammunition was destroyed by Russia, which would confirm the statements of its staff.

The M-142 and M-270 are probably more sophisticated than the equivalent Russian systems in terms of their design. Like the rest of the Western weapons produced in the last quarter century, they were designed for projected operations. They are modular and can be adapted to different operational requirements, but they are very expensive and complex to produce. Today, Lockheed-Martin produces 10,000 GMLRS missiles per year. With additional investment, it will reach 14,000 units by 2024, but it will not be able to double its production until 2026[547]. In fact, the United States simply does not have the physical and personnel capacity to expand production to meet both Ukraine's needs and those of its other customers.

---

542. John Ismay, "The Missile Ukraine Wants Is One the U.S. Says It Doesn't Need," *The New York Times*, October 6, 2023 (https://www.nytimes.com/2022/10/06/us/ukraine-war-missile.html)

543. Michael R. Gordon & Gordon Lubold, "U.S. Altered Himars Rocket Launchers to Keep Ukraine From Firing Missiles Into Russia," The Wall Street Journal, December 5, 2022 (https://www.wsj.com/articles/u-s-altered-himars-rocket-launchers-to-keep-ukraine-from-firing-missiles-into-russia-11670214338)

544. Brad Dress, "US secretly modified HIMARS for Ukraine to prevent Kyiv from shooting long-range missiles into Russia," *The Hill*, December 5, 2022 (https://thehill.com/policy/defense/3762042-us-secretly-modified-himars-for-ukraine-to-prevent-kyiv-from-shooting-long-range-missiles-into-russia/)

545. Russia/Ukraine Joint Staff J3/4/5 Daily Update (D+369) (February 28, 2023) (SECRET/NO FORN)

546. "U.S. Security Cooperation with Ukraine - Fact Sheet, *Bureau of Political-Military Affairs, State Department*, April 19, 2023 (https://www.state.gov/u-s-security-cooperation-with-ukraine/)

547. Sam Skove, "Why It's Hard to Double GMLRS Production," *Defense One*, March 30, 2023 (https://www.defenseone.com/business/2023/03/why-its-hard-double-gmlrs-production/384646/)

The equivalent Russian systems are more numerous, but simpler and therefore less expensive to produce. This is why Russia can easily increase its production and play on a greater density of systems deployed in the field.

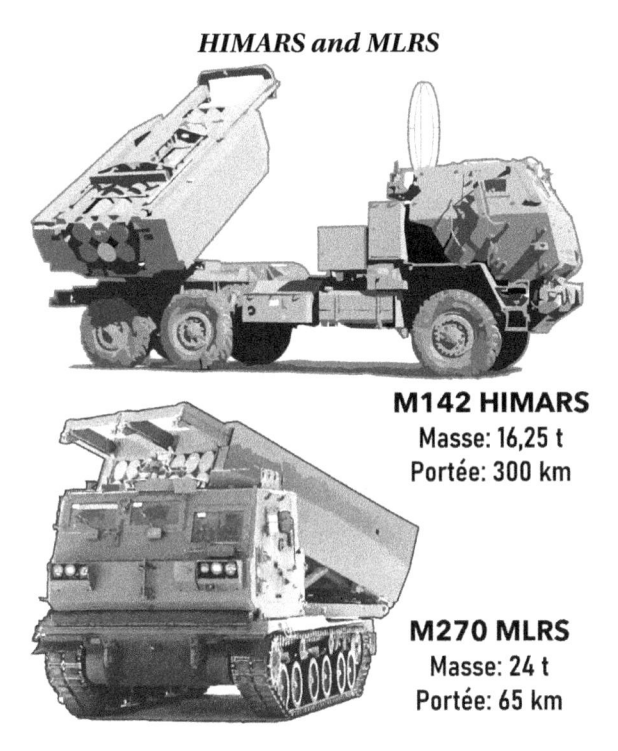

HIMARS and MLRS

M142 HIMARS
Masse: 16,25 t
Portée: 300 km

M270 MLRS
Masse: 24 t
Portée: 65 km

Figure 68 - American multiple missile launchers supplied to Ukraine

4.8.9.3. Counter-battery systems

The Russians have developed particularly effective counter-battery fire capabilities and are able to destroy Western equipment almost as it arrives in the theater of operations.

The Russians need 2 minutes between the detection of a Ukrainian shot and the transmission of its coordinates to trigger a counter-battery shot[548]. On the Ukrainian side, moving an American 155mm M777 howitzer requires 2-3 minutes for a trained crew in optimal conditions[549].

---

548. https://eng.mil.ru/en/special_operation/news/more.htm?id=12449739@egNews
549. http://www.military-today.com/artillery/m777.htm

In theory, this not only means that a Ukrainian artillery piece can only fire one shot in each firing position, but that it can be destroyed each time before it can even move.

This ability to instantly fire counter-battery fire has significantly limited the capabilities of Ukrainian artillery. With the gradual advance of Russian troops, Ukrainian artillery is almost unable to reach the city of Donetsk. What the West was unable to stop by negotiation, the Russians have achieved by force.

4.8.9.4. Conventional artillery versus precision artillery

In order to help Ukraine reduce its consumption of artillery shells, the West has opted to supply precision weapons to reduce the volume of ammunition used. In addition to 155mm howitzers/gunners, they began supplying Ukraine with 155mm precision ammunition in July 2022[550].

Guided artillery ammunition
M982 Excalibur 155 mm (USA)

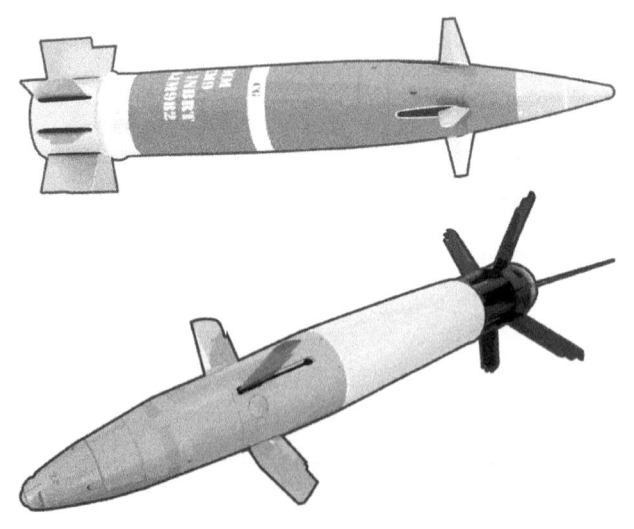

2K25 Krasnopol 152 mm (Russie)

Figure 69 - 155 mm and 152 mm guided munitions used by Ukraine and Russia respectively. These munitions are extremely expensive in relation to their effectiveness.

---

550. "Ukraine to receive new precision-guided 155-mm artillery rounds from USA," Ukrainian Military Center, July 9, 2022 (https://mil.in.ua/en/news/ukraine-to-receive-new-precision-guided-155-mm-artillery-rounds-from-usa/)

These systems allow the shell to remain on its intended trajectory and thus reduce its dispersion (Circular Error Probable - CEP). This improves the hit probability and reduces the number of shells needed to destroy a target.

Numerous systems exist and have been supplied to Ukraine, such as the 155 mm EXCALIBUR self-guided shells, which make it possible to hit targets very precisely.

With a unit cost of $68,000, these precision shells are 85 times more expensive than a 155 mm shell at $800. This is why the Americans have been testing alternative solutions in Ukraine, such as the M1156 Projectile Guidance Kit (PGK).

The M1156 Projectile Guidance Kit (PGK)

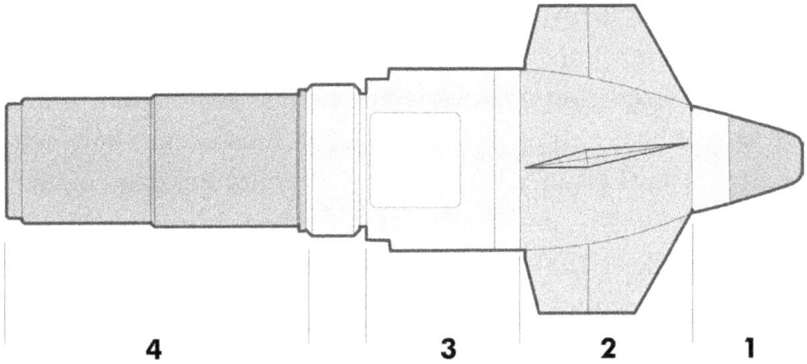

Figure 70 - M1156 PGK 155 mm artillery shell accuracy improvement kit. It consists of: (1) Telemetry module and proximity sensors; (2) Guidance module; (3) GPS module; (4) Rocket and trigger mechanism.

The M1156 PGK is an artillery projectile accuracy enhancement kit consisting of a fuse with steerable fins, which attaches in place of "normal" shell fuses. After reaching its peak, the fins keep the shell on its trajectory and compensate for the effects of wind, temperature, etc. The M1156 PGK is very simple and relatively inexpensive (about $20,000 each).

Precise ammunition is an advantage, but also has constraints. It requires very precise target designation and the ability to guide the projectile to the target. Guidance is usually provided by a GPS module, while target designation is provided by American reconnaissance systems, such as the MQ-9 REAPER or RQ-4 GLOBAL HAWK.

However, after the destruction of most of its potential in the spring of 2022, the Ukrainian army has become a heterogeneous assembly of equipment from different sources, with different capabilities and logistical chains. The problem of the Ukrainians is not really the lack of weapons, but the ability to integrate them into an optimal and efficient structure.

Moreover, the Russians have unparalleled electronic warfare capabilities and are able to jam or disrupt these systems. That said, Russia also has equivalent systems, such as the laser-guided 2K25 KRASNOPOL, which is delivered by a drone. That being said, Russia seems to prefer the use of aerial bombs, which are more powerful.

4.8.9.5. Inadequate equipment

Ukraine's problem is not so much the number of weapons, but the way they are used. For the weapons the West has provided are not designed for this type of war. Since the 1990s, the "big" Western armies have been equipped to wage colonial-style wars against adversaries with little in the way of heavy equipment. Ukraine is thus caught between two different conceptions of artillery: the traditional Russian conception, based on massive fire, and a more tactical Western conception, based on sniping artillery. The idea is to reduce the number of shots needed to destroy an objective.

This is the case for systems such as the French *Camion Équipé d'un Système d'Artillerie* (CAESAR) or the American M777 howitzer. Their main qualities are precision and range. But these are demanding qualities. Their accuracy depends largely on efficient and integrated reconnaissance and target designation systems, but also on the way the equipment is maintained.

Both capable of firing the NATO 155 mm ammunition, they are excellent, more accurate than the Russian howitzers, but more fragile. Intended to "hit the bull's eye" with every shot, their guns were not designed to fire large volumes of fire and do not withstand wear and tear. The *New York Times* cites the example of an M777 howitzer in Syria that fired 23,000 rounds in 5 months (or 150 rounds per day) and had to be completely overhauled to be operational.

A few weeks after their arrival in Ukraine, the CAESARs are proving unable to keep up with the high rates of fire imposed by the Russians.

Already by the end of 2022, France plans to deploy a workshop near the Ukrainian border for repairs as reported by the Ukrainian military website *Militarniy*[551]. As for the American M777 howitzers, 30 percent of them must be regularly removed for repairs[552].

Our media has presented them as "miracle weapons," but in reality, these weapons do not have the desired effect, as they cannot be engaged in the manner in which they were designed[553]. Despite enormous assistance from Western countries, these weapons cannot be integrated into battlefield management systems and are therefore used inefficiently.

4.8.10. Electronic warfare

A field systematically ignored by our "experts" and often confused with cyber warfare is *electronic warfare* (EW), which the Anglo-Saxons call *"Electronic Warfare"* (EW). Referred to as "Radio-Electronic Warfare" (радиоэлектронная борьба) (REB) in Russia, this is an area where it excels and probably has a greater lead than the West. It is also an area of quiet success.

At the beginning of its intervention, in February 2022, Russia was able to neutralize all the Ukrainian military means of transmission.

Ukraine was able to restore its transmissions thanks to the donation of about 20,000 Starlink terminals, financed by the American, British and Polish governments. Implemented by Elon Musk's company SpaceX, the *Starlink* system allows the transmission of data through a network of satellites. It is thus particularly useful in a country as vast as Ukraine, for the conduct of combat, including the piloting of drones or the designation of goals. The operation of this network in Ukraine costs about 400 million USD per year.

Starlink thus quickly became one of the priority targets of the Russian electronic warfare. Initially, SpaceX was able to prevent jamming of

---

551. https://mil.in.ua/en/news/the-ministry-of-defense-wants-to-create-a-service-center-for-caesar-self-propelled-howitzers/
552. Stew Magnuson, "Ukraine to U.S. Defense Industry: We Need Long-Range, Precision Weapons," *National Defense Magazine*, June 5, 2022 (https://www.nationaldefensemagazine.org/articles/2022/6/15/ukraine-to-us-defense-industry-we-need-long-range-precision-weapons)
553. Alex Hollings & Sandboxx News, "Ukraine's troops have been highly effective with the M777 howitzer, but US troops can turn it into a 'giant sniper rifle," *Business Insider*, September 18, 2022 (https://www.businessinsider.com/us-targeting-system-makes-m777-howitzer-highly-accurate-2022-9)

its satellites[554], but the Russians had not said their last word[555]. In early October 2022, massive *Starlink* failures had "catastrophic" consequences for combat formation transmissions. According to General Valeriy Zaloujny, head of the Ukrainian forces, the Russians would destroy 500 terminals per month[556].

STRIJ anti-drone system

Figure 71 - The Russians have developed a range of electronic systems to neutralize drones before they become a threat. The STRIJ is one of these systems that can protect tactical units.

The destruction of Starlink terminals forces command posts to exchange fire data by voice via the *Iridium* satellite telephone network. This slows down the reaction time of the artillery which is then more vulnerable to counter-battery fire.

---

554. Michael Kan, "Pentagon Impressed by Starlink's Fast Signal-Jamming Workaround in Ukraine," *PC Magazine*, April 21, 2022 (https://www.pcmag.com/news/pentagon-impressed-by-starlinks-fast-signal-jamming-workaround-in-ukraine)
555. Elizabeth Howell, "Elon Musk says Russia is ramping up cyberattacks on SpaceX's Starlink systems in Ukraine," *Space*, October 14, 2022 (https://www.space.com/starlink-russian-cyberattacks-ramp-up-efforts-elon-musk)
556. Xander Landen, "Starlink Outages Put 'Dent' in Ukrainian Counteroffensive Against Putin," *Newsweek*, October 8, 2022 (https://www.newsweek.com/starlink-outages-put-dent-ukrainian-counteroffensive-against-putin-1750116)

The Russians have also developed ways to jam the GPS signal and thus disrupt the use of drones and guided missiles. According to the American magazine *Forbes*, Russia is able to shoot down 90% of Ukrainian drones with its electromagnetic systems[557]. In *The Economist*, a Ukrainian official states[558]:

> *The Russians are very, very good at what they do [...] They do black magic in electromagnetic warfare. They can jam frequencies, fool the GPS system, send a drone to the wrong altitude so that it just falls out of the sky.*

RANETS-E electromagnetic protection system

Figure 72 - The RANETS-E is a Mobile Microwave Protection System (MMPS). It generates a centimeter wave with a duration of about 20 nanoseconds and a power of up to 500 MW. It can fry all the electronics of an aircraft at a distance of 15 kilometers and cause failures in its operation at distances of 15 to 40 km.

Russia also has a whole arsenal of systems which allow it to jam or even destroy the adversary's electronic systems and thus render their

---
557. David Axe, "Russia's Electronic-Warfare Troops Knocked Out 90 Percent of Ukraine's Drones," *Forbes*, December 24, 2022 (https://www.forbes.com/sites/davidaxe/2022/12/24/russia-electronic-warfare-troops-knocked-out-90-percent-of-ukraines-drones/?sh=2b8c98a9575c)
558. "Ukraine is betting on drones to strike deep into Russia," *The Economist*, March 20, 2023 (https://www.economist.com/europe/2023/03/20/ukraine-is-betting-on-drones-to-strike-deep-into-russia)

4. Military considerations

transmissions or their devices inoperative. This is the case of the RANETS-E system.

4.8.11. Anti-aircraft weapons

At the beginning of the SVO, Ukrainian anti-aircraft defence relied mainly on its S300 systems supplied by Russia. The Ukrainian air force was quickly grounded by the first Russian strikes, but the Ukrainian anti-aircraft capabilities were then little affected. Russia's objective was not to take over Ukraine, so it did not need to have control of the skies over the entire territory. Its missiles allowed it to act in depth without having to risk its aircraft and their pilots.

By the end of the summer of 2022, seeing that the West was leading them into a war of attrition by delivering weapons to Ukraine, the Russians decided to complete the destruction of Ukrainian forces. This is to prevent Ukraine from reconstituting its forces for the great offensive it has been promising since the spring of 2022. But they realize that for the destruction of buried infantry positions, aviation is the most effective solution.

In order to reduce the anti-aircraft threat, the Russians decided to push the Ukrainians to exhaust their stock of long-range missiles. This is why they carry out missile strikes against the electrical infrastructure, which they had not done until then. This forces the Ukrainians to use their S-300 and BUK missiles, and even several for a single target. This is why some of these missiles end up aimless and end up landing in Poland.

The Russian tactic is to send a first wave of cheap drones or obsolete missiles as decoys, which cause the Ukrainians to activate their radars. Simultaneously, with an A-50U MAINSTAY early warning aircraft monitoring the airspace from Belarus, the Russians analyze the Ukrainian response patterns. They can then send a second wave of cruise missiles that can destroy Ukrainian air defense positions.

Our media claimed that the Russians had no more missiles and were forced to use obsolete ones. Moreover, the results announced by the propaganda suggested that the Ukrainian air defenses were efficient! This explains why the West neglected to provide anti-aircraft weapons and concentrated their efforts on artillery. Thus, ironically, by seeking to minimize Russian successes, our media and military experts have amplified the effectiveness of the Russian strategy and directly contributed to the weakening of Ukrainian resources.

The A-50U MAINSTAY, stationed at the military airfield of Matchulishchy, near Minsk, is an essential part of this system. That is why Ukraine tried to destroy it.

On February 26, 2023, *Le Figaro*[559] and the Swiss *RTS* announced *"a Russian plane destroyed on an airfield in* Belarus*"*[560], by the Belarusian opposition[561]. The next day, *Le Point* declared that the success was *"confirmed"* and specified that it was the *"most successful sabotage operation*[562]*"*. However, despite their decisive tone, our media know absolutely nothing about it. British military intelligence (DI) announced no action on 26 and 27 February, but mentioned the incident on the 28th, specifying that neither the incident, nor the perpetrators, nor the damage was confirmed[563]. The DI was right to be cautious, because on February 28, satellite images of the Russian aircraft, published by *Maxar Technologies*, show that it is intact. [564]

By saturating air defenses with a combination of missiles, drones, and decoys, the Russians are forcing the Ukrainians to use hundreds of thousands of dollars worth of missiles to hit drones worth a few thousand. Secret U.S. documents "leaked" in April 2023 indicate that the SA-10/S-300 and SA-11/BUK anti-aircraft systems and their ammunition were depleted between late March and late May 2023.

According to the American magazine *Forbes*, Ukraine had 300 SA-10/S-300 systems in February 2022. A year later, according to "leaked" US classified documents, it had only 25 systems left. According to Volodymyr

---

559. "A Russian plane destroyed on an airfield in Belarus, according to the opposition", *Le Figaro / AFP*, February 26, 2023 (https://www.lefigaro.fr/international/un-avion-russe-detruit-sur-un-aerodrome-au-belarus-selon-l-opposition-20230226)
560. https://www.rts.ch/info/monde/13820148-attaque-mortelle-dune-dizaine-de-drones-iraniens-sur-khmelnytsky-dans-louest-de-lukraine.html
561. "Russian plane worth 330 million euros destroyed on an airfield in Belarus: 'The most successful sabotage operation', rejoices the opposition", 7 of 7/ BELGA, February 27, 2023 (https://www.7sur7.be/monde/un-avion-russe-a-330-millions-deuros-detruit-sur-un-aerodrome-au-belarus-loperation-de-sabotage-la-plus-reussie-se-rejouit-lopposition~a1f4bb60/)
562. I.M. / AFP, " L'opposition biélorusse annonce avoir détruit un avion russe ", *Le Point*, February 27, 2023 (https://www.lepoint.fr/monde/l-opposition-bielorusse-annonce-avoir-detruit-un-avion-russe-27-02-2023-2510106_24.php)
563. https://twitter.com/DefenceHQ/status/1630453726304518144
564. Tyler Rogoway, "Russian A-50 Radar Jet Intact After Claimed Drone Attack In Belarus," *The War Zone*, February 28, 2023 (https://www.thedrive.com/the-war-zone/first-image-of-russian-a-50-radar-jet-after-claimed-attack-in-belarus)

Omelyan, former Ukrainian Minister of Infrastructure between 2016 and 2019, 200 anti-aircraft systems would be needed to effectively protect the country's 50 largest cities[565].

A-50 MAINSTAY

Figure 73 - A-50 MAINSTAY long-range warning aircraft. This is the Russian equivalent of the AWACS used by NATO countries in Romania and Poland. It can simultaneously detect and process some 150 targets up to a distance of 650 km in the air and up to 300 km on the ground.

The Russian strategy worked well because in late 2022 - early 2023, the West must urgently send anti-aircraft systems to Ukraine. The United States promised a unit of MIM-104 PATRIOT. In March 2023, France decided to send two CROTALE systems with a range of 11 km and joined

---

565. Brendan Cole, "NATO's Patchwork Air Defenses Failed Ukraine. What Now?", *Newsweek*, October 14, 2022 (https://www.newsweek.com/ukraine-russia-air-defense-zelensky-1751511)

Italy in sending a MAMBA SAMP/T system in the summer. Despite the quality of these systems, these efforts are very insufficient to allow Ukraine to restore the balance.

State of the Ukrainian air defense

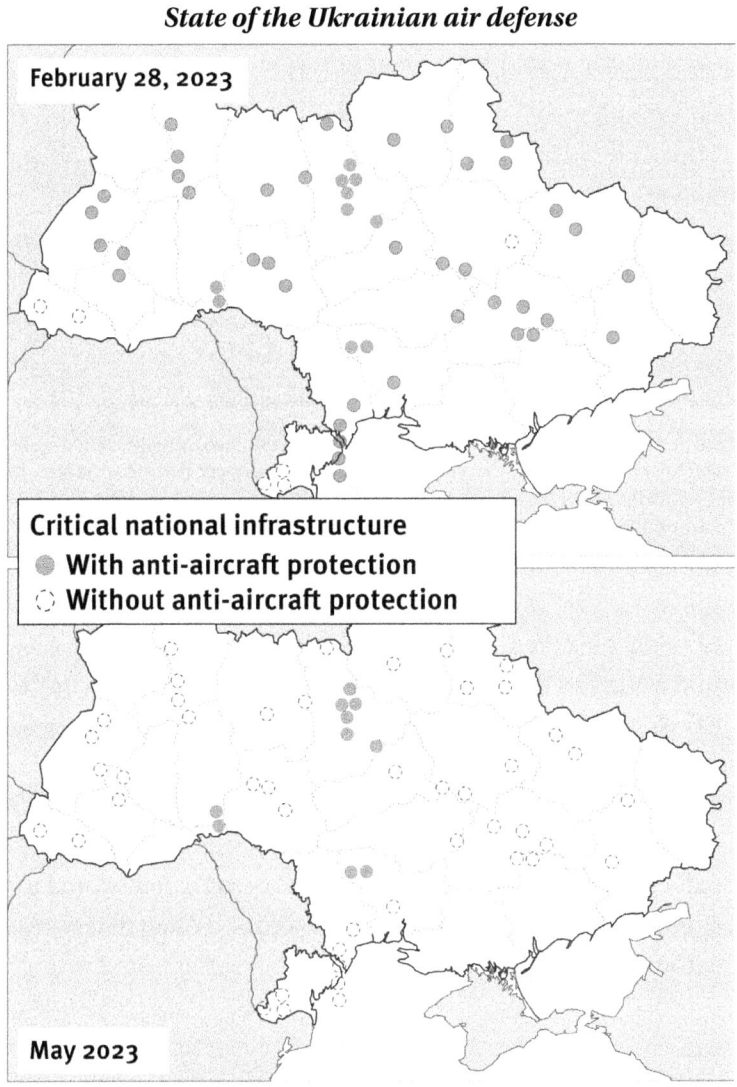

Figure 74 - Information from "leaked" classified documents in early April 2023. They show that in May, practically all anti-aircraft systems will run out of ammunition and Ukraine will be defenseless. This is the consequence of the statements of Ukrainian propaganda and our media that Russia had no more missiles and aircraft.

4. Military considerations

Anti-aircraft systems supplied by the West in early 2023

System	Number	Country	Altitude range [km]
S-300	?	Russie	200 / 40
MIN-104 PATRIOT	3	USA / Allemagne	60 / 24
NASAMS	8	USA	50 / 20
IRIS-T	3	Allemagne	40 / 20
ASTER 30 SAMP/T	1	France / Italie	120 / 40

Figure 75 - Number of systems. At the time of writing, the characteristics of the systems supplied to Ukraine are not clear. However, it does not appear that these systems can match the performance of the S-300 systems. With an air defense system that is out of breath, the Western systems do not provide a decisive advantage.

It has been observed that these systems are insufficient to ensure uniform coverage of the more than 600,000 km² of Ukrainian territory. In other words, the Ukrainian command must choose between protecting strategic areas (such as Kiev) or its ground operations.

In addition to this, in an Interview with *Associated Press* in late March 2023, Volodymyr Zelensky said that the systems received "from a European country" did not work and had to be repaired several times[566]. Here, as elsewhere, Westerners send obsolete and often defective equipment to Ukraine.

---

566. Julie Pace, Hanna Arhirova & James Jordan, "Takeaways from AP's interview with Ukraine's Zelenskyy," *AP*, March 30, 2023 (https://apnews.com/article/ukraine-zelenskyy-russia-putin-war-78f55fbf4fb7e57711c2fadaf914fd45)

4.9. Diversion

For weapons to be effective, they have to get to the front! In technical terms, diversion is the detour of weapons from their original purpose. It is a well-known phenomenon when a market is saturated with weapons. This was the case in Iraq and Afghanistan.

What journalists (liars or corrupt?) referred to as *"Russian disinformation"* in July 2022[567], seems to be verified by a *CBS News* documentary film, "Arming Ukraine", which finds that only 30-40% of the weapons sent reach their recipients[568]. After protests from Kiev, this documentary was quickly censored[569]...

It now seems to be confirmed that Ukrainians sold American HIMARS multiple missile launchers and French CAESAR self-propelled guns to the Russians. This allowed the latter to analyze the systems that fell into their hands and to develop countermeasures: software for anti-aircraft missiles and electronic countermeasures. As a result, the HIMARS so highly touted in the West have become commonplace threats.

This is why the Americans refused to supply Ukraine with four MQ1C GRAY EAGLE drones because of the risk of technology leakage[570]. This was also the reason for not supplying M1 ABRAMS tanks, whose armour is made of a particular alloy classified[571].

Believing their own propaganda, our journalists have totally ignored the diversionary phenomenon. While the *RAND Corporation* report

---

567. Gilles Sengès, "La Russie instille le doute sur la destination des armes occidentales livrées à l'Ukraine", *L'Opinion*, July 15, 2022 (https://www.lopinion.fr/international/la-russie-instille-le-doute-sur-la-destination-des-armes-occidentales-livrees-a-lukraine)
568. Adam Yamaguchi & Alex Pena, "Why military aid in Ukraine may not always get to the front lines," CBS News, August 7, 2022 (https://www.cbsnews.com/news/ukraine-military-aid-weapons-front-lines/)
569. Sinéad Baker, "CBS partially retracts documentary that outraged Ukraine by claiming that US weapon shipments were going missing", Business Insider, August 8, 2022 (https://www.businessinsider.com/cbs-partially-retracts-ukraine-docuemtnary-alleging-missing-us-weapons-2022-8)
570. Inder Singh Bisht, "Pentagon Postpones Armed MQ-1C Drone Sale to Ukraine," *The Defense Post*, June 21, 2022 (https://www.thedefensepost.com/2022/06/21/pentagon-postpones-mq1c-drone-ukraine/)
571. Joseph Trevithick, "M1 Abrams Tanks In U.S. Inventory Have Armor Too Secret To Send To Ukraine," *The War Zone*, January 25, 2023 (https://www.thedrive.com/the-war-zone/m1-abrams-tanks-in-u-s-inventory-have-armor-too-secret-to-send-to-ukraine)

warned of this problem in 2019 already[572], no verification mechanism was put in place by the Westerners[573].

In April 2023, investigative journalist Seymour Hersh published an article on the corruption of American and Ukrainian elites[574]. In it, he showed that Zelensky and his entourage had shamefully enriched themselves with the funds paid to him, to an amount estimated by a CIA analyst at 400 million dollars, by trafficking diesel from... Russia! The weapons supplied to Ukraine found their way to other countries, through front companies in Poland, the Czech Republic and Israel, which resell these weapons, leaving substantial "commissions" to Zelensky and his team.

Sometimes it seems that the war has become an opportunity for some in Ukraine. In July 2022, by the law 2425-IX[575] the members of the Verkhovna Rada[576], the Parliament of Ukraine, grant themselves a salary increase of 70%, which is to be financed by the budget of Ukraine. This is not a new or unique phenomenon, and Ukrainians are no worse than others in this regard. The problem is that this corruption is done with our financial support.

In January 2023, during his meeting with Zelensky, William Burns, director of the CIA, expressed his displeasure and gave him a list of 35 generals whose corruption was a little too conspicuous in the eyes of the American government. A few days later, Zelensky dismissed ten of them...

These dismissals come at a time when tensions are building in the Ukrainian leadership over the Bakhmut situation. In February 2023, Zelensky dismissed Ruslan Dzyuba, deputy commander of the National Guard[577], and then Major General Eduard Moskalyov, commander of Ukrainian forces in the Donbass (Forces of the Operational Command

---

572. James Dobbins, Raphael S. Cohen, Nathan Chandler, Bryan Frederick, Edward Geist, Paul DeLuca, Forrest E. Morgan, Howard J. Shatz, Brent Williams, "Extending Russia: Competing from Advantageous Ground," RAND Corporation, 2019, p. 101
573. "A Case for More Oversight of Military Aid to Ukraine," *Arms Control Association*, Volume 14, Issue 6, August 9, 2022 (https://www.armscontrol.org/issue-briefs/2022-08/case-more-oversight-military-aid-ukraine)
574. Seymour Hersh, "Trading with the Enemy," *Seymour Hersh Substack*, April 12, 2023 (https://seymourhersh.substack.com/p/trading-with-the-enemy)
575. https://zakon.rada.gov.ua/laws/show/2425-IX#Text
576. https://itd.rada.gov.ua/billInfo/Bills/Card/40038
577. Katerina Tishchenko, "Зеленський звільнив заступника командувача Нацгвардії," *Ukraïnska Pravda*, February 11, 2023 (https://www.pravda.com.ua/news/2023/02/11/7388966/)

"East")[578]. At the same time, Zelensky recomposed the Security and Defence Council by adding Ihor Klymenko, the new Minister of the Interior, and Vasyl Malyuk, the new head of the Ukrainian security service.

The dismissals that reflect the dilemma created by the situation in the Donbass

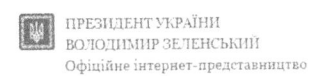

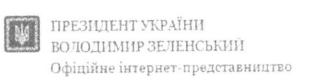

Figure 76 - The dismissals of the deputy commander of the National Guard and the commander of Ukrainian forces in the Donbass illustrate the tensions that exist in early 2023 within the Ukrainian leadership. The strategy of nibbling away at Ukrainian capabilities announced by Russia in the wake of massive Western arms deliveries is working.

---

578. Kateryna Tyshchenko, "Zelensky fired commander of joint forces," *Ukraïnska Pravda*, February 26, 2023 (https://www.pravda.com.ua/eng/news/2023/02/26/7391121/)

5. The information war

5.1. Failing Western media

As in any conflict, each belligerent tries to convince of the merits of its action. The problem that since 2014, our reading of the Ukrainian conflict is *exclusively* based on Ukrainian propaganda. This is what leads, in early 2023, to contradictory discourses about a Russia that "loses" and a Ukraine that fails to "win". Everything we are seeing today was predictable as early as June 2022. But the hatred of Russia and Russians has stifled reason and common sense.

A great lesson of the Ukrainian conflict is that our media - which boast of journalistic professionalism - *never* verify their information. The whole of the Belgian, French and Swiss traditional media work *exclusively* with the information spread by the Ukrainian propaganda, without verifying anything.

When we compare afterwards the information given by our media and the reality, we see a deliberate effort to give a perception of reality that is not aligned with facts, but with the politics of Western countries (Figure 78). Several observations can be made.

First of all, the main French-language media examined here (*RTBF* in Belgium, *France 5* and *LCI* in France, and *RTS* in Switzerland) have virtually only Ukrainian propaganda as their source. Even unofficial Ukrainian media, and even Russian opposition media, are excluded when they give a more nuanced picture of the conflict.

Evaluating information - the main problem of our media

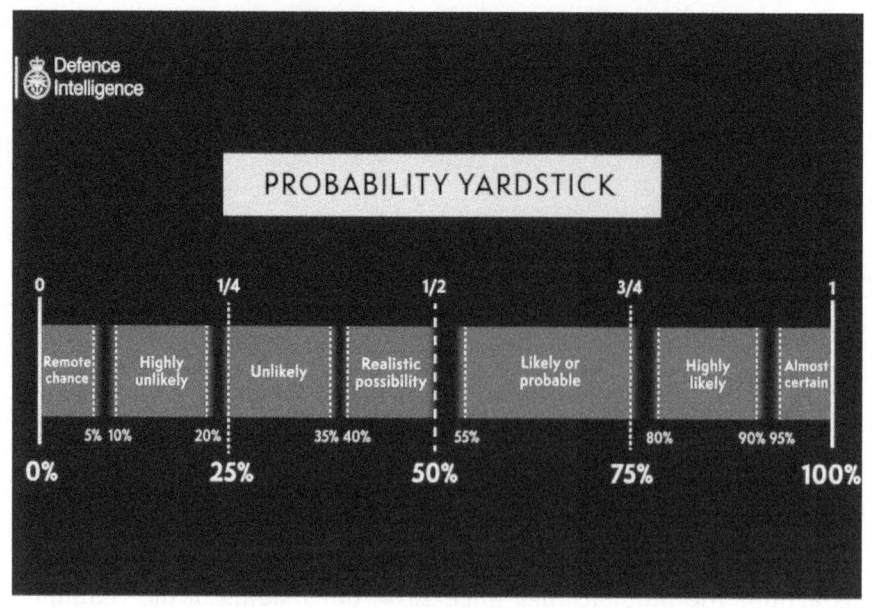

Figure 77 - Our journalists have yet to understand that words have meaning. In the world of intelligence, terms like "probable" or "improbable" have a quantifiable meaning. Here, the scale of terminology used by British military intelligence. Media like BFM TV, RTBF, France 5 or RTS have no rigor in the way they present information and the degree of realization of the information they give us. [Source: Defence Intelligence]

Then, when we look back a few weeks or even months later at the information given by our media, we see that the vast majority of it (>90%) was simply wrong. This could be explained by the "fog of war", but the examples we have given in this book show that this is not the case. In reality, the correct information was available at the time of broadcast by our media.

Moreover, the term "false" must be qualified. Because information is not composed of elements that are all false. In fact, we notice that the information served by our media is most often "recomposed", a bit like a poor quality cooked ham. In other words, media such as BFM TV, LCI or RTS provide us with information from which we have kept only the elements that support a given discourse. This is for example the case with nuclear weapons: they systematically omit to remind us of the Western threats, in order to make us believe that Vladimir Putin launched his threats without reason.

Comparison of the media used in this book

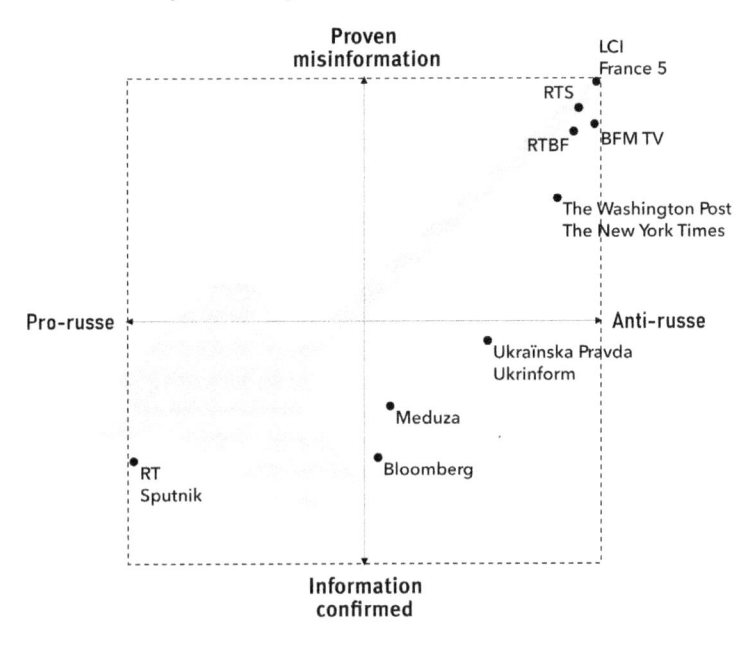

Figure 78 - Comparing the information given by the main media used in this book and comparing their information with the reality a few days later, taking into account the information available at the time of publication, we can see that they have systematically misinformed us. As we show in this book, media like LCI, RTS, France 5 and BFM TV work without respecting the Munich Charter on Journalism.

Thus, by systematically discarding elements of information that interfere with the official rhetoric, our media only retain information that supports a political approach: this is a practice that meets the technical definition of conspiracy.

The *"fact checkers"* rely on certain elements to accredit the information given by the media, but systematically ignore the elements left out by our media: we are therefore going in circles.

The inability of our leaders to understand the conflict, its real dynamics and therefore to develop strategies to end the crisis is the result of the image given by our media:
- By systematically generating a succession of incitements to hatred, polarizing minds and stifling all voices that tried to bring reason and dispassion to the reading of the facts.

- By misrepresenting Russia's stated objectives - which have proven to be consistent - our media have deliberately kept our governments and Ukraine from the right solutions.
- By suggesting a defeat of Russia based on *no* factual elements, which justified not engaging in a negotiation process.

In the spring of 2023, the Western narrative increasingly clashes with the reality on the ground. We can see that the West has trapped itself. Having judged Russia according to prejudices and not facts, they acted against an adversary they had largely underestimated.

Comparison of crisis communication in Ukraine and Russia

	Ukraine / West	**Russia**
Main axes	• Glorification of Ukrainian actions • Maximizing Russia's losses and failures	• Denunciation of « Russophobia ». • Absurdity of the Western accusations.
Channel axes	Communication largely based on social networks	Mainly based on institutional networks.
Style	Very contemporary and offensive. Emotional approach.	Sober and defensive. Rational and technical approach.
Form	Modern and using young codes, aiming more to influence than to inform.	Conventional, more academic, but more factual and reliable than in Ukraine.
Architecture	Zelensky is the keystone of the information strategy and all political and military communication goes through him.	Operational information is provided by the military, while information of a political and strategic nature is the responsibility of the presidential communication team (Maria Zakharova).
Approach	Volodymyr Zelensky fights in the information space.	Vladimir Putin fights in the material and real space.

Figure 79 - Two approaches to communication. If Ukrainian communication "catches on" more, it is probably the Russian approach that will pay off in the long run.

As we have demonstrated with many examples in this book, it appears from our observations that the policy of these media is to polarize the perception of the conflict. In other words: to maximize the hatred of Russians.

For example, on April 15, 2023, in front of the building housing the Parliamentary Assembly of the Commonwealth of Independent States (CIS) were displayed the flags of the member countries of the organization, including that of Ukraine. Officially it is still part of the organization and the Russian authorities wanted its flag to be present. It was removed by the people of St. Petersburg, causing the disapproval of the authorities[579]. This example illustrates the more mature and dispassionate nature of the official Russian approach to the conflict. Perhaps this is why no Western media reported on this incident, which was widely reported in Russia.

5.2. The role of intelligence

5.2.1. Strategic intelligence

Once again, we see the distressing understanding of the role of intelligence in the French media. Probably more used to the press of boulevard than to reflection, our journalists continue to understand intelligence, as in a James Bond movie[580]!

There are three levels of intelligence: strategic, operational and tactical. The role of strategic intelligence is to inform strategic political and/or military decisions. But it can only fulfill its mission under certain conditions:
- The first is that the decision-maker makes his decision after consulting and listening to his intelligence services. Today, however, our leaders live and decide at the pace of Twitter, and the speed of the decision takes precedence over its relevance. This is all the more true with weak personalities, but convinced of their superiority, such as Anthony Blinken in the United States, Emmanuel Macron (and many of his ministers!) in France, Annalena Baerbock in Germany, Sanna Marin in Finland or Kaja Kallas in Estonia.

---

579. "В России не поддержали сорвавших украинский флаг возле штаб-квартиры МПА СНГ", Lenta.ru, April 16, 2023 (https://lenta.ru/news/2023/04/16/nosupport/)
580. https://youtu.be/c44ZdBhcuno

- The second is the extent to which intelligence has the independence (and the courage) to formulate analyses that run counter to the expectations of the decision maker.
- The third is the capacity of the intelligence services to analyze the situation. This implies having the analytical capacity to process all the elements of information.

Depending on the nature of the conflict, it is 90-97% based on open sources, provided that care is taken to have a sufficiently wide range of sources to ensure impartiality of analysis. And that is the problem.

Our ministries and administrations feed the decision of the governments mainly on the basis of what the media say. However, these media have in the end one and only one source: propaganda (not media) from Ukraine. That is why our image of the conflict has little relation to reality, and our journalists are so surprised when they are confronted with the facts.

The publication, in April 2023, of classified documents (up to TOP SECRET) sheds unexpected light on the conflict and on the perception that the United States has of it. These documents are very controversial, because they provide a more nuanced picture of the operational situation in Ukraine than our media claim.

Without going into detail, what these documents reveal is that the Americans depend exclusively on the Ukrainians and the media for strategic analysis. They have a relatively accurate picture of what is deployed on the ground, thanks to their RQ-4 GLOBALHAWK and MQ-9 REAPER strategic drones. On the other hand, their casualty assessment seems to rely almost exclusively on Ukrainian information and open sources (such as the ORYX website). Larry Johnson, a former CIA agent, made exactly the same observation in January 2023[581].

This lack of information is confirmed by an article by Seymour Hersh on April 12, 2023, in which he explains that in January 2023, convinced of the Ukrainian victory, General Mark Milley, head of the Joint Chiefs of Staff, had a surrender plan drawn up for Russia after its defeat on the ground[582]. This initiative is all the more surprising given that in January,

---

581. Larry Johnson, "Blinded by the Lies - The U.S. Military is Relying on Ukrainian Intelligence," *Sonar 21*, January 4, 2023 (https://sonar21.com/blinded-by-the-lies-the-u-s-military-is-relying-on-ukrainian-intelligence/)
582. Seymour Hersh, "Trading With The Enemy," *Seymour Hersh Substack*, April 12, 2023 (https://seymourhersh.substack.com/p/trading-with-the-enemy)

the situation of Ukrainian forces in the Donbass was extremely precarious. This confirms that beyond *"bean counting"*, the Americans have a very poor understanding of the conflict.

The same phenomenon can be observed in France and Germany, where the intelligence services seem to be "lagging behind". However, I think that in both countries, the intelligence services have a more accurate picture of the conflict than their leaders. The problem comes essentially from the latter.

Switzerland is no exception. The Swiss ambassador to Ukraine described in our media a situation that was the direct result of Ukrainian propaganda, with no real connection to reality[583]. The problem is repeated in the *Annual Swiss Security Report*[584] published in September 2022 by the Swiss *Federal Intelligence Service* (SRC). It literally contains no analysis and only reports the situation as it comes from the Ukrainian services.

In May 2022, Sauli Niinisto, the Finnish president, was surprised that Vladimir Putin was not angry on the phone after his country's announcement to apply for NATO membership[585]. This means that his intelligence service was not able to "brief" him on the personality of his interlocutor or gave him false information.

The biggest mistake you can make in war is to underestimate your opponent and overestimate your own capabilities. Our media has pushed us to do this, while at the state level, strategic intelligence, whose role is to help politicians make rational decisions, has been unable to do so.

As Sir Jeremy Fleming, Director of the *Government Communication Headquarters* (GCHQ), the United Kingdom's electronic intelligence service[586], notes, a trend has been emerging in the West over the past twenty years to use intelligence services as organs of information for the public. In fact, intelligence services have become organs of communication, intended to support political discourse.

---

583. https://www.rts.ch/play/tv/redirect/detail/13567586?startTime=383
584. https://www.newsd.admin.ch/newsd/message/attachments/72369.pdf
585. Peter Aitken, "Finland President surprised at Putin's 'calm' response to NATO membership news," *Fox News*, May 15, 2022 (https://www.foxnews.com/world/finland-president-putin-calm-nato-membership)
586. Evie Coffey, "GCHQ head says Ukraine conflict marked 'sea-change' in release of intelligence," *Gloucestershire Live*, December 29, 2022 (https://www.gloucestershirelive.co.uk/news/uk-world-news/gchq-head-says-ukraine-conflict-7976536)

5.3. Russian disinformation

The main weakness of the West in today's complex world is that it seems to perceive situations only through its own prejudices. Since the Cold War, everything that comes from Russia (and the USSR before that) is perceived in the West as propaganda or disinformation (which in the minds of journalists is exactly the same thing).

In the middle of the Ukrainian conflict, to convince us of the Russian disinformation, the Swiss journalist Jean-Philippe Schaller did not find a better example than the operation INFEKTION of the KGB, dating from... 1985[587]!

As the Soviets acknowledged in August 1987[588], INFEKTION was a disinformation operation blaming the United States for the creation of the AIDS virus[589]. According to Yevgeny Primakov, then director of the Central Intelligence Service (TsSR)[590], the aim was to divert attention from the attempted assassination of Pope John Paul II, so as not to "lose" Catholic populations in developing countries, where the USSR was fighting against "Western imperialism.

It is symptomatic that Jean-Philippe Schaller is reduced to looking for KGB operations from the 1980s to demonstrate Russian disinformation today. The choice of our journalist shows that even during the Cold War examples of Soviet (or Russian) disinformation are rare. The communist system favored propaganda (literally: "what is worth spreading") that emphasizes positive points (as in a commercial), but is (usually) not false. The same philosophy can be observed today.

For our journalists, the notion of "disinformation" is variable geometry. Trolling on social networks coming from Russia is automatically attributed to the Russian government and qualified as disinformation. On the other hand, examples of Western disinformation are ostensibly implausible ("Putin would take bloodbaths"). What is qualified as "disinformation" for Russia, becomes *"story telling"* for Ukraine[591]!

---

587. https://youtu.be/bEv4-IJsl9k?t=1337
588. Thomas Boghardt, "Operation INFEKTION - Soviet Bloc Intelligence and Its AIDS", *Studies in Intelligence* Vol. 53, No. 4, CIA, December 2009
589. https://cia.gov/resources/csi/studies-in-intelligence/volume-53-no-4/soviet-bloc-intelligence-and-its-aids-disinformation-campaign/
590. The former 1st Main Directorate of the KGB, which will become the *Foreign Intelligence Service* (SVR).
591. https://youtu.be/bEv4-IJsl9k?t=285

The information disseminated by the Russian media, such as RT or Sputnik, focuses - quite logically - on the elements that work against Ukraine. However, we can see that the information given is very often correct, unlike the official Ukrainian information which is very often false. In technical terms, Russia tends to favor propaganda, while Ukraine uses disinformation.

5.4. The Ukrainian and Western information war

5.4.1. Information structures

Ukrainian communication on the conflict is extremely complex. It is being developed with the support of the *NATO Center of Excellence for Strategic Communication* (COE *StratCom*) based in Riga, Latvia, which was established in January 2014 in the wake of Euromaidan[592]. On July 1st, 2014, a Memorandum of Understanding between Germany, Spain, Italy, Lithuania, Latvia, Poland, and the United Kingdom made the center an international organization. It was accredited as a NATO Center of Excellence on September 1, 2014 by the North Atlantic Council, with the stated goal of supporting Ukraine[593]. Today, it is one of the centers that coordinates disinformation and propaganda about the Ukrainian conflict.

Created in the aftermath of the 2014 Ukrainian crisis, the UK *Integrity Initiative* (II) was only revealed to the public in late 2018 by an *Anonymous* hack[594]. At that point, Russian intelligence was naturally accused of running a disinformation campaign against NATO. This is not impossible, but there is no evidence of it at this stage, as the documents revealed - including lists of names of NI agents and correspondents abroad - appear to be authentic. In November 2018, the British government actually confirmed that it was funding this initiative[595].

---

592. www.stratcomcoe.org/
593. "Latvia shares NATO STRATCOM experience with Ukraine," LSM.lv, October 27, 2015 (https://eng.lsm.lv/article/society/society/latvia-shares-nato-stratcom-experience-with-ukraine.a152152/)
594. telegra.ph/OP-HMG-Trojan-Horse-Part-4-Undermining-Russia-I-02-04
595. *Foreign and Commonwealth Office: Integrity Initiative, Question for Foreign and Commonwealth Office*, UIN 196177, November 27, 2018.

The II was created under the aegis of the British Foreign Office (FCO), which is also responsible for the *Secret Intelligence Service* (MI-6) and the *Government Communications Headquarters* (GCHQ) in charge of cyber warfare, which are associated with this initiative. It is funded by the British Ministry of Defence and the army, the Lithuanian Ministry of Defence and NATO, and aims to *"combat Russian disinformation in Europe".* It uses the *BBC* and *Reuters* to promote an "official" narrative. It includes computer marketing networks and private intelligence agencies such as Bellingcat, and relies on national "clusters" composed of correspondents in each participating country.

The national clusters are the most disturbing aspect of the II. Its members, belong to official or reputedly independent institutions. Thus, in France, British officials made the first contacts with government officials in early 2016. After a meeting in Paris in May, they note:

> *The French are very nationalistic, anti-American. There is also admiration for brute force ("the Napoleon complex"). As a result, there is a clear tendency to admire Putin, combined with a historical feeling of closeness to Russia that makes them sympathize with Russia.*[596]

This will result in the creation, *"independently of the government",* of the *"Integrity France"* cluster. How complete and still correct are the lists of names revealed in 2018? This is uncertain, but they question the integrity of the institutions that inform or inform our politicians. They include journalists, officials from the Ministry of Foreign Affairs, the *General Secretariat of Defense and National Security* (SGDSN), Rudy Reichstadt and several collaborators of *Conspiracy Watch*[597], Françoise Thom (who denounces the foreign-paid media (!) and opponent of a diplomatic dialogue with Russia[598]) or Galia Ackerman, who regularly intervenes on *France 5* about Russia. In the Belgian cluster (2019), there are NATO and

---

596. CND Paris & Brussels May 2-4, 2016 (https://www.pdf-archive.com/2018/12/13/cnd-paris--bxl-may-2016-v2/).
597. Benoît Bréville, "Chasseur de 'conspis'", *Le Monde diplomatique*, April-May 2018; Brice Perrier, "Conspiracy Watch de Rudy Reichstadt: les contradictions de l'anti-complotiste professionnel", *Marianne*, November 23, 2019; Laurent Dauré, "Quand les 'complotologues' de Franceinfo font l'impasse sur la principale théorie du complot de l'ère Trump", *Acrimed*, March 10, 2021.
598. Isabelle Mandraud, "Françoise Thom, la procureur de Poutine," *Le Monde*, October 21, 2019.

EU officials, as well as researchers from the *Free University of Brussels*; in the Swiss cluster (2019), there are people paid by the Swiss Ministry of Defense. In the British cluster, unsurprisingly, there is *Bellingcat* and Vladimir Achourkov, a close collaborator of Navalny.

As for *Bellingcat* - which is regularly referred to by far-right conspiracists, *Conspiracy Watch*, and many Western media outlets - an internal UK *Integrity Initiative* document from June 2018 on countering Russian disinformation judges it as follows:

> *Bellingcat has been somewhat discredited, both by spreading misinformation itself and by being willing to produce reports for anyone willing to pay.*[599]

Technically, individuals employed by one government, but simultaneously working underhandedly for the benefit of another, as part of an influencing activity, fit the definition of *"agents of influence"*[600]. This is a situation where employees of national governments may have conflicts of interest with the policy decisions of their employer. This contributes to what some call the "deep state," which can generate dynamics different from those intended by the elected authorities. This can lead to situations comparable to that of France towards Germany, when Clément Beaune, Secretary of State for European Affairs, publicly spoke out in favour of abandoning the *Nord Stream 2* project[601] because of the Navalny affair, forcing Yves Le Drian, and then Emmanuel Macron, to clarify that France considers the two cases to be separate[602].

The II is essentially a structure of influence, which has little in common with "fact-checking". As described in its *"guide,"* its role is essentially to discredit Russia's responses to attacks on it, which have never been demonstrated, remain unexplained, or only partially described (the Skripal affair, the MH-17 disaster in Ukraine, the "annexation" of

---

599. *Upskilling to Upscale: Unleashing the Capacity of Civil Society to Counter Disinformation*, Final Report, June 2018, p. 72.
600. en.wikipedia.org/wiki/Influencer
601. "Affaire Navalny: la France favorable à l'abandon du projet de gazoduc Nord Stream 2, selon le secrétaire d'État chargé des Affaires européennes", *franceinfo.fr*, February 1st, 2021.
602. "France will not intervene with Germany on Nord Stream 2, says Le Drian," *Reuters*, February 3, 2021.

Crimea, cyber attacks...)[603]. In June 2018, during a meeting organized by the FCO to mobilize support for influence operations, the objective of the operation is clearly stated: *"The program aims to weaken Russia's influence on its neighbors"*[604], without mentioning once the rule of law or human rights.

This type of structure is a threat to the rule of law, because the problem is not so much responding to information coming from Russia, but rather the spirit and ethics we put into it. For example, II is a tool that can be used rather quickly, for example when it comes to campaigning against the Labour Party in Great Britain[605]. If organizations like *Conspiracy Watch* in France are the subject of controversy, it is less because of their fight against conspiracy than because of a lack of intellectual rigor and ethics in the way they do it.

The problem is that by dint of seeing disinformation in everything that might seem favorable or positive for Russia, media outlets like RTS, LCI or BFM TV and outlets like Conspiracy Watch, working outside the principles of the Munich Charter, end up doing disinformation themselves. As a June 2018 UK *Integrity Initiative* document[606] puts it:

> *Another obstacle to combating disinformation is the fact that some Kremlin-backed stories are factually true [...]. Responding to inconvenient truths, as opposed to pure propaganda, is naturally more problematic.*

This explains why the strategy of these media is to carry out personal attacks against discordant voices, in order to reinforce their own discourse.

---

603. The Integrity Initiative Guide to Countering Russian Disinformation (https://www.pdf-archive.com/2018/11/02/untitled-pdf-document-1/)
604. *Supplier Event, Support for Independent Media in Eastern Partnership Countries, Support for Independent Media in the Baltic States*, Foreign & Commonwealth Office, London, June 26, 2018.
605. Chris York, "How A Murky Row Over Russia, Jeremy Corbyn And A 'Psyops Campaign' Went Mainstream," *huffingtonpost.co.uk*, February 2, 2019; Mark McLaughlin, "Hacker-hit research group the Integrity Initiative is sorry for Jeremy Corbyn tweets," *The Times*, April 6, 2019.
606. *Upskilling to Upscale: Unleashing the Capacity of Civil Society to Counter Disinformation*, Final Report, June 2018, p. 55 (paragraph 5.3).(https://www.pdf-archive.com/2019/03/22/untitled-pdf-document-1/)

5.4.2. Different philosophies

The analysis of the communication on the conflict in Ukraine and Russia shows different philosophies of information.

As for the form, Ukrainian communication is very "young. It is based on the dissemination of "messages" and not on the reflection of reality: it does not matter if what is said is verified on the ground, the important thing is that people believe it. Propaganda films seem to be straight out of electronic games. Everything is communication, just like Volodymyr Zelensky, who acts by his very presence and not by his content. An effort is made on the tone of voice that mark the will to fight and determination. A huge work is done on social networks to disseminate the official Ukrainian propaganda, which feeds our media, to the exclusion of any other source.

The Ukrainian LGBT Battalion

Figure 80 - Shoulder badge of the LGBT battalion. It includes a unicorn (right) fire (lower left) and trident (upper left). The establishment of an LGBT battalion illustrates Ukraine's communication philosophy, which is based on popular codes in the Western political class. This battalion was observed in Kremennaya, Donbass[607].

The communication codes (smileys, but in heart, etc.) and dress codes (battle dress and T-shirt) are also young and directed at an uncritical audience with a low cultural level, used to receiving "ready-made" information and incapable of analysis. For the European Union summit in Kiev in early February 2023, guidelines for participants asked to avoid the

---
607. https://lgbtmilitary.org.ua/eng

color khaki (the color of President Zelensky's outfit[608]) as well as bright colors (in order to keep the attention on Zelensky)[609].

In contrast, Russian communication has a more austere, factual and traditional form; some would say "old-fashioned". It relies heavily on the traditions and values of Eastern European populations, such as the family, the church and respect for elders. Dress codes remain traditional (suit, tie). The difference in approach was evident during the discussions initiated by Ukraine at the end of February 2022, when the two delegations faced each other in Belarus: on the one hand, the Ukrainians in combat gear, and on the other, the Russians in suits and ties[610].

As for the substance, Ukrainian communication uses younger themes, often taken from the world of electronic games, and is also more juvenile in its content. In contrast, Russian communication is less prolific, more restrained and less attractive, but more mature and reliable.

If we take a step back, the differences in approach lead us to different conceptions of society. Strongly supported by the Western communication apparatus, Ukraine seems to espouse a lighter society, without real values, where the immediate is opposed to the long term, where the individual is opposed to the collective.

Russia is playing less on emotions and more on facts. If we look at the information disseminated by the official Ukrainian and Russian media, we can see that the Russians have systematically provided correct information. Generally speaking, Ukrainians are ready to falsify the truth to maintain their image, while Russians would rather hide what does not serve them. While the Ukrainian information is very often wrong, the Russian information tends to be incomplete.

In technical terms, Ukraine tends to practice disinformation, while Russia is more about propaganda. Disinformation is the spreading of

---

608. James Crisp, "Don't dress like Volodymyr Zelensky when in Kyiv, EU officials warned," *The Telegraph*, February 2, 2023 (https://www.telegraph.co.uk/world-news/2023/02/02/dont-dress-like-volodymyr-zelensky-when-kyiv-eu-officials-warned/)
609. Florian Eder, "The EU's Ukraine trip dress code: Wear a suit, not green like Zelenskyy", *Politico*, February 1st, 2023 (https://www.politico.eu/article/eu-ukraine-summit-trip-dress-code-brussels-military-volodymyr-zelenskyy-russian-invasion-solidarity-kyiv/)
610. "Russia, Ukraine set to resume negotiations via video link Monday," *The Times of Israel*, March 14, 2022 (https://www.timesofisrael.com/russia-ukraine-set-to-resume-negotiations-via-video-link-monday/)

false information, while propaganda is the spreading only of "what is worth spreading".

Western communication tends rather to accept the image of war

Figure 81 - NATO tweet: "Ukraine is the scene of one of the greatest epics of this century - We are Harry Potter and William Wallace, the Na'vi and Han Solo. We escape from Shawshank and blow up the Death Star. We fight with the Harkonnens and challenge Thanos." [Source: https://twitter.com/NATO/status/1628687961477750790/photo/1]

5.4.3. Principles of Ukrainian and Western communication

5.4.3.1 Isolating the opponent

This method is widely used by Western countries and Israel to try to remove all credibility from the opponent. The most famous examples are the Palestinians, Iran, China and Venezuela. This is obviously the objective of sanctions, but information warfare extends their effects.

As with the sanctions, the objective is to reach the population, in order to instrumentalize their anger or humiliation to provoke a change in their leaders. This is why, from the beginning of the Russian intervention, the language adopted by our media and our leaders has clearly incited hatred.

This explains the exclusion of Russians from competitions like Eurovision, or even cats from cat shows. Moreover, in Belgium there is concern about the racism[611] of which[612] people of Russian origin are victims[613]. A phenomenon that seems to worry neither France nor Switzerland... two countries where racism is becoming a culture!

The isolation of the opponent is not only a foreign policy tool, but also a way to fight against free speech. By stigmatizing dissenting opinions, they are pushed aside to make room for the official narrative. This is the objective of the list published in July 2022 by the *Center for Combating Disinformation* (CPD) of the National Security and Defense Council of Ukraine. It lists international speakers who *"promote narratives in line with Russian propaganda"*, which include members of the U.S. Congress, politicians, journalists, ex-agents of Western intelligence services. At the time, it listed my name[614], but in the latest version of the list published in December 2022 my name was removed, along with that of Tulsi Gabbard[615].

---

611. Ludovic Jimenez, "Rentre chez toi rejoindre ton peuple de barbares": les Russes de Belgique victimes de harcèlement et de racisme", DHnet.be, March 10, 2022 (https://www.dhnet.be/actu/belgique/2022/03/10/rentre-chez-toi-rejoindre-ton-peuple-de-barbares-les-russes-de-belgique-victimes-de-harcelement-et-de-racisme-USQWGLLUZZB6VIT5C4KIZE7F6U/)
612. Romain Van Dyck, "'He gets picked on at school because he's Russian' says a student", RTL.be, March 5, 2022 (https://5minutes.rtl.lu/actu/luxembourg/a/1870898.html)
613. "Harassment and racism: the Russians of Belgium collateral victims of the Russian invasion", *Metro/AFP*, March 10, 2022 (https://fr.metrotime.be/belgique/harcelement-et-racisme-les-russes-de-belgique-victimes-collaterales-de-linvasion-russe)
614. https://cpd.gov.ua/reports/спікери-які-просувають-співзвучні-ро/
615. https://cpd.gov.ua/reports/spikery-yaki-prosuvayut-spivzvuchni-rosijskij-propagandi-naratyvy-2/

This practice is still widely used by the European state media. Ironically, the only authorization of a narrative aligned with Kiev's propaganda has made them completely ignore the difficulties of the Ukrainian army. Thus, paradoxically, by wanting to protect Ukraine, media such as RTS (Switzerland), France 5, LCI, BFM TV (France) or RTBF (Belgium) have largely contributed to maintain its failures. By wanting to establish a form of censorship, these media have become largely responsible (with others) for the evolution of the situation.

5.4.3.2. Putting down and humiliating the opponent

Systematically belittling Russia or presenting it as weak and inefficient. This ranges from assertions - never substantiated - about the lack of ammunition, the inefficiency of logistics, the incompetence of military commanders, to the poor quality of materials and armaments, through the lack of willingness of Russians to fight.

The preferred method of Ukraine and the West to misinform the Western population is the "mirror" effect, also called "projection". It is a matter of projecting one's own defects, problems or mistakes onto the opponent and appropriating his successes.

At the end of March 2022, the Russian troops advancing in Ukraine discover many cases of war crimes: revenge against the civilian population, killing of "collaborators", killing of supporters at a negotiation, etc. The images begin to circulate on social networks. Zelensky fears that these revelations will call into question Western support[616]. But these Ukrainian crimes are real.

The evocation of a massacre in Boutcha comes at the right time, on April 2, 2022. What exactly happened there? Nobody knows[617]. But some civilians were executed, others appear to have been collateral victims of the fighting. As for who was responsible, Ukraine accuses the Russian army, while Russia claims that it was a falsification. Ukrainian

---

616. "Zelenskyy Worried About Western Financial Support After Video Surfaces Showing Ukraine Military Torturing Russian POW's," www.theconservativetreehouse.com, March 27, 2022 (https://theconservativetreehouse.com/blog/2022/03/27/zelenskyy-worried-about-western-financial-support-after-video-surfaces-showing-ukraine-military-torturing-russian-pows/)

617. "Pentagon can't independently confirm atrocities in Ukraine's Bucha, official says," *Reuters*, April 4, 2022 (https://www.reuters.com/world/pentagon-cant-independently-confirm-atrocities-ukraines-bucha-official-says-2022-04-04/)

socialist MP Ilya Kiva[618] reveals on his Telegram channel that the tragedy of Butcha was planned by the British MI6 special services and implemented by the SBU[619].

The point here is not to determine responsibility - which should be the task of a neutral and impartial international commission - but to note that we are systematically in a duel of narratives. What is at stake for Ukraine is to maintain the level of interest - and therefore of support - of the West. This is why it has a more aggressive communication strategy, which is not based on veracity, but on its emotional content.

Our state media have become tools of propaganda, asserting without ever proving anything. In Switzerland, the RTS even denounced Russian war crimes in Ukraine, which the Ukrainians themselves considered as falsifications. This is the case of the rapes committed by Russian troops. It is very likely that rapes were committed by soldiers on both sides. But at the beginning of April 2022, suddenly, there was an upsurge in these accusations. They came from the Ukrainian Commissioner for Human Rights, Lyudmila Denisova[620]. RTS reports on these rapes, stressing that these crimes have been carefully verified[621] and that they *"are part of the Russian war arsenal"*, while acknowledging that *"complaints are rare"*[622]. But RTS does not exactly have a reputation for honesty and integrity. The problem is that it's all false[623] Denisova was sacked because the accusations were not supported by evidence and her allegations damaged Ukraine's image, according to Ukrainian media outlet *Ukrinform*[624].

---

618. https://en.wikipedia.org/wiki/Illia_Kyva
619. https://t.me/intelslava/24353
620. https://www.francetvinfo.fr/monde/europe/manifestations-en-ukraine/guerre-en-ukraine-apres-le-massacre-de-boutcha-les-temoignages-glacants-des-victimes-de-viols-commis-par-l-occupant-russe_5145007.htm
621. https://www.rts.ch/audio-podcast/2022/audio/multiplication-des-accusations-de-viols-en-ukraine-interview-de-lea-rose-stoian-25813937.html
622. https://www.rts.ch/info/monde/13005321-les-viols-de-civils-font-partie-de-larsenal-de-guerre-russe-en-ukraine.html
623. https://hromadske.ua/posts/deputati-zibrali-pidpisi-za-vidstavku-ombudsmenki-denisovoyi-vona-nazivaye-mozhlive-zvilnennya-nezakonnim
624. https://www.ukrinform.fr/rubric-ato/3496821-la-commissaire-aux-droits-de-lhomme-ukrainienne-demise-de-ses-fonctions.html

Figure 82 - Here on the site of the Ukrainian military intelligence (GUR), the word "Russia", (which is always written with a capital letter in English) is deliberately and systematically written with a lower case. This somewhat primitive and very Western type of communication is not observed in Russian communication. [https://gur.gov.ua/en/content/rosiia-bilshe-ne-stanovyt-viiskovoi-zahrozy-svitu.html]

5.4.3.3. Minimizing fanaticism and extremism in Ukraine

In his speech on February 24, 2022, Vladimir Putin stated the two main objectives of the SVO: "demilitarization" and "denazification." In fact, he used two of the "four Ds" of the 1945 Potsdam Declaration concerning defeated Germany: *demilitarization, denazification, decentralization* and *democratization*. It should be noted that *decentralization* and *democratization* were at the heart of the philosophy of the Minsk agreements, which would have made it possible to resolve the crisis in Donbass. But the West has de facto refused to implement these agreements.

With the objective of "denazification", "Nazism" is making a strong comeback in the communication and propaganda of both sides. The result is a cacophony, in which "Nazism" is sometimes associated with Ukraine, sometimes with Russia. The opacity created by the incapacity of our media and pseudo-experts has made it impossible to read the problem intelligently.

For it is not easy to see. We have trouble grasping the fact that Zelensky is a Jew, and that his henchmen are neo-Nazis. To simplify and not to enter into vast historical controversies, "Nazi" refers to a political ideology, while "neo-Nazi" refers more to a behavior.

For Ukrainians, these two notions tend to be confused: the SS of the Panzer Division "Das Reich" liberated Kharkov in 1943, while those of the 14th Grenadier Division "1. Galizien" defended the short-lived independence of Ukraine. As in the Baltic states, the troops of the Third Reich retained a prestige not known in Western Europe. On the other hand, for the Russians, the Nazis were responsible for some 25 million deaths.

In Ukraine, the issue is less "Nazi" than "neo-Nazi," a difference our journalists avoid making. In February 2022, the goal of "denazification" was to eradicate the threat of ultra-nationalist and neo-Nazi militias against the people of Donbass. They were created as early as 2014 to supplement the lack of combativeness and brutality of the Ukrainian army, and the objective of the Minsk agreements was precisely to stop their exactions. But the West had no intention of doing so[625].

---

625. "Civilian casualties in the conflict-affected regions of eastern Ukraine," *Organization for Security and Co-operation in Europe*, November 9, 2020 (https://www.osce.org/special-monitoring-mission-to-ukraine/469734)

At the end of March, with the encirclement of Mariupol - the cradle of neo-Nazi militias - Colonel-General Sergei Rudskoy, head of the Main Operations Directorate of the Russian General Staff (GOU), announced that the objectives of the first phase of the SVO had been achieved[626]. The *Financial Times*[627] and *Business Insider*[628] state that the Russian command considers the objective of "denazification" to have been achieved and will not be subject to further negotiations.

Today, the fate of the Tatar community is frequently used to stigmatize the role of Russia. In 2016, the Eurovision Grand Prix was awarded to the Ukrainian Jamala, who sang about the deportation of Tatars, by the Soviets in 1944. According to *Franceinfo*, "*a minority of Tatars apparently collaborated with the Nazis*"[629]. The word "*apparently*" tends to suggest that it could be false information: the role of collaboration with the Nazis is relativized and minimized, the better to castigate Russia, as in the newspaper *La Croix*[630].

In fact, the several tens of thousands of voluntarily enlisted Tatars formed seven large units of the Waffen SS[631]. In 1944, after having surrounded them in Crimea, Stalin wanted to keep them away from the front by deporting them to the East. They were not allowed to return to the Crimea until the early 1980s.

626.. "Ukraine: EU doubles military aid to €1 billion - as it happened," dw.com, March 23, 2022 (https://www.dw.com/en-ukraine-eu-doubles-military-aid-to-1-billion-as-it-happened/a-61226171; https://p.dw.com/p/48tit).
627.. "Russia no longer requesting Ukraine be 'denazified' as part of ceasefire talks," *Financial Times*, March 28, 2022 (https://www.ft.com/content/7f14efe8-2f4c-47a2-aa6b-9a755a39b626).
628. Matthew Loh, "Russia is prepared to drop its demand for Ukraine to be 'denazified' from its list of ceasefire conditions," *Business Insider*, March 29, 2022 (https://www.businessinsider.com/russia-nazi-demand-for-ukraine-dropped-in-ceasefire-talks-2022-3?r=US&IR=T)
629. Jacques Deveaux, "Who are the Tatars sung by Jamala, the Eurovision winning singer?", *Franceinfo*, May 15, 2016 (https://www.francetvinfo.fr/monde/russie/qui-sont-les-tatars-chantes-par-jamala-la-chanteuse-vainqueur-de-leurovision_3063393.html)
630. Olivier Tallès, "Les Tatars de Crimée sous la pression de Moscou," *La Croix*, September 13, 2017 (https://www.la-croix.com/Monde/Europe/Tatars-Crimee-pression-Moscou-2017-09-13-1200876387)
631. The Tatar volunteers formed 7 militias and units attached to the Waffen-SS: SS-Waffengruppe Idel-Ural, Waffen-Gebirgs-Brigade der SS (Tatar Nr. 1), 30. Waffen-Grenadier-Division der SS (russische Nr. 2), Wolgatatarische Legion, Tataren-Gebirgsjäger-Regiment der SS, Waffen-Gruppe Krim, Schutzmannschaft Battalion. In all, it can be estimated that 40,000-60,000 Tatars fought with the German forces.

Main Tatar units of the Waffen SS

| 30. Waffen-Grenadier-Division der SS (russische Nr. 2) | Waffen-Gebirgs-Brigade der SS (Tatar Nr. 1) | SS-Waffengruppe Idel-Ural Wolgatatarische Legion |

Figure 83 - It is fashionable today to minimize the role of the Tatars in the service of the Third Reich. The "afficionados" of the latter try to minimize their role in order to legitimize the opposition to Russia.

5.4.3.4. Reductio ad-Hitlerum

Since the end of World War II, Hitler has been used as a "unit of measure" of evil for the enemies of the West: Slobodan Milosevic[632], Saddam Hussein[633], Ali Khamenei[634]. Vladimir Putin is no exception to the rule. The media get carried away, but remain incapable of providing facts[635] that could support their accusations with a disturbing intellectual

---

632. Ken Livingstone, "Comment: Why we are not wrong to compare Milosevic to Hitler," The Independent, April 21, 1999 (https://www.independent.co.uk/arts-entertainment/comment-why-we-are-not-wrong-to-compare-milosevic-to-hitler-1088574.html)
633. Tom Raum, "Bush Says Saddam Even Worse Than Hitler," *AP News*, November 1st, 1990 (https://apnews.com/article/c456d72625fba6c742d17f1699b18a16)
634. Arash Azizi, "Khamenei's Open Dream: Finishing Where Hitler Left Off," *Iranwire*, May 21, 2020 (https://iranwire.com/en/special-features/67072/); Jas Chana, "Was Hitler's anti-Semitism different than Khamenei's?", The Times of Israel, September 18, 2015 (https://www.timesofisrael.com/was-hitlers-anti-semitism-different-than-khameneis/)
635. Laurence Piret, "Putin and Hitler, similar profiles? La comparaison qui fait débat !", *Sudinfo.be*, June 10, 2022 (https://www.sudinfo.be/id467294/article/2022-06-10/poutine-et-hitler-des-profils-similaires-la-comparaison-qui-fait-debat)From a very Western perspective, Ukraine relies more on the number of weapons, while the Russians place more emphasis on how they are used. This explains, among other things, Ukraine's pressing demands for modern Western weapons, while the Russians seem to make better use of the strengths of their various weapons systems, including those that appear obsolete, as we shall see.

poverty. In fact, they have gone beyond politics to propaganda of the lowest order[636].

For the comparison is dangerous: Milosevic was cleared in 2016 by the Criminal Tribunal on Yugoslavia[637]. Saddam Hussein was convicted of being responsible for the death of "only" 148 people. Certainly, this is a crime, but 148 remains quite modest compared to the "score" of George W. Bush, Barack Obama, Tony Blair, Nicolas Sarkozy, François Hollande, Emmanuel Macron and many other Western leaders. One can therefore draw two possible conclusions: either the comparison is exaggerated, or Hitler was not so bad after all!

As we can see, easy invective, thrown out into the open, can have perverse and counter-productive effects. We observe in France the same flaw as in the United States: the conviction that only our way of thinking is right. From then on, the facts, and their perception by others, are insignificant and we arrange reality as we perceive it. Because in Ukraine, Vladimir Putin is not Hitler. As one Euromaidan activist said: *"Putin is not even a Russian. He is a Jew!*[638]*"*

In the French magazine *Le Point,* the journalist François-Guillaume Lorrain sketches a parallel between the special operation and the German intervention in the Sudetenland in 1938[639]. The comparison would be interesting, provided that it is honest... which it is not.

The Sudeten crisis was triggered by the anger of the German minority, whose language had been banned by the Czech government, contrary to the provisions of the Treaties of Versailles and St. Germain. It was after the violent repression suffered by the German-speaking minority that Germany intervened. Ironically, when Bernard-Henri Lévy addressed the population of Kiev on March 2, 2014, he explained that *"Hitler (...) argued that the Sudeten Germans spoke German in order to invade*

---

636. "Putin as Hitler in his bunker: 'Russia is losing,'" *Courrier International*, September 20, 2022 (https://www.courrierinternational.com/une/vu-de-tchequie-poutine-en-hitler-dans-son-bunker-la-russie-est-en-train-de-perdre)
637. Patrick Besson, "Le triomphe modeste," Le Point, September 17, 2016 (https://www.lepoint.fr/editos-du-point/patrick-besson/besson-le-triomphe-modeste-17-09-2016-2069084_71.php)
638. Shaun Walker, "Azov fighters are Ukraine's greatest weapon and may be its greatest threat," *The Guardian*, September 10, 2014 (https://www.theguardian.com/world/2014/sep/10/azov-far-right-fighters-ukraine-neo-nazis)
639. François-Guillaume Lorrain, "Poutine-Hitler, même combat?", *Le Point*, February 23, 2022 (https://www.lepoint.fr/debats/poutine-hitler-meme-combat-23-02-2022-2465943_2.php)

Czechoslovakia[640]," when in fact it was precisely the suppression of this right that was at the origin of the crisis.

It is thanks to journalists like this that history stutters, because the same causes often have the same effects. Thus, on February 24, 2014, Ms. Astrid Thors, OSCE High Commissioner on National Minorities, warned the new Ukrainian government that emerged from Mayan, against *"quick decisions that could lead to an escalation of the situation"* in a context where *"languages are a divisive issue"*[641]. She was right, and we knew it! If our journalist from Le *Point* had sounded the alarm at that moment, we would not be here today... But he did not!

While the linguistic question is at the origin of the Ukrainian conflict, it is totally absent from the analyses in France. Because this question is inconceivable for a French brain: France has maintained its unity by harshly repressing the use of regional languages seen as the expression of nationalisms opposed to the power of Paris.

In fact, the puerile "Hitler-Putin" comparisons mask our inability to learn from history. And France should know this. Munich in 1938 was the consequence of a bad treaty of Versailles, resulting from France's vengeful spirit. One hundred years later, the same causes have the same effects with Ukraine. Yet, France could have avoided this "stuttering" of History by enforcing the Minsk agreements that it had signed. But we know today that François Hollande never had the intention to make Ukraine apply these agreements. He thus endorsed the discriminatory policy of the Ukrainian government, which led to the Russian intervention.

5.4.4. Losses

From the beginning of the Russian intervention, the Western narrative revolves around the Russian defeat, the unexpected resistance of Ukraine and the inability of Vladimir Putin to assess the risks in a rational manner. It is therefore necessary to show that the Russians are losing more men than the Ukrainians in this operation. To do this, our media use the oldest weapon in the world: the lie.

---

640. "March 2, 2014, BHL, Kiev, second address at Maidan," *YouTube*, March 5, 2014 (https://youtu.be/w3jpkzdBTlY)
641. http://www.osce.org/hcnm/115643

This war of numbers is only possible because the real numbers are unknown: the Ukrainian government does not communicate them, and the Russian authorities do so only sparingly. From then on, estimates become facts and facts become language.

Thus, some "officials" (we don't really know what this means) speak of a ratio of 1 Ukrainian for every 5 Russians killed. Oleksei Danilov, secretary of the Ukrainian Security and Defense Council, estimates this ratio at 1 to 7[642].

5.4.4.1. Russian losses: confusion of terms and war of influence

From the examination of the figures on Russian losses, we observe that Ukraine systematically applies the technique of "projection" or "mirroring" to communicate. Thus, the numbers announced by Ukraine on the losses of each other must be reversed to give a picture closer to reality.

Since February 2022, the Western media has been trying to demonstrate that Russia is losing the war and a permanent confusion of terms is used for propaganda purposes.

The vocabulary itself has thus become a way of misinforming and manipulating information. The term *"casualties"*, which is a generic term that includes the dead, the injured and the missing, is itself often misused as a synonym for *"fatalities"*.

An example of lying and manipulation of information is given by the *Swiss Radio-Television* (RTS). On August 22, 2022, the Swiss media states:

> *Russia, in particular, has conceded very few casualties since the beginning of its invasion (1,300 dead, the last death toll established in March), while the United States estimates Russian losses at about 80,000 dead and wounded, recalled French senior official Cyrille Bret in the program Tout un monde. "Between 80,000 and 1,300, we measure the extent of possible manipulations"* on both sides, he stressed.

---

642. Roman Olearchyk, Ben Hall & John Paul Rathbone, "Bakhmut: Ukrainian losses may limit capacity for counter-attack", *The Irish Times/The Financial Times*, March 9, 2023 (https://www.irishtimes.com/world/europe/2023/03/09/bakhmut-analysis-ukrainian-losses-may-limit-capacity-for-counter-attack/)

In an attempt to show the Russian "manipulation", RTS cheats on two aspects: the time, the sources and the nature of the figures.

First, the 1,300 figure comes from the Russian Ministry of Defense's March balance sheet, which is actually 1,351[643], so higher than RTS claims, while the 80,000 estimate was published in August 2022, five months later[644].

Then, the sources are obviously different. The figure of 80,000 is given by the Pentagon, based on Ukrainian information, as stated by the American website *military.com*[645]. Note that while the Anglo-Saxon media speak of an estimated range of 70,000-80,000, the RTS automatically takes the higher figure.

As for the nature of the figures, the balance of 1,351 published by Russia represents "deaths", while 80,000 represents "losses", which allows for all sorts of suppositions. RTS is comparing apples and pears here. We are therefore here in a work of which is technically situated between propaganda and disinformation. In any case, unworthy of a public service... because RTS could have also consulted the Mediazona site.

As soon as the Russian offensive began, the Russian opposition media Mediazona - close to Aleksei Navalny - joined forces with the BBC to publish the figures of Russian deaths in Ukraine based on the death notices published in Russia. As the media is fiercely anti-Putin, one can imagine that its figures are overestimated and that they are rather unfavorable to the Russians. Nevertheless, for August 9, Mediazona and the BBC mention 5,185 deaths (counted as of July 29)[646].

On September 23, 2022, the "Checknews" of the French newspaper Libération headlined: "*War in Ukraine: were there 6,000 Russian deaths as Moscow claims, or 55,000 as Kyiv claims*? Of course, our "fact checkers" substitute one elucubration for another to arrive (we don't know how, but probably by simply averaging the two numbers) at 20,000-30,000

---

643. "Some 1,351 Russian troops killed since start of special operation in Ukraine - top brass", *Tass*, March 25, 2022 (https://tass.com/politics/1427515)
644. Caroline Anders, "Russia has lost up to 80,000 troops in Ukraine. Or 75,000. Or is it 60,000?", The Washington Post, August 9, 2022 (https://www.washingtonpost.com/politics/2022/08/09/russia-has-lost-up-80000-troops-ukraine-or-75000-or-is-it-60000/)
645. Travis Tritten, "Russia Has Suffered Up to 80,000 Military Casualties in Ukraine, Pentagon Says," military.com, August 8, 2022 (https://www.military.com/daily-news/2022/08/08/russia-has-suffered-80000-military-casualties-ukraine-pentagon-says.html)
646. https://zona.media/casualties

dead[647]. However, if one consults the media outlet Mediazona, one finds 6,129 Russian deaths on this date (counted as of September 9).

This example would tend to demonstrate two things: a) that our media are only relying on Ukrainian propaganda, and b) that the figures produced by the Russian military authorities are probably close to the truth.

By the end of November 2022, the Ukrainian General Staff claims that Russian casualties total more than 86,000 men[648] (a figure that *Yahoo News* increases to 88,800 men!) and Zelensky predicts that they will reach 100,000 dead by the end of 2022[649]. His statement was clearly prescient, since three weeks later he claimed that the Russians had almost 100,000 dead[650]. On December 22, the 100,000 Russian dead mark was celebrated in Kiev by projecting the number "100K" on a building in the city[651]. However, on that same date, the Russian opposition media Mediazona reported 10,229 dead[652].

An examination of the casualty figures gives a good indication of how Ukrainian propaganda works. Assuming that Mediazona and the BBC are likely to be unfriendly to the Russian government, one can assume that their figures would tend to overstate Russian losses.

Of course, one can question Mediazona's methods. However, at least Mediazona has a method, while media like *RTS* or *Libération* have none, except slavishly passing on the Ukrainian propaganda without checking it.

The media that we finance with our taxes try to manipulate us. This is true with the state media, such as RTBF in Belgium, RTS in Switzerland and France 2, France 5 and France 24 in France, but also through the so-called "private" media, such as LCI or BFM TV in France, which are widely known for giving poor quality information and whose journalists do not have the ethical level that we could expect.

---

647. https://www.liberation.fr/checknews/guerre-en-ukraine-y-a-t-il-eu-6000-morts-russes-comme-laffirme-moscou-ou-55000-comme-le-revendique-kiev-20220923_AL4JKOEZ4BFQDJWMEKPJSF-ZYEI/
648. "Russian troop losses in Ukraine exceed 86,000, says Ukraine's General Staff," *The New Voice of Ukraine*, November 25, 2022 (https://english.nv.ua/nation/russian-troop-losses-in-ukraine-exceed-86-000-says-ukraine-s-general-staff-50286593.html)
649. https://news.yahoo.com/von-der-leyen-statement-death-163600213.html
650. Jimmy Nsubuga, "Almost 100,000 Russian soldiers killed in war, Ukraine says," Yahoo News, December 21, 2022 (https://news.yahoo.com/almost-100000-russian-soldiers-killed-in-war-ukraine-says-180208808.html)
651. Meghan Roos, "Ukraine Marks Russian Troop Death Milestone With '100K' Light Projection," Newsweek, December 22, 2022 (https://www.newsweek.com/ukraine-marks-russian-100000-troop-death-milestone-100k-light-projection-kyiv-library-building-1769193)
652. https://web.archive.org/web/20221222025542/https://zona.media/casualties

Comparison of Russian loss figures

Date	Ukraine / Occident	Opposition russe
12.03.2022	rtbf.be — 1300 soldats ukrainiens tués, 12.000 russes	С 24 фев 2022 по 12 мар 2022 подтверждена гибель как минимум 1 316 военных
23.09.2022	Libération — CheckNews Guerre en Ukraine: y a-t-il eu 6 000 morts russes comme l'affirme Moscou, ou 55 000 comme le revendique Kyiv?	Медиазона — Потери России в войне с Украиной. Сводка «Медиазоны» 6 219 смертей российских военных подтверждено по открытым источникам на 9 сентября
22.12.2022	Newsweek — WORLD Ukraine Marks Russian Troop Death Milestone With '100K' Light Projection BY MEGHAN ROOS ON 12/22/22 AT 7:02 PM EST	Медиазона — Потери России в войне с Украиной. Сводка «Медиазоны» 10 229 смертей российских военных подтверждены по открытым источникам на 16 декабря
12.02.2023	TF1 INFO — 7 février, 910 entre le 8 et le 9 février, ou encore 900 entre 12 février. Soit au total 137.780 décès de militaires russes ... un an.	Медиазона — Потери России в войне с Украиной. Сводка «Медиазоны» 12 538 смертей российских военных подтверждены по открытым источникам на 27 января

Figure 84 - Comparison of Russian deaths announced by Ukrainian propaganda and repeated uncritically by our media with the figures given by the Russian opposition media Mediazona associated with the BBC. The apparent "fact-check" of the newspaper Libération is, as we have also seen on many subjects, only a misleading analysis. Overall, it is not a very serious work, which serves above all to support or legitimize prejudices or even false information. (NB: the extracts are those that were published on the date indicated)

These falsifications tell us something else: the Russian propaganda (that is, the Russian government's propaganda, not that of small bloggers and other twitterers!), which our media harp on without ever demonstrating, appears to be a myth designed to pave the way for the Western narrative.

5.4.4.2. Ukrainian losses

5.4.4.2.1. Military losses

The number of dead Ukrainian servicemen is unknown, because Ukraine does not give any figures. It fears - and rightly so - that if Western public opinion knew the number of deaths, they would oppose their governments' support for the war.

Observations on the ground and testimonies of returned Western volunteers tend to confirm that Ukrainian forces are suffering considerably higher losses than the Russians. Our media never give estimates of Ukrainian casualties, because it is necessary to maintain the illusion of a victory against Russia, which justifies arms deliveries.

This policy of discretion about the number of dead has unexpected consequences. Thus, in Izyum at the end of March 2022, when the Russians offered the Ukrainians the possibility of collecting their dead, the latter refused to do so. Some claimed that this refusal was to avoid paying widows' pensions, but it was more likely to avoid having to report the number of dead. It should be remembered that Mediazona estimates the number of Russian dead from the obituaries. These dead on the battlefield were buried by Russian soldiers because their Ukrainian brothers refused to do so[653]. This did not prevent the Swiss state channel *RTS* from attributing - without any verification - these same bodies that were seen buried in March in the same place, to Russian "massacres", at the end of September 2022[654] !

This policy of communication leads to some contradictions, because on the one hand, negligible Ukrainian losses are presented, but on the other hand, it is the Russians who are trying to destroy the country and make as many deaths as possible.

---

653. https://youtu.be/I6ngm-QUn4M
654. "In the ruins of Izum, a traumatized Ukrainian city", *rts.ch*, September 29, 2022 (https://www.rts.ch/info/monde/13419199-dans-les-ruines-dizioum-ville-ukrainienne-traumatisee.html)

The Ukrainian strategy of defending every square meter of territory by holding on until the end only leads to the destruction of its own forces. This is what the French and Germans did in 1914-1918. But this time the Russians are mobile. If we take up a historical comparison, we have the situation of a 1914 defense and a 1940 attacker. The result: by the summer of 2022, the Ukrainian military potential is destroyed.

The West then took fright and began to supply Ukraine with weapons, hoping to turn the situation around. The Russians then understood that the West would not let the Ukrainians negotiate and that they would try to prolong the conflict until Russia was exhausted. They then changed their approach: if the influx of weapons could not be stopped, those who were using them had to be destroyed.

Then begins another form of war. The objective remains the military potential, but instead of destroying the weapons have destroyed their servants. Thus, at the beginning of June 2022, President Zelensky mentions daily losses of 60 to 100 men[655]. On June 9, Mykhailo Podoliak, an adviser to Zelensky, said on the BBC that Ukrainian forces were losing 100 to 200 men a day[656]. In mid-June, David Arakhamia, Zelensky's chief negotiator and close adviser, spoke of 200-500 deaths per day and mentioned a total loss (dead, wounded, captured, deserters) of 1,000 men per day[657]. According to *Business Insider*, Ukraine lost the equivalent of the entire British infantry, or more than 18,000 men[658].

It is not clear whether these figures are accurate. On the one hand, experts close to the intelligence services believe that these figures are far below reality. On the other hand, the Ukrainian figures are higher than the estimates given by the Russian army. Some claim that the Ukrainian forces have suffered 60,000 dead and 50,000 missing. We are now in June 2022 and the former American general Stephen Twitty estimates the losses of the Ukrainian army at 200,000 men[659].

---

655. Mazurenko Alona, "Подоляк: Щодня гине 100-200 українських захисників," Ukraїnska Pravda, June 9, 2022 (https://www.pravda.com.ua/news/2022/06/9/7351600/)
656. "У війні гине 100 - 200 українських військових щодня - Офіс президента", BBC News, June 9, 2022 (https://www.bbc.com/ukrainian/news-61752749)
657. Dave Lawler, "Ukraine suffering up to 1,000 casualties per day in Donbas, official says," Axios, June 15, 2022 (https://www.axios.com/2022/06/15/ukraine-1000-casualties-day-donbas-arakhamia)
658. Katie Anthony, "Ukraine has lost more troops during the Russian invasion than there are infantry in the British army, defense expert says," Business Insider, June 28, 2022 (https://www.businessinsider.com/ukraine-has-lost-more-troops-than-there-are-in-the-british-army-expert-2022-6)
659. "US-General verwundert: "200.000 Ukrainische Soldaten verschwunden"", Exxpress.at, June 8, 2022 (https://exxpress.at/us-general-verwundert-200-000-ukrainische-soldaten-verschwunden/)

A group that would do the same work as the BBC and Mediazona, but for Ukrainian casualties based on death and burial announcements, estimates Ukrainian casualties at 402,000. What is pompously called "OSINT" (open source intelligence) has largely developed with the Ukrainian conflict. But the methodology and professionalism of these amateur "analysts" often leaves much to be desired, so these figures should be treated with caution. It is, however, an indication that the figures given by our media are very likely to be far below the reality. For example, the *Washington Post* quotes the testimony of a commander of the 46th Ukrainian paratroop brigade in Bakhmut who claims that he is the only survivor and that the members of his units are new conscripts with no experience[660]. He was dismissed three days later[661].

This is most likely an exaggeration, but it shows that despite the losses attributed to Russia, Anglo-Saxon military circles are beginning to wonder.

In October 2022, General Surovikin declared that the Russian army was not looking for large-scale operations, but to crush the opponent without exposing itself. The West and our media see this as a sign of the Russian army's weakness and proof that we must continue in the same direction. In November 2022, the Swiss ambassador in Kiev declared that it was Russia that was asking to negotiate, because it was in a weak position[662]. This is not true!

On November 30, 2022, Ursula von der Leyen, President of the European Commission, declared that *"more than 20,000 civilians and more than 100,000 Ukrainian soldiers have been killed to date[663]."* It immediately triggers the anger of Kiev, who demand to withdraw this figure. This is done on the spot[664]. But this indicates several things. First, the sensitivity of the death toll for internal stability in Ukraine. Second, Ms. von der Leyen certainly did not invent this figure, which is probably circulating

---

660. Isabelle Khurshudyan, Paul Sonne & Karen DeYoung, "Ukraine short of skilled troops and ammunition as losses, pessimism grows," *The Washington Post*, March 13, 2023 (https://www.washingtonpost.com/world/2023/03/13/ukraine-casualties-pessimism-ammunition-shortage/)
661. Olga Kyrylenko & Olena Roshchina, "Battalion commander of 46th Brigade demoted after Washington Post interview and resigns", Ukraïnska Pravda, March 26, 2023 (https://www.pravda.com.ua/eng/news/2023/03/16/7393733/)
662. https://www.rts.ch/play/tv/redirect/detail/13567586?startTime=383
663. https://twitter.com/AZgeopolitics/status/1597913370023579648
664. "Von der Leyen statement about death of 100,000 Ukrainian soldiers cut from speech," *The New Voice of Ukraine*, November 30, 2022 (https://english.nv.ua/nation/von-der-leyen-statement-about-death-of-100-000-ukrainian-soldiers-cut-from-speech-50287771.html)

confidentially in Western chancelleries. Third, given Ms. von der Leyen's tendency to downplay Ukrainian casualties, the 100,000 dead figure is probably an underestimate.

It would seem that this hypothesis is verified by figures from the Israeli Mossad published by the Turkish media *Hürseda Haber*[665]. How accurate are these figures, how authentic their origin and how reliable the media? This is difficult to determine. In any case, Mossad seems to estimate the Ukrainian death toll at 157,000, which seems realistic.

As we have seen, Ukrainian propaganda seems to attribute to Russia the number of its own casualties and to itself the number of Russian casualties. We see that the ratio of the number of dead between Ukraine and Russia is about 10-11 to 1. Assuming that the Russian opposition site *Mediazona* is reliable, given the 14,000 dead announced for Russia in February 2023, it would not be incongruous to estimate the number of Ukrainian dead at more than 150,000 men.

Another way to look at it would be to relate the consumption of artillery ammunition to get an indication of the casualty ratio on both sides of the front line. Taking the figures given by Ukrainian and Western military officials, the Ukrainians fire about 2,000-4,000 artillery shells per day and the Russians about 40,000-50,000, one can estimate a casualty ratio of 1 to 10-25. In other words, for February 2023, we would have between 140,000 and 350,000 dead on the Ukrainian side. This is difficult to confirm, but it is probably more likely than the crazy figures that our media throws at us without justifying them.

Another way to look at this is by looking at the size of the armed forces. In May 2022, President Volodymyr Zelensky stated that the Ukrainian army had 700,000 men[666]. This figure was confirmed two months later by Oleksei Reznikov, Ukrainian Minister of Defence[667]:

> We have about 700,000 military personnel and if you add the National Guard, the police and the border guards, we are close to one million.

---

665. "İddia: MOSSAD'a göre Ukrayna ve Rusya kayıpları," *Hürseda Haber*, January 25, 2023 (https://perma.cc/FD7T-LQU8)
666. "700,000 soldiers defending Ukraine now, Zelenskyy says, as battles rage in the Donbas," Euronews/AP/AFP, May 21, 2022 (https://www.euronews.com/2022/05/21/live-sievierodonetsk-shelling-brutal-and-pointless-zelenskyy-says-as-russia-continues-offe)
667. Emily McGarvey, "Ukraine aims to amass 'million-strong army' to fight Russia, says defence minister", *BBC News*, July 11, 2022 (https://www.bbc.com/news/world-europe-62118953)

But in September 2022, the German newspaper *Frankfurter Allgemeine Zeitung* called the Ukrainian army "the *second strongest army in Europe*," with 250,000 men[668].

In early 2023, the battle around Bakhmut took on a tragic aspect. At first, the West sees the heroic resistance of the Ukrainian army and an accumulation of deaths on the Russian side. Then our media claimed that there were equal losses on both sides and the image of Verdun in 1916 was revived. But slowly the truth is coming out: it is the Ukrainian army that is suffering. In *Newsweek* magazine, a former American volunteer in the Ukrainian ranks states that the life expectancy in Bakhmut for Ukrainians is about 4 hours[669]. We do not know how this figure was calculated, nor do we know if it reflects reality; however, it does give an idea of the perception of the Ukrainian military.

At the beginning of March 2023, our media declare that the Russians destroy the bridges in Bakhmut. As always, our journalists confuse their prejudices with the facts[670]. In reality, it is the fanatical Ukrainian militia that destroys the bridges that would allow to leave the then almost surrounded city, in order to force the fighters to fight[671]. For, contrary to what our media tell us, the Ukrainian military are not prepared to be massacred for towns that we already know will be abandoned.

5.4.4.2.2. Civilian losses

Obviously, the Russians can only be brutal. On March 22, 2022, on the set of *RTS*, Gennady Gatilov, the Russian ambassador, spoke of the efforts of Russian troops to carry out this operation "delicately", seeking to minimize collateral damage[672]. The Swiss journalist Philippe Revaz ironizes and claims that the Russian military massacred women and children.

---

668. Lukas Fuhr, "Die zweitstärkste Armee Europas", Frankfurter Allgemeine Zeitung, September 16, 2022 (https://www.faz.net/aktuell/politik/ausland/armee-der-ukraine-ist-die-zweitstaerkste-in-europa-18318445.html)
669. Anna Skinner, "Bakhmut Life Expectancy Near Four Hours on Frontlines, Fighter Warns," *Newsweek*, February 20, 2023 (https://www.newsweek.com/bakhmut-life-expectancy-near-four-hours-frontlines-ukraine-russia-1782496)
670. Mehdi Bouzouina, "Bakhmout continues, two bridges were destroyed by the Russians", Le Parisien, March 5, 2023 (https://www.leparisien.fr/international/guerre-en-ukraine-la-bataille-de-bakhmout-se-poursuit-deux-ponts-ont-ete-detruits-par-les-russes-suivez-notre-direct-05-03-2023-35L4I4NJGRFY7JIPS54SZDAIRM.php)
671. Isobel Koshiw, "Ukrainians blow up bridge in Bakhmut amid reports Russia closing in", The Guardian, February 14, 2023 (https://www.theguardian.com/world/2023/feb/14/ukrainians-blow-up-bridge-in-bakhmut-amid-reports-russia-closing-in)
672. https://www.rts.ch/play/tv/redirect/detail/12960214

However, on the same day, in the American magazine *Newsweek*, an analyst from the *Defense Intelligence Agency* (DIA), the American military intelligence, declared[673]:

> *I know it's hard to swallow that the slaughter and destruction could be much worse than it is (...) But that's what the facts show. It suggests to me, in any case, that Putin is not intentionally attacking civilians, that he may be aware that he has to limit the damage in order to leave a way out for negotiations.*

So the Swiss journalist is lying. He simply has no professional ethics: he is not doing journalism, but propaganda.

The objective of the Russians was not to destroy or occupy the country, but to destroy its potential threat to the Donbass. That is why they did not accompany their advance by massive bombing that could affect the population, as the West did in Iraq or Afghanistan.

Moreover, in January 2023, Oleksei Arestovitch, then ex-personal adviser to Volodymyr Zelensky, interviewed on the Ukrainian media *Mriya*, uses almost the same words as Ambassador Gatilov to describe the Russian intervention[674]:

> *They [the Russians] did not want to kill anyone (...) They tried to wage an intelligent war... A special operation as elegant, as beautiful, as fast as lightning, where polite people, without causing any harm to the kitten or the child, liquidated the few resisters. And not even eliminated, but offered to surrender, to defect, to understand, etc. They did not want to kill anyone. It was enough to sign a waiver.*

So we can see that the Swiss journalist contradicts the findings of the Ukrainians themselves. He is a manipulator and this confirms that the Swiss channel does not follow the principles of the Munich Charter, which has the effect of propagating a message of hate. It should be noted

---

673. William M. Arkin, "Putin's Bombers Could Devastate Ukraine But He's Holding Back. Here's Why," Newsweek, March 22, 2022 (https://www.newsweek.com/putins-bombers-could-devastate-ukraine-hes-holding-back-heres-why-1690594)
674. https://en.mriya.news/58331-they-didnt-want-to-kill-anyone-arestovich-spoke-about-the-beginning-of-the-nwo

that neither the *RTS* nor its journalist reacted to the torture and elimination of Russian-speaking civilians between 2014 and 2022[675]... But if they had done so, probably Russia would not have felt obliged to intervene in 2022! Because obviously, for them the Russians are "sub-humans" who deserve neither our interest nor our compassion!...

5.4.4.3. The issue of losses in Western propaganda

The loss communication shows two axes:
- The idea that Ukraine is victorious and that Western support is effective;
- Ukraine is much less affected by the conflict than is Russia.

Western unity is achieved only by accentuating the negative consequences of the war for Russia and by hiding those affecting Ukraine. This is why the mention of the 100,000 deaths mentioned by Ursula von der Leyen was immediately removed from official communications.

By concealing the number of deaths that Ukraine is suffering because of its disastrous management of the fighting, it gives the impression that it is victorious. The Western countries thus justify the continuation of their arms deliveries and their refusal of a negotiated solution. For if the public opinion knew the figures of Ukrainian losses, they would oppose the prolongation of the conflict by sending arms.

In fact, if we take a step back, we can see that the losses suffered by Ukraine have been systematically minimized, or even ignored, so as not to prejudice the Western discourse. This is the case with the civilian casualties in the Donbass since 2014, which are the reason for the Russian intervention, and which are considered "negligible quantities" for our media and the governments that support war crimes. This is also the reason why Westerners date the start of the war to February 24, 2022, and not February 23, 2014. Because the victims of this period contribute to the legitimacy of the Russian intervention, especially since the West has admitted that it never intended to implement the Minsk agreements.

A neo-Nazi politician from the French-speaking part of Switzerland had called me a "Putinolater" for having mentioned the suicides in the

---

675. "You Don't Exist" - Arbitrary Detentions, Enforced Disappearances, and Torture in Eastern Ukraine," *Human Rights Watch*, July 21, 2016 (https://www.hrw.org/report/2016/07/21/you-dont-exist/arbitrary-detentions-enforced-disappearances-and-torture-eastern#)

Ukrainian army before 2022. Today, he can hurl his insults at British parliamentarians, because in January 2023, they themselves noted that the suicide rate there is alarming[676]. Our politician would have been more inspired to encourage our diplomacy to enforce the Minsk agreements, which he did not do...

So we have foolish politicians, who blind themselves with their lies, instead of anticipating the problems!...

Forced recruitment seems to be primarily directed at minorities, especially the Magyar minority[677]. This is what has provoked the anger of Hungary[678]. Today, 97% of Hungarians are opposed to European sanctions against Russia[679].

5.4.4.4. The myth of the "waves of infantry"

In our media, as the figures on Ukrainian losses accumulate, they try to show that the Russians are losing an equivalent number of men. The old myth of Russian attacks by "waves of humans" who attack chest to chest in order to be slaughtered is then brought out. As is to be expected from the pseudo-military experts on television, this is not true.

This is a myth that emerged at the end of World War II, when the Red Army adapted its operations to break through the powerful German defenses. In 1984, the U.S. Army's manual on Soviet tactics described Soviet breakthrough operations as follows[680]:

> For example, in one case, a Guards Infantry Corps was assigned a 22-kilometer-wide advancing spindle, but concentrated 80 to

---

676. "Ukrainian soldiers are committing suicide due to war stress, says Duncan-Smith," *Politics.co.uk*, January 16, 2023 (https://www.politics.co.uk/parliament/ukrainian-soldiers-are-committing-suicide-due-to-war-stress-says-duncan-smith/)
677. Füssy Angéla, "Mint a barmokat, úgy fogdossák össze a férfiakat Kárpátalján - Nézze meg helyszíni videóriportunkat!", *PestiSracok*, January 23, 2023 (https://pestisracok.hu/mint-a-barmokat-ugy-fogdossak-ossze-a-ferfiakat-karpataljan-nezze-meg-helyszini-videoriportunkat/)
678. Chris King, "Shocking claims of ethnic Hungarians being forcibly drafted into Ukrainian military in Transcarpathia," *Euro Weekly News*, January 24, 2023 (https://euroweeklynews.com/2023/01/24/shocking-claims-of-ethnic-hungarians-being-forcibly-drafted-into-ukrainian-military-in-transcarpathia/)
679. Robert Semonsen, "97% of Hungarians Reject Brussels' Sanctions Against Russia," *The European Conservative*, January 17, 2023 (https://europeanconservative.com/articles/news/97-of-hungarians-reject-brussels-sanctions-against-russia/)
680. "Field Manual 100-2-1, The Soviet Army: Operations and Tactics," *Department of the Army* Washington, DC, July 16, 1984 (https://irp.fas.org/doddir/army/fm100-2-1.pdf)

90 percent of its forces on a width of less than one-third of its total spindle width. Thus, within a width of 7 kilometers, the Corps massed 27 battalions, 1,087 artillery pieces and towed mortars, and 156 tanks and self-propelled artillery weapons, giving it a 4-to-1 infantry superiority, 10-to-1 artillery superiority, and 17-to-1 tank superiority.

This concentration of forces on a very narrow front seems contrary to common sense. Any infantry corporal knows that to avoid casualties, soldiers must be dispersed as much as possible. This was the lesson learned the hard way by the infantrymen of World War I (but not their officers). One hundred years later, the officers have understood, but are not able to adapt their thinking, as can be seen on the French television channel LCI. What is true at the tactical level is not necessarily true at the operational level.

For example, assuming that an anti-tank weapon fires a projectile every ten seconds, if it is presented with one tank every ten seconds, each tank will be hit. On the other hand, if it is presented with ten tanks together, the first tank will be hit, but not the other nine. This is the principle of saturation of the opponent's defense.

It should be noted in passing that the fact of giving weapons to Ukraine in dribs and drabs facilitates the destruction of these weapons by Russia as they arrive in the theater. In other words, no matter how good the weapons supplied are, their quantity will never reach the critical mass that would allow Ukraine to make a difference. This shows that the West is not trying to help Ukraine, but to prolong the war in order to exhaust Russia.

As for the "waves" of Russian soldiers, this is a legend, created by Ukrainian propaganda. In April 2023, Christopher Perryman, a British veteran, fighting for Ukraine, explains in *The Spectator*, that he has hardly ever seen a Russian fighter. In fact, the Russians act with artillery, then come in to clear the ground afterwards, but hardly ever expose themselves to infantry fire. Perryman notes of the Russians, "*Their artillery teams are really good. You can't compare Iraq to that, it's much more intense.*[681]"

---

681. Colin Freeman, "'Iraq does not compare to this': the British soldier on Ukraine's front line," *The Spectator*, April 15, 2023 (https://www.spectator.co.uk/article/iraq-does-not-compare-to-this-the-british-soldier-on-ukraines-front-line/).

In Ukraine, neither the Ukrainians nor the Russians are fighting with *"waves of infantry"*. This is pure propaganda, as can be seen on the French channel LCI, which relies on a few images that have nothing to do with *"human waves"*, unverified figures and with "experts" who know nothing[682].

5.5. Refugees

Western disinformation is on the rise and our media show an incredible lack of integrity. The Swiss daily *Le Temps* published a map showing the distribution of Ukrainian refugees[683]. In January 2023, the map gives the figure of 9,076,773 refugees in Poland and 2,852,395 refugees in Russia. The Swiss newspaper lies and cheats. In order not to show that the majority of Ukrainian refugees have chosen to go to Russia, it gives figures of different kinds. Thus, for Poland, it gives the number of border crossings and for Russia, the number of refugees. In reality, at that time, the number of refugees in Poland was 1,353,338, which is less than half of the refugees who chose Russia[684]!

As we have said, neo-Nazis consider Russian-speaking Ukrainians as subhuman. This is also true of the media, which is inspired by nauseating ideologies. Since 2014, Westerners have followed Ukraine and considered the population of Donbass as subhumans who were not worthy of attention. This is why no one has condemned the exactions against them. This is also why, when we talk about refugees, we only talk about refugees since February 24.

Moreover, between 2014 and February 2022, 1,044,862 Ukrainians went to Russia as refugees, which gives a total of no less than 3.8 million Ukrainian refugees in Russia at the beginning of 2023[685]. Obviously, our media do not mention this because it would show that these millions of Ukrainians have chosen neither to stay in the country nor to go to Europe!

---

682. https://youtu.be/pe2khpEykc4
683. https://labs.letemps.ch/chat/custom/guerre-russie-ukraine-2704/
684. https://data.unhcr.org/en/situations/ukraine
685. https://data.unhcr.org/en/dataviz/107?sv=0&geo=0

Distribution of Ukrainian refugees (as of January 20, 2023)

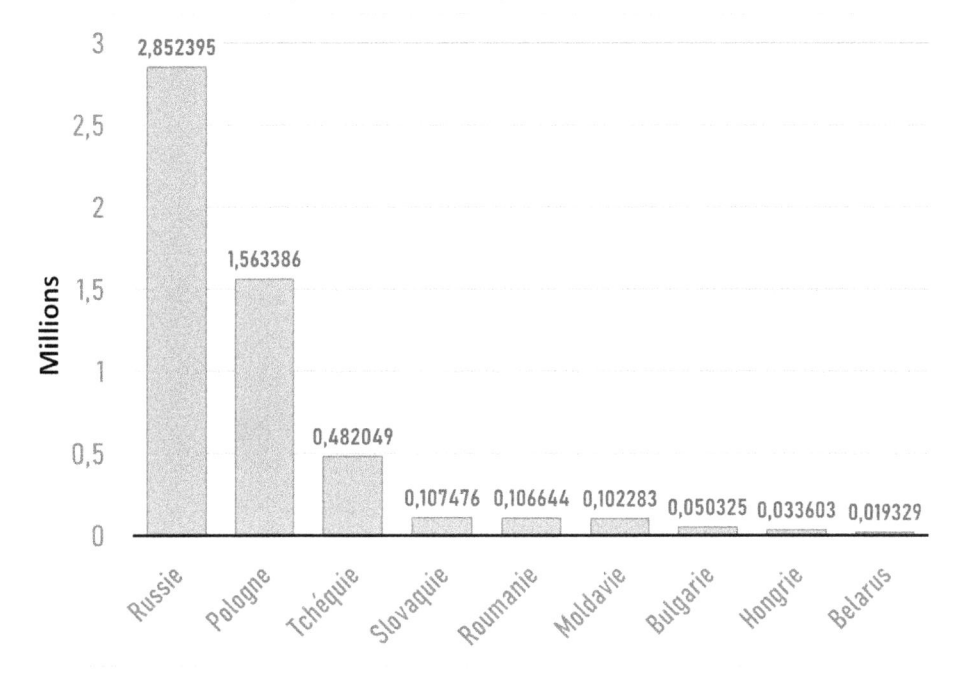

Country	Refugees (millions)
Russie	2,852395
Pologne	1,563386
Tchéquie	0,482049
Slovaquie	0,107476
Roumanie	0,106644
Moldavie	0,102283
Bulgarie	0,050325
Hongrie	0,033603
Belarus	0,019329

Figure 85 - Distribution of Ukrainian refugees in Ukraine's neighboring countries since February 24, 2022. [Source: United Nations High Commissioner for Refugees (UNHCR)

Western manipulation

Au moins 17 688 845 réfugiés ont déjà fui l'Ukraine

Réfugiés d'Ukraine depuis le 24 février 2022. Statut au: 17/01/2023

Figure 86 - Map published by the Swiss daily Le Temps[686]. *In reality, according to UNHCR figures, there are a total of 7,977,980 Ukrainian refugees in Europe as of January 17, 2023, and only 1,563,386 refugees in Poland. The figure of 17,688,945 is not a number of refugees, but the number of crossings of the Ukrainian border and back. The real numbers are bad enough, but our media systematically tries to overdramatize the situation. The Swiss daily newspaper simply tries to hide the fact that Russia was the first choice of the Ukrainians.*

---

686. https://labs.letemps.ch/chat/custom/guerre-russie-ukraine-2704/

6. The upheaval of the world

The term "rest of the world" is deeply distasteful, as it implies a kind of ranking among nations and underlines the disdain of Westerners for anything outside their sphere. But it is interesting, because it alone explains the upheavals in the world order that we are witnessing in the wake of the Ukrainian conflict.

The various crises that the world has experienced in recent years, from the overthrow of Gaddafi to the Ukrainian conflict, from the CoViD-19 crisis to the American defeat in Afghanistan, have highlighted both the incompetence, inefficiency and arrogance of the West.

6.1. De-dollarization

One of the major consequences of the conflict in Ukraine is the loss of confidence in the West by the "rest of the world". The phenomenon is not completely new and some countries in the Sahel had already shown the way with the expulsion of Western forces from their territory.

The incredible virulence of the Western reaction to the Russian intervention contrasts with the complacency that accompanied Western interventions in the Middle East and Africa. This was all it took to arouse the mistrust of the "rest of the world" which sees, more than a "double standard", the expression of a profound contempt of the West for anything that does not come from them.

In November 2019, then in the midst of an election campaign, Joe Biden said about Saudi Arabia and the Khashoggi affair[687]:

We were going to make them pay the price and make them the outcasts they are.

We can certainly debate the Khashoggi affair, but such a promise coming from one of the leaders of a country that overthrows governments, practices torture, extra-judicial killings and openly commits war crimes is obviously not reassuring. Especially since the American president made the same promise to Russia[688]. Managing the world through sanctions and confiscation, if not attempted overthrow, is not conducive to harmonious relations.

The sanctions against Russia have reminded the countries of the "rest of the world" that they are at the mercy of the West. They have understood that the West adapts the rules according to their interests. Therefore, it is a matter of getting rid of the dollars that are the leverage of the sanctions. In fact, this is what Republican Senator Marco Rubio says[689]:

Just today, Brazil, the largest country in the Western Hemisphere, signed a trade agreement with China. From now on, their trade will be in their own currencies, avoiding the dollar. They are creating a parallel economy in the world, totally independent of the United States. Within 5 years we won't be talking about sanctions. There will be so many countries trading in currencies other than the dollar that we won't be able to sanction them.

This fear is the driving force behind the "de-dollarization" that is coming at great speed. Already in February 2023, the Chinese yuan has

---

687. Alex Emmons, Aída Chávez & Akela Lacy, "Joe Biden, in Departure From Obama Policy, Says He Would Make Saudi Arabia a 'Pariah,'" *The Intercept*, November 21, 2019 (https://theintercept.com/2019/11/21/democratic-debate-joe-biden-saudi-arabia/)
688. Olivier Knox, "Biden warns Russia will be a pariah as long as Putin's in charge," *The Washington Post*, April 5, 2022 (https://www.washingtonpost.com/politics/2022/04/05/biden-warns-russia-will-be-pariah-long-putins-charge/)
689. https://twitter.com/i/status/1642727525800460290

replaced the dollar as the most widely used currency in commercial transactions in Russia[690].

Countries like Russia and even Iran, which export essential raw materials, can undoubtedly withstand sanctions, but not all countries can. Moreover, Europe's alignment with the United States raises fears that dependence on the euro could lead to the same problems.

The challenge is therefore to reduce dependence on the dollar (and the euro), which is the main lever the United States has to impose its will. But this is not without consequences for the American economy.

In 1972, the inflationary pressure created by the financing of the Vietnam War pushed the United States to leave the Bretton Woods system and abandon the convertibility of the dollar into gold. In order to prevent the dollar from collapsing, they then maneuvered with the Gulf States (1973), and then with all the oil-producing countries (1975), to have oil paid for exclusively in dollars.

The idea was to force the countries of the world to obtain dollars to buy oil. This created a demand for dollars that allowed the United States to print dollars almost indefinitely without being caught in an inflationary loop. It is a kind of "Ponzi scheme[691]" that allows the American economy - which is essentially a consumer economy - to be supported by the economies of other countries around the world. This is the "petrodollar" system, the disappearance of which would be a considerable threat to the American economy and could lead to its collapse.

At a time when the United States was the only major economic power, the countries of the "rest of the world" had little choice. But today, with the rise of a dynamic China that does not try to export its "values" but simply trades without judgment, the situation is very different. For it is not simply a question of "values", but a problem of "alignment". As we have seen with Nord Stream 2, being an ally of the United States is not enough: you have to be in line. However, the vast majority of countries in the world have national interests that do not coincide with those of the United States and do not wish to have an "American-style" society.

---

690. "China's Yuan Replaces Dollar as Most Traded Currency in Russia," *Bloomberg*, April 3, 2023 (updated April 4, 2023) (https://www.bloomberg.com/news/articles/2023-04-03/china-s-yuan-replaces-dollar-as-most-traded-currency-in-russia#xj4y7vzkg)

691. Wikipedia: A Ponzi scheme is a fraudulent financial arrangement in which clients' investments are paid for primarily by funds provided by new entrants.

They have their own values, traditions and cultures that they wish to manage in their own way. In order to avoid the sword of Damocles that western sanctions represent, they prefer to distance themselves from the dollar.

Dedollarization

Countries seeking to reduce the use of the dollar

Figure 87 - Countries reporting use of non-dollar currencies for trade transactions (as of April 20, 2023)

Many countries are looking for alternative means of payment and arrangements to escape the dollar. The use of the Chinese yuan, the ruble or national currencies for trade - including for oil products - is growing. However, one must remain cautious: the dollar remains the most widely used currency for trade in the world (88% of trade according to the World Bank) and as a reserve currency. De-dollarization is a trend that is accelerating, but still far from threatening the U.S. economy.

6.2. The failure of diplomacy

6.2.1. The failure of Western diplomacy

The function of diplomacy is to maintain channels of communication between the various actors in a crisis and to create the conditions for a solution. But from the beginning of the Ukrainian conflict, instead of taking a step back, Western diplomacy sided with one of the belligerents. The EU has favored the supply of arms over diplomatic action. This is an unprecedented role for a multilateral structure.

This commitment remains misunderstood in the world. While the EU is expected to play the role of a referee, it has taken on the role of a player. To what end? Assuming that it is a way to show its willingness to support international law, why did it not supply arms to Iraq or Afghanistan?

Since the end of 2021, Western diplomacy is focused on the situation in Ukraine. It is making every effort to keep the herd of Russia's enemies together and is trying to push others to follow them by fuelling the conflict with weapons. Our diplomacy seems to have lost sight of the world's problems and, probably for the first time since the end of the Cold War, is losing the initiative on all fronts.

Worse, at a time when the countries of the southern hemisphere are worried about the carrot-and-stick policy of the West, Josep Borrell, head of European diplomacy, stands out for his untimely and childish statements. His comparison between Europe, which would be a "garden" coveted by the rest of the world disdainfully described as a "jungle" was very badly received in Africa, which saw - with good reason - an essentially racist speech. It would be difficult to find a more awkward way for a diplomat to put it.

Concerned about the turn of events on the Taiwan issue, China has issued a foreign policy paper condemning the hegemonic attitude of the United States around the world[692], and has developed a *Comprehensive Security Initiative* (CSI)[693]. It has also proposed a conceptual framework

---
692. "US Hegemony and Its Perils," Ministry of Foreign Affairs, February 20, 2023 (https://www.fmprc.gov.cn/mfa_eng/wjbxw/202302/t20230220_11027664.html)
693. "The Global Security Initiative Concept Paper," Ministry of Foreign Affairs, February 21, 2023 (https://www.fmprc.gov.cn/eng/wjbxw/202302/t20230221_11028348.html)

for normal relations between states and peaceful settlement of disputes[694], which could be applied to the resolution of the conflict in Ukraine.

But after Xi Jinping's visit to Moscow, Western countries fear that these initiatives will lead to a ceasefire or peace[695]. While our diplomats[696] declare *urbi et orbi* that the decision to negotiate belongs to Ukraine[697], the White House declares from the start that any attempt to start negotiations would be unacceptable[698]. The West is in complete contradiction.

Negotiation is seen as a reward to Russia and not as a way to preserve the existence of Ukraine and Ukrainians. Our diplomacy is more concerned with punishing Russia than with finding a solution to the problem, so it is both judge and jury and cannot play a mediating role.

Because we fail to support Ukraine logistically, it has become common to think that we have disarmed ourselves and that it was a mistake to believe in a peace dividend. This is not true. Our military apparatus could be reduced at the end of the Cold War because we had the opportunity to rethink our security policies. We had the opportunity to ensure our security through cooperation and not through confrontation. That is the shift we have missed.

Our security is not related to the number of weapons we have, but to the consistency with which we use a combination of force and diplomacy. Russia is holding NATO in check despite a defense budget that represents only 3.1% of global military spending, while the West is accumulating 50%. The problems we have today are not related to the number of weapons we have, but to our inability to build strong ties and keep our commitments, as we have seen. The old adage of Vegetius "Si vis pacem para bellum" does not mean that peace depends on our

---

694. "China's Position on the Political Settlement of the Ukraine Crisis," *Ministry of Foreign Affairs*, February 24, 2023 (https://www.fmprc.gov.cn/mfa_eng/zxxx_662805/202302/t20230224_11030713.html)
695. Charles Hutzler, "U.S. Seeks to Head Off Any Chinese Call for Cease-Fire in Ukraine," *The Wall Street Journal*, March 17, 2023 (https://www.wsj.com/articles/u-s-seeks-to-head-off-any-chinese-call-for-cease-fire-in-ukraine-ef456819)
696. https://www.rts.ch/play/tv/redirect/detail/13567586?startTime=508
697. Michael Birnbaum, "NATO says Ukraine to decide on peace deal with Russia - within limits," *The Washington Post*, April 5, 2022 (https://www.washingtonpost.com/national-security/2022/04/05/ukraine-nato-russia-limits-peace/)
698. Tim Hains, "NSC's John Kirby: Any Call For A Ukraine Ceasefire That Comes From Xi's Trip To Russia This Week Will Be 'Unacceptable,'" Real Clear Politics, March 19, 2023 (https://www.realclearpolitics.com/video/2023/03/19/nscs_john_kirby_china_and_russia_are_chafing_against_the_us-led_international_rules-based_order.html)

ability to wage war, but on our wisdom in preventing it. War and peace are intimately linked.

A smart security policy is to integrate diplomacy and defense seamlessly. If we had helped Africa more effectively, and contributed effectively to its development, we would not have refugees today. In Ukraine, if we had respected our commitments and enforced the Minsk agreements, we would not have a war today. While Western diplomacy seems to remain hung up on the Ukrainian conflict, Russia's is active. Not only that, but Russia has managed to shift the balance of power between the West and the "rest of the world."

6.2.2. The end of Swiss neutrality?

One of the most significant developments in the Ukraine conflict was Switzerland's abandonment of its policy of neutrality. This development is not entirely surprising, as careful observers have noted that the foundations of Swiss foreign policy have slowly drifted since 2019. That year, a report on the future of Swiss foreign policy spoke of the predominance of a *rules-based international order*[699]. An orientation confirmed by Ambassador Jürg Lauber, Switzerland's permanent representative to the United Nations in Geneva, in the midst of the Ukrainian crisis[700].

On November 23, 2022, Claude Wild, Swiss ambassador in Kiev, confirmed that Switzerland "*is not neutral*" in the Ukrainian conflict, but applies "*the law of neutrality*", a subtle nuance, which consists of not joining an alliance and not delivering arms to the belligerents[701]. He explains that one cannot be neutral in the situation where there is "*a war of aggression and a* clear *aggressor*"[702].

This is a bit short and even shocking. One might ask why Switzerland did not have the same attitude during the conflicts in Afghanistan, Iraq or Libya, where it even supported the attacker. But we knew that they were

---
699. https://www.eda.admin.ch/dam/eda/fr/documents/aktuell/dossiers/avis28-bericht-190619_FR.pdf
700. Jürg Lauber, "In the future, we will always need a rules-based international order", *Le Temps*, September 29, 2022 (https://www.letemps.ch/opinions/lavenir-aurons-toujours-besoin-dun-ordre-international-fonde-regles)
701. https://www.rts.ch/play/tv/redirect/detail/13567586?startTime=547
702. https://www.rts.ch/info/suisse/13567448-claude-wild-la-suisse-nest-pas-neutre-dans-le-conflit-en-ukraine.html

illegitimate, because they were based on accusations *that we already knew were lies.*

This is a radical change in the application of neutrality by Switzerland. Its neutrality is substantially different from those of other Western countries, in that it was imposed - and guaranteed - by the great powers at the time of the dismantling of the Napoleonic empire in 1815, and in that it is permanent. In contrast, U.S. neutrality at the outbreak of World War II was a unilaterally decided policy, which was abandoned after the attack on Pearl Harbor on December 7, 1941.

In other words, in spirit and letter, Swiss neutrality is not a policy of circumstance, but applies regardless of the nature of the actors involved in a conflict. This is how it is perceived in the world, and it is precisely this characteristic that gave it a unique credibility.

Although Switzerland has always acted as if it were part of the Western world, its policy of neutrality allowed it to act as an intermediary throughout the Cold War. Today, the "à la carte" application of neutrality depending on whether it considers the attacker "good" or "bad" robs it of all credibility.

In February 2022, it was Switzerland that Zelensky turned to for mediation. At this stage, it had not yet adopted sanctions against Russia and would be ideal for this role. The West then forced Zelensky to give up negotiating.

In March, when the situation in Mariupol turned sour, Zelensky revived the idea of negotiations and sent a proposal to Russia. But this time, Zelensky turned to three countries to find a mediator: China, Turkey and Israel. Yet none of these countries is a model of neutrality, and Turkey is even supplying arms to Ukraine. So why does Russia trust Turkey more than Switzerland, which has refused to deliver ammunition to Ukraine?

Conspiracy theorists will say that "only dictators can understand each other. But a less primitive explanation is that Turkey has a less passionate analysis of the conflict. As the *Kyiv Independent* writes[703]:

> *Turkey strongly supports the territorial integrity of Ukraine, while opposing any incitement to tensions in the region through an "incomprehensible policy" towards Russia.*

---

703. "Erdogan announces new talks with Zelensky, Putin," *The Kyiv Independent,* December 9, 2022 (https://kyivindependent.com/news-feed/erdogan-announces-new-talks-with-zelensky-putin)

Thus, while Switzerland positions itself as a judge, Erdogan seeks to solve a regional security problem and stop the loss of life[704]. This is the difference between an ideological and a pragmatic approach. For effective mediation work, one should not adapt facts to conclusions, but conclusions to facts.

Switzerland was then one of the Western countries that had applied the most sanctions to Russia and probably even Zelensky thought that it was no longer credible enough towards Russia to be able to mediate effectively. This is why, in August 2022, Russia refuses to grant Switzerland accreditation to represent Ukrainian interests in Moscow, explaining that it *"has lost its status as a neutral state and can act neither as a mediator nor as a representative of Ukrainian interests"*[705].

6.2.3. Respect for international law

This brings us to the question of respect for international law. We consider Russia's action to be illegal and illegitimate and thus justify the delivery of arms to Ukraine. Seen from afar this seems coherent, but it is not.

Because our respect for international law cannot be limited to a criticism of the conflict since February 24, 2022. It was necessary to act since 2015 to prevent the bombardments of the populations of Donbass by Kiev and to make respect the agreements of Minsk. These were part of international law and should prevent the conflict from escalating. As we did not do so, and as the Russians saw that we had no intention of doing so, they decided to settle the situation by applying the UN principle of R2P.

In order not to legitimize the Russian position, the French-speaking media remained very discreet about the confessions of Petro Poroshenko, Angela Merkel, François Hollande and Volodymyr Zelensky not to have wanted to apply these agreements. But these confessions have not gone unnoticed by the "rest of the world". They show that our conception of international law is variable geometry and that we use the law only when it is in line with our interests.

---

704. "Turkey's Erdogan announces meetings with Zelenskyy, Putin," *The New Voice of Ukraine*, December 9, 2022 (https://english.nv.ua/nation/turkey-s-erdogan-announces-meetings-with-zelenskyy-putin-50289792.html)

705. "Moscow refuses that Ukraine be represented in Russia by Switzerland", *rts.ch*, August 11, 2022 (https://www.rts.ch/info/monde/13300549-moscou-refuse-que-lukraine-soit-representee-en-russie-par-la-suisse.html)

When one invokes "values" and "principles" with such intransigence for others, one must do so for oneself. Inconsistency is not acceptable. We would be credible in invoking international law if we had put the same energy into sanctioning those who have lied in order to wage totally illegitimate wars. Why have sanctions not been adopted against the United States, Great Britain and France? Why were their assets not confiscated for the reconstruction of the countries they destroyed? Why have Western leaders not been tried for their crimes? The fact that the Western interventions in Afghanistan, Iraq, Libya and Syria have been treated differently from the one in Ukraine tends to demonstrate the political nature of our use of international law. Not only does this fact discredit us in the "rest of the world", it also discredits international law. This is the case of the International Criminal Court, which is perceived by African countries as a means to put pressure on them.

6.3. Africa

Africa's distrust of Western countries is not new. It was largely stimulated by the disastrous 2011 operation to overthrow Gaddafi. By destroying the governance of the country that had the highest human development index in Africa at the time, the West destabilized the Sahel for good. This is what necessitated operations SERVAL and BARKHANE. The African countries then understood that we were moving from one military crisis to another, without worrying about the regional consequences and their effects on the populations.

Without a clear strategy and objectives, our operations are doomed to failure, leading to a permanent state of war. Carried out without real inclusion of the African countries concerned, our actions bring apparent short-term successes, but solve nothing. This explains the expulsion of French military contingents from Mali[706] and Burkina Faso[707], after France

---

706. Elian Peltier & Ruth Maclean, "French Soldiers Quit Mali After 9 Years, Billions Spent and Many Lives Lost," *The New York Times*, August 15, 2022 (updated August 19, 2022) (https://www.nytimes.com/2022/08/15/world/africa/mali-france-military-operation.html)

707. "Burkina Faso confirms demanding France to withdraw troops," *Africanews*, January 24, 2023 (https://www.africanews.com/2023/01/24/burkina-faso-to-expell-french-troops//)

has already withdrawn its military from the Central African Republic following a series of scandals[708].

4.6 billion that the EU spent on Ukraine in one year under its *European Peace Facility* (EPF)[709], with the 2.7 billion euros it spent on African Union peace and security activities between 2007 and 2019[710], to gauge the bitterness of Africans. Not only does Africa have to deal with the consequences of conflicts that we have often created through unfortunate policies, but we are pressuring them to adopt our policy towards Ukraine.

On March 21, 2023, Alain-Claude Bilie-By-Nze, Prime Minister of Gabon, gave an interview to journalists Marc Perelman of France 24 and Christophe Bobouvier of RFI. With consummate impertinence, they questioned him about Gabon's abstention from the United Nations General Assembly vote on the situation in Ukraine. With intelligence, the Prime Minister declared himself to be *"always surprised that people ask [African countries] to justify the choices they make; nobody asks that of other countries, especially* Western countries"[711].

Today, African countries are finding that dialogue with the BRICS countries, especially China and Russia, is easier and free of the increasingly oppressive Western paternalism.

We always come back to a fundamental question: Why is the Ukrainian conflict more reprehensible than the others we have provoked? The problem for the West is that the expected collapse of Russia could only be achieved if the whole world followed them. But African countries have concerns far removed from the European regional conflict.

As S. Jaishankar, India's Minister of Foreign Affairs, said in response to a journalist as unaware as her French colleagues[712]:

---

708. Nur Asena Erturk, "France withdraws last troop from Central African Republic," *aa.tr*, December 15, 2022 (updated December 16, 2022) (https://www.aa.com.tr/en/africa/france-withdraws-last-troop-from-central-african-republic/2764958)
709. "Ammunition delivered to Ukraine: Council approves €1 billion support under the European Peace Facility", *Council of the EU*, April 13, 2023 (https://www.consilium.europa.eu/fr/press/press-releases/2023/04/13/ammunition-for-ukraine-council-agrees-1-billion-support-under-the-european-peace-facility/)
710. "As More Conflicts, Problems around World Mount, European Union High Representative Tells Security Council World Must Invest in Revitalizing Multilateral System," *un*.org, February 23, 2023, SC/15210, 268th session (https://press.un.org/en/2023/sc15210.doc.htm)
711. https://youtu.be/C__MvkcmYEQ
712. https://youtu.be/8U5LeXjyyOM

Somehow, Europe must evolve from the mindset that Europe's problems are the world's problems, but the world's problems are not Europe's problems. If it is you, it is yours, if it is me, it is ours.

In July 2022, a paper written by the head of the EU delegation to the African Union (AU) was presented in Brussels, which expressed concern about the widening gap between the two continents[713]:

The EU's reputation as a mediator and peacemaker is being eroded by the Union's military assistance to Ukraine. In Africa, the EU is seen as fuelling conflict, not facilitating peace.

The conflict in Ukraine and the billions invested by the West have highlighted its inability to put its priorities on a peaceful solution of the disputes. What the West has paid to support Ukraine militarily (instead of promoting the solution of the Minsk agreements that would have avoided the conflict) will be as much less investment in the "rest of the world". The latter needs infrastructure that currently only China is able to finance.

6.4. The Near and Middle East

The conflict in Ukraine has highlighted the inability of the West to manage its own crises other than by force. The pressure and threats exerted on the countries of the "rest of the world" to align themselves with Western policy have been very poorly received in the Middle East.

The "values" that Westerners use as criteria for imposing sanctions or interfering in the internal affairs of countries are not perceived in the region as compatible with their cultures. The latter know that - as in the case of Iran - their way of seeing the world and society can quickly serve as a pretext for regime change. Saudi Arabia has understood that the United States is an ally to be wary of. It knows that its promise to make the kingdom a pariah state is a sword of Damocles that could come down at any time.

---

713. Vince Chadwick, "Exclusive: Internal report shows EU fears losing Africa over Ukraine," *devex.com*, July 22, 2022 (https://www.devex.com/news/exclusive-internal-report-shows-eu-fears-losing-africa-over-ukraine-103694)

The countries of the region tend to see Western interference as existential for their societies. This dimension tends to bring them together beyond ideological differences.

While Western diplomacy is busy with the Ukrainian conflict, Russian diplomacy is bringing Syria back on the international scene, China is multiplying its initiatives in the Middle East.

The Ukrainian conflict - or, more precisely, the sanctions that accompanied it - seems to have encouraged the Iranians and Saudis to continue their secret dialogue under the aegis of China. No doubt taking advantage of the inattention of Western chancelleries, diplomacy in the "rest of the world" has sought to resolve the problems. In the Near and Middle East, Chinese diplomacy strikes a historic blow. On March 10, 2023, Iran, Saudi Arabia and China signed a tripartite declaration[714] for the resumption of diplomatic relations between the two major Middle Eastern powers and the reopening of embassies[715]. This event is followed by King Mohammed bin Salman's (MBS) invitation of Iranian President Ibrahim Raissi to Saudi Arabia for an official visit[716].

At the same time, Iraq and Iran signed a security cooperation agreement to put an end to the actions of the Kurds, who were used by the West to foment unrest on both sides of the border[717].

But this rapprochement was frowned upon in Washington. On April 6, 2023, William Burns, director of the CIA, made an impromptu visit to Riyadh to express the "frustration" of the United States at seeing relations with Iran restored[718]. The West has lost its footing and the "rest of the world" tends to see them as troublemakers.

Syria, isolated by Western diplomacy, is back on the international scene. In February 2023, President Bashar al-Assad was received in the Sultanate of Oman. In March, he was invited with his wife to the United

---

714. Henry Austin, "Regional rivals Iran and Saudi Arabia agree to restore their ties after years of tensions," *NBC News*, March 10, 2023 (https://www.nbcnews.com/news/world/iran-saudi-arabia-agree-restore-diplomatic-relations-china-rcna74314)
715. https://www.spa.gov.sa/viewfullstory.php?lang=fr&newsid=2433248#2433248
716. Kathryn Armstrong, "Saudi Arabia invites Iran's President Raisi to visit, Tehran says," BBC News, March 20, 2023 (https://www.bbc.com/news/world-middle-east-65010185)
717. "Iran, Iraq sign security cooperation agreement," IANS/Investing, March 20, 2023 (https://in.investing.com/news/iran-iraq-sign-security-cooperation-agreement-3566648)
718. Alex Marquardt, "CIA director makes unannounced visit to Saudi Arabia," *CNN*, April 6, 2023 (https://www.cnn.com/2023/04/06/politics/cia-director-william-burns-saudi-arabia/index.html)

Arab Emirates to meet Sheikh Mohammed[719]. Syria renewed its ties with Tunisia in March[720], with Egypt in April[721] and was invited by MBS to the Arab League Summit on May 19 in Riyadh[722]. At the same time, Moscow is engaging its diplomacy to settle the Syrian issue and a quadripartite meeting of the deputy foreign ministers of Russia, Syria, Iran and Turkey was held on April 3-4, 2023 under the leadership of Moscow.

As for the conflict in Yemen, it seems to be moving towards a negotiated solution thanks to the efforts of Chinese diplomacy in the wake of the rapprochement between Saudi Arabia and Iran[723]. In other words, it is the diplomacy of the BRICS that is taking the lead in the Middle East with trade as a unifying factor. While the West is bent on escalating the conflicts it has created (and reaped the benefits of with terrorism), Eurasian diplomacy is focused on solving the problems.

In sum, there is a trend toward a calming of the Middle East conflicts. With the "Silk Roads" as a common thread, the countries of the region may well see an interest in putting their quarrels on the back burner and joining their energies to shape the future. The foreseeable reduction in hydrocarbon consumption in the West is a challenge for these countries to rethink their economies.

This regional upheaval could well have repercussions for Israel and its increasingly intransigent policy towards the Palestinians. The hebrew state has always viewed the disunity of the Arab world and the alliance between the Saudi kingdom and the United States as a guarantee of its security. It is probably time to resume more cooperative diplomatic activity while there is still time.

---

719. "Syria's Assad in UAE for second post-quake Gulf visit," Al Jazeera, March 19, 2023, (https://www.aljazeera.com/news/2023/3/19/424)
720. "Tunisia - Syria: the restoration of diplomatic relations confirmed by Said," *Le Temps*, March 11, 2023 (https://www.letemps.news/2023/03/11/tunisie-syrie-le-retablissement-des-relations-diplomatiques-confirme-par-saied/)
721. Summer Said & Benoit Faucon, "Egypt, Syria in Advanced Talks to Restore Diplomatic Relations," The Wall Street Journal, April 2, 2023 (https://www.wsj.com/articles/egypt-syria-in-advanced-talks-to-restore-diplomatic-relations-e569dfae)
722. Aziz El Yaakoubi & Maya Gebeily, "Saudi Arabia to invite Syria's Assad to Arab leaders summit, ending regional isolation," *Reuters*, April 2, 2023 (https://www.reuters.com/world/middle-east/saudi-arabia-invite-syrias-assad-arab-leaders-summit-sources-say-2023-04-02/)
723. Ryan Grim, "To Help End the Yemen War, All China Had to Do Was Be Reasonable," *The Intercept*, April 7, 2023 (https://theintercept.com/2023/04/07/yemen-war-ceasefire-china-saudi-arabia-iran/)

7. Getting out of the crisis

7.1. The inability to overcome prejudice

For several years now, Westerners have been known to make decisions based on rumours, unverified information or even false information. This is the case of the Skripal or Navalny cases, where decisions and sanctions were taken even before serious, impartial and inclusive investigations were conducted.

The Ukrainian crisis has shown the same phenomenon, but at its most extreme. The strategy of the Western countries was totally based on a narrative that they themselves had created and not on the facts. They literally invented the idea of a faltering Russian economy that would quickly be brought down by sanctions. This was not the case. It was claimed that Russia was just a "gas station" and that stopping buying hydrocarbons from it would cause it to collapse. This was not the case. It was said that the popular opposition to Vladimir Putin in Russia was considerable and that he was isolated. His popularity, already high, has increased.

Ukraine was given the prospect of a chimerical victory, which divided Ukraine and strengthened cohesion in Russia at the cost of hundreds of thousands of Ukrainian deaths.

The initiatives of Volodymyr Zelensky to start a negotiation process were systematically prevented by the same Western countries that encouraged and took part in the massacre of the civilian population of the Donbass between 2024 and 2022 (United States, Great Britain,

Canada and France). Because the objective was not to help Ukraine, but to bring down Russia.

In other words, either these decisions deliberately used Ukraine to achieve objectives that were contrary to Ukraine's interests (which the European populations certainly did not want), or they were taken without measuring the consequences. An examination of the facts shows that the second explanation dominates, but partially covers the first.

In Europe, and particularly in France, whether one is for or against Ukraine or Russia, the analysis of the conflict is extraordinarily poor. On the left as well as on the right, the analysis of the Ukrainian conflict suffers from the prejudices of those who see in it a moral requirement to support it and of those who think that it shows the limits of supranationality.

Now, justified or not, these prejudices cannot replace the facts, and we notice that they are terribly badly known. Those who intervene in our media only imperfectly repeat what they have heard and assemble pieces of facts that allow them to stick with their prejudices. What is understandable from a person in the street can no longer be understood from a director of IRIS.

Even personalities like Emmanuel Todd, whose comments have had a worldwide echo, have an analysis of the conflict based on his own perception and not on facts. In reality, Todd has misunderstood the Russian position. His contribution has less to do with the relevance of his analysis than with an approach that attempts to appeal to reason.

Whether one is for Russia or for Ukraine, the quality of the analysis is very poor in France and in Europe, and a little better in the United States. However, some trends can be identified: the pro-Russia analysis seeks appeasement, while those who express a pro-Ukrainian position seek to "punish" Russia.

Negotiation is perceived as a reward. As the Swiss ambassador in Kiev said, negotiating would be giving "*a bonus to the aggressor*[724]"! This reading poses three problems.

First of all, it contradicts the idea that it is up to Ukraine to find its own way. But so far, we have done everything to ensure that the negotiations Ukraine wanted did not succeed. We have also supported the Ukrainian

---

724. https://www.rts.ch/info/suisse/13567448-claude-wild-la-suisse-nest-pas-neutre-dans-le-conflit-en-ukraine.html

government's efforts to remove - literally and figuratively - all the personalities who were in favor of a negotiation.

Secondly, it is based on the fallacious idea, totally fabricated by our media, that Ukraine is in the process of winning and that the time is not ripe for negotiations. This is what Boris Johnson said in August[725], then Ursula von der Leyen in September 2022[726] and Emmanuel Macron in April 2023[727]. This is a position that is supported only by fantasies, because from the beginning, Ukraine has been in a situation of failure.

Thirdly, it poses a problem of ethics and coherence. To give priority to the idea of "punishing" the aggressor over that of resolving the conflict means that one leaves the role of referee and takes on the role of vigilante. The idea of "punishing" the Russian state and population would perhaps be acceptable if the same logic had been applied against the United States, Great Britain, France and Israel, which have triggered multiple conflicts in the Middle East. These countries are the instigators of wars and conflicts, regularly violate international law, and commit crimes that are at the root of the terrorism that strikes our populations. Moreover, by admitting this role of vigilante, who are we really punishing? Are we not condemning Ukraine rather than Russia? Here again, the myth of the victorious Ukraine holds surprises for us.

Third, it raises the question of our integrity. Regardless of how the Ukrainians feel about the Russians, we must not take sides, but rather stand on our own two feet. In reality, we have put ourselves in the conflict, whereas to play a mediating role, we would have to stay out of it. This explains why China, Turkey and even Russia have been able to help bring together adversaries considered irreconcilable, such as Turkey and Syria, or Saudi Arabia and Iran.

In early April 2023, with a Ukrainian counteroffensive looming, the West must realize that its ambitions were exaggerated. The *Washington Post* wonders about the likely *"modest gains"* of such an offensive. And yet, with many signs pointing to failure, Zelensky would not be forgiven for

---

725. Roman Romaniuk, "Possibility of talks between Zelenskyy and Putin came to a halt after Johnson's visit", *Ukrainskaya Pravda*, May 5, 2022 (https://www.pravda.com.ua/eng/news/2022/05/5/7344206/)
726. "State of the Union Address 2022 by President von der Leyen", *European Commission*, September 14, 2022 (https://ec.europa.eu/commission/presscorner/detail/fr/speech_22_5493)
727. Nicolas Barré, "Emmanuel Macron: 'Strategic autonomy must be Europe's fight,'" *Les Echos*, April 9, 2023 (updated April 14, 2023) (https://www.lesechos.fr/monde/enjeux-internationaux/emmanuel-macron-lautonomie-strategique-doit-etre-le-combat-de-leurope-1933493)

entering into a negotiation when Western countries have been dangling a total victory over Russia[728]:

> But opening negotiations with Russian President Vladimir Putin could be risky for Ukraine's leader, President Volodymyr Zelensky, given the acute animosity toward the Kremlin among the Ukrainian people, who have endured extraordinary levels of violence and deprivation during the conflict, but who have remained united by the promise of total victory.

The repeated narrative of a losing Russia and a victorious Ukraine is now turning against Zelensky. Broken promises are the lot of politicians, but when the population has made the sacrifice of blood for these promises, it is not sure that it will forgive those who have deceived it. This concerns Zelensky here, but also all those who relayed a speech that was known to be false from the start: journalists from media such as LCI, BFM TV, RTS, RTBF, Le Monde, and many others could become the legitimate targets of those who felt deceived by their speech.

In the United States, despite the generally unfavorable prejudices towards Russia, a growing polarization of the population and the pressure of the traditional media, the analysis of the conflict has remained somewhat more rational than in Europe, notably because the military has a better perception of the situation. In France, we think, then we refer - eventually - to the facts. In the United States, you look at the facts, then you think. This is why there are fundamental differences between institutions like the RAND Corporation and IRIS in France. Although RAND has developed the elements of a strategy to weaken Russia through the conflict in Ukraine, it had already warned that this strategy would be dangerous for Ukraine, for the United States and for Europe.

---

728. Alex Horton, John Hudson, Isabelle Khurshudyan & Samuel Oakford, "U.S. doubts Ukraine counteroffensive will yield big gains, leaked document says," *The Washington Post*, April 10, 2023 (https://www.washingtonpost.com/national-security/2023/04/10/leaked-documents-ukraine-counteroffensive/)

7.2. The Russian perception

The Russian concept of war is derived from Clausewitz's thinking. This means that one moves seamlessly from the military to the political and seeks to transform operational success into strategic success. In this perspective, diplomatic action is not antinomic to military action. There is therefore a willingness to negotiate, as we have seen with the positive responses to Ukraine's demands in 2022.

But on the other hand, the Russians have understood that even if there is a negotiation process, the West will use it to freeze the conflict and resume it later, as they did with the Minsk agreements. They know that the word of the West is worthless. In 1990, April Glaspie, the American ambassador to Iraq, told Saddam Hussein that the Americans would not object to an invasion of Kuwait[729]. She had lied. In 2015, the United States, Russia, China, France, the United Kingdom, Germany, the EU, and Iran signed the Vienna Agreement (JCPOA). Iran, Russia and China complied[730], not the West[731]. In 2020, the Americans and the Taliban agreed on a date for the US withdrawal[732]. The Americans did not keep their word and unilaterally postponed the date by more than 4 months. This is the reason for their pitiful departure. Finally, since November 2022, we know that the signature and the word of Angela Merkel and François Hollande were worthless. And these are only a few examples…

Moreover, the Russians have understood that Volodymyr Zelensky and the West are prisoners of their discourse. After promising Russia's defeat and entry into the EU and NATO to Ukraine, the West has withdrawn any possibility of ending the crisis without a prolonged conflict. Thus, Russia

---

729. "Confrontation In The Gulf - Excerpts From Iraqi Document on Meeting With U.S. Envoy," *The New York Times*, September 23, 1990) (https://www.nytimes.com/1990/09/23/world/confrontation-in-the-gulf-excerpts-from-iraqi-document-on-meeting-with-us-envoy.html).
730. Daniel Larison, "IAEA Confirms Iranian Compliance for the Fifteenth Time," *The American Conservative*, May 31, 2019 (https://www.theamericanconservative.com/iaea-confirms-iranian-compliance-for-the-fifteenth-time/)
731. Mark Landler, "Trump Abandons Iran Nuclear Deal He Long Scorned," *The New York Times*, May 8, 2018 (https://www.nytimes.com/2018/05/08/world/middleeast/trump-iran-nuclear-deal.html)
732. *Agreement for Bringing Peace to Afghanistan between the Islamic Emirate of Afghanistan which is not recognized by the United States as a state and is known as the Taliban and the United States of America*, state.gov, February 29, 2020 (https://www.state.gov/wp-content/uploads/2020/02/Agreement-For-Bringing-Peace-to-Afghanistan-02.29.20.pdf)

knows that the flow of Western weapons will continue and that the only way to stop the hostilities is for the fighting to stop because of the lack of (Ukrainian) fighters. The West thinks it is wearing down Russia, but it is wearing down its only asset in the region.

Russia will probably not seek to extend its territorial gains, but it will not take the initiative for negotiations. It has realized that Ukraine is the plaything of Western countries and will only engage in negotiations if it perceives a sincere desire to resolve the problem and stick to the agreements reached. For this reason, it will undoubtedly be very demanding in setting the terms of an agreement with Ukraine, and will require a commitment from the West.

It is likely that a negotiated solution will be more unfavourable to Ukraine than it would have been in February or March 2022, before the West prevented it from continuing the talks.

7.3. Towards a negotiated solution?

On November 23, 2022, Claude Wild, Swiss ambassador in Kiev, declared that the decision to negotiate *"belongs to the Ukrainians"*[733]. He is right. The problem is that *we* prevented Zelensky from doing so in February, March and August 2022 by pressing him to abandon his proposals. On April 9, 2022, Josep Borrell, the head of European diplomacy, said that *"this war will be won on the battlefield*[734]*."* In other words, not only is the European Union excluding itself from a solution, but if there is one, it will not be diplomatic.

So we are not honest with either the Ukrainians or the Russians.

In 2022, it seems that a large part of Ukrainian public opinion was in favour of negotiations with Russia. But as we have seen, negotiating is perceived as a betrayal and the purges observed in Ukraine in March 2022, in August 2022[735], and then in January 2023, show that divergent voices on this issue were systematically silenced. On August 27, 2022,

---

733. https://www.rts.ch/play/tv/redirect/detail/13567586?startTime=508
734. https://twitter.com/JosepBorrellF/status/1512778418445860864
735. Max Hunder, "Ukraine's President Fires Spy Chief and Top State Prosecutor," *Reuters/US News*, July 17, 2022 (https://www.usnews.com/news/world/articles/2022-07-17/ukraines-president-fires-security-service-chief-and-prosecutor-general)

Mikhail Podolyak, a close adviser to Volodymyr Zelensky, declared that the war could only end in one way: the military defeat of Russia, the return of the occupied territories, the judgment of the criminals and the beginning of the transformation of Russia[736].

But the situation on the ground is becoming more difficult for Ukraine, which is struggling to renew its equipment and personnel capabilities. This is why, in November 2022, some voices in the United States, such as that of General Mark Milley, who chairs the Joint Chiefs of Staff, suggested that Ukraine engage in a negotiation process[737]. His proposal caused an outcry in the West, but he was well placed to see that the situation in Ukraine was deteriorating, and he renewed it in February 2023[738]... without success!

The problem is that, as the Swiss ambassador in Kiev explains, the West believes that Ukraine should engage in a negotiation process only after it has been able to "*capitalize*" on its "counter-offensives"[739].

Thus, the weapons delivered to Ukraine are not intended to take back the lost territory, but only to obtain successes - the nature of which has never been defined - which would allow to save face during a negotiation. This is clearly a proxy war.

This is what we can learn from Emmanuel Macron's interview of April 9, 2023, on his return from his trip to China, when he declared that *"the time is not for negotiations [...] the time is* military[740]". The tone is set.

Ukraine has become a victim of its own propaganda. Those who - like François Hollande[741] - advocate the continuation of the fighting with the deep conviction that Ukraine is winning are very likely to be wrong. They understand the situation as they would like it to be and not as it is. They believe that Russia, fearing Ukrainian recapture, is seeking to negotiate, and therefore that this is not the right time for Ukraine.

---

736. https://www.pravda.com.ua/news/2022/08/27/7365021/
737. Alexander Ward, Lara Seligman & Erin Banco, "U.S. scrambles to reassure Ukraine after Milley comments on negotiations," *Politico*, November 14, 2022 (https://www.politico.com/news-/2022/11/14/u-s-ukraine-milley-negotiations-00066777)
738. "General Milley: Russia-Ukraine war will end with negotiations", *The Kyiv Independent*, February 16, 2023 (https://kyivindependent.com/general-milley-the-war-will-end-with-negotiations/)
739. https://www.rts.ch/play/tv/redirect/detail/13567586?startTime=478
740. "Now is not the time for negotiations, now is the time for military action - Macron", *Ukraïnska Pravda*, April 9, 2023 (https://www.pravda.com.ua/eng/news/2023/04/9/7397114/)
741. https://youtu.be/D8FDgJsrRt0?t=549

Since February 2022, the Ukrainians have advanced only on territories that the Russians had decided to abandon earlier. They advanced without fighting, and then they were slaughtered in "pockets of fire" (огневой мешок) by the artillery of the Russians, without the Russians having any losses. The capture of the territory of Kharkov, which the Russians had left beforehand, was deadly for the Ukrainians despite the absence of fighting: they arrived in a pocket of fire and were destroyed by Russian artillery without being able to exploit their "success." The same thing happened in Kherson. This is the reason why Zelensky was skeptical about the Russian withdrawal in Kherson and had feared (with reason) a trap[742]: he had learned the lessons of what happened in Kharkov!

The vast majority of experts agree that the "spring counter-offensive" will not fulfill its promises. Variable successes are attributed to it, but at no time do the Westerners put them in relation to the risks incurred. The West and Ukraine are caught in the "sunk cost" syndrome: the sacrifices have been so great that a negotiation would be considered a betrayal of those who have given their lives so far. The Ukrainians are thus caught between common sense and a feeling of betrayal. This is what Oleksiy Danilov, secretary of the Security Council of Ukraine, says when he says that negotiating would be political (and probably physical) suicide for Volodymyr Zelensky[743].

Because our media claims that the price paid by Ukrainians is lower than that paid by Russians, our governments encourage Ukraine to continue to fight. But this is exactly the opposite of the reality and we know that Ukraine has never been and is not in a position to prevail. Therefore, it is no longer a question of "winning", but of losing with more dignity. That is why Ukraine is being pushed towards a "last stand".

The outcome of the spring counteroffensive (which is getting closer and closer to summer[744]) cannot be predicted, but the fact that equip-

---

[742]. https://www.dailymail.co.uk/news/article-11411551/Is-Russias-retreat-Kherson-actually-trap-laid-Ukraine.html

[743]. Safak Costu, "Zelensky Averts 'Political Suicide' by Rejecting Peace Talks with Russia, Says Ukrainian Defense Council, Secretary Danilov," *BNN*, April 6, 2023 (https://bnn.network/breaking-news/zelensky-averts-political-suicide-by-rejecting-peace-talks-with-russia-says-ukrainian-defense-council-secretary-danilov/)

[744]. "The anticipated Ukrainian counter-offensive: When, where and how?", *Euronews*, April 22, 2023 (https://www.euronews.com/2023/04/22/the-anticipated-ukrainian-counter-offensive-when-where-and-how)

ment planned for this offensive is being used in the Bakhmut sector suggests that the Ukrainian army is running out of steam before it has even begun[745].

Our lack of hindsight in the way we approached the conflict forced us to take a position and to make a judgment that is now difficult to reverse. It was not a question of renouncing the sympathy that one might have for one or other of the belligerents, but of maintaining a link with Russia in order to maintain a dialogue. The total exclusion of Russia from international forums has excluded this possibility and Ukraine is now condemned to win (which seems difficult) or be destroyed. This is what Peter Maurer, Secretary General of the *International Committee of the Red Cross* (ICRC) and former Swiss ambassador for peace policy, says in the Swiss weekly *Die Weltwoche*:

> *Wars do not end with labels like "good" and "bad", but with concrete work of reconciliation and mediation.*

For sticking labels is only a way to exclude dialogue. In this case, Western diplomats would have been well advised to consider the following question:

> *What makes this conflict more reprehensible than those we have created before?*

However, to my knowledge, no Western diplomat, journalist or politician has once raised this question or even attempted to answer it…

---

745. "La Republica: M109 howitzers delivered by Italy already in use Ukraine", *The Kyiv Independent*, April 16, 2023 (https://kyivindependent.com/la-republica-italy-delivers-m109-howitzers-to-ukraine/)

Table of contents

1. Understanding the conflict 7

2. The actors 9
    2.1. The United States 9
        2.1.1. The Wolfowitz doctrine.. 10
        2.1.2. The trap of Thucydides... 12
        2.1.3. The RAND Corporation Strategy (2019)............................. 20
    2.2. The Ukraine.. 22
        2.2.1. The objectives of Ukraine.. 22
        2.2.2. The Ukrainian strategy.. 24
    2.3. Russia 25
        2.3.1. Russia's objectives 25
        2.3.2. War as a continuation of politics.. 43
        2.3.3. Russia ready to negotiate from the start 45

3. Geostrategic considerations 51
    3.1. The Russian threat to Europe.. 51
    3.2. The "values" 53
        3.2.1. From "law-based international order" to "rules-based international order".. 53
        3.2.2. A new look at neo-Nazism and extremism............................. 62
        3.2.3. A new perception of terrorism... 67
    3.3. The sanctions 68
        3.3.1. The effectiveness of sanctions on the Russian economy 71
        3.3.2. Sanctions on petroleum products.. 77
        3.3.3. The lack of microprocessors.. 79

  3.3.4. The sanctions on Nord Stream 80
  3.3.5. Fertilizers and cereals 82
  3.3.6. The isolation of Russia 84
  3.3.7. The stability of Russia 91
 3.4. Strengthening NATO and the EU 94
  3.4.1. Relations between NATO and Russia 96
  3.4.2. Ukraine's membership in NATO and the EU 98
  3.4.3. Sweden's and Finland's membership in NATO 101
  3.4.4. The sabotage of the Nord Stream 1 and 2 gas pipelines 103

4. Military considerations 119
 4.1. The return of conventional warfare 119
  4.1.1. Cyberwarfare 124
  4.1.2. The disappearance of hybrid warfare 126
  4.1.3. The nuclear question - The core of the problem 127
  4.1.4. The Russian nuclear threat 130
 4.2. The Ukrainian conduct of the war 143
  4.2.1. Communication dominates the conduct of operations 143
  4.2.2. The absence of popular resistance 145
  4.2.3. Conduct of operations 150
 4.3. The spring counter-offensive (2023) 161
 4.4. The "leaked" American secret documents 165
  4.4.1. Military documents 167
  4.4.2. The CIA's documents 169
 4.5. The Russian conduct of operations 170
  4.5.1. Driving structures 171
  4.5.2. The Russian mastery of the operative art 175
 4.6. Russian failure or success? 181
 4.7. The role of "volunteers" 184
  4.7.1. Individual volunteers 184
  4.7.2. Private Military Companies (PMC) 186
 4.8. The myth of the role of Western armaments in Ukraine 187
  4.8.1. Western investment 188
  4.8.2. An industrial war 189
  4.8.3. The Wunderwaffen 191
  4.8.4. Training 192
  4.8.5. Drones 193
  4.8.6. "Smart" weapons 197

    4.8.7. Hypersonic weapons.. 200
    4.8.8. Combat tanks 202
    4.8.9. Artillery 215
    4.8.10. Electronic warfare 225
    4.8.11. Anti-aircraft weapons 228
  4.9. Diversion 233

5. The information war 237
  5.1. Failing Western media 237
  5.2. The role of intelligence 241
    5.2.1. Strategic intelligence.. 241
  5.3. Russian disinformation 244
  5.4. The Ukrainian and Western information war............................245
    5.4.1. Information structures 245
    5.4.2. Different philosophies.. 249
    5.4.3. Principles of Ukrainian and Western communication 252
    5.4.4. Losses 260
  5.5. Refugees 274

6. The upheaval of the world 277
  6.1. De-dollarization 277
  6.2. The failure of diplomacy 281
    6.2.1. The failure of Western diplomacy 281
    6.2.2. The end of Swiss neutrality? 283
    6.2.3. Respect for international law... 285
  6.3. Africa 286
  6.4. The Near and Middle East..288

7. Getting out of the crisis 291
  7.1. The inability to overcome prejudice 291
  7.2. The Russian perception...295
  7.3. Towards a negotiated solution?...296

Best sellers Max Milo Editions

Hitler's banker, Jean-François Bouchard

Confessions of a forger, Éric Piedoie Le Tiec

The Koran and the flesh, Ludovic-Mohamed Zahed

Governing by fake news, Jacques Baud

Governing by chaos, Collectif

A political history of food, Paul Ariès

Mad in U.S.A.: The ravages of the "American model", Michel Desmurget

Mondial soccer club geopolitics, Kévin Veyssière

Putin: Game master?, Jacques Braud

Treatise on the three impostors: Moses, Jesus, Muhammad, The Spirit of Spinoza

TV Lobotomy, Michel Desmurget